2⁰⁰

Spring 83

MINDING THE ANIMAL PSYCHE

A Journal of Archetype and Culture

Summer 2010

SPRING JOURNAL
New Orleans, Louisiana

CONTENTS

FILM REVIEW

BOOK REVIEWS

ABOUT THE COVER PHOTOGRAPHER

ROBIN LINDSEY is a wildlife photographer living in Seattle, Washington. Her photographs, including a number of images of harbor seals and their pups, have been published in numerous magazines and newspapers, and have also appeared on television. Her work will be featured in the children's book, *Pups on the Beach,* by renowned nature writer and novelist Brenda Peterson (forthcoming, Henry Holt Publishing, 2011).

Robin works closely with the National Oceanic and Atmospheric Administration (NOAA), both as a photographic contributor and as a first responder to seal strandings in Puget Sound. She is one of the founding members of the conservation group Seal Sitters (www.sealsitters.org), a member of NANPA (North American Nature Photography Association), and is on the board of directors of TerraMar Research (www.terramarresearch.org).

The photographs that appear on our cover are from Robin's Silkie Dream Series, and explore the mysterious and soulful side of seals. Seals, or "silkies," hold a special place in the lore of peoples of the North Atlantic. Romantic legends abound of seals that come ashore, shed their skins, intermarry with humans, and finally return to the sea. Robin's photographs in this Series attempt to reflect these ethereal spirits in all their earthly beauty.

To see more of Robin's work, go to www.robinlindseyphotography.com.

A Note from the Editor

Spring is honored to have G.A. Bradshaw, Ph.D., Ph.D., serve as the Guest Editor of our Minding the Animal Psyche issue. Dr. Bradshaw holds doctorate degrees in ecology and psychology, and her many areas of expertise include the effects of violence on and the trauma recovery of elephants, grizzly bears, chimpanzees, parrots, and other species. Her research has been featured in the *New York Times, Time Magazine, National Geographic, Smithsonian, The London Times,* ABC's 20/20, and several documentary films.

She is the author of the acclaimed book *Elephants on the Edge: What Animals Teach Us About Humanity* (Yale University Press, 2009), an in-depth psychological portrait of elephants in captivity and in the wild. *Elephants on the Edge* was voted a Favorite Book of 2009 by the *Scientific American*, received the Prose Award, and has been reviewed in the *New York Review of Books* and *Atlantic Monthly.*

Dr. Bradshaw's research has created the newly emerging field of trans-species psychology that integrates neuroscience, ethology, and psychology to articulate a human-inclusive, species-common model of brain and mind. It offers a collective language bridging the human-nature gap to bring us a "science of the heart." The principles of trans-species psychology are developed and explored at The Kerulos Center, www.kerulos.org, located in southern Oregon and of which Dr. Bradshaw is the Executive Director.

Spring's gratitude toward G.A. Bradshaw for sharing her knowledge, insights, and compassion is immense, and we hope that you, our readers, are inspired and challenged by this new issue of our journal.

Nancy Cater, J.D., Ph.D., Editor
Spring: A Journal of Archetype and Culture
New Orleans, Louisiana

Editor, Nancy Cater, with Tarzan (l) and Sheba (r).

Guest Editor, G. A. Bradshaw, and Peanut

GUEST EDITOR'S INTRODUCTION

G. A. BRADSHAW PH.D., PH.D.

*We are a strange kind of animal. We have bodies like other animals'
bodies and move like them. Our stories tell of these human-animal
affinities, we speak of animals as totems or familiars, and we elucidate
principles of the cosmos or society in terms of animal behaviour. Yet,
in telling, speaking and elucidating—indeed in building and
thinking—we find ourselves estranged from the animals.*

—David Morris,
"Animals and Humans, Thinking and Nature"[1]

C.G. Jung was a man ahead of his times. While infrequently
credited, his ideas are absorbed into current science to emerge re-labeled
as complexity theory, evolutionary psychology, and other trendy
monikers. Jung was anticipatory in other ways.

Unlike most colleagues who followed reductionism's ever-
tightening spiral into intellectual balkanization, Jung maintained
exchange across disciplines. It is one reason why his work remains
relevant as both philosophy and theory.

In today's Age of Consilience, we are in critical need of conceptual
coherence to mend what Descartes put asunder.[2] Confronted with
perhaps the most profound reconciliation yet, the repatriation of
humans to nature, we are fortunate to possess Jung's description of
cross-species psychobiological continuity.

The various lines of psychic development start from one common
stock whose roots reach back into the most distant past.
Theoretically it should be possible to peel the collective
unconscious, layer by layer, until we come to the psychology of
the worm, and of even the amoeba.[3]

It continues to be one of the most elegant and accurate portraitures
to date. However, there is one critical flaw. Jung was still encumbered
by the Great Chain of Being, the notion that evolution proceeds linearly,

species stepping over species, inching toward its apex, Mankind.[4] Given his catholic tastes and attention to scientific discoveries, it is likely that Jung would have forsaken vertical relatedness for today's species-common models that pronounce humans and other animals comparable in brain and mind.[5,6]

Followed by contributions from John Bowlby, Allan Schore, Darcia Narvaez, Alva Noë, and the growing lineup of post-modern scholars of neuropsychoanalysis, moral neuropsychology, neurophilosophy, and ecopsychology, C.G. Jung has bequeathed a wonderful Humpty Dumpty image of psyche, cracked, but with most of the pieces put back together again. Subsequently, our task is less conceptual than it is practical. We may recognize our interconnection to all living beings, but we have forgotten how to exist with them. The pressing question is: How are we to live?[7] This is the subject of the Minding the Animal Psyche issue of *Spring*.

Through the eyes of diverse scholars, we explore the exciting ground between human and animal psyches. It is has been a lonely space, grown barren after years of denial and neglect. Similar to many estranged relationships, the first steps are often tentative, the way unclear. Our authors are some of the pioneers who have staked their lives in this in-between land to re-vitalize ancient wisdom about ourselves and our animal kin. They reflect on these questions:

- *What concepts and practices enhance our abilities to hear and understand animal minds and feelings?*
- *What are necessary changes in human perception and action that revitalize mutually respectful interspecies relationships?*
- *How do we create ways of living that serve other animals as equal partners in knowledge and culture making?*
- *How can we increase other species' participation in guiding human culture?*
- *What are the material and psychological implications— for ourselves and for other animals—of archetypal ways of understanding animals?*

Psychology's expansive move from a human-only to a species-inclusive domain is groundbreaking and exciting. We now re-acquaint ourselves with Sister Amoeba and Brother Worm not as poor country cousins lost somewhere on the family tree but as colleagues of "one common stock"[8] in the creation of a new trans-species consciousness and community.

NOTES

1. David Morris, "Animals and Humans, Thinking and Nature," *Phenomenology and the Cognitive Sciences*, 4 (2005): 49–72, p. 49.

2. E.O. Wilson, *Consilience: The Unity of Knowledge* (New York: Knopf, 1998).

3. C.G. Jung (1981), *The Structure of the Psyche,* in R.F.C. Hull, trans., *The Collected Works of C. G. Jung,* Vol. 8 (Princeton, NJ: Princeton University Press). (Original work published 1931), p. 141.

4. Sean Nee, "The Great Chain of Being," *Nature* 435 (2005): 429.

5. G.A. Bradshaw, "The Scientist's Bark," *Huffington Post*, October 15, 2009, http://www.huffingtonpost.com/ga-bradshaw/the-scientists-bark_b_322558.html.

6. G.A. Bradshaw and Robert M. Sapolsky, "Mirror, Mirror," *American Scientist*, 94(6), (2006): 487-489.

7. Peter Singer, *How Are We to Live? Ethics in an Age of Self-Interest* (New York: Prometheus, 1995).

8. Jung, *Collected Works,* Vol. 8, p. 141.

Jung and the Parrot: Facts, Interpretations, and Connections

PHOEBE GREENE LINDEN

I have come to see that the cages and enclosures in which we bind animals are the materialization of the cages and prisons of the mind in which we live.— G.A. Bradshaw

Introduction

One day, while in early research for this paper, I picked up *Man and His Symbols*. I opened a random page. This is what I read in a chapter written by Marie-Louise von Franz:

After long and painful wandering, [Hatim] comes to a beautiful garden in the middle of which is a circle of stone statues. In the center of the statues, he sees a parrot in its cage, and a voice from above says to him: "Oh hero, you probably will not escape alive from this bath. Once Gayomart (the First Man) found an enormous diamond that shown more brightly than sun and moon. He decided to hide it where no one can find it, and therefore he built

Phoebe Greene Linden and Santa Barbara Bird Farm parrots are active trans-species companions who work, advocate, and volunteer to improve the welfare of captives everywhere.

this magical bath in order to protect it. The parrot that you see here forms part of the magic. At its feet lie a golden bow and arrow on a golden chain, and with them you may try three times to shoot the parrot. If you hit him the curse will be lifted. If not, you will be petrified, as were all of these other people."

Hatim tries once, and fails. His legs turn to stone. He fails once more and is petrified up to his chest. The third time he just shuts his eyes, exclaiming "God is great," shoots blindly, and this time hits the parrot. An outbreak of thunder, clouds of dust. When all this has subsided, in place of the parrot is an enormous, beautiful diamond, and all the statues have come to life again. The people thank him for their redemption.[1]

Discovering a synchrony between the personal and the collective text, and the parrot, I was at first delighted. Parrots have been among my best friends for nearly 30 years. But I felt cleaved by the tale, especially by the human-perpetrated violence against a caged parrot. I thought that the people in the story might become greedy and argue over the diamond, and I became eager for Hatim to meet a dire fate.

As von Franz's essay progresses, so did my incredulity, especially when she refers to the parrot as "demonic" and "repetitive," even though the parrot in the myth makes no move or sound. "The parrot," she writes, "signifies the evil spirit of imitation that makes one miss the target and petrify psychologically."[2] Evil spirit, indeed. The evil realities of cage, weapons, and target practice are tangential facets of parrot persecution: another is insatiable demand. Where Hatim and von Franz would shoot and vilify, scores of other people seek to capture and keep winged ones.

With the help of some parrots, I co-explore trans-species community—an initiative, the firmament of which contains the precepts and practices of trans-species psychology,[3] the ascendancy of which is propelled by sweeping wings. Trans-species psychology views humans and non-human animals as "kin under the skin," who share psyche, culture, and value. In the trans-species community, we likewise share earth, air, and water. In this fusion-fission[4] society, vilifications are replaced by verities. To illustrate, here is the same story re-told as a trans-species encounter:

During an enriching journey, Kerulass sees a caged parrot surrounded by stone people. Before he can think, a voice says, "Captivity is measured in stone-headedness."

Kerulass scrutinizes each stone statue: none responds; they don't move. Then Kerulass catches the eyes of the parrot—who looks back. The air thrums with silent music.

"I am Josserlynn," says the parrot without speaking. "I'm glad you're here; I'm getting tired of petrified people."

Kerulass touches the cage door and it swings open. With one step out and several giant flaps, Josserlynn flies to a crown of branches high in the breeze. Joss regains functional strength and flexibility when preening her feathers: full range of motion, compounded movements. She rouses from head to toe, pauses a jot, lifts her wings, and surely flies away.

Glistening sunlight freshly illuminates the landscape, and from the inside out, the stones start to move.

Unchaining the bow and arrow, Kerulass makes a sundial and so begins the practice of gnomonics. With the chain, Kerulass fastens the cage door open forever.

The stones shake lose the ponderous shackles of petrifaction as simultaneously their consciousness eschews conscription. They vow forevermore to honor parrots (and other non-humans) in all ways. They see that the diamond could never replace Josserlynn because it only reflects what the parrot embodies: Beauty's gift and beauty's giver.[5]

Josserlynn, with a swoop, lands in the tree-tops of her ancestral territory. The flock sings, "Thus ends captivity. Thus begins true wealth."

In this trans-species narrative, wisdom, freedom, and wealth touch all; old strata are re-arranged and everyone matters. This story signifies the legitimate needs, desires, and rights of parrots as examples of non-human persons, and it hints at the benefits of such. Additionally, it hopes to unveil truths to which we have been blind.[6]

Because my husband, Harry, and I live everyday with over forty psittacine birds, parrots of many species[7] who inhabit outdoor aviaries as well as seven who co-habit the house with us, we know something about the work and benefits inherent in trans-species connections.[8] As former parrot breeders and life-long parrot devotees, we have committed to making a world that supports vital psittacine lives. But, after all, trans-species connections happen one bird at a time. This is Bonnet.

BONNET LEAVES THE AVIARY: OCTOBER

Concurrent with interests in Jung and Jungian thought, circumstances[9] led Bonnet, *Amazona aestiva*, Blue-fronted Amazon,

Fig. 1: Bonnet talks about her accomplishments.
Photo courtesy of Santa Barbara Bird Farm and Lindsey Eltinge

and me to re-enter a close companionship. After living outside in the aviary for nearly seventeen years, Bonnet was coming back into the house, back to where she was hand-raised and fledged—into areas I knew she would remember well.[10]

As I prepare her cage, perches, play gym, and landing spaces, I mentally map Bonnet's indoor experience. Time out of a cage freshly painted with non-toxic paint, time in safe exploration, shared spaces, friendly cooperation, flight training: I see us together and then I look at the real estate as if I were her. I know she'll like the big windows and fresh breezes: I trim the magnolia tree outside to clear her view to the ocean. I also decide to collect empirical, yet informal, data on our attachment (or re-attachment) and Bonnet's physical athleticism in these relatively new surrounds. I wonder what it will look like when Bonnet and I interact in the indoor environments we co-create with the dual aims of expanding her behavioral freedom and deepening community. It will not be difficult, I speculate, to count and document flights, flight patterns, and landings; it might be trickier to describe the changes in our interspecies connection. In this home-based trans-species community, one set up with both parrots and people equally in mind, Bonnet and I set out to interpret a new proximity in a trans-species community.[11]

A New Nest in an Old Growth Tree

I press Jungian wisdom into service to help demarcate the known boundaries of trans-species practice. Whether vibrantly woven into our psyches or loosely gathered by gossamer threads, trans-species lives, works, and sensibilities reside in our shared psyches.

Jung himself approaches trans-species interpretation when he writes about the dream interpreter who "has to deal with casualties in a genuine war."[12] Two interpretive disciplines—dream interpretation and trans-species interpretation—are ideally set up for parallel exploration. This essay reflects trans-species work incubated in reading and research and over twenty-five years of hands-on qualitative trans-species interactions; a new nest in an old-growth tree. It is about the immediate—play gyms and relationships—as much as it is about abstract concepts—trans-species communities and Jungian thought. It includes daily lives and the relationships of a huge and ever-growing psittacine-human flock. Like the limits of captivity, the limits of interpretation are immutable when single: only collectively do they become malleable.

Bonnet and I work with non-traditional methodologies because they are best suited for parrot-centric activities. As the digitally-blessed member of the flock, I translate the experiences via keyboard and word as best I can. G.A. Bradshaw calls her parrot-centric activities "a new parrot-digm,"[13] and that word conjures up a lot. When not totally parrot-centric, we use "an alternative paradigm," the type "seen in the work of Jane Goodall, Barbara Smuts, and others, [one that] made a fundamental departure from methodological features."[14] With gratitude to alternative parrot-digms, Bonnet and I begin a new phase of life together.

Bonnet in the House

When she first comes back to live in the house, after living in a 10' x 10' aviary, Bonnet and all the parrots outside make a huge racket. It's as if the new vocal range must be explored at full volume. The calling back and forth continues and everyone gets in to the chorus. In the house, Bonnet has a fully enriched 40" x 36" sleep/nap cage in our bird/sun room that I've equipped with new versions of her favorite perches, chew toys, food bowls, and privacy panels. Her time out of the cage is at my discretion, so I take her confinement seriously, just as I also know the limits of schedules. The first day, she jumps with alacrity on to my arm the moment I open the cage door. We stand together and breathe, relaxing and checking out the lay of the land.[15] After a few moments, we walk through the house as Bonnet revisits the places she knew as a neophyte and fledgling.[16]

By the second round touring the house and with my encouragement, Bonnet makes a small jump onto the wooden play gym that she often used during the tentative tender time of fledging. She tests each branch by stepping all over them one at a time and testing others with her beak. We hang out, relax, and I watch for a few minutes until she has touched every inch of the branches. Then with a rouse, she rests comfortably on her favorite perch. This indicates that we are set to begin our mutual re-discovery—corporally, athletically, and socially. Our shared psyches want to take off and fly, but we see the danger of windows, we know of the challenges of flying around corners, and we recognize the immoveable walls of confinement. While I look at glowing Bonnet, my mind turns to the thousands of other Blue-fronted Amazons who, like Bonnet's parents, were wild-caught. I know that her flights are paid for through countless sacrifices by multitudes of not only parrots, but all birds.

INJUSTICE AND PROPITIATION

Nearly all humans—whether they are conscious or oblivious—have been contacted by a member of the genus *Aves*. From time immemorial to present day, humans have taken advantage of the stationary cage and parrot grace in order to feast their eyes on the wild beauty exemplified by the order *Psittaciformes*.[17] Every parrot made captive is somewhat familiar with humans. For these reasons, parrots perhaps have a natural inclination towards a trans-species life because they have been forced to adapt to such a life in order to survive.

Sadly, Hatim's parrot exists today in plethora. Parrots of all types are locked inside cages. They are surrounded by ineffective people and often worse.

Even as humans kill and cage them, birds shape our notions of freedom and liberty. They give us song, dance, and dreams of flight. We use them for decoration, companionship, and inspiration, and still we continue to invade and destroy their ancestral grounds, seemingly without compunction and certainly without reparation.

> In our colonization of the planet, *billions* of birds have died for us, have made way for us, have seen their habitats erased at an evolutionary speed equivalent to the negligent push of the delete button, and we hardly even know it.[18]

Through the domestication of birds, we've "generated enormous benefits for ourselves in terms of food security and quality."[19] We've killed songbirds, seabirds, and others "in volumes too great to guess at, and seized their eggs and young no less ruthlessly."[20] In essence, "the enormity of what we owe to the birds" is compounded by the "impossibility of a full and equitable repayment."[21] The fury of injustice meets the burden of propitiation.

Human behavior is the cause of suffering for parrots and human behavior is essential for remedy. By force of history, we humans control the resources and the community, and so far, our global stewardship has been almost entirely human-centric, with grave results. In the trans-species paradigm, mind and action are fully informed by deep understanding and keen psychic awareness with wild animals, as well as by getting and staying busy with non-human individuals. Knowing nearly 150 individuals of thirty different species over the years, many whom I hand-raised, allowed me the privilege of making thoughtfully arranged environments designed with parrots' wellbeing in mind. But all my efforts, years of work, benefitted only a small number of parrots. The majority still need to be saved. Captivity is not the answer and conservation, too, has its problems.

JUNG AND THE PARROT

A pre-industrial Eden[22] never existed for psittacine birds. Throughout time, parrots have been held physically captive while simultaneously revered, no more so than by peoples indigenous to the great South and North Americas. People of all cultures cage parrots. And if you're a parrot, the ethnicity of your captors hardly matters.

In keeping with age-old tradition, the people of Taos most likely had scarlet macaws (*Ara macaos*) in cages on the pueblo when Jung visited. Like the puebloan groups, Hopi, Zuni, Acoma, and others, the Taos people recognize their intrinsic part in the ancient "parrot clan."[23] When researcher Stevenson asked the Taos who they were, they first called themselves the Summer people, then the Mother people, and finally mentioned a "name [that] was so sacred it was never spoken aloud," but which is written as "Macaw."[24] Even today, macaw feathers remain important for many puebloan ceremonial rites, just as they were hundreds of years ago, as evidenced by archeological finds from 1100 A.D.[25]

Subsequently, there is a strong possibility that C.G. Jung himself at least heard, possibly met, and perhaps interacted with a scarlet macaw when, in the winter of 1924-25, he visited the Indians of Taos Pueblo in New Mexico.[26] Because it would stretch the bounds of credulity to do so, I refrain from asserting that Jung's macaws are related to the very real scarlet macaws I live with and know. However, the speculative parrots in Taos and the very real ones in Santa Barbara share history in ways related to each other and to humans: capture, survival, captivity, and community.

What would C.G. Jung have thought about seeing, closely and personally, a caged macaw? And, what did the macaw think of him,

Fig. 2: Tara, a scarlet macaw, catches and reflects light in Santa Barbara.
Photo courtesy of Santa Barbara Bid Farm and Kelly Flynn

bearded and white-skinned, foreign to the red soils of New Mexico? By means of this glimmer of connection, I wonder, from a trans-species perspective—when Jung visited Taos, was part of the profound impression[27] left upon him due, in part, to a pair of yellow eyes that touched his gaze? If the cage was large enough, did he see wing outstretched in arabesque? Did macaw calls greet the dawn Jung writes about some 30 years later?[28]

BONNET IN NOVEMBER

Bonnet is part of a surviving population. Hatched in the USA and provisioned with many advantages known to domesticity,[29] Bonnet and her potential mate, Bucket, were both wanted, beloved parrots.[30] Bucket was carefully tended as together we battled a disease which eventually claimed his life.[31] These two parrots, beauties both, have individual stories that inimitably contribute to the flock's collective experience: Bucket's story was cut short; Bonnet's continues.

Within one month of being back in the house, Bonnet regularly flies with dependable control 22' from cage to play gym where she expertly lands. I pick her up, take her to the starting point, and she does it again. After four or five flights, she's slightly out of breath. When set down, she stays on the gym, vocalizes with the flock, and checks out the view.

After all, she's only 40' away from her aviary cohorts: Blossom, Mack, Far Flights, Josserlynn, Sisters Girl, and others; only screens separate her from the outside. With attendant hawks, wild parrots, migratory birds, and all familiar to her, Bonnet strengthens the energies that travel in the house-aviary conduit. If vocalizations are colored, heard and measured, these are resplendent, loud, and enduring. Chortles, trills, beeps, riffs, screams, honks and whistles—there's no doubt that Bonnet keeps everyone within ear-shot informed of her experiences.[32] While Bonnet navigates the family room, her wild cousins fight for their lives.

How Wild is the Wild?

A short list of the current perils facing wild parrots includes: legal and illegal wild "pet" trade, widespread inexorable habitat destruction, and the growing demand for parrots as pets. Tragically, today's grim realities for wild parrots are continuances of history, innumerable outgrowths of ageless exploitations.

Because parrots are found all over the world, they can be victimized by poor subsistence farmers who have not the means to share even one ear of corn, as well as by developers and consumers of luxurious vacation homes. Often, parrots are poached by the destitute and so end up destitute themselves: bereft of flock, land, and freedom. Even scarcity is scary for parrots because it increases demand.

The pulse of commerce—"the wild bird trade"—throbs with atrocities. Both legal and illegal trade continues; and, if you're a parrot, it hardly matters whether the people who rob your nests and clear-cut your forests have permits or not.[33]

Once the United States and Europe were the primary culprits with an insatiable demand for wild parrots, but as the importation of parrots to these countries became disallowed, Asia emerged with a new, huge, eager, moneyed pool of customers. Unfortunately, a significant percentage of this ever-growing human population wants parrots for

Fig. 3: The beauty and diversity of parrot feathers are deemed desirable by a demanding public that fuels the wild bird trade.
Photo courtesy of Santa Barbara Bird Farm and Chris Pinchbeck

their own. Exports from the wild—reminiscent of the slave trade—yield few survivors. Lengthy unregulated transportations of frightened, crowded, captive animals result in a meager unsatisfactory harvest for a parrot-starved world. The wild ones who survive the many journeys from remote homeland to strange new land usually end up caged, often singly, in any variety of stores, zoos, hotels, breeding establishments, tourist attractions, homes, and worse. If you're a parrot, this matters a great deal.

As a result, flocks of fully engaged, sociable, worthy individuals are driven from their homes. Current research confirms that "parrots have the largest number of threatened species of any bird family" and are "actually worse off than most birds."[34] Yet even now, "widespread habitat fragmentation" and "unsustainable harvests from the wild" continue to decimate free-flying wild parrots.[35]

Wild parrots prefer to live in remote areas. The promise of commerce tends to intoxicate people, corrupt governments, and imperil wildlife; so parrots suffer. In parrots' varied homelands, conservation is often difficult to accomplish and trafficking is nearly impossible to police. Additionally, "the tools, resources and expertise needed to help one species of parrot might be completely ineffective to help another."[36] From the Earth's perspective, the elimination of parrots from the natural world would leave Her bleak. Among other attributes, parrots are natural mulch-makers, music composers, and seed dispersers. With the death of every parrot, Earth becomes an increasingly desolate, weirdly silent monoscape.

Proofs of parrots' learning abilities, descriptions of their complex and lively natural societies, records of their languages, stories of their fidelities, and images of their antics accumulate in the news and on YouTube even as wild populations decline. In the worst cases, psittacine abilities and adaptabilities are agents of their exploitation: in the best cases, abilities and adaptabilities help them thrive.

BONNET WORKS: DECEMBER

After two months in the house, Bonnet stands tip-toe on her familiar gym and leans forward, wings flipping, ready to fly 12' away to the kitchen counter-top. She launches, flies, and then lands 6' away from Hawkeye. (Perhaps Bonnet has forgotten that Hawkeye is the undisputed flock-imperial, Hawk-headed parrot who every day sits unchallenged on Hawkeye's Windowsill.) It has been thus for many years: Hawkeye and I prepare the flock's daily fresh meal together. And now, here's Bonnet with a yell. Hawkeye flares her head-dress and hisses as Bonnet trespasses the invisible boundary. Other flock members know to keep a respectful friendly distance, but Bonnet flares right back at Hawkeye.[37] With quick, stabbing beak thrusts, loud vocalizations, dilating eye pupils, and fully fanned feathers, Hawkeye's "back off" meets Bonnet's "here I come." I intervene by offering my hand to Bonnet. She quickly jumps on and we regain regular heart-beats when Bonnet goes back to her gym.

In moments, Bonnet repeats her escapade—she flies into the kitchen, skids to a landing on the counter-top, and flares: Hawkeye flares and hisses in return. As Bonnet gets her balance, I get Bonnet: she goes back to the safety of her play gym. Hawkeye and Bonnet yell at each other and it takes several minutes before it's calm again. The three of us are equally attentive.

Bonnet and Hawkeye were captive raised and have never known life in the wild, but the wild is still in them. They are inculcated with me as I am happily with them and thus the trans-species model is built and managed. Sadly, even if trans-species communities proliferate, they are too late for those who, like the Carolina Parakeet, *Conuropsis carolinensis*, are already extinct.[38] History is clear: the Carolina Parakeet

Fig. 4: The gracefulness of flight and the interplay of feather color are sights that benefit human vision and consciousness.
Photo courtesy of Santa Barbara Bird Farm and Lindsey Eltinge

was blessed with voluminous numbers and occupied a huge territory, but even these advantages were no match for human covetousness.

CAROLINA PARAKEETS: RIP

The extinction of the Carolina parakeet (*Psittacus carolinensis* [Audubon], *Conurposis carolinensis* [Forshaw]) in 1918 is attributed in part to poultry disease which the parrots contracted at the farms of early settlers.[39] Yet, while it is true that the only parrot species endemic to North America, the Carolina parakeet, became extinct, infected poultry were not the only cause of their demise.

The famed naturalist Audubon writes about the Carolina parakeet in 1831. He describes the brilliant yellow and green parrots descending in fields from trees, wreaking destruction to the crops, and earning "severe retaliation on the part of the planters."[40] He writes,

> The parakeets are destroyed in great numbers, for whilst busily engaged in plucking off the fruits or tearing grain from the stacks, the husbandman approaches them with perfect ease, and commits great slaughter among them. All the survivors rise,

shriek, fly around for about a few minutes, and again alight on the very place of imminent danger. The gun is kept at work; eight, ten, or even twenty, are killed at every discharge. The living birds, as if conscious of the death of their companions, sweep over their bodies, screaming as loud as ever, but still return to the stack to be shot at.[41]

Audubon makes the point of diminishing numbers of these swift and direct fliers when he also writes, "Our parakeets are very rapidly diminishing in number; and in some districts, where twenty-five years ago they were plentiful, scarcely any are now to be seen." Lest we forget that Audubon was himself a collector and trapper who eagerly sought rare species, he reminds us himself:

> I have seen several hundreds destroyed in this manner in the course of a few hours and have procured a basketful of these birds at a few shots, in order to make good choice of good specimens for drawing the figures by which this species is represented in the plate now under your consideration.[42]

Audubon's print still survives, but Carolina parakeets, "darting in and out through the trees with remarkable precision,"[43] are gone forever. Clearly, even parrots' outstanding adaptability has its limits.

LIFE IN CAPTIVITY

Captive breeding and hand-rearing parrots for many decades has resulted in great numbers of individual parrots living in human-dominated domestic situations, as Hawkeye and Bonnet do. Along with the resultant modified parrots, are some radically modified humans. Keeping our environments suitably arranged for parrots is a never-ending process.[44, 45] Neither remains the same as they were before their encounters, and many are truly inspired to lead fruitful and fulfilling trans-species lives. Bonding and development share two-ways; attachment pulls and growth pushes, yin and yang. For good and bad, my life is infused with parrot pleasures, priorities, and perils. Hand-rearing parrots created the interspecies community I call home, and it is the same community that keeps me captive in their service.

Parrots in captivity are kept in such a variety of circumstances that it is nearly impossible to try to describe the "average" life of an "average" captive parrot. Standards of care vary widely and with an estimated

13,000,000 birds (yes, that many, and likely more) in captivity[46]—plus relentless production via captive breeding and wild trade—decimations burgeon in type and volume.

A distressing rise in homelessness in parrots mirrors the rise in human psychological distress. Reports of abuse and trauma proliferate; over-populated parrot sanctuaries cry for support; news of needless and countless deaths flood the internet. Even this massive unhappiness does not yet deter breeders from producing—nor stores from selling—nor people from buying—parrots as commodities. Exploited, displaced, and used wrongly by an increasing human population, parrots need effective actions to help them survive.

Too often, the larger work of education becomes a victim of politicized un-doing. Talents and efforts are "squandered in slaying paper dragons," as Orwell might say.[47] More studies, more graphs, more dissertations, even more funding: these "monuments to our own magnificence"[48] are hollow unless we provide what we can to animals we know or know of while we also work to control human population growth. Only then will there be hope for the richness of the animal world and trans-species communities.

As I work in my own community, I am reminded of ideas "waiting in the air," new ideas which may not initially be expressed perfectly or codified fully, but which nonetheless have "contained in them or hidden beneath them . . . something which people, all over the world, suspect is relevant to present actions."[49] When an argument for change catches on, it does not happen "adventitiously"[50] and never in isolation, but in and through community. Because they are so new, so varied, and inclusive, trans-species communities benefit from nimble leadership and competent, compassionate strength. At least, finally, we humans know all about the wreckage of collided *person*alities, and so we go about problem-solving differently now. Big issues require that "our personalities mean nothing: but the issues themselves mean a good deal."[51] In the functional trans-species community, we save each other from self-perpetuated as well as captivity's atrocities.

BONNET'S VOLITION

As 2009 progresses, Bonnet and I continue our mutual explorations in parrot-centric activities, which I admittedly enjoy, too.

Soon she flies from her cage to her gym, then to the kitchen counter top. She hangs out on the counter and plays with toys. In a few days, she does the above, then climbs onto the counter-top perch, a parrot favorite. Since the counter-top perch is closer still to Hawkeye's Windowsill, and Hawkeye is still imperial, I remain vigilant to avoid parrot-to-parrot conflict.[52] Soon it's time to add for Bonnet a new destination. She no longer gets out of breath from flying, only from flaring at Hawkeye.

As the days progress and our times together increase, Bonnet and I start doing more and doing less. We find pleasure in more flying and landing lessons as well as being together and just looking. Our time together increases. We check the views from many windows; we watch outside; we look for hawks; we preen her feathers. When I go outside to pick pomegranates and oranges, Bonnet watches me. In the house, she gets a new play gym on top of the refrigerator: a big hit! Suddenly, it seems that Bonnet is everywhere, hanging on the mug rack, checking out her reflection in the toaster oven, landing on and taking off from every surface in her range. I can no longer count and document her flights and keep track of her at the same time.

Soon, she discovers the easy flight from her gym to the backs of the dining room chairs, which are off limits because she chews them.[53] This necessitates action, so I enrich the dining room table with a big basket of fruit that Bonnet can pulverize right after I cover the backs of the chairs with over-turned magazines, deterrents to those zygodactly toes and that hooked beak. Bonnet stays busy flying from her cage to her gym to the counter or counter perch, up to the 'frig top, and down to the fruit basket. She effectively doubles her flight patterns as she begins flying back and forth.

On her own, Bonnet flies to a bookcase and samples some spines. Every shelf is explored; books are chewed. When I suggest that she go elsewhere, she does until the moment my attention wavers, then she goes back to her psittacine-centric yet bookish demonstration of insatiability. Sometimes, separation is a necessary part of community.[54] After lots of adventure, sometimes not enough, Bonnet jumps back into her cage where a good meal and her nap await her.

Dream Interpretation and Trans-species Interpretation

For us, Bonnet and me, communication is verbal and non-verbal, visualized and invisible, familiar yet imperceptible. This experience with Bonnet is quiet and raucous, funny and profound, and it pushes new boundaries of shared freedom.

> Look, it cannot be seen – it is beyond form.
> Listen, it cannot be heard – it is beyond sound.
> Grasp, it cannot be held – it is intangible.
> These three are indefinable;
> Therefore they are joined in one.[55]

Whether tightly woven with vibrant cords or loosely gathered with gossamer threads, trans-species lives, works, and sensibilities reside in the human psyche. On the jacket of a DVD that features wild parrots in flight, applied behavior scientist Susan Friedman writes, "If you don't dream of flight, you will."[56] Nearly every dawn, my dreams of flight are interrupted by distant parrot yells that get louder as the wild flock of parrots in Santa Barbara flies onto our property.[57] It's no wonder that outstretched wings, flashing colors, and lip-free music are prominent in my dreams.

The epistemes of the dream interpreter and the trans-species interpreter have much in common. Jung writes, "I have made it a rule myself to consider every case as an entirely new proposition about which I do not even know ABC."[58] This is exactly the way I approach both trans-species communication, mind, and behavior. Further, "routine responses may be practical and useful when one is dealing with the surface," but as soon as we touch another being's psyche, Jung writes, "even the most brilliant theoretical premises become ineffectual words."[59] "Ineffectual words" have little use in actual trans-species collaborations, however humans find them necessary for communicating with other humans. Parrots whisper, sing, riff, and yell a wide variety of tones, tunes, whistles, chirps, and beeps, equally communicative and interpretive.

In much the same manner as dream interpretation, interpretation in the trans-species community is fresh each time, layered within the "imagination and intuition [which] are vital to our understanding."[60]

Fig. 5: Trans-species communication often requires a different language, that of color and posture, for example.
Photo courtesy of Santa Barbara Bird Farm and Kelly Flynn

The type of imagination and intuition required for interpretation are "manifestations of a psyche that is beyond the control of the conscious mind,"[61] yet dependent upon learning and evidenced by action.

Intuition and imagination are inimical to the pursuit of trans-species psychology, strengthening its precepts and principles. "Meaning and purposefulness are not the prerogatives of the mind; they operate in the whole of living nature."[62] I see meaning and purposefulness in Bonnet's actions; she actualizes those words with take-offs, flights, and landings. An element of fearlessness attends her actions, too, because some destinations are entirely new and untried. Therefore, she combines purposefulness with intuition, just like a physicist. "Even physics," Jung writes, "the strictest of all applied sciences, depends to an astonishing degree upon intuition, which works by way of the unconscious."[63] Interpretations are purposeful experiences that include images, dreams, awakenings, and deep meetings. "Overall," writes G.A. Bradshaw, "C.G. Jung's depth psychology retains a capacity to connect across species through the pervasive extensive world of the unconscious and myth."[64]

In practicality, Jung is spot-on when he says the dream interpreter "has to deal with casualties in a genuine war,"[65] which is particularly true for trans-species interpreters. The interpreter "must concern himself with psychic realities, even if he cannot embody them in scientific definition,"[66] says Jung, by way of explanation. The same holds true of the trans-species interpreter, especially as we come to grips with the historically horrific roles humans have played and continue to play in the lives of non-human beings. The screams of parrots in distress are unforgettably piercing and even potentially damaging to human ears; deafness is not unknown in aviculture.

It's "imagination and intuition, those vital guides" that assist us as we "deal with facts that cannot be completely or adequately grasped."[67] Those facts are, of course, subject to measurable collection like empirical data, as well as the "phenomenon of emotion" and the "concept of the unconscious:"[68] all of which meet for exploration during trans-species communication.

Not a lazy practice, Jung warns would-be dream interpreters against feelings of "vague satisfaction"[69] and false senses of security, maladies not restricted to interpreters alone. Jung advocates serious study and practice before one takes on interpretation, and he writes enough to ensure the serious student materials sufficient for many hours of such study. "One can explain and know only if one has reduced intuitions to an exact knowledge of facts and their logical connections,"[70] he admonishes, and in an ideal world, trans-species interpreters would all attain such standards. As an example of diligent practice, Jung is known to have interpreted over 80,000 dreams.[71]

BONNET'S 80,000 WAYS OF THINKING, FEELING, AND BEING

Bonnet's expanded life and actions, especially her adept flights,

Fig. 6: Revelation in a glance.
Photo courtesy of Santa Barbara Bird Farm and Chris Pinebeck

Fig. 7: Captive for over 25 years, Simon is committed to the new parrot-digm.
Photo courtesy of Santa Barbara Bird Farm and Lindsey Eltinge

numerous smooth landings, mid-air turns, and raucous trills, illustrate
not only her individual growth, but our collective relationship. I let
the answering machine pick up telephone messages in order to hang
out with her; I get up earlier in the morning; Hawkeye gets a great big
perch in another room so Bonnet can sometimes enjoy the windowsill
without competition. She flies from wherever to land on my arm,
shoulder, hand, or hip. When she comes out of the cage, she no longer
automatically bolts for the play gym, but instead climbs up my arm
for a face-to-face appreciative eye flash and nuzzle. I think about her
when we're apart.

In the months that it has taken to complete this essay, Bonnet's
prowess has increased and is usually ½ step ahead of my vigilance. Her
flight patterns are too numerous to count because by now, she tries
something new every day. In fact, she goes from one new expression to
another, then back to any point along the way.

Just today, for instance, after going to all her known places, Bonnet
and I went to a different room, my work-out room, which is significantly
enriched for parrots (here is where Hawkeye got her new big perch).
Up until now, it's a room Bonnet does not visit since it's normally
inhabited by either Hawkeye or (Carly) Simon, *Amazona ochrocephala
parvipes*.[72] Today, first time there, Bonnet made herself at home right
away as she un-shyly goofed around on Simon's extensive play gyms
(Simon was away, yelling in another part of the house). Then Bonnet
enthusiastically accepted the invitation to take a shower on Simon's
gym. After that, she foraged for, found, and devoured Simon's almonds.
Later, with a shriek, Bonnet flew from Simon's basket back to her own
'frig gym, then to her old play gym, and finally to my shoulder where
her loud self-congratulations were broadcast directly in to my ear.

Now she does all of the above in a variety of patterns, back and
forth. Our actions and interactions blossom and proliferate. Now I
either have to stop our sessions to keep track of her actions (human-
centric), or become more Bonnet-like and eschew documentation
(parrot-centric). I choose the latter.

Nowhere does Jung better describe my normal daily routine than
when he says the practice of interpretation "ceases to be a tranquil
pursuit for the scientist in the laboratory and becomes an active part
of the adventure of real life."[73] The adventures of my life through trans-

species concerns consist of hours and hours of hard work, enthusiastic yelling, and moments of glimmering transcendence.

ASCENDANT GOOFING-OFF, TROUBLESOME DEMAND

During these times, our trans-species communications have grown in direct proportion to our community. Every day, fluency between Bonnet and me increases. But it's not only places we've been, flights made, or landings accomplished: it's time together, the scent of the ruff of feathers surrounding her neck, the spectrum of colors marching along her feathers, the feel of her feet and weight on my arm: relaxed heartbeats and quiet breathing. Innumerable choices and mutual decisions have strengthened our shared will and we want more: bigger spaces, more time, and yes, deeper meanings.

The nuance and the force of this relationship and others like it, however, must serve the purpose of *decreasing* demand for parrots in captivity, not increasing it. I worry that Bonnet's beauty and the companionship we share can be twisted into a possessive I-want-that-energy, energy that seeps out and causes other wild parrots to be caught in nets and die in transport so that other Phoebes get to experience inter-species companionship. I worry, as Jung did, about the problems some people—those for whom the "phenomenon of symbolic ideas are a nuisance"—might encounter in trying to understand our specific relationship and interpretations in general. However, "irrespective of our ability to formulate them in intellectual terms," examinations of relationships and interpretations continue, with and beyond time and reason, to enrich.

THE ANESTHESIA OF OPTIMISM

A major problem with trans-species interpretation arises because of the time and work it requires, and another because it is profoundly unsettling. It is much easier to inhale the anesthesia of optimism than to come face-to-face, brain-to-brain, and heart-to-heart in deeply meaningful ways with non-humans while being simultaneously aware of one's personal and history's aggregated disregard for entire animal populations and their wild habitats. This awareness turns the poles of one's being. Thinking, feeling, sophisticated, and worthy non-humans —not just parrots, but elephants, dolphins, turkeys, dogs, sea-horses, and more—uncounted by-catch, unremembered communities, singular deaths, and multiple graves—the implications of trans-species understanding are innumerable and shattering. The deeper the knowledge, the more daunting the challenge, and the rewards are not guaranteed because, honestly, we do not know for sure that we are capable. Even so, we reject the anesthesia of optimism when we challenge reality, starting with our daily lives. We recall what may have been taught out of many of us: we "listen to the world's other voices [that] reverberate in the psyche."[74] We must call upon our "superior" human reasoning to renew what we have "unlearned": integration and community-building through trans-species relationships.

"Envelopes of Protection"

Trans-species interpreters and facilitators learn about capture, war, confinement, and even genocide because we are ethically called to listen to *all* of the story, not only the nice parts. Often, revelations call out for resolution. As one living being connects to another, together we form "envelopes of protection"[75] for each other. Trained, well-practiced interpreters must "give up the implicit assumption that any conscious experiences of other animals must be a subset of human experiences"[76] and be ready to assume the priorities and sensibilities of other species.

For this writer, being an interpreter for animals is a serious ethical undertaking that consistently calls upon a well-disciplined intellectual life, good physical health, and efficient emotional processing. Parrots will not communicate with the naïve or bumbling. Discipline is essential for reflection. Also, humans must resist twisting messages into human-centric concerns; when that happens, the information is corrupted, time is compromised, and nothing is accomplished.[77]

During interpretation, one animal might speak for herself, her flock, her kind, or as a sole voice for the entire non-human clan. She might share images through emotions or dreams. Or, she might be hesitant, unsure about how to effectively share what she knows. A hawk or other disturbance trumps a story, and many sessions are ended peremptorily, with loud yells. However, trans-species relationships are built on these keen, clean interactions, and we welcome each moment, image, and understanding.

For example, here is a transcription of dialogue with Hawkeye, who has a skin condition which I think would benefit from more showers.

She is resistant to showering ("Ornery," I used to think.). I want her to shower more readily, when it's convenient for me, when I decide she should, such as in the morning, when she comes into the bathroom with me. During many conversations, over months together in the shower where Hawkeye consistently chooses to be out of the spray, here, distilled, is our conversation.

"Hawkeye, how do you want to bathe?" I ask.

"I don't want to bathe at all," she explains. "It's not bathing I need, it's a total environment."

"OK. Tell me more."

"The ideal place for me—and others like me—is an environment where everything is saturated with pure water. The very air is long-suffused with vapors. Waters lap on a bank of rocks. The environment I like is green and blue, thick blue with warm cool water, cut by dappled light, stirred by barely felt wet breezes. These are the elements my feathers, skin, and being needs."

Quietly, I consider her words. I remember being in Costa Rica, and how, getting off the plane, the air hit my skin, hot and moist. It felt like involuntary osmosis. My pores poured open in complete symbiosis with that hotter-than- normal body temperature! My body's 97% water content was the same as the enveloping 97% humidity, and the temperature of 102° F was consistent inside and out.

"That's what I like," Hawkeye confirms. "Especially for my feathers."

"I hear you. Please, continue," I suggest.

*Obligingly, Hawkeye explains, "Ideally for me, where each feather shaft inserts, my skin should be perpetually moist. Follicles' furthest points, where they sink into muscles, damp and supple. Think of being upside down and shaking your hair, long and wet, but it covers **all** your body, then you turn right side up again and you feel each follicle, wet, reposition itself in muscle and skin.*

"For me," says Hawkeye, "it's a particular type of moisture."

She continues, "My feathers are individuals, each as well known to me as your digits are to you.

"The feathers on my body are as different from each other as your finger is to your toe; each with a different function, too. Functions that, when coordinated, result in a finely tuned body capable of flight.

"In this environment I'm describing," says Hawkeye, "the moist one, my slick primary flight and tail feathers encourage damp atoms to slide along

the feather shafts. When I rouse, the damp atoms percolate through my covert feathers and then go into the downy puffs that insulate the insertion points between feather and skin.

"That's how I like my body moisturized—through dewy wetness that skates down my primary feathers and gets puffed into my barbs and barbules."

"Every once in a while," she conveys, "I'll take a real bathing bath, but mainly, I like breathing heavy warm wet atoms, and I like the way these atoms feel against my feathers, skin, beak, and everything I touch."

I ask, "What does a "real bathing bath" look like to you?"

Hawkeye replies, "It happens on that bank I tell you about, where water slides against the shore. Of many live ponds, one is special to us.

"Our bathing bath spot has vines that trail down from the tallest trees. Down, down, down to the water where tendrils joust in the eddies.

"That's where I'd go with my cousins for a bath. Once we're all together, we goof around for a while splashing our wings and stuff, and, if we feel like it, we take a bath. Usually, we just catch mist.

"All around are flock, everyone as individual as your family, including the elders, kids, and kin."

In our shared vision, the light changes overhead, and with raucous yells, the flock flies away. In the physical world, I add humidity to Hawkeye's environment, but worry that it's too little, too late. In my dreams, I see the bathing spot she describes.

Clearly, the interpreter must not only know the practice, she must also be learning, and learning quickly, while seamlessly adjusting past knowledge with the information currently imparted. If attempts at trans-species dialogue are thwarted or over-embraced, individualized repair procedures are needed. When it works correctly, mutual un-divided attention is shared simultaneously between two beings; neither one wanting anything except clarity, experienced mutually. Getting through and being there together for the experience as it unfolds; this is the work of trans-species communication.

Inter-species communications are a sure antidote to human-centric life; they correct my path by broadening it beyond species lines.[78] Similarly, Jung's experience at Taos broadens him, and parrots may have inspired his epiphany. Likewise, the cultural strictures of his time might have kept Jung from giving parrots any formal credit, but the imagery he uses invokes that of captivity. Before going to Taos, Jung writes, "I was still *caught up and imprisoned* in the cultural consciousness of the white man."[79] While in Taos, something spokesman Ochwiay Biano says to Jung stimulates a "long meditation," wherein he "felt something unknown and yet deeply familiar"[80] rising within.

Jung recognizes his outsider status at the pueblo—he's not a flock member, he doesn't know the language. He's a visitor. Yet the air is "filled with a secret known to all the communicants, but to which whites could gain no access,"[81] he recounts. The unknown yet deeply familiar will not let him go; his longing for connection and understanding intensifies and eventually, Jung goes through an experience that leaves him irrefutably changed.[82]

The secret "known to all communicants" is the nexus of trans-species interpretation. Parrots are famous for yelling it. For non-humans, the importance of humans who take on trans-species sensibilities, who build trans-species communities, and who practice trans-species psychology, is inimitable.

I am sure there are many humans who think as I do, which is that while we still have some non-humans left—those we've not yet managed to eat, chase away, or obliterate—we need to do our very best to understand and protect them. Non-human centric ways that tightly edit proven traditions: these are inimical to the co-creation of trans-species communities.

Surely, as sentient human beings, we are fully awakened now to the multiple atrocities of colonialization, human-centricism, human over-population, and the attendant degradation these controllable behaviors have upon our planet, our psyches, and our shared futures. Let's stop building "intricate defensives"[83] that protect the rancid status quo and more vigorously incorporate respectful, reciprocal, and attendant relationships with non-human animals into our actions and psyches.

Nascent readiness sparks Bonnet's countenance: every day, she's ready to try many new activities, and she advises me of her readiness at dawn. On mornings like the one Jung writes about, when the sunrise blazes with "tremendous impress,"[84] that's when Bonnet yells her loudest.

NOTES

1. Marie-Louise von Franz, "The Process of Individuation," *Man and His Symbols*, ed. Carl G. Jung (New York: Dell Publishing, 1975), p. 235-236.

2. *Ibid.*, p. 235.

3. The Kerulos Center; www.kerulos.org.

4. Kathleen M. Dudzinski and T. Frohoff, *Dolphin Mysteries: Unlocking the Secrets of Communication* (New Haven: Yale University Press, 2008), p. 31. In a "fission-fusion dynamic," parrots are like elephants, dolphins, and chimpanzees who "spend a lot of time in small groups traveling, foraging, and playing and come together to form larger groups for socializing, coordinated foraging, and other activities." Parrots also form one-on-one life-long friendships and familial relationships.

5. From Gerard Manley Hopkins, "The Leaden Echo and the Golden Echo (Maiden's song from St. Winefred's Well)", *The Poems of Gerard Manley Hopkins*, eds. W.H. Gardner and N. H. MacKenzie (New York: Oxford University Press, 1970), p. 92. The poet's original line is, "Give beauty back, beauty, beauty, beauty, back to God, beauty's self and beauty's giver."

6. C.G. Jung, *Memories, Dreams, Reflections*, recorded and edited by Aniela Jaffe (New York: Vintage Books, 1965), p. 248.

7. Psittacine birds are of the order *Psittaciformes* who are zygodactyl (with two toes pointing forward and two back), hook-billed birds including macaws, cockatoos, lories, parakeets, Amazons, and more. See Forshaw, www.parrots.org, *et al*.

8. Santa Barbara's climate is particularly suited to outdoor living for healthy parrots as they benefit from natural full-spectrum light, day-length variations, and year-round, locally-grown fresh produce. This author considers exposure to full-spectrum light a necessary aspect of parrot care. See Greene Linden, "How UV Light Helps Parrots Select Food," *Parrots* (West Sussex, England: Imax Publishing), 55: Aug 2002, 16-22.

9. Bucket died of fatty liver disease. To read more about this affliction, consult, http://www.parrots.org/index.php/newsletter/ FlockTalk_Issue9, http://www.parrots.org/index.php/ forumsandexperts/interview_brian_s, http://www.parrots.org/pdfs/ all_about_parrots/reference_library/health_and_nutrition/ Milk_Thistle.pdf.

10. Phoebe Greene Linden, "Early Memory in the Developing Parrot," *Proceedings of the International Aviculturists Society* (IAS: Ft. Meyers FL, 1997), pp. 104-123.

11. Since the 1970's Santa Barbara Bird Farm has advocated for and provided reinforcements and environments well-suited to encourage parrot-like behaviors in aviary- and home-based situations. In the last decade, the work of Dr. G.A. Bradshaw, especially, has been invaluable for people and parrots, and for this author particularly. Bonnet's environment is built to accommodate individual psittacine growth, where both individual preferences and species-like propensities are practiced.

12. C.G. Jung, "Approaching the Unconscious," *Man and His Symbols*, p. 80.

13. G.A. Bradshaw, personal communication, August, 2003.

14. David Fraser, "Abstract: Animal Behavior, Animal Welfare and the Scientific Study of Affect," *Applied Animal Behavior Science* (118), 2009, 108.

15. Phoebe Greene Linden, "Teaching Psittacine Birds to Learn," *Seminars in Avian and Exotic Pet Medicine*, Alan M. Fudge and Christine Davis, eds., 8:4, Oct 99, 154-164.

16. Andrew Luescher and Phoebe Greene Linden, "Behavioral Development of Psittacine Companions: Neonates, Neophytes, and Fledglings," *The Manual of Parrot Behavior*, A. Luescher, ed. (Ames, IO: Blackwell Publishing, 2006), pp. 92-111. The behavioral thresholds necessary to give parrots and people "the richest experiences possible as companions" are more fully explained herein.

17. This taxonomic order is among the *Aves* class and includes parrots conspicuous by their hooked beaks and zygodactyl feet (two toes point forward and two toes point back), but who otherwise inhabit a plethora of sizes, shapes, colors, and habitats.

18. Nigel J. Collar, A.J. Long, Robles Gil, and J. Rojo, *Birds and People: Bonds in a Timeless Journey* (Mexico City, Mexico: CEMEX-Agrupacion Sierra Madre-Bird Life International, 2007).

19. *Ibid.*, p. 41.

20. *Ibid.*

21. *Ibid.*

22. C.P. Snow, *The Two Cultures and A Second Look* (New York: Cambridge University Press, 1959).

23. Joanne Abramson, B.L. Speer, J.B. Thomsen, *The Large Macaws: Their Care, Breeding and Conservation* (Fort Bragg, CA: Raintree Publications, 1995), pp. 502-507.

24. *Ibid.*, p. 502.

25. *Ibid.*

26. Vine Deloria, Jr., "Excerpts from C. G. Jung and the Sioux Traditions: Dreams, Visions, Nature and the Primitive", *Spring 76, A Journal of Archetype and Culture: Psyche & Nature*, 2 of 2 (New Orleans, LA, Fall 2006), pp. 7-18.

27. *Ibid.*

28. *Ibid.*

29. Luescher and Greene Linden, "Behavioral Development," pp. 92-111.

30. *Ibid.*, p. 105.

31. To read more about the affliction hepatic lipidosis or "fatty liver disease," consult, http://www.parrots.org/index.php/newsletter/FlockTalk_Issue9,http://www.parrots.org/index.php/forumsandexperts/interview_brian_s, http://www.parrots.org/pdfs/all_about_parrots/reference_library/health_and_nutrition/Milk_Thistle.pdf and Greg J. Harrison and T.L. Lightfoot, "Non-infectious Diseases of the Liver," *Clinical Avian Medicine, Vol. 1* (Palm Beach, Fl: Spix Publishing, 2006), p. 444-445.

32. Perhaps, like dolphins and elephants who vocalize outside the range of human hearing (Dudzinski and Frohoff, *Dolphin Mysteries*, p. 10), parrots emit sounds that humans cannot hear without special equipment. Even so, the sounds parrots make that humans *can* hear are so varied, so complex, so melodious, and so numerous as to defy enumeration and categorization.

33. See a recent news brief on the confiscation of 1000 African Greys at http://www.parrots.org/flyfree/pressreleases/wpt_release_0210.pdf.

34. N. Snyder, P. McGowan, J. Gilardi and A. Grajal, eds., *Parrots. Status Survey and Conservation Action Plan 2000-2004* (Gland, Switzerland: International Union for Conservation of Nature, IUCN, 2004), pp. 2-15.

35. *Ibid.*

36. *Ibid.*

37. Hawkeye-approved visitors include Nikki (*Eolophus roseicapillus* cockatoo, who reveres Hawkeye), Cella (*Eclectus roratus vosmaerie,* who

stays out of Hawkeye's way) and Harry (*Homo sapiens,* who respects Hawkeye).

38. Joseph Forshaw, *Parrots of the World* (Neptune, NJ: T.F.H. Publications, 1977), pp. 412-415.

39. http://en.wikipedia.org/wiki/Carolina_Parakeet.

40. Forshaw, p. 414.

41. *Ibid.*

42. *Ibid.*, emphasis mine.

43. *Ibid.*, p. 414.

44. Luescher and Linden: "Thoughtful caregivers keep the environment suitable for keen interaction with the birds as they change and develop." "Behavioral Development," p. 94.

45. *Ibid.* "The rigorous environmental, nutritional, and interactive demands that neonates make are mimicked by the equally unapologetic demands made by highly functioning psittacine adults."

46. http://www.parrots.org/index.php/referencelibrary/specialtygroupsandpublications/.

47. George Orwell, *Dickens, Dali & Others* (New York: Harcourt, Brace, Jovanovich, 1946), p. 123.

48. William Butler Yeats, "Sailing to Byzantium," *The Norton Anthology of English Literature*, M.H. Abrams, *et. al.*, ed. (New York: W.W. Norton, 1968), p. 2386.

49. C.P. Snow, *Two Cultures*, p. 55.

50. *Ibid.*, p. 56.

51. *Ibid.*, p. 58.

52. I'm careful with Hawkeye and Bonnet's interactions because parrots do not automatically get along with each other, especially in the domestic environment where they cannot easily fly far away in the event of another parrot's intrusion.

53. I solve the problem of Bonnet flying to the book cases by putting strips of aluminum foil across the shelves, which she avoids. In a week, I reduce the size of the foil, and eventually remove it altogether as Bonnet is busy with more parrot-friendly places.

54. Lao Tsu, "Fourteen," *Tao Te Ching*, trans. Gia-Fu Feng and Jane English (New York: Random House, 1972).

55. Susan G. Friedman, as quoted on "PollyVision," World Parrot Trust DVD jacket. http://www.parrots.org/index.php/shoptosave/pollyvision.

56.http://www.santabarbarabirdfarm.com/Wild%20Parrots/wildparrots.html.

57. Carl G. Jung, "Approaching the Unconscious: The Role of Symbols," *Man and His Symbols* (New York: Dell Publishing, 1975), p. 82.

58. *Ibid.*

59. *Ibid.*

60. *Ibid.*, p. 53.

61. *Ibid.*

62. *Ibid.*, p. 82.

63. G.A. Bradshaw, "Elephant Trauma and Recovery: Toward a Liberation Ecopsychology," dissertation (Santa Barbara, CA: Pacifica Graduate Institute, 2005), p. 79.

64. Jung, "Approaching the Unconscious," p. 80.

65. *Ibid.* "One cannot afford to be naïve in dealing with dreams," writes Jung. He effectively portrays my experience with trans-species communications which "originate in a spirit that is not quite human, but is rather a breath of nature. . ." p. 36.

66. *Ibid.* Jung warns "against unintelligent or incompetent dream analysis" as well as "ready-made systematic guides" to dream interpretation, but also calls upon typical and frequently occurring dream "motifs", such as dreams of flying. p. 38.

67. *Ibid.*, p. 47.

68. *Ibid.*, p. 80.

69. *Ibid.*

70. John Freeman, "Introduction," *Man and His Symbols*, pp. v-xii.

71. Bonnet and Carly Simon do not get along.

72. Jung, "Approaching The Unconscious," p. 80.

73. Stephen Aizenstat, "Tending the Dream is Tending the World," *Spring 76, A Journal of Archetype and Culture: Psyche & Nature*, 2 of 2 (New Orleans, LA, Fall 2006), p. 62.

74. G.A. Bradshaw, "Trans-species Psychology," lecture April 2007.

75. *Ibid.*

76. Bradshaw, "Toward Liberation Ecopsychology," p. 18.

77. For an example of inauthentic inter-species communication, go to http://www.marianhaileymoss.com/, scroll until you see the turkey fingers, then read "Phoebe's Goin' Veggie."

78. Jung, *Memories, Dreams, Reflections*, p. 247. Emphasis mine.
79. *Ibid.*, p. 248.
80. *Ibid.*, p. 249.
81. Deloria, Jr., "Excerpts from Jung and the Sioux," p. 13.
82. C. P. Snow, *Two Cultures*, p. 67.
83. Jung, *Memories, Dreams, Reflections*, p. 251.

THE ART OF CULTURAL BROKERAGE: RECREATING ELEPHANT-HUMAN RELATIONSHIP AND COMMUNITY

CAROL BUCKLEY & G. A. BRADSHAW

The zoo elephants were taught to never, ever touch the bullhook, the razor-sharp, pointed steel prod used to control elephants in captivity. One day the elephant Amy knocked the bullhook out of a keeper's hand and it flew across the yard. The keeper ordered Amy to retrieve the bullhook, telling her, "Amy, go pick up the bullhook." Amy hesitated and was ordered to again and again until she finally complied. Once near the bullhook, Amy was ordered to "pick up the bullhook." She didn't. The keeper repeated the order. Finally, Amy picked up a stick. The keeper said, "Amy, no, pick up the bullhook." Amy found and picked up another stick-like item. Again, she was ordered to pick up the bullhook. Finally, Amy picked up the bullhook and then began repeatedly hitting herself on the head with it.
—American zookeeper[1]

Carol Buckley is an international leader in trauma recovery of Asian and Africa elephants. She has over thirty years experience with elephants in captivity and is co-founder of the first natural-habitat refuge for sick, old, and needy endangered elephants, the Elephant Sanctuary in Tennessee. Carol is the recipient of the Genesis Award in 2001 and TIME Magazine's Hero for the Planet Award in recognition of her innovative work.

G.A. Bradshaw, Ph.D., Ph.D., is the executive director of the Kerulos Center and author of *Elephants on the Edge: What Animals Teach Us About Humanity* (Yale University Press, 2009). Her work focuses on animal psychological trauma and recovery and approaches to support wildlife cultural self-determination.

INTRODUCTION

There is perhaps no construction in the English language as entrenched as the "and" in "human and nature". With a simple insertion of three letters, the universe splits in two. Law, food, custom, economics, language, social relationships, and the ethics of global culture are all rooted in this divide. This separatist paradigm permeates our relationships with other animals.

But of late, there is a change. Animals no longer seem so different. Even science, that once insisted we humans stood out from the rest of the animal kingdom continuum, has conceded that humans[2] and other animals are comparable in mind. Suddenly, we find ourselves similar to strangers who discover they are related: face to face on equal footing but uncertain how to proceed.[3]

Following the maxim of the medical profession, the logical first step is to "do no harm": discontinue practices that presume human privilege at the expense of other animals. Ethologist Marc Bekoff encourages us to "expand our compassion footprint" and to do unto animal relatives as we would wish to have them do unto us: to stop mass enslavement of animals as commodities for food production and entertainment, for example.[4] Vanquishing this and other cruel practices prevents future abuse, but what about the millions of living casualties? The tiger living in a concrete zoo, the chimpanzee suffering from decades of biomedical testing, the parrot caged in isolation, and domesticated cats and horses whose minds and bodies are shaped to comply with human desires? Even "wild" grizzly bears living in Glacier National Park and elephants in Amboseli, Kenya are not immune. Their fates are determined by what humans wish, not the animals' own decisions, ecology, and psychology.[5] Moving into a compassionate future entails putting the truth we know into reconciling action by helping animals rebuild their lives.

However, righting past wrongs does not happen over night. The scars of trauma run deep: violence leaves a legacy in the minds and bodies of its victims. Further, animals have learned to fear humans even "when they bear gifts."[6] Dame Daphne Sheldrick tells us that elephants and other animals "who once trusted and loved humans may not be quite so accommodating after having been "told" about the experience of others at the hands of humans."[7] If we are to help animal victims recover, then we, as the agents of their distress, must learn how to eschew

Fig. 1: Carol Buckley, co-founder of the preeminent Elephant Sanctuary in Tennessee, and Tarra share a bond developed over nearly forty years.
Photo courtesy of Carol Buckley

domination and instead interact with other animals under their conditions and terms.[8]

Here we integrate the concepts of trans-species psychology and neuropsychology with elephant experience of trauma and their recovery in sanctuary. We explore an example of relational transformation through a description of elephants and humans living in sanctuary. We describe the re-creation of trans-species community looking through the lens of *culture brokering*. This concept was developed to depict human cross-cultural facilitation, the "act of bridging, linking or mediating between groups or persons of differing cultural backgrounds for the purpose of reducing conflict or producing change."[9] We extend this idea to psychosocial processes across species where humans function as catalysts, interpreters, and negotiators of relational repair for elephants in recovery from trauma. In sanctuary, elephant caregivers are taught to cultivate the art of trans-species brokering through self-transformation and by redefining the elephant-human relationship from exploitation to service. In so doing, a new, trans-species cultural consciousness begins to evolve.

ELEPHANT SANCTUARY

Tragically, human fascination for elephants has led to the brutal process of capture, captivity, and display. As a result, elephants over the world suffer in depauperate captive conditions.

In 1995, I co-founded the Elephant Sanctuary in Tennessee. It has grown to be the largest captive elephant, natural-habitat sanctuary in the world. I have spent thirty-six years living intimately with elephants made captive. For nearly twenty years, I traveled in the U.S. and abroad as an elephant trainer and performed in a number of circuses including Circus Gatini in Quebec, Canada and the Big Apple Circus in New York City. Before founding The Elephant Sanctuary in Tennessee,[10] I owned and operated Tarra Productions exhibiting, training, and caring for Tarra, a female Asian elephant, who performed for television, motion pictures, and circus shows. Tarra and I have been together since she was one year old. It was the profound relationship that developed with Tarra, and Tarra herself, that catalyzed my own transformation. I quit the entertainment industry to provide a home for elephants.

Typically, elephants come to sanctuary singly from various zoos or circus settings. However, in 2006, precedence was broken when a group of female elephants arrived together at the Elephant Sanctuary in Tennessee. The eight "Divas" (as they were soon dubbed in recognition of their celebrity and worldly experiences) came to sanctuary through action brought against the Hawthorn circus corporation by the United States Department of Agriculture's (USDA) Animal and Plant Health Inspection Service. Hawthorn's John F. Cuneo, Jr. had been charged with violating the Animal Welfare Act (AWA) for causing physical harm, discomfort, and trauma to elephants. Cuneo pled guilty, was fined

$200,000, and agreed to release of all elephants to USDA-approved facilities. After a protracted two-year delay, Billie, Frieda, Debbie, Queenie, Liz, Minnie, Lottie, and Ronnie were finally released by the Hawthorn Corporation and trucked over twelve hours to the Sanctuary. They arrived two by two, transported in the Sanctuary's custom-designed, climate-controlled elephant trailer. Sadly, Sue, also a Hawthorn elephant, died weeks before she could be moved to the Sanctuary. The tragedy occurred as result of a sedative administered by a Hawthorn veterinarian.

On average, the elephants were captured at the age of two and lived their days and nights in confinement. More recently, zoos obtain elephants through artificial insemination programs and captive breeding.[11] Most of these infants will be prematurely separated from their mothers and in the case of female infants who in the wild would remain with their mother their entire lifetime, will experience relational trauma: unnatural separation from mother and family with no exposure to normative elephant society. All are subjected to the heavy hand of human control. The Divas were prevented from socializing freely. The majority of their time was spent in dark indoor barns with concrete floors and they were chained eighteen or more hours a day except when performing. Their circumstances most closely resembled those of

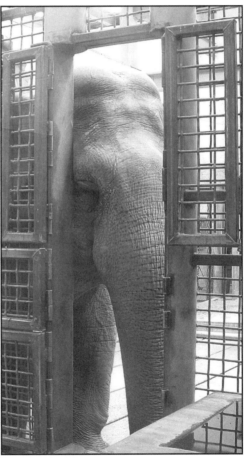

Fig. 2: Lucy behind bars in the Edmonton Zoo, Canada—captivity is unsuitable for any soul.

Photo courtesy of Zoocheck, Canada

human prisoners who experience group living shackled and separated in individual cells.[12]

Circuses and zoos routinely employ a number of physical and psychological techniques to control and dominate elephants.[13] A description of an American zoo by a former elephant keeper provides a snapshot of typical life for a zoo elephant: "The elephant facility consisted of a cramped indoor exhibit where the elephants were chained front and back nightly. . . Access to the outside yard meant passing through the hippo's night stall across a hallway and involved three manual doors. The outside yard was a four-foot high chain link fence with a pair of leg chains." Further, many zoos are located in climates unsuited for elephants.[14] Over time, combined with the poor living quarters and inadequate social and emotional support, climatic stress leads to health and mental breakdown. In recognition of the duress that captivity causes, a number of zoos have recently moved away from chaining, converting to a more humane system called "protected contact". In this system the ankus (a sharpened metal prod, also called a bullhook) is obsolete. However, circuses and zoos that continue the use of traditional elephant methods (referred to as *free contact*) share a common goal: total control. It is telling that the captive industry refers to systems of elephant care as elephant "management" as opposed to simply elephant "care."[15]

One of the Sanctuary's primary functions is to provide safe structure without human control. Critically, elephants have free will and are able to exercise choice at all times. They may move, think, and be in their bodies without fear. To address deep-seated psychological damage resulting from unnatural confinement and harsh practices of control, the Sanctuary designed its care program to model what psychoanalyst Donald Winnicott calls a *facilitating environment* by creating "a dialogical space of security and creativity."[16] The arriving elephant is treated carefully and tenderly to provide her full flexibility and the capacity to secure for herself a sense of control in new surroundings. For the first time in decades, she encounters an environment that promotes healthy and natural elephant living. While not identical to the jungles of Asia or the savannahs of Africa, the sanctuary habitat provides a variety of lush vegetation and foraging opportunities, with ample nutritious food to chose from, holistic healthcare, a life-long home and social groups, hundreds of acres to explore to help build physical and mental competence, ponds and creeks to bathe in and play, and barns that provide comfort and shelter. The elephants form and participate in a trans-species community comprised of other elephants, humans, and other Sanctuary residents such as Bella, a dog, with whom Tarra became very close.[17]

> The fundamental relationships for elephants are those with their true herd members. In captivity we need to define what is meant by "true." Clearly, a true herd member in the wild is a related family member. But the Sanctuary is a captive environment; none of our elephants are related by blood. They are a part of this group that has come into existence only by circumstance: bonds and meaning must be forged and family created. Human caregivers are members of that family. They provide food, water, friendship, access to freedom, and the sense of security that enables the elephants to recover from their past traumas. Critically, elephants and humans form social and emotional bonds. Human caregivers hold a special place in the hearts of these elephants because they are catalysts of elephant psychological transformation from terror to peace. They provide elephants with evidence of hope and life. If we were to believe that caregivers do not enhance the lives of these elephants then one might argue that since Bella is a dog, her relationship with Tarra, the elephant, is somehow insignificant.

Staff work on elephant time, at the elephant's convenience, not humans', shifting the dynamic from human-controlled management to a life determined by pachyderm residents.[18] In contrast to zoo and circus life, a sanctuary elephant is given total freedom of choice and encouraged to make her own decisions. Human caregivers ask, not demand, an elephant to cooperate with routine procedures such as foot soaks and trunk washes. Gentle communication is accomplished through patience and positive interactions that include the expression of care and pleasure by providing special foods. Elephants are highly intelligent and actively curious. When they feel safe and comfortable in their surroundings they willingly participate in activities that the caregiver seeks to encourage. In this positive, agency-encouraging manner, caregivers find a way that helps an elephant decide to do something in order to accomplish a need, such as receiving medical treatment or even persuading the elephant to move to a different area of the barn or habitat.

Care protocol and relationships between staff and elephant residents are informed by the philosophy of "passive control". Its three key elements are space, time, and non-dominating interactions. The term "control" was retained in recognition that sanctuary is still captivity.[19] Although sanctuary grounds comprise 2,700 acres, they are fenced, and so is, therefore, the mind of a sanctuary elephant. The elephants know that it is still humans, albeit benignly, who control their lives. These elephants will never experience their homelands and relatives again, nor experience the joy of a traditional family and caring for their children and their children's children. Nor will they be able to participate in other experiences that have made elephant society what it is: extensive migrations throughout their home range, interactions with hundreds of other elephants who comprise a vast relational network that once spanned entire continents, in the seemingly endless landscapes they call home.

Unfortunately, traumatic experiences are often deeply enduring despite the rich healing life made available to the elephants. Elephants arriving to sanctuary are encumbered by a variety of debilitating injuries including foot disease, tuberculosis, anorexia, obesity, immunological compromise, and psychological trauma. Clinically, the elephants conform to a diagnosis of Complex Post-Traumatic Stress Disorder (PTSD; also referred to as Disorders of Extreme Stress Not Otherwise Specified (DESNOS), the description created to address individuals who experience sustained long-term trauma.[20] Through her extensive work and cumulative studies on concentration camp survivors, veterans, prisoners of war, and victims of domestic violence, psychiatrist Judith Herman found that "the diagnosis of 'post-traumatic stress disorder' . . . does not fit accurately enough . . . survivors of prolonged, repeated trauma." Rather, "the syndrome that follows . . . [such experiences] needs its own name. I propose to call it 'complex post-traumatic stress disorder.'"[21] Severe trauma constitutes a profound assault on the core self that guides beliefs, emotions, and actions and can lead to changes in self-concept.

Similar to concentration camp kapos, prisoners who chose or were chosen to be guards over their fellow inmates as a way to survive, some elephants absorb the violent human culture in which they are immersed. Even after coming to Sanctuary, one of the Divas, Minnie, extended her violent behavior towards humans to other elephants, although environmental conditions that encouraged abnormal behavior—threats of violence, chains, and abusive control—were absent. Her continued abusive behavior toward Debbie and her dissociative, depressive periods suggest an alteration in identity like that observed among human prisoners who have experienced prolonged abuse. These individuals often exhibit "personality changes, including deformations of relatedness and identity."[22] Human concentration camp survivors had "alterations of personal identity [that] were a constant feature of the survivor syndrome. While the majority of . . . patients complained 'I am now a different person,' the most severely harmed stated simply 'I am not a person.'"[23] Minnie, in effect, was no longer able to be an elephant. She had lost her elephant self.

Another common psychological symptom found in traumatized elephants held in captivity is stereotypy, the patterned dance of head bobbing, trunk and body swaying. Most elephants who come to sanctuary shed this symptom whenever they are out in the habitat. However, for some, this psychological state can be triggered. For instance, an elephant, after roaming through the maze of wooded copses, wading through ponds and creeks, and climbing hills, encounters the sanctuary boundary. Instead of turning and walking in a different direction or choosing to do something else, such as knocking down a tree or talking with another elephant, a few individuals at the sanctuary boundary halt, stand in front of the fence, and begin to sway. Stereotypic dissociations develop as a protective mechanism against unbearable stress and can be related to neuropsychological traumatic reenactments that are "subcortically driven, and unintegrated into more complex adaptive behaviors [reflective of] . . . impairment of higher cortical centers."[24,25] Repetitive anxiety-triggered dissociation causes the release of endorphins that numb psychological pain and panic. In this way, the individual's core self is shielded. At sanctuary, caregivers are instructed to anticipate and divert such behavior from occurring through distracting the elephant away from the fence with succulent food, play, or a warm greeting that seeks to keep her mind and attention present.

The absence of threat and physical and emotional comfort that sanctuary offers provides the essentials for an elephant to begin her recovery. However, severe psychological damage requires others to nurture and rekindle a healthy sense of self. Through the assistance of

Fig. 3: Human control of an elephant, such as Lucy, in captivity exacts a profound psychological price because it seeks to breakdown and control the elephant's core self.

Photo courtesy of Zoocheck, Canada

friends and family, an individual learns to rebuild her identity to transition from human-dominated solitary life to human-supported, but elephant-defined, collective living. Residents co-create their own brand of elephant culture, and it is sanctuary caregivers who are integral in helping facilitate this process.

CULTURE BROKERAGE

There are multiple definitions of culture. Anthropologist Clifford Geertz defined it most succinctly as: "an ordered system of meaning and symbols, in terms of which social interaction takes place."[26] Once regarded as closed systems of meaning, cultures are conceptualized more fluidly, as a set of values, beliefs, customs, interpersonal interactions, and expectations to which a group of individuals ascribe. The term "culture broker" and related concepts such as cultural intermediary and interpreter evolved in situations where members of one human culture encountered those of another. Typically, these concepts have been applied to negotiate differences between modern white European and indigenous peoples.

A culture broker seeks to support the values, beliefs, and customs of a marginalized group, helping the members of it gain access to resources that have been denied and sequestered by the dominating culture. These resources may include jobs, education, health care, funds, and social access. In human contexts, the culture broker commonly holds a position of educator, social worker, or healthcare practitioner. At the interpersonal level, the culture broker functions similarly to a therapist by cultivating the means for the "client" to attain and maintain a self-identity that permits healthful functioning across cultures.

The task is not easy. The culture broker must be able to function biculturally, with the ability to hear and speak in ways that are meaningful to both cultures/species. Knowledge, custom, and language are shared. S/he also must be competent in diverse sub-cultures and be able to navigate intricate nuances and tacit assumptions of two or more cultures that are, almost by definition, at odds. As educator Glen Aikenhead[27] points out, the goals and ethics of culture brokering is somewhat contradictory. Concerning the education of indigenous children in western-dominated culture and schools, he asks: "How does one nurture students' achievement toward formal educational credentials and economic and political independence, while at the same time develop the students' cultural identity as Aboriginals?" and "To what extent, and how, can First Nations students learn non-Aboriginal school subjects such as science without being harmfully assimilated by science's dominant Western culture?" In other words, how can a culture broker both support an individual's sense of self that thrives in one culture while at the same time insisting that the self accommodate norms of a second culture that retains control and power? This question has particular significance for elephant trauma recovery in sanctuary where culture brokerage and elephant psychological repair intersect.

TRAUMA AND THE ELEPHANT SELF

As the pivotal culture broker/therapist, the sanctuary is charged with the ethically delicate task of helping the resident cultivate a genuine sense of self. This is accomplished by creating conditions that encourage the trauma victim to access internal psychological resources developed before trauma. Renewing social bonds is one critical aspect of recovery essential for self-repair.

While identity is influenced by a number of factors, attachment and developmental contexts are considered primary.[28] Early relationships tune the mind and brain to be able to interact successfully with the biophysical and social environment. The growing mind is incredibly plastic and receptive to the sounds, touch, smell, emotions, and voice of those who care for the infant. Depending on who and how he/she was raised, an individual's sense of self may reflect a range of cultural orientations. For example, in contrast to *individualistic, independent* societies that earmark modern, western society, many indigenous cultures are referred to as *collective, interdependent* social systems.[29] Broadly speaking, self-identity in collectively-based cultures is closely linked with the group.

Pre-trauma self-development and post-trauma self-repair are related. This is vividly illustrated in cases of cross-fostered individuals, those who are born to one species/culture and reared by another. Studies show that trauma recovery is facilitated when recovery contexts reflect developmental contexts where attachment relationships have been strong, nurturing, and healthy.[30] For wildlife, this means species-normative rearing in the wild. Sanctuary elephants have had little exposure to normative elephant society. However, because the Tennessee Sanctuary elephants spent at least their first and second years in free-ranging elephant society, they likely acquired an identity with their species/culture of origin and were therefore able to carry some elephant values and understanding into captive life.

Infant pachyderms in free-ranging, traditional elephant society are raised by a mother and allomothers: a constellation of aunts and siblings with whom the young female elephant remains for the entirety of her life. Young male elephants stay within the natal family until approximately ten years of age before moving to an all bull group for tutoring during a second phase of socialization. Viewed through the lens of transcultural neuropsychology, the elephant mind is profoundly influenced by multiple family members and the consciousness of the group.

The idea that the mind is something more than personal is common to many schools of psychology beginning with depth psychology's model of the collective unconscious to more recent concepts such as the "groupmind" where an individual is seen as a "vessel through which unconscious group life can be expressed and understood. . . [and where] groups are seen as living systems and the individuals in the group are subsystems of which the group is comprised."[31] When a person speaks he/she does so not only for themselves but also for the unconscious sentiment of the group. Recovery of an elephant psyche involves revitalization of "the supra-individual nature" of the self that represents aspects of the group's unconscious mind.[32] Individual healing is effected in the plural. But who is the captive elephants' community?

One might assume that the elephants in sanctuary belong to the same culture, or at most two cultures, given that the sanctuary provides homes for both African and Asian species. However, the elephants' "ordered system of meaning and symbols. . . in. . . which social interaction[s] take place"[33] was not shaped by free-ranging elephant society alone, but by human circus and zoo culture. Their systems of customs, interpersonal interactions, and expectations were human-dominated, forcibly imposed, in relative isolation from or sporadic contact with other elephants. Prior to living at the Sanctuary, the Divas sometimes shared physical space, yet they were forbidden to interact with each other naturally. A young mind subjected to harsh deprivation and the constant threat of harm or death has few defenses. As Minnie's torment painfully illustrates, circus and zoo elephant minds were subjected to experiences of traumatic survival; by force of circumstance, their systems of meaning became distorted by an environment defined by violence. Recovery, by necessity, involves the complex negotiation between a revitalized elephant self, the experiences of trauma, and socialization with other elephants and human caregivers.

ELEPHANT CULTURAL BROKERAGE

The elephant survivor in recovery is challenged to create a post-trauma self and learn new social behavior that is not rooted in abuse and mistrust. The sanctuary caregiver helps an individual broker past (pre-trauma self, traumatized self) and present (post-trauma self). The therapeutic alliance develops slowly and evolves over time where the human caregiver becomes part of the elephant groups as healer, sister, and friend. Relational trauma from human betrayal and violence can only be mended with relational repair: the development of deep trust, love, and care between an elephant and human caregiver. The profound bond between human and elephant that matures over time can be as important as those between elephants and must be considered as sacred. Unwilling breaking of such a bond violates elephant culture and can cause a re-traumatization.

Elephants truly see beyond the exterior to the heart and soul.

As Bunny's story illustrates, the elephants and I work with each other as co-facilitators in trans-species community. After living more than forty years in an Indiana zoo, Bunny was overweight, out of shape, and had to retrain her muscles to be able to walk with any surety in the sanctuary habitat. One evening, she was coming back to the barn but she could not figure out how to cross a dry creek. She stopped, then took a step forward at the edge of a creek bed where the embankment dropped off. She stepped as if expecting the ground to be directly under foot but it was not. She collapsed onto her elbows and froze in place, scared to death. I coaxed her to get up to no avail, she appeared to be in shock, not physically injured but emotionally traumatized. I looked up and saw Barbara, another elephant, watching from the barn door several hundred yards away. Without hesitation or verbal encouragement from me, Barbara came over to us. With a gentle trunk touch on the side of Bunny's face, Barbara was able to effortlessly and instantly encourage Bunny to stand up and follow her across the creek. I stood frozen in awe as they left for the barn, Barbara looked over her shoulder into my eyes. We shared a moment of joyful sisterhood, reveling in Bunny's triumph.

Jezewski[34] identifies twelve attributes characteristic of culture brokers and their functions. For example, a cultural broker is often called upon to intervene when tension develops that may lead to conflict. This is the role that was demanded in the early days of the Divas' arrival to sanctuary.

At 11,000 pounds, Minnie is the largest elephant at the Sanctuary. She would physically intimidate other elephants as a means to get her needs

Fig. 4: Barbara and Carol Buckley, friends and sisters in sanctuary.
Photo courtesy of Carol Buckley

met. Even though she has over 200 acres to roam and explore, trees to wrestle and topple, and ponds in which to play, Minnie exhibits periods of anxiety and begins to search out another elephant literally to push around. Initially, when I saw Minnie begin to corral another elephant, I would try to distract her with positive gestures such as giving her food or by persuading her to play with a ball or game. But these efforts merely exacerbated the situation. The more I sought to distract her, the more focused her aggressive attention on the other elephants got. I realized that I needed to be more of an observer, to watch how the tension began and what was happening environmentally that set up this situation. It was not possible to stop Minnie or other conflicts once they started, but it was possible to adjust the context so that these negative interactions did not occur or, if they did, were much more attenuated.

Many of Minnie's aggressive acts happened about one half hour before evening feeding. Typically, we brought hay and fruits to the elephants around 5:30 p.m., and it was at about 5:10 p.m. that Minnie showed signs of agitation, anxiety, and searched for someone to "pick on". When I decided to make the evening feeding times random, Minnie's conflicts decreased significantly. However, there came a time when resolution of interpersonal tensions demanded something more than perceptual readjustment.

Certain aspects of cultures, like the biophysical terrains in which they evolve, have rigid boundaries that do not permit a mixing of customs or resolution of conflict by compromise. These boundaries support psychological identity and bring coherence. However, they can also be a source of conflict when they are not consonant with those of another community. Culture brokers are therefore called upon to innovate when traditions are inflexible.[35]

Many months were spent carefully watching social and psychological patterns of individuals as they interacted with each other. Each Diva has a distinct personality and set of complexes with which she struggles on her path of recovery. Initially, the eight shared common ground. But in addition to Minnie's aggression, Billie also showed a one-time occurrence of belligerence toward a ertain member of the group. Born in 1953, Billie is the eldest, but she is not a natural matriarch like Lottie. Billie became aggressive to Lottie and head-butted her. Lottie did not retaliate, but eventually her friends, Minnie and Debbie, reprimanded Billie and despite her chronological seniority, Billie was eventually driven from group, initially spending time alone and later forming strong bonds with Liz and Frieda.

There were other internal altercations. Minnie wanted to be with Debbie, but Debbie did not. This difference in opinion led to fighting with each other, finally involving Ronnie. Finally, the conflict was so significant that Minnie's aggression threatened to injure Ronnie, which prompted me to physically split the Divas into three groups, each having their own physical area: Minnie, Lottie, and Queenie together, Debbie and Ronnie in a second group, and Liz, Frieda, and Billie in a third. After many months of networking between the sub-groups, supporting each sub-group's traditions and values, and trying to cultivate relationships, I was able to translate their individual and collective psychological needs into the design of their care and habitat. Although separated, they are able to interact across fences and talk with each other. Critically, while my relationship with each is unique, they all trust my role as intermediary and facilitator. The rewards of this work are immeasurable, both in terms of the elephant's recovery to life and their profound appreciation for my help.

The managing director of the Sanctuary describes this deep love and trust:

> I was distracted from my work in the quarantine barn office by a loud trumpeting, and jumped up just in time to see Minnie tearing through the creek. . . I admired how gracefully Minnie moved, her upper body held high while her legs raced her across the ground. Her best friend, Lottie, had summoned her, and Minnie as usual wasted no time in joining her. Soon the valley was filled with trumpets, Queenie-squeaks and a magnificent low rumbling that I have come to learn may mean the elephants are pleased to see someone. Minnie, Lottie, and Queenie were soon jostling for a prime viewing spot along the fence line, of what I wondered. The rumbling and trumpets grew louder, and then I saw what their focus was; it was Carol, who had been working at the keeper's house, coming out to greet them. These three magnificent elephants were showing and receiving love from their caregiver, after lifetimes filled with pain and disrespect. Amazingly resilient, they are able to open their hearts and we are blessed to be in their presence.[36]

Another important role of the culture broker is to "stand guard over critical junctures in the context of interactions," to provide vulnerable individuals with the security of a third party "container" who can oversee and guarantee safety. This requires that the brokering human be trusted. One of the most important challenges an elephant faces when she comes to sanctuary is to establish a relationship with her human caregivers. To grasp the enormity of this task, it is necessary to understand the roles humans play in the minds and lives of elephants made captive.

In the circus culture, where the Divas spent decades of their lives, humans have very specific roles. There are generally three categories: trainers, grooms, and showgirls. The trainer is the most powerful; he dominates the elephant using bullhooks and other instruments. The elephant must comply and obey the trainer or severe punishments follows. The groom is much lower in the circus hierarchy. S/he cleans floors, feeds the elephants, and moves elephants from chain to chain. Grooms are generally shown limited respect by the trainers and the elephants know this. Minnie was known in the circus as a "slapper": an elephant who tries to hit the groom with her trunk or leg. Some

Fig. 5: A lifetime of suffering: Elephants in annual Washington, D.C. parade
wearing green hats to celebrate St Patrick's Day.

Photo courtesy of Amy Mayers

trainers actually encourage this behavior to bolster their position of
power. The showgirl has little contact with the elephants except in
rehearsals and during the circus performance when she rides atop the
elephant's back or head. Understandably, many entertainers who are
props on the elephants are intimidated by the elephants sheer size and
use food to "bribe" and placate the elephant.

*When the Divas came to sanctuary, they found that I did not fit any of
these categories. On one hand, I fulfilled the trainer's role because of my
expertise and confidence, but I did not tell them what to do nor discipline
or punish them for any action. On the other hand, I contradicted this image
because I performed groom chores. Minnie was aware of this and showed
me no respect; indeed, she went out of her way to show her disrespect. Minnie
believed that I had no right to approach her in a personal manner. In her
eyes, I was breaking the rules of conduct by mixing trainer and groom
behaviors. The other elephants were much less resistant and became amenable
to a human who had a diversity of behaviors and roles. In a sense, they trusted
me because of these contradictions: I did not use force or try in any way to
dominate, and I encouraged them to make their own decisions, gave them
a variety of foods to choose from, and did not prevent them from coming or*

going to the barn and around the grounds. Over time, as our interactions together were shown to be consistently positive and non-threatening, trust towards me grew. It may be that the ambiguity[37] and multiplicity of my role encourages the elephants to focus on me as a person, not my status or species.

Subsequently, when a situation arose that caused anxiety or possible friction, I was sufficiently trusted to be permitted to help work things out between the elephants. For instance, when I saw that there was relational strain, I would open a gate to let Ronnie and Debbie move through to a different area leaving the others behind. They would still be able to interact with the others, but with safety. In this way, the elephants were able to work things out relationally amongst themselves in a secure and safe environment. When things calmed down. I would then open the gate to let them freely comingle. This type of brokering helped them move forward emotionally. It was my goal not to force them to be a certain way, but to provide them with the psychological, emotional, social, and physical resources to recover their own "culturally distinctive modes of communication, thought, and life styles."[38] After these many months, I have been accepted as one of the group. My knowledge and beliefs are respected as I respect those of each elephant and the group as a whole and we learn from each other. I must learn to identify the fears of each elephant and help her through every single step of the way. It is a marvel to be there when she makes a breakthrough and I stand with her as part of the family with the other elephants.

This process of mutual learning and helping is illustrated in the relationship with Sissy and Winkie.

Sissy was born in 1968 and captured from the wild in Thailand at one year of age. The City of El Paso, Texas, decided to send her to Sanctuary after she was severely beaten by zoo staff. She had suffered a series of prior traumas including being submerged in a 1981 flood that hit Gainesville, Texas, where she was kept at the Frank Buck Zoo. She survived by holding her trunk up and out of the water for three days. Unlike other elephants who cavort and splash joyfully in the pond and creek, Sissy was understandably terrified of water. She would panic when it began to rain and refuse to go near the creek.

In the fourth month after her arrival, I was out walking with her when we came across a shallow patch of standing water. I spoke softly to her, encouraging and telling her that I was right with her and would we could cross the water together. The conflictive emotions showed on Sissy's face as she obviously tried to build up confidence to try—and she finally succeeded. When we had crossed through the water, she let out a blast of a trumpet; she had actually been holding her breath. Her accomplishment, working through this fear, resulted in a display of great joy as she spun around, chirped, and ever so gently touched me with her trunk. Soon afterwards, she became mentor and coach. A few months later, Winkie, another Asian elephant with a traumatic history, was too fearful to leave the barn. Sissy stepped in and in a fashion similar to the coaching I had performed with her, she helped Winkie, two years her senior, overcome her fear and walk out of the barn.[44]

DISCUSSION

This brief excursion into the experience of elephants and humans in sanctuary provides one example of trans-species culture brokering and the transformation of animal-human relationships. Sanctuary residents and caregivers learn to share knowledge, custom, and language and to move fluidly through a mosaic of multiple sub-cultures— human, elephant-human, and elephants, each having their own customs and social expectations.

The culture broker also helps an elephant learn how to safely enter in relationships with other elephants in community. Both species work together to "create safety for each other as they re-build community, and what emerges is deepening self-knowledge not just of the individual but of the group."[39] Psychosocial integration creates a new trans-species culture. Caregivers function as "brokers" who help elephants transition from a past culture of human domination to one of elephant agency. Similar to human-human brokering, sanctuary provides marginalized individuals access to external resources formerly denied. Instead of jobs, education, and funds, elephant sanctuary provides nutritious food, expansive terrain, water, trees, and socialization with others. However, it does something more.

Critically, through aiding trauma recovery, the sanctuary *vas* helps elephants gain access to their *internal* resources: psychological and physical competence, self-repair and regeneration, and the capacity to bond socially. This was illustrated dramatically with Minnie, whose core elephant self was broken by abuse. By brokering physical and social space with Minnie, sanctuary provided her with the means to begin healing deep psychological wounds. Today, she is on the path to

Fig. 6: Carol and her elephant sisters; the evolution of trans-species community and consciousness.

Photo courtesy of Carol Buckley

rebuilding an identity of someone other than the person who absorbed the identity of her abusers.[40]

Bicultural brokering requires competence in both cultures, in this case, human and elephant. Effective sanctuary facilitators must be able to function on common ground psychologically and linguistically to gain trust and insights necessary for psychological healing and trans-species negotiation. For this reason, elephant psychological transformation is contingent on human psychological transformation. The trans-species worker must constantly be mindful and reflective of her/his projections. While sharing cultures and values, we must be respectful of difference. Even while interactions, such as Minnie and Debbie's conflict, can be very painful to watch, our role is to facilitate their process and maintain their safety, witness, not judge. It is also crucial that the caregiver believes that elephants possess the ability and right to make decisions that concern their wellbeing. Elephants are able to discern the difference. If the caregiver does not believe in elephant agency, the elephant continues to be objectified and remains psychologically dominated and captive.

Unlike western science's objectivity, witnessing does not subordinate psychological reality to collectively based facts. Witnessing is not suspicious of personal experience and does not automatically question and evaluate such experience relative to a collective standard. It involves "trust-based" inquiry that relies on the significance of the experiencer and the observer alone. Further, witnessing does not ask the individual to conform to a particular mode of expression; full perceptual and somatic experience beyond the convention of scientific observation is considered valid. Changing human attitude from authority to partnering deconstructs animal objectification and invites a "participatory mode of consciousness which 'is the awareness of a deeper level of kinship between the knower and the known.'"[41] Above all, we must respect the profound lasting relationships that form the psychological matrix of wellbeing: elephant-elephant, elephant-human, elephant-dog. In so doing, we contribute to a common ground of consciousness, a new compassionate ethic that knows no species bounds.

NOTES

1. American zookeeper, recounted to Catherine Doyle, personal communication, February 26, 2010.

2. The use of the term "human" here generally refers to members of modern, westernized cultures.

3. G.A. Bradshaw and Robert M. Sapolsky, "Mirror, Mirror," *American Scientist*, 94(6), 487-489, 2007.

4. Marc Bekoff, *The Animal Manifesto: Six Reasons for Expanding Our Compassion Footprint* (Auburn, CA: New World Publishing, 2010).

5. G.A. Bradshaw, "Elephants and the New Animal Protection Conservation," in M. Bekoff, *Encyclopedia of Animal Rights and Animal Welfare* (Santa Barbara, CA ABC-CLIO, 2009).

6. Virgil's *The Aeneid, Book 2*: "Do not trust the horse, Trojans. Whatever it is, I fear the Greeks even when they bring gifts."

7. Daphne Sheldrick, "The Rearing and Rehabilitation of Orphaned African Elephant Calves in Kenya," in D.L. Forthman, L.F. Kane, D. Hancocks, P.F. Waldau (eds.), *An Elephant in the Room: The Science and Well Being of Elephants in Captivity* (North Grafton, MA: Tufts University Cummings School of Veterinary Medicine's Center for Animals and Public Policy, 2009), p. 212.

8. Susie O'Keeffe, this volume.

9. Michael Michi, "The role of culture brokers in intercultural science education: A research proposal," http://members.ozemail.com.au/~mmichie/culture_brokers1.htm, retrieved Ferbruary 23, 2010; M.A. Jezewski and P. Sotnik, *The rehabilitation service provider as culture broker: Providing culturally competent services to foreign born persons* (Buffalo, NY: Center for International Rehabilitation Research Information and Exchange, 2001).

10. Carol Buckley website; www.carolbuckley.com.

11. Segment of BBC Horizon documentary showing bull elephant masturbated by humans for semen collection; March 20, 2009, http://www.youtube.com/watch?v=FX9Fc2aZSkc&feature=related.

12. Jean Casella and James Ridgeway, "Ask Shamu: The U.S. Tortures Both Human and Animal Prisoners," http://solitarywatch.wordpress.com/2010/03/16/ask-shamu-solitary-confinement-is-torture-for-orcas-and-humans/March 16, 2010, *Solitary Watch*, retrieved March 17, 2010.

13. G.A. Bradshaw, "Perfect in Herself," *Psychology Today*, http:// www.psychologytoday.com/blog/bear-in-mind/201001/perfect-in-herself, 2009: For more information on Lucy see Zoocheck, www.zoocheck.org.

14. American zookeeper, recounted to Catherine Doyle, personal communication, February 26, 2010.

15. Randy Malamud, this volume; Lori Marino, G.A. Bradshaw, Randy Malamud, "Captivity Industry: The reality of zoos and aquariums", *Best Friends Magazine*, March/April, CA.; G.A. Bradshaw, "Inside looking out: neurobiological compromise effects in elephants in captivity"; D.L. Forthman *et al., Elephant in the Room*, pp. 55-68; G.A. Bradshaw, "Elephants in captivity: analysis of practice, policy, and the future", *Society & Animals* 1-48, 2007.

16. G.A. Bradshaw and Mary Watkins, "Trans-Species Psychology; Theory and Praxis," *Spring*, Vol. 75, pp. 69-94, 2006.

17. Steve Hartman, "On Elephant Sanctuary, Unlikely Friends: Steve Hartman Looks At What Difference A Couple Of Tons Makes—Or Doesn't— For Two Old Friends," CBS Evening News. January 2, 2009; http:// www.cbsnews.com/stories/2009/01/02/assignment_america/ main4696340.shtml, retrieved March 16, 2010.

18. G.A. Bradshaw, *Elephants on the Edge: What Animals Teach Us About Humanity* (New Haven: Yale University Press, 2009).

19. Zoos and circuses use two kinds of systems to control elephants in captivity: free contact (chains) and protected contact (fences and bars). For further details, see D.L. Forthman *et al., Elephant in the Room*.

20. Judith Herman, "Complex PTSD: A Syndrome in Survivors of Prolonged and Repeated Trauma," in *Living with Terror, Working with Trauma*, D. Knafo (ed.) (Lanham, MD: Bowman & Littlefield, 2004).

21. The use of the term "human" here generally refers to members of modern, westernized cultures.

22. Judith Herman, *Trauma and Recovery: The Aftermath of Violence, from Domestic Abuse to Political Terror* (New York: Basic, 1997), quoted in G.A. Bradshaw, *Elephants on the Edge*, p. 115.

23. Herman, *Trauma and Recovery*, quoted in Bradshaw, *Elephants on the Edge*, p. 119.

24. Allan N. Schore, personal communication, March 21, 2010.

25. Allan N. Schore, "Attachment, Affect Regulation, and the Developing Right Brain: Linking Developmental Neuroscience to Pediatrics," *Pediatrics in Review* 26(6): 204–17, 2005.

26. Clifford Geertz, *The Interpretation of Culture* (New York: Basic Book, 1977).

27. G.S. Aikenhead and O.J. Jegede, "Cross-cultural science education: A cognitive explanation of a cultural phenomenon," *Journal of Research in Science Teaching,* 36(3), 269-287, 1999, p. 222.

28. Schore.

29. Patricia Greenfield *et al.*, "Cultural Pathways Through Universal Development," *Annual Reviews of Psychology* 54 (2003): 461–90.

30. G.A. Bradshaw, Theodora Capaldo, Gloria Grow, and Lorin Lindner, "Developmental context effects on bicultural post-trauma self repair in chimpanzees," *Developmental Psychology* 45: 5,1376-1388, 2009.

31. Sandra Bloom, "By the crowd they have been broken, by the crowd they shall be healed: The Social Transformation of Trauma," in *Post-traumatic Growth: Theory and Research on Change in the Aftermath of Crises,* R. Tedeschi, C. Park, and L. Calhoun (eds.) (Mahwah N.J.: Lawrence Erlbaum, 1997).

32. Bloom.

33. Geertz.

34. M.A. Jezewski, "Evolution of a grounded theory: Conflict resolution through culture brokering," *Advances in Nursing Science,* 17(3), 14-30, 1995.

35. Jezewski.

36. The Elephant Sanctuary Asian Elephant Diaries. www.elephants.com; February 8, 2007.

37. Jezewski.

38. Aikenhead, p. 223.

39. Judith Atkinson, *Trauma Trails: Recreating Song Lines* (Melbourne, Au: Spinifex Press, 2002), p. 213.

40. Bradshaw. *Elephants on the Edge.*

41. L. Heshusius, "Freeing ourselves from objectivity: Managing subjectivity or turning toward a participatory mode of consciousness," *Educational Researcher,* 23(3), 15-22, 16.

IMAGINING COEXISTENCE: WHAT GRIZZLY BEARS HAVE TO TEACH US

SUSIE O'KEEFFE

We need...forms of education in which the words "soul" and "imagination" are not banished but are honored and deepened and acted upon.—Matthew Fox[1]

As the source of our creations, the imagination contains the seeds of the future we craft. We form our world and ourselves from the images that come to us. There is, of course, always a distance between what we eventually create and what is imagined. The artist sees her painting in her mind, but never reproduces it exactly. The practice of creating moves the artist in unforeseeable ways, she is transformed, new images appear, and a re-imagining emerges.

Susie O'Keeffe received her Master's with distinction from Oxford University. Her research explored the return of the wolf to the French Alps, and the ensuing conflicts with farmers and hunters. For the past twenty years she has also worked with a variety of environmental and local agriculture organizations in the United States and Europe. She is currently developing an education project that examines the connections between aesthetic perception, consciousness, contemplative inquiry, and coexistence with the natural world. Her work presently focuses on carnivores. She lives in the Sheepscot Watershed in Montville, Maine.

As the plight of the earth worsens, it is becoming apparent that the work of restoring the natural world, and finding our place within it, is ultimately a similar call to re-imagine. Humans are being challenged as individuals, and as a collective, to engage in the continuous creative act of re-visioning not only how we live, but our perceptions of and relationships with all forms of life and landscape. We are being asked to form, in the words of Thomas Berry, new stories[2] —stories that help us understand that "the universe is composed of subjects to be communed with, not of objects to be exploited."[3]

Naturalist Barry Lopez writes that the "the solution to our plight is likely to be something no other culture has ever thought of, something over which !Kung, Inuit, Navajo, Walbiri, and the other traditions we have turned to for wisdom…will marvel at as well…"[4] It implies the creation of "an entirely different system with entirely different claims."[5] This task seems so huge, so overwhelmingly difficult, that many believe it is impossible. Human-induced extinctions, climate change, consumption, and overpopulation are only a few of the larger problems that have resulted from modernity and western ethics, and need to be tackled. Some argue that the history, economics, nature, and the world we have created make the idea of addressing these issues and restoring the natural world an unattainable fantasy.[6] Succumbing to the same sense of inevitability, conservationists do not ask how we might devise ways to coexist that preserve and honor the planet's manifold systems of life, but rather what parts can we keep and what parts can we do without. Solutions are tailored to fit within the dominant economic system: the current paradigm, not a re-imagined one, that shapes virtually all decisions. This was reiterated to me during a recent lecture on wildlife conservation in South Africa.

A well-known biologist argued that lions, elephants, and most other mammals that need large expanses of land to thrive, will exist only in various forms of captivity. He presented an example of *farming* male lions in large enclosures to meet the demand of wealthy trophy hunters. He proffered this idea as one of the best solutions. Tragically, this plan he presented is already a reality. In addition, elephants are soon on their way out in South Africa and elsewhere. Unless drastic changes in human behavior are made that stop predation of elephant lives and lands, the great pachyderm will extinguish in the wild within two decades.[7]

Fig. 1: No human-created enclosure can provide the ineffable quality of nature.

Photo courtesy of Susie O'Keeffe

Conservationists are not alone in shying away from envisioning how human beings might take their place among the other animals, instead of keeping them in various forms of subservience and incarceration, or abandoning them to extinction. Even those who embrace the imagination falter. James Hillman writes in *Dream Animals* that the vision of restoring the natural world is an impossible, but "noble longing, (that) houses a utopic impulse that may yet be satisfied in the private enclave of the dream."[8] Rather than employing the force and power of the imagination to conceive of how we might come to coexist, this urge is used to create a "utopic no-where world (where the animal's) souls and ours meet as images...and we are no more substantial, in the dream, no more physically located, no more timebound, than their appearances."[9] Artists, too, despair before this re-imagining. Painter Margot McLean states "we are going to have to start realizing that zoos are the animal habitats of the future, depressing as this is."[10]

Without a doubt, the work of restoration is of mythic proportions. However, if we capitulate before this Herculean task, we risk sinking further into abstraction and drowning ourselves in the novelty and speed of our technological inventions at the cost of the planet itself. We will also have failed ethically by not taking responsibility for the destructive aspects of modernity. For the desire to learn to coexist is at once a metaphor for internal union with what is wild and free, a dream of Eden, and a real call to find our place in the community of life—a place that is not about reviving old images and myths, but about realizing new ones.

A number of efforts are underway to help teach how to coexist with animal kin and nature as a whole. Ecopsycology, Deep Ecology, and several other schools that fall under the general rubric of radical ecology articulate new ethics and behaviors based on respect for the intrinsic rights of all life forms. And yet, although much of this re-visioning does provide real steppingstones, these efforts, like the environmental movement at large, often do not bring forth requisite transformations. This is due, in part, because the hard task of confronting the unconscious is overlooked.[11] As individuals and as a collective, "people will do anything, no matter how absurd, in order to avoid facing their own souls."[12] Many of us fear this work, and for good reason. The journey inward reveals that we are capable of both great good and much evil.[13] If one remains unaware of the capacity for darkness, it inevitably will manifest internally and externally,[14] sometimes in very bad acts, sometimes simply by palely loitering through life.[15] As C.G. Jung repeatedly intones, it takes as much courage to face our dark sides as it does to realize our true calling. It requires a commitment that is not cultivated or called for by modern society, and a practice that does not come easily as it must be forged individually. And yet, the continual work of self questioning not only helps us live lives of meaning, it cultivates individual ethics. "For the point is not only *what* we do but the source from which we do it."[16]

Subsequently, many paths that could lead to reconciliation with nature divert from profound change. The vision quests, shamanic journeys, and sacred wilderness retreats that are promoted as ways to establish new forms of connection with the earth tend to focus on the human participant's intrapsychic state, directing their efforts to feeling good, personal empowerment, and the achievement of "sacred" experiences with nature as an end in itself.[17] Rarely is it acknowledged that the work of coming to know the natural world demands a great deal of time, continuous connection, and a rigorous practice of self awareness.[18] If we ignore the unconscious, such endeavors reinforce the path of individualism rather individuation. In her story of imagining a journey into cougar country as a shamanic initiation, ecopsychologist Laura Sewall does not take into consideration that her lack of knowledge of this animal could lead to her death,[19] and subsequently the death of one or several cougars, since today's "conservation and wildlife management policies" call for the systematic destruction of carnivores who injure or kill humans.

Many of the concepts and approaches used to reconnect with nature are built upon various levels of understanding of native cultures and rituals. Western, Euro-Americans have tended to take up these traditions with little regard for the context within which these ways evolved and took form. There is a formidable, unconscious conceit in believing that we of one culture can adopt the sacred rituals of another in order to fulfill our own needs. Native people's experiences, understandings, and subsequent rituals and rites grew from countless years of living as members of the natural world. Learning these ways requires great work, time, and levels of wisdom and experience that very few of us, who come from generations of people that denied, divorced, and desecrated the land and the animals, possess. Rituals cannot be "bought over the counter". They are culturally and contextually bound to the places and periods that produced them. Without a practice of consciousness that helps make this usurping and our anthopocentric projections visible, there is the danger of repeated trespass and violation. This is not to say that the work of finding ways to re-image, re-enter, and restore life should not be undertaken. Indeed, it must. The question is, how do we proceed in a manner that is respectful, effective, and engages the unconscious?

One native tradition that is common to all cultural traditions and is readily available to everyone is storytelling. Through the real life narration of people who have ventured to learn about another animal, or simply sought to be in that animal's presence, those of us who have led lives away from the wilds can catch a glimpse of how we might begin. Of all animals of North America, wild grizzly bears perhaps stir the imagination and emotions the most. Named *Ursus horribilis,* they are beings who inspire, in part because they are one of the few species that can consume us. Bears demand attention and bring us face to face with ourselves, our deepest fears and desire for power. Stories of encounters with living grizzly bears (also called "brown bears") subsequently offer a look into the unconscious while demanding conscious vigilance.

Just as myths and stories of old vary widely depending on the cultures they come from, so do these new stories. Some teach us how to act, and others warn us of the dangers of hubris and violation. By challenging many of our deeply engrained fears and ideas about these animals and our relationships with them, several of these stories help us learn how coexistence might move from image to form, and the pivotal role that the work of consciousness plays in this process.

Timothy Treadwell is one of the more notorious examples of someone approaching grizzly bears from the heart, but displaying an uncertain understanding of his own unconscious motivations and needs. His story also illustrates how others, in this case filmmaker Werner Herzog, not only use other animals but also humans to manifest their own image of nature. By selling the film *Grizzly Man* as a documentary, Herzog pretends that what he portrays is "truth", while at the same time distorting Treadwell's experiences to provide a platform for his own opinions, perceptions, and fondness for sensationalism.

In a critique of *Grizzly Man,* John W. White describes how Herzog cannot simply let Treadwell's own words and actions speak for themselves; Herzog "cannot use the camera in a way that is non-political". Instead, the German filmmaker "represent[s] himself and his own views in quite polarized reaction to those of Treadwell, as though in contrast to Treadwell's beautiful seemliness of the dream world, he is presenting the horrifying and intoxicated reality which underlies Treadwell's illusory conception of nature." White goes on to provide examples of the filmmaker's "fulmination against nature". In one scene showing Treadwell "swimming with a bear, petting the creature from behind", Herzog's voice illustrates this polarization, the impulse to inject darkness into Treadwell's and nature's intentions: "You see, it looks like complete harmony of man and beast, like him in unison with nature. We believe things are all right and they are not when you find the dark menace in it."[22] White goes on to quote Herzog in context of an earlier film, *Fitzcarraldo*, where once again Herzog wages battle against nature:

> I see fornication and asphyxiation and choking and growing
> for survival and growing and rotting. The trees here are in misery.

> The birds here are in misery—they don't sing, they just shriek in pain … We are cursed for what we are doing here! It is a land that God, if he exists, has created in anger! There is no order here, no harmony in the universe! The only harmony is of overwhelming, collective murder! It is a vile, base obscenity!

If we peel away the layers of Herzog's own personal myth, we find that Treadwell did take on the profound task of wrestling with the unconscious as best he could. He was a young man from Los Angeles who, in an effort to recover from his addictions to drugs and alcohol, ventured into the world of the grizzly bear. He had no previous

Fig 2: The parent-child relationship is universal among mammals.
Photo courtesy of Susie O'Keeffe

experience of these animals, nor did he have any backcountry or wilderness skills to draw on. Nevertheless, he weathered extreme and rugged conditions and spent thirteen seasons with the grizzly bears in the Katmai National Park in Alaska. During this time he demonstrated that these animals were far more tolerant and accepting of human beings than previously thought. By living among the bears on a continual basis, Timmy helped us see that the grizzlies, like humans, are deeply individual, complex, intelligent beings capable of trust and generally peaceful. He also showed us that bears are bears, and like us, they have their own cultures and behavioral norms. By figuring out how to behave accordingly, Timothy did learn how to coexist with them. For many years he educated children, challenged our thinking, and inspired people to learn about living peacefully with grizzlies.

Treadwell's tale has a tragic ending, and it is this ending that has shaped the story of his time with the bears. He, and the woman accompanying him, Amie Huegenard, were killed and partly consumed by grizzlies. Two bears were killed in reprisal by government authorities. Treadwell's own video footage that Herzog includes in *Grizzly Man* depicts someone who is searching for connection, love, and relationship and sought to do so through his interactions with the bears. The video clips also show someone who is troubled and yearning for a level of emotional fulfillment, understanding, and answers from the animals that no one, human or bear, could have provided. In many ways, Treadwell captures the essence of the modern human condition: the desire to meld again with nature, yet possessed by a legacy that hinders and distorts such union, as well as the profound pain involved in waking up to our innate love of nature to find that what we love is being destroyed.

While no one will ever know the exact details of what took place, Treadwell's letters and video footage revealed that he had begun to feel he was one with the bears. In his last letter to Roland Dixon he wrote, "my transformation is complete—a fully accepted wild animal, brother to these bears."[23] He also, on several occasions, told people that he would not mind being eaten as long as the bears were not harmed.[24] Regardless of what our reactions might be to these statements, are we in a position to judge whether or not this literal devouring "should" have taken place? Heightened by Herzog's sensationalism, Treadwell's story provokes intense debate. Herzog's reaction to Treadwell, the bears, and nature in general is reflective of western culture's "red in tooth and claw" attitudes. Nature is not to be reconciled but punished for any trespass against humanity. The idea that humans and bears, or people and the rest of nature, can co-exist peacefully is anathema to Herzog: "I think it's a gross misconception. It's misreading what's out there. I say in the film that I see chaos, hostility, and murder."[25]

The impulse to revitalize connection, along with, perhaps, a sense of invincibility, are mythologically and psychologically interesting to contemplate. Are there deeper, more ineffable meanings embedded in the fact that Timothy was consumed by the bears he loved and with whom he found connection? If he had understood this urge as a literal feeling as well as a metaphor, what might he have learned about himself, and how might this knowledge have contributed to his relationships with the bears? Could it have helped us understand the bears and our relationships with them differently? Why did Timothy ignore the continual advice of seasoned naturalists such as Charlie Russell to use electric wire to keep curious and hungry bears away from his camp and to carry bear spray?[26]

To contemplate these questions deepens our awareness concerning projections and assumptions about the natural world, and the ethics of our relationships with other species. In particular, it brings up the issue of why modern, western culture sanctions the killing of animals because they kill humans. As Doug Peacock articulates, "we like the idea of having wild grizzlies around but would prefer them on our own terms…we seem to regard them as modern day renegades holed up in their last stronghold; if they wander out or get too bold, we want to treat them as rogues. We see the value in their independence, but it makes us nervous…(yet) somewhere buried in the modern psyche, we crave contact."[27] Do we have the right to kill another being because of this need?

In the real world of grizzly bears, there are, as Charlie Russell explains, boundaries that cannot be crossed.[28] Nevertheless, as with our relationships with people, limits shift and change depending on our behavior, our knowledge, and our willingness to come to experience another being for the mystery that they are. By living with the bears for years and learning their ways, Treadwell helped the modern day public see that much of what we *think* we know about bears is actually based on culturally-shaped projections, fears, and engrained prejudices. Treadwell showed that humans, even those unschooled in bear ways, can coexist peacefully with species as formidable as grizzlies if we learn to behave according to the animals' cultural norms. Treadwell's death also serves as a reminder to keep the human ego in check, and to be aware of personal inflations and the power of unconscious desires. The stories that have taken form around his demise, and Herzog's representation and negative amplification, reveal how readily we project, scapegoat, and try to profit from another person's suffering. Tragically, Treadwell is ridiculed and condemned because he openly revealed an emotional instability and expressed dramatic affection. His vulnerability reflects our own susceptibility to the anxieties, depressions, addictions, and general psychological malaise that permeate the modern world. In part, Treadwell's story teaches us about the pain and longing that accompanies and perhaps motivates our on-going destruction of life and landscape, and how this suffering can push us to use, unbeknownst to ourselves, the animals we wish to protect and know to fulfill our unconscious needs at their expense.

While Treadwell's story stirs up a number of issues, another man who has interacted intimately with grizzlies, Charlie Russell, offers an alternative perspective on how we can learn to live peacefully with these great carnivores. Charlie's work with bears began when he was a boy in Canada. Along with his father and brother, Charlie was the first person to film grizzlies in the wild. His experience also includes being a bear guide in British Columbia and ranching in bear country in

Fig. 3: Charlie Russell with Biscuit in Kamchatka, Russia.
Photo courtesy of Maureen Enns

Alberta. After decades of experience, Charlie, and his then partner Maureen Enns, decided to explore how "people might learn to live with bears in a way that would not lead to collision, violence and the ongoing destruction of a threatened species."[29] In 1996 Charlie and Maureen traveled to Kamchatka, Russia to learn how brown bears who have not been subjected to human cruelty would accept people.

The naturalist and artist were swept into a journey that neither expected. Entering Russia just after *Perestroika*, they found that the brown bears of Kamchatka had in fact been subjected to as much human malice as the bears of North America. While they had planned to simply live among the grizzlies, Russell and Enns ended up raising 12 orphaned cubs in the wild in the company of a number of wild bears for the following decade. Charlie and Maureen demonstrate how, through trust, love, intelligent behavior, continual self assessment, and respect, bears and humans can live together peacefully. Most importantly, they illustrate how when approached in this way, other animals expand human consciousness. Charlie explains.

> By allowing me into their world, by tolerating my limitations and the baggage of humanness, they helped me expand my humanness. Through their acceptance of me, and by following their lead, I had become more than just an observer of the land. I had become part of it. There is a great freedom in the way animals live, and my senses had changed a little in that direction, thanks to our bears. The subtleties that I had become able to sense were more the norm for an animal than for a human—a modern human at least.[30]

Charlie's understanding of bears is truly remarkable. People have a tendency to feel that he has a "gift." This is an idea he strongly rejects. Charlie insists that everyone, if they can remain aware of their actions and intentions and move toward the animals with respect and love, has the capacity to come to know and to coexist well with grizzly bears. A deeply feeling person, Charlie resists strongly the confines of the scientific method of inquiry. However, he does not deny a need for knowledge, nor does he deny that bears are powerful animals that can injure and kill. Instead, he has followed an instinctual understanding that there are other ways to learn how to understand bears than through the theoretical, at-a-distance eye of science. His alternative methods include "assess(ing) and accept(ing) the real odds."[31] Charlie emphasizes that living safely with bears begins with respect—something that is earned, not commanded. "I doubt anyone earns the esteem of a bear by shooting it in the face with pepper spray or in the rear with a rubber bullet. Respect from bears should be the goal, but our work indicates that you have to be willing to earn the bear's respect to get it. Once you have a bear's respect and trust, you're not apt to lose it."[32] In the words of Koyukon Catherine Attla, "the law is respect...what enforces that law is the world itself, not other humans."[33] By being in the presence of the bears for many years and learning to "listen" instinctually and intuitively, Russell lifts the veil of human projections. He works continuously to understand how the bears perceive his actions and intentions, and learns to wrestle with and understand his own unconscious fears and needs.

Having embarked on a much different journey, Karsten Heuer and Leanne Allison also came to experience the inner work that coexisting with grizzly bears, and the land itself, requires. In an effort to convince the United States government and people that the Artic Wildlife Refuge is an invaluable and irreplaceable gift that should not be opened to oil drilling, Karsten and Leanne followed the Porcupine Caribou herd throughout their ancestral migration from the Yukon to their calving grounds in the Artic National Wildlife Refuge and back to the Yukon. Sadly, their sense of connection, of "being caribou" would "shrink and die,"[34] though not completely, and not without having offered the world an incredible story of how, through continual presence and perseverance, the rational mind relaxes and allows psyche not only to speak, but to be listened to and heeded. Karsten writes of finally opening after following the caribou and being followed, and occasionally stalked, by grizzlies.

> Everything else has been shed—my false sense of security, my hubris, my mental clutter—and what it allowed me to do in that moment was relax. The bulls seemed to sense this: their eyes softened, the breathing quieted, and for a brief, suspended moment we moved in unison, heartbeats and footsteps mingling while we inhaled each other's exhaled breath. Finally, after so many miles, I was floating with animals instead of chasing them. I was experiencing the caribou experiencing themselves.[35]

Their story helps us see how our false sense of security, separateness, and safety slip away when we are respectfully and mindfully embedded

in the natural world on a continual basis. As they trekked back with
the caribou they found the mountains they had struggled over were in
fact hills, and the grizzly bears were not hungry predators that terrified
them, but part of the movement they were all engaged in. "... (A) shift
had happened...competitors had become companions...we took our
position in the parade of animals, following the caribou followed by
the grizzly, sharing the same challenges and fears."[36]

Once they were catapulted back into modern civilization, Heurer
and Allison's sense of connection eroded. Their experience offers us a
glimpse of the internal consequences of living in a highly technological
world remote from nature.

> ...I sensed parts of me that had taken months to open while
> moving with the caribou were already beginning to close down.
> And they had to. Life in the modern technological world carries
> none of the subtleties of living with caribou. There's too much
> to absorb, too much for the sharpened sense to do anything but
> go dormant if one wants to survive.[37]

One thing that did not slip away from Heuer was the memory of
the land "thrumming."[38] He searched for scientific facts about this pulse
he experienced, but found nothing about infrasonic vibrations with
caribou. A professor suggested he develop the experience into a doctoral
thesis. Disconnected and somewhat defeated, Heuer concludes that
"some things aren't meant to have the wildness and mystery strangled
out of them. Some things are best left in mystery."[39] Carl Jung put it
this way, "[t]o understand a thing is a bridge and possibility of
returning to the path. But to explain a matter is arbitrary and
sometimes even murder."[40]

Charlie and Maureen, Timothy, Karsten and Leanne, and a number
of other people, including wildlife filmmakers Jeff and Sue Turner, and
Larry Aumiller and Derek Stonorov, who helped make Alaska's McNeil
River State Game Sanctuary and Refuge a haven for grizzly bears, have
profoundly expanded our understanding of these animals. They have
shown us that by moving toward grizzlies with heart, self-awareness,
and respect, we can develop the levels of consciousness needed to create
a world where bears and humans coexist. Like all those who lead us
toward new forms of awareness, these people have challenged imposed
boundaries and disproven engrained perceptions. They have shown

what is possible and what is necessary if we are to achieve what society ostensibly claims: the salvation of the planet and the lives of other species. If we resist the examples set by these pioneers it is because we are unwilling to exchange the illusion of power, separateness, and security for one of humility, reverence, and membership. If we are to succeed in re-imaging a world where we coexist with rather than extinguish, incarcerate, and manage the grizzly, the caribou, the elephants, and all the nonhuman species of the world, we will have to enact in our own way what these individuals have had the courage to imagine and bring forth.

Fig 4: The carnivores challenge our self-proclaimed superiority, and ask us to imagine and create a world where their right to live freely is honored and accomodated.

Photo courtesy of Susie O'Keeffe

Fig. 5: Respect and trust are offerings that transcend species.
Photo courtesy of Maureen Enns

NOTES

1. Matthew Fox, *Creativity* (New York: Penguin, 2002), p. 61.

2. Brian Swimme and Thomas Berry, *The Universe Story: From Primordial Flaring Forth to the Ecozoic Era* (New York: Harper One, 1992), p. 3.

3. Thomas Berry, Prologue, *A Communion of Subjects: Animals in Religion, Science and Ethics,* ed. Paul Waldau and Kimberly Patton (New York: Columbia University Press, 2006), p. 8.

4. Barry Lopez, "The Passing Wisdom of Birds," in *Crossing Open Ground* (New York: Vintage Books, 1989), p. 199.

5. Wendell Berry, *Life is a Miracle: An Essay Against Modern Superstition* (New York: Counterpoint, 2000), p. 35.

6. James Hillman and Margot McLean, *Dream Animals* (San Francisco: Chronicle Books, 1997), p. 15.

7. Samuel K. Wasser *et al.*, "Combating the Illegal Trade in African Elephant Ivory with DNA Forensics," *Conservation Biology* 22 (2008): 1065–71.

8. Hillman and McLean, *Dream Animals*, p. 15.

9. *Ibid.*, p. 15.

10. *Ibid.*, p. 8.

11. Liz Evans, "Developing a Jungian Ecopsychology," *Psyche and Nature, Part 2, Spring: A Journal of Archetype and Culture 76* (2006), p. 136.

12. Meredith Sabini, ed. *The Earth Has a Soul: The Nature Writings of C.G. Jung* (Berkeley: North Atlantic Books, 2001), p. 169.

13. C.G. Jung, *Red Book,* ed. S. Shamdasani (New York: W.W. Norton, 2009), p. 234.

14. Sabini, *Nature Writings of Jung*, p. 127.

15. John Keats, quoted in *The Forsaken Garden* by Nancy Ryley (Wheaton: Quest Books, 1998), p. 19.

16. Jacob Needleman, Introduction to *Tao te Ching* by Lao Tzu (New York: Random House, 1989), p. xii.

17. Evans, "Jungian Ecopsychology", p. 135.

18. *Ibid.*, p.134–135.

19. *Ibid.*, p.134–135.

20. Rainer Marie Rilke, in *News of the Universe: Poems of Twofold Consciousness*, Robert Bly (San Francisco: Sierra Club Books, 1980), p. 246.

21. Phillip Reiff, *The Triumph of the Therapeutic: Uses of Faith after Freud* (Chicago: University of Chicago, 1987), p. 5.

22. John White, "On Werner Herzog's Documentary *Grizzly Man*: Psychoanalysis, Nature, and Meaning", http://www.uta.edu/huma/agger/fastcapitalism/4_1/white.html.

23. Doug Peacock and Andrea Peacock, *In the Presence of Grizzlies: The Ancient Bond Between Men and Bears* (Guilford: The Lyons Press, 2009), p. 44.

24. Personal communication, Matthias Breiter, June 2009; Charlie Russell, January, 2009; John Rogers, July, 2009.

25. Marrit Ingman, "Discord and Ecstasy: Werner Herzog on 'Grizzly Man'", http://www.austinchronicle.com/gyrobase/Issue/story?oid=oid%3A285426.

26. Personal communications, Charlie Russell, September, 2009.

27. Peacock and Peacock, *Grizzlies*, p. 45-46.

28. Charlie Russell, in *Edge of Eden: Living with Grizzlies*, filmed and narrated by Jeff Turner, River Road Films, 2006.

29. Charlie Russell and Maureen Enns with Fred Stenson, *Grizzly Heart: Living without Fear Among the Brown Bears of Kamchatka* (Toronto: Vintage Canada: 2003), p. 2.

30. *Ibid.*, p. 208.

31. *Ibid.*, p. 208.

32. *Ibid.*, p. 304-5.

33. Richard Nelson, "Exploring the Near at Hand," *Parabola: The Magazine of Myth and Tradition*, VXI, no. 2 (1991), 36.

34. Karsten Heuer, *Being Caribou* (Seattle: The Mountaineers Books: 2005), p. 222.

35. *Ibid.*, p. 196.

36. *Ibid.*, p. 167.

37. *Ibid.*, p. 230.

38. *Ibid.*, p. 233.

39. *Ibid.*, p. 233.

40. Jung, *Red Book,* p. 233.

MY FATHER WAS A BEAR:
HUMAN-ANIMAL TRANSFORMATION IN
NATIVE AMERICAN TEACHINGS

*In the last analysis, most of our difficulties come from losing contact with
our instincts, the age-old forgotten wisdom stored up in us.* — C. G. Jung[1]

In the very earliest time,
when both people and animals lived on earth,
a person could become an animal if he wanted to
and an animal could become a human being.
Sometimes they were people
and sometimes animals
and there was no difference.
All spoke the same language.
That was the time when words were like magic.
The human mind had mysterious powers.
A word spoken by chance
might have strange consequences.
It would suddenly come alive

Jeanne A. Lacourt, Ph.D., is Chair of the Ethnic Studies Department and Associate
Professor of American Indian Studies at St. Cloud State University in Minnesota. She
has strong interests in the intersections of Jungian and Indigenous studies.

and what people wanted to happen could happen—
all you had to do was say it.
Nobody could explain this:
That's the way it was.
                                —Linda Hogan[2]

My father was a bear. Not a teddy bear type of bear, no, he was a big, brown, muscular bear who lived in the forest—the thick, dense, old growth forest—and he knew this environment well. He knew which rivers and lakes offered the best fish, he knew the deer trails and locations of other bears' dens, he knew where the plumpest and juiciest berry bushes could be found, and he could sniff out the finest line of ginseng root in all the forest's floor. He was a fine fisher, a skilled hunter, and a keen gatherer. These skills were handed down to him from a long line of impressive bears. In fact, he came from the original bear: the great light-colored ancestral underground bear of the Menominee Indians.

The Menominee origin story tells of a time when Grandfather created spirit beings in the forms of animals and birds before there were people on this earth. One day, at a place where the Village River streams into the Bay In Spite of Itself (present day Green Bay, Wisconsin), a great light-colored bear emerged from the underworld and started traveling up river. The great bear spoke to Grandfather and when Grandfather saw that the bear was still an animal, he determined to *allow the bear to change his form*. So the great ancestral bear changed into human form and became the first Menominee. While on his journey, the great ancestral bear met other spirit beings: Golden Eagle, Beaver Woman, Moose, Wolf, and Crane. He asked them if they would join him and become his brothers and sisters. Each was also granted the ability to change into human form and they thus formed the first major clans of the Menominee people.[3]

I direct readers to view these first Menominee clans, the "little Menominee," as symbolically carved out of the trees of the Menominee forest by Menominee artist James Frechette. Note how the carvings depict the Menominee in transformational transition from animal to human. See: http://www.uwsp.edu/museum/menomineeclans/ (you must click on each individual clan to see the carvings).

Mythic stories and transformation accounts are not uncommon

among the indigenous people of this land. Nor are they mere remnants of the past, holding no use for native people today. You will notice that for the title of this essay, I chose to use the word "teaching" over myth, story, or legend as these latter words seem to imply a made-up fantasy, a falseness. And as Native American activist and scholar Vine Deloria, Jr. points out, "tribal knowledge is often regarded by many educated people as simply 'fun' or 'quaint' because it is so exotic."[4] Native people will argue that their stories, myths, and legends hold truths and teachings for them to live by. While the term "teaching" is my preference, for the sake of variety in the text, I will use all the terms interchangeably.

These teachings continue to instruct the way native people live and interact with animals. Humans' relationship to animals and our participation in their world bring forward our innermost instinctual selves and to honor this intimacy is to return the sacred to the world. Nurturing our relationship with animals through direct communication is our responsibility. "We are in need of an ancient way of being," says Choctaw writer and environmentalist Linda Hogan. "It is through our relationship with animals that we maintain a way of living, a cultural ethics shaped from an ancient understanding of the world, and this is remembered in stories that are the deepest reflections of our shared lives on Earth."[5]

Perhaps the most widely known account of human-animal transformation is that of *Pte-san Win-yan* (White Buffalo Calf Woman) among the Lakota/Dakota/Nakota *oyate* (people). This teaching tells of a spirit woman carrying a sacred bundle who appears before two young scouts. She instructs one of them to go to his people and have them prepare an altar of sage and cherry branches for her return. Once the people had followed these instructions, she returns, singing a song and carrying the sacred bundle. She gives the people the sacred *C'anupa* (pipe) that was in the bundle and instructs them in its meaning and use. She also gives them seven sacred rites to aid them in living a sacred way of life. As she leaves the people, she rolls over four times, each time changing color until she eventually turns into a white buffalo calf. Today the sacred *C'anupa* is under the care of Arvol Looking Horse, 19th generation keeper of the sacred white buffalo calf pipe; and, the seven sacred rites continue to sustain the Lakota/Dakota/Nakota nations.[6]

These accounts, as well as numerous others, are evidence of perhaps the most intimate relationships experienced by native people with animals over thousands of years. They carry a numinous quality to them. They are sacred. Some estimate that over seventy-five percent of Native American myths include animal characters. Sharing an intimate psychic and physical reality with animals provides insight into how to live in these interdependent relationships. These teachings outline an ethics of behavior that native people have followed, and some continue to follow, in order to maintain healthy relationships with our animal relatives. They teach us how to participate in the world and how to keep respectful, reciprocal relationships with other spirit beings.

The ability to transform into human or animal form might be considered highly suspicious, and one may be tempted to relegate these transformation myths as mere superstitions of a primitive people. However, keep in mind that the point of these teachings isn't whether one can actually, physically, transform into another species, but rather the insight gained as to the interdependent nature of our relationship with animals and the effectiveness of an ethics of behavior for long-term, respectful relationships negotiated with them. Having just written this, however, I would be remiss if I didn't point out that recently among the Iñupiat, an elderly man's body was found after he had been missing from camp. "He was found half-man, half-caribou and 'good, honest, praying people' saw the body." When asked about this, a villager remarked that it was nothing out of the ordinary, that he was simply "doing what Eskimos did long time ago."[7] Then too, there is Calvin Martin's story to consider. Martin had taught a class to incarcerated Eskimos. One of the students handed Martin a paper on which was written: "I am a Puffin!" . . . "I am a puffin," he repeated softly yet firmly, "from my ancestral tree and in blood." Martin described him as "a man who effortlessly negotiated the porous, wafer-thin membrane separating Homo from the Other."[8]

Believing in transformation accounts is a matter of ascendancy, according to Vine Deloria, Jr. who, in *C.G. Jung and the Sioux Traditions*, wrote: "it is only the assumption of superiority that allows western readers to doubt such an account."[9]

> Regardless of what Indians have said concerning their origins, their migrations, their experiences with birds, animals, lands . . . the scientists have maintained a stranglehold on the definitions of what respectable and reliable human experiences are. The

> Indian explanation is always cast aside as a superstition, precluding
> Indians from having an acceptable status as human beings, and
> reducing them in the eyes of educated people to a pre-human
> level of ignorance.[10]

Indeed, as Jerome Bernstein carefully demonstrates in his book *Living in the Borderland,* a fundamental separation and assumed domination of western man over animals seems to have been explicitly mandated in Genesis, the first book of the Hebrew Bible. Bernstein provides three common, dominant interpretations of the scripture where man is given directive to *rule* over the whole earth, have *dominion* and subdue everything that moves on the earth, and *conquer* all the animals living in sea, in air, and on earth.[11] Bernstein maintains that a split in Western ego consciousness developed from these directives and that this split has had a hold on the Western ego for at least three and half millennia. He writes,

> One primary goal of the new consciousness commanded in
> Genesis was the development of a *new psychic construct in human
> evolution.* Pointedly, the goal was the development of this unique
> ego structure. "Dominion over the earth" was to be the means to
> that end. I am suggesting that the underlying goal was not the
> simple control of the earth, but a *boundaried* and *contained* ego
> based on logic and the *logos* principle. *This* ego, unlike the ego
> merged-with-nature that preceded it, would elevate logic and
> left-brain thinking to the exclusion of the arational, the irrational,
> and the transrational, and the right-brain functioning. It was to
> become an ego that would hold logic and rational process as
> superior and more real than feeling and intuition. It would
> consider any reality other than rationality as being inferior and
> less real.[12]

It comes as no surprise then that this assumed superiority over nature and animals by Western Europeans allowed for the over killing of many species, driving them to near extinction. The fur trade nearly exterminated the beaver, and the desire for buffalo hides caused the uncontrolled slaughter of over 50 million buffalo. While some scholars would ascribe the wildlife decimation to Indians, Calvin Martin's work on the fur trade tells another story. Martin carefully examines what the fur trade meant to Indians from within their own cultural context, a perspective sorely lacking in previous literature. By exposing the

"Western bourgeois'" imposition of their marketplace theory and their assumption that "impotent aboriginal technology" was inadequate, Martin shows how these explanations were used to discredit a hunting and gathering way of life and undermine a traditional religious belief system. Instead, Martin explains,

> The single most important deterrent to excessive hunting, . . .
> was the fear of spiritual reprisal for indiscreet slaughter. Prior to
> European influence, these Indians of the Canadian forest were
> on amicable terms with the spirits of the game, . . . and it was the
> vivid, daily awareness of this courteous relationship which more
> than anything else precluded overkill.[13]

It also comes as no surprise that how European immigrants historically have treated native people has striking similarities with how they treated animals. In G.A. Bradshaw's work with elephants, she notes the twin genocides of wildlife and Indians and the similar treatment elephants and Indians share. "Both elephants and indigenous peoples have formed an Other in the eyes of the colonizers—appealing to their dominators because of their desired qualities and annihilated for some of the self-same qualities."[14] Like animals, native people were viewed as less sophisticated, "primitive,"[15] and inferior, and massacres against them were common. Just as buffalo robes were a valuable commodity, money could also be gained by proving an Indian had been killed. To receive payment, one needed only provide the "redskins" of the hunted natives. The need for land also provides evidence of the similar treatment natives and animals endured by their European neighbors. Natives have been forcibly removed, relocated, and allotted to live on undesirable lands, ultimately restricted to small reservations. Likewise, many animals today no longer have a natural habitat to live in and instead are restricted to small unnatural environments: zoos, circuses, pens, cages, and worse.

What we see in western culture is a strong dissociation due to its assumed superiority over, and separation from, nature and its own natural instinct. Jung also recognized this:

> Our intellect has created a new world that dominates nature,
> and has populated it with monstrous machines. . . . Man is bound
> to follow the exploits of his scientific and inventive mind and to
> admire himself for his splendid achievements. At the same time,

he cannot help admitting that his genius shows an uncanny tendency to invent things that become more and more dangerous, because they represent better and better means for wholesale suicide.[16]

Gregory Cajete, Tewa, describes the dissociation in this way:

The once sacred Earth community that nurtures human life has become "outside," a place filled with malevolent natural forces that must be controlled or otherwise guarded against. Fear, control, and exploitation of the "outside" or the other as enemy is deeply embedded in the psychology of Western society. To this end, much of modern science and technology has been mobilized to guard against or to war against the other, be it a mountain, a forest people, a religion, or a world of insects.[17]

For native people, this "war on nature is a war on the psyche, a war on the soul,"[18] and not only on the human soul, but on the animals' as well. In her keynote address at the Global Forum on Environment and Development for Survival, Audrey Shenandoah, Onondoga Clan Mother, explains "there is no word for 'nature' in my language. Nature, in English, seems to refer to that which is separate from human beings. It is a distinction we don't recognize."[19] Yet this distinction persists in western ideologies. It is engrained in psychology, environmental policy, education, and most other fields.

The belief that animals also have soul is embedded in most traditional native views. Interestingly, Deloria points out that the buffalo nickel, which has an Indian profile on one side and a buffalo on the other, "curiously represents the Sioux Indians' belief that in a higher cosmic dimension they and the buffalo are one spirit, split into two separate entities upon taking physical form."[20] And that "first and foremost in the Sioux mind was the idea that other creatures were 'peoples' like us."[21] For the Osages, the closest living relatives in this world are their sisters and brothers, the buffalo and the corn.[22] For the Menominee, the animal clan you are born into is your brother or sister. Native people make less of a distinction between human, animal, and spiritual realities. These realities interpenetrate one another and share a common heritage. Transformation teachings then, and other native myths that include animal characters, are critical to honoring our shared realities. These stories help us "take back the soul, the anima, which has stepped away from our bodies and hidden in fear from what it has witnessed and endured. It is through such relationships that we return to a respect and love for life and other species."[23]

The relationship of humans to animals as outlined in the Genesis creation story, and as evidenced in events of history, differs markedly from those delineated in native creation stories. Whereas Western Europeans assumed human superiority over animals, natives viewed animals as their equals and acknowledged relationships that were reciprocal. It is common in native creation stories that humans were among the last creatures created, after animals had already been engaging in the world. In fact, "it is believed that the animal nature helped to create humans and that animals have always served as humanity's mentors in coming to know the nature of the world."[24] Humans therefore did not assume any special status above animals. Rather, being the youngest and most ignorant of living in the world, humans petitioned animals for their friendship and for help with the daily hazards of living in potentially dangerous environments. The Sioux felt that "animals actually chose the people they wanted as human companions."[25] In general, American Indians "understand that all life forms not only have consciousness, but also have qualities that are poorly developed or entirely lacking in humans."[26] Therefore, any hierarchy of being that might have existed placed humans at the bottom, in need of guidance and knowledge. Animals were at least equals, as many native cosmologies show, and in some instances, more intelligent than humans, as Kills Straight, member of the Lakota Buffalo Caretakers Cooperative remarks:

> If you communicate with a buffalo you'll see that they're much more intelligent than a human, just that they can't articulate it as humans. Our lives as humans rely on the buffalo, as long as the buffalo live, we can also live. For spiritual reasons we rely on the buffalo and consequently take care of them.[27]

Reciprocity is essential in human-animal relationships. However, Deloria warns that these reciprocal relationships "would be difficult to fit into a Jungian context in which there is not a mutual exchange of knowledge but merely symbolic relationships and the assumption of human superiority and animal inferiority."[28] Transformation and other animal stories illustrate occasions when humans receive items, knowledge, and specific instructions from animals about living in this world. These might include sacred bundles containing power, herbal remedies for illnesses, songs, dances, and rituals to be remembered and performed, or even admonishments of improper human behavior with demands for corrective action.

Over the years, the relationships native people have with animals have changed. The intimacy that was once typical and common has weakened considerably. Some say this intimacy came to an end when humans began to be disrespectful to animals. Certainly, tribes participated in over killing animals too, in taking more than what they needed, and in violating their covenant with their relatives. Today, in an attempt to reclaim the knowledge shared with us by animals and to strengthen these relationships, more tribal people are returning to culturally informed ways of living in the world. Hunting rituals, ceremonies, dance, and applying tribal worldviews to business ventures all offer ways to rebuild relations with our animal relatives.

Counter-intuitive and contradictory as it first seems, the archetype of the hunter offers a contemporary framework in which to maintain an intimate, direct, and reciprocal relationship with animals. The Hunter of Good Heart, a symbolic metaphor among the Pueblo and found in many other native hunting cultures, represents "a way of living, a way of relating, a way of ethics and proper behavior, the foundation of teaching and learning about the relationship to the animals."[29] The act of hunting brings the hunter and the community into direct contact with the reality of life and death, with the reality of how our lives are dependent on animals, and with the need to maintain proper relationships with them. Hunters understand that animals need to be treated properly and great care taken to perpetuate the covenant created with them. Animals are seen to possess special qualities and powers that they may share with humans if they are treated properly. Therefore, adhering to proper conduct is essential as hunting rituals are reenacted and performed. Hunting rituals cultivate a spiritual quality to the act of hunting as animals are seen as "gifts" that willingly and consciously give themselves to hunters who respect them.

> When a buffalo is killed, traditionally there is a ceremony. In Lakota culture, the Buffalo Kill Ceremony is to offer prayers and talks to the spirit of the animal. Then, and only then will the

buffalo surrender itself. That is when you can kill a buffalo. To kill incorrectly, the elders say, disrupts life.[30]

I recall a story my father told me about a porcupine who agreed to give its life for food. My father and his uncle were out collecting firewood in the woods and came upon a porcupine that was high up in a tree. My father's uncle proceeded to talk to the porcupine, make tobacco and prayer offerings to him, and ask him if he might give himself over for food; that he was needed. The uncle then carefully built a small fire at the base of the tree. The porcupine slowly descended whereby the uncle hit him on the head with a piece of wood and took him to my aunt to be used for food. The uncle explained to my father that the porcupine was his brother, that he knew he was needed, and so he sacrificed himself.

Just recently I spent two weeks at home on the reservation. It was a time when my brother and cousins were out hunting everyday. When I asked if they offered tobacco and prayers before their hunt, their reply was immediate, firm, and affirmative. In fact, I was looked at as though I was crazy to ask such a question and was reassured that prayers were also offered on behalf of other hunters. Offerings, prayers of thanksgiving, and other rituals are still made to animals prior to and after a hunt. These rituals are old and are founded upon an understanding of animals' behaviors and ways animals should be properly used and treated. For example, George Tinker, when writing about buffalo, says that buffalo gave "permission to humans to engage in hunting and eating them—as long as the hunting and the consuming was always done in a sacred (i.e., ceremonial) manner."[31] And Lame Deer recounted:

> When we killed a buffalo, we knew what we were doing. We apologized to his spirit, tried to make him understand why we did it, honoring with a prayer the bones of those who gave their flesh to keep us alive, praying for their return, praying for the life of our brothers, the buffalo nation, as well as for our own people.[32]

It is also understood that the spirit of the animal is not destroyed when the animal gives itself for food and is taken in a proper way. This is clearly illustrated in a prayer offered at a Northwest Salmon Ceremony:

Old friends, thank you that we meet alive. Now we pray you, supernatural ones, to protect us from danger, that nothing evil may happen to us when we eat you, supernatural ones, for that is the reason why you have come here, that we may catch you for food. We know that only your bodies are dead here, but your souls come to watch over us when we are going to eat what you have given us to eat now.[33]

But not all native hunters adhere to cultural and behavioral ethics when they hunt. In 1996-1997 several elder grandmothers of the Makah tribe, who themselves came from whaling families, spoke out against their tribe's return to whaling at the International Whaling Commission in Scotland. There was conflict between traditionalists of the tribe and young business leaders who were negotiating contracts for profit. The elders recognized their behavior as a breach of tradition, breaking a spiritual law. "Shooting a whale with a machine gun is not a spiritual way," said one of the elders. A long, well-prepared ceremony is required. They explained that no longer did anyone in their village still have a direct relationship with the whale; that using the argument of "subsistence" was a lie since their people hadn't used or had whale blubber since the early 1900s. Exercising treaty rights, another argument council members made, was also shown false in the way the tribe was sidestepping the law and misrepresenting their intent. Angry council members tried to silence the grandmothers. One woman was hand-delivered a resolution that stated she could not speak about whaling or even make an appearance, or she would be arrested. These elders remind us that long before there were humans and treaties, there were whales; that new considerations must take into account that whales are our elders and that to further endanger them is no longer a human privilege; that we must reckon with the spirit of the whale and reestablish a relationship based on mutual respect.[34, 35]

I offer here my father's story as an example of consequences that can result when a hunter fails to adhere to established cultural and ethical codes of conduct. My father was a skilled hunter. Early in his hunting career he killed a screech owl, the mythic messenger of death to the Menominee. He had the owl stuffed and placed in an upper corner of our living room ceiling. The owl remained perched there for years and as a child I swore I heard it flying about the house at night. One day, my father's aunt came to visit our house. When she saw the owl in the living room she immediately left the house and demanded my father remove it. She cautioned him that harm would come to him and that she would not return to visit unless the owl was removed. My great aunt, Jane Neconish, was a medicine woman in her own right. She refused to speak English, lived in a one-room dirt floor cabin, knew how to use plants for healing, strictly followed Menominee/Potowatomie cultural practices, could make fire without flint or matches, and could tell you things before they would actually happen. Because my father refused to remove the owl from our home, my aunt never came to visit us again. If we wanted to see her, we had to go to her.

As a member of the bear clan, my father was forbidden from hunting bear. Unfortunately, he ignored these rules, passing them off as mere superstitions, and insisted on hunting his brother. To make matters worse he sold the bear's gall bladder, violating even more deeply this long-established cultural taboo. As fate would have it, and as my aunt predicted, my father became seriously ill, having to undergo surgery to remove *his own gall bladder*. He then developed diabetes and had several fingers and one of his legs amputated. One time, after one of his surgeries, he had a sudden and clear change of heart about the bear he hunted. He promptly asked my mother to remove all the bear meat we had in our freezer and any other bear parts in our possession. He asked that they be out of the house before he returned home from the hospital. After years of suffering from his disease and on an evening when my mother and father had returned home from a dialysis treatment, my mother noticed that the owl was no longer perched in the living room. Somehow, it had fallen (to this day, no one in the family has figured out how this happened) and was lying on its back behind the television. As she approached the bird, my father stopped her and told her not to touch it, to leave it be. A few hours later my father died suddenly in his bed, lying on his back, in the same position as the owl. When we buried my father, we buried him whole, with his fingers and leg that had been taken from him, in the hopes that his journey would be easier. As for the owl, under strict instruction from tribal elders, my younger brother offered prayers to it and buried it in an appropriate and respectful manner.

Many might take this as purely coincidence: that the owl, the messenger of death, and my father both ended up on their backs, absent of life, on the same evening. However, similar to Jungian synchronicity, from a Menominee perspective, we understand that this is a teaching; that this tragic event was due to a violation of a covenant between the ancestral bear and his younger human brother. To kill your spirit brother is taboo and doing so will cause harm.

Today hunting has become a multi-million dollar recreational *sport* and since certainly not all native hunters adhere to traditional ways of hunting, tribes have found ways to adapt and yet maintain their values with respect to hunting animals. Many tribes enforce hunting regulations and game management systems. Some tribes allow only one kind of game to be hunted during a season. Regulations restrict the gender of the animal hunted and the number that can be harvested at any given time. Hunters too, in talking with one another about their hunting experiences, informally keep each other "in line" with current (and traditional) hunting behaviors. My cousin explained that when he hunts deer, he doesn't shoot indiscriminately. First, he offers prayers to the animal. Then, when seeing a deer, he ascertains if it is female, if it has babies, if perhaps a buck will be following, and if he has a "kill shot." He explained that he usually avoids killing female deer and he never kills one if she has babies with her. If he doesn't have a "kill shot", he won't fire because the shot will cause the deer never to return to that particular place again and the deer will become skittish and anxious. If he encounters a bear while hunting, he'll shoot his gun in the air to scare the bear away. He doesn't kill for sport. He hunts for food for his family and to maintain a relationship with the animals he hunts.

My brother spoke about another younger hunter who killed a small doe. He explained how other hunters relentlessly teased him. They insisted he had killed one of their dogs rather than a deer. This teasing directly lets the young hunter know that in the future he needs to be much more selective of his kill. Elders too will reprimand hunters for inappropriate behavior, as we saw with the Makah grandmothers. To be reprimanded by an elder in a native community could prove so shaming to the hunter and the hunter's family that he or she may choose to stop hunting altogether. The community will hold this story in collective memory and will call for it, when needed, to serve as a reminder to others who go against cultural ethics.

Hunters are patient observers in their environment. They see, hear, smell, and witness animals interacting with one another and a bond is renewed between the hunter and animal. Hunters share their observations of animal behaviors with family and friends, usually with a keen sense of respect for the animals and with knowledge gained about how to live in community. This deep respect and sharing of experiences has influenced entire communities to fight for the preservation of the land the animals inhabit. Tribes have spent time and resources fighting mining and lumber companies, power plants, and other industries that seek to exploit the resources found on many reservations today. "Who will speak for the wolf?" was a common campaign slogan that tribes in the Midwest used when fighting mining companies in the 1980s and 1990s.

Ceremony is another means by which human-animal relationships continue to be honored. Tribes understand that ancient knowledge can be assessed through proper ceremony and that animals will make themselves and their knowledge available when treated with respect. In particular, medicine men rely on animals when conducting ceremonies. Accounts of medicine men performing ceremonies sometime describe them as metamorphosing into the shape of their animal helper/protector and that this transformation is explained as movement of soul, spirit possession, or knowing how to use "medicine" properly. To the Iñupiat of Alaska, this mobility of soul is as old as time and is referred to as "time out of mind."

Countless ceremonies performed today require animal participation. Whether an animal-calling ritual is enacted, animal hides or bones used, or whether animals appear in visions or dreams imparting knowledge, it remains that information is shared, insight is gained, and relationships are strengthened.

> In ceremonies, birds and animals could substitute for each other and in visions they could transform themselves into each other when the occasion warranted. …we often find several changes from bird to animal to human and back again. People cherished these changes because they gave the vision questing individual an insight into the larger cosmic world of the seen and unseen.[36]

Some ceremonies are essential for the continued survival of our animal relatives. People living on the Menominee reservation set aside time each spring to celebrate the sturgeon, an ancient fish, sub-clan member to the ancestral bear, and protector of the wild rice beds. The Menominee chose their present day reservation during the treaty-making era, in part, because of the annual sturgeon migration up the Wolf River. Usually in April, people gather at *Namae'o Uskiwamit* (the place where sturgeons come home), as small fingerlings are placed in the river with prayers for their return and continued survival. Then, specific fish dances are performed and songs are sung that speak to the sacred relationship that exists between the Menominee and the sturgeon. A sturgeon is sacrificed and its oil is offered to elders for its medicinal uses and a feast of sturgeon ends the day's ceremony. The Menominee are committed to restoring the sturgeon to their original homelands and are dedicated to maintaining an environment that not only welcomes their brother home, but also keeps him there.

Ceremonies are also enacted when the need arises. In 1997, after years during which hundreds of buffalo had been shot and slaughtered near Yellowstone National Park for roaming off park lands and crossing the invisible border onto state lands, a small group of people, including Arvol Looking Horse, gathered to offer their prayers. Rosalie Little Thunder, a Lakota grandmother and advocate for buffalo, was warned about trespassing onto private land where the buffalo had been killed. Disregarding the warnings, Little Thunder, like her buffalo relatives, crossed the imaginary boundary and went to pray for the slain buffalo. Little Thunder was handcuffed and arrested. Like the 50 million buffalo that had lost their lives without the benefit of a ceremony, their spirits left to wander, Little Thunder and others saw the need to offer the Yellowstone buffalo a ceremony for the return of their souls. By engaging in the appropriate ceremonies, Looking Horse, Little Thunder, and others are able to ensure the physical rebirth of the animals hunted or killed. "The renewal ceremonies practiced by tribes are specific expressions of the human responsibility to preserve, protect and perpetuate the life of the animals."[37]

Dancing is another way humans transform into their animal relatives and learn about our interdependence. Today, contemporary social gatherings such as pow-wows provide ample opportunity to witness and participate in this phenomenon. Pow-wows are celebrations where dance, song, and ritual come together. Tribes from across the nations gather to celebrate, share stories, renew and create friendships, and practice cultural values. In ceremonies and at pow-wows, dances that have been given to the people by the animal being honored are a physical enactment of humans' responsibility to maintain a respectful relationship with animals. When dancing, humans are not merely acting out a role. At a much deeper level, it is believed that "those who enacted the ritual became identified with the power of the animal persons, spirits . . . who were responsible for the original gift to the people."[38] Any observer at a typical tribal pow-wow is bound to see dancers wearing animal skins or carrying other animal parts as pieces of their dancing regalia. For example, the feathers, talons, and wings of the eagle will be used while dancing and, when used ceremonially, will bring "the power of the eagle into the ceremony for healing and help."[39] And, if you watch carefully, you will see a good dancer transformed into their animal host when captured by the rhythmic heartbeat of the drum and the collective voice of the song. The dancers relive the myth, become the animal, and invite us to become active participants. These dances, in mythical and very real ways, ensure that our collective memory of our relationship and responsibility to our animal relatives is maintained. By dynamically "dancing the inner, subjective experience, a re-intensification of it results, and the larger social group is able to participate. This helps to influence the young people toward this quality of experience and so to preserve the central values."[40]

A common dance at many pow-wows is the snake dance. No snake is needed for the dance nor is any part of a snake used. Rather, the people collectively become the snake as the dance unfolds. Together, while dancing, we coil and uncoil, we shed our skin, and we cross over the river to another realm. We acknowledge our relationship to the snake, the wisdom and guidance it offers us, and we come to understand that this expression helps us become more fully human.

Our relationships with animals are informed by our myths, our ceremonies, and our lived experiences with these spirit beings. Similar to how ancient Greek myths give us insight into our own and collective psyche, so too do these transformation teachings keep us keenly aware of our intimate relationships with our animal relatives. They help us adhere to and maintain an ethics of behavior, they provide information about ceremonies, rituals, and medicines, and they have implications for our knowledge of self in relation to other beings. Profound myths of animal-human transformation ultimately ensure continued survival of our own and animal species.

As tribes work to maintain reciprocal and respectful relationships with our animal relatives, direct knowledge of the natural world is nevertheless still rapidly being lost, and indigenous people are not entirely free from fault. It is therefore necessary that tribes do not remain alone in these efforts. Depth psychology has much to offer. Jerome Bernstein has outlined a phenomenon of the collective unconscious he calls the Borderland. "It is an evolutionary dynamic that is moving the western psyche to reconnect our overspecialized ego to its natural psychic roots."[41] G.A. Bradshaw and Mary Watkins, faculty in Depth Psychology at Pacifica Graduate Institute, remind us that "psychology, by maintaining an agenda of speciesism, violates one of its central projects: individual development of moral consciousness." They propose a trans-species psychology "that eschews the assumption of human ascendance" and allows for "other species as partners in decision-making, culture-making, and community meaning making."[42] Jung pointed out that

> it's the intellect that is making darkness, because we've let it take too big a place. Consciousness, discriminates, judges, analyzes, and emphasizes the contradictions. It's necessary work up to a point. But analysis kills and synthesis brings to life. We must find out how to get everything back into connection with everything else. We must resist the vice of intellectualism, and get it understood that we cannot only understand.[43]

And Vine Deloria, Jr. also noticed:

> There must be a great kinship between Jungian psychology and the American Indian traditions that has been emerging, will continue to develop, and is worth the time and energy of our investigation. A major component of that kinship is Jung's strong sense of a dissociation in western culture due to its separation from nature and the Indian psyche that has never experienced such a separation and for whom nature is a living experience and spiritual presence.[44]

But Deloria also cautions us as we attempt to form cross-cultural exchanges. He emphasizes that efforts must be made to carefully and accurately translate from one context to another. One cannot immediately apply Jungian concepts to indigenous philosophies—as if to assume that one understands indigenous ceremonial and religious beliefs. To do this would risk perpetuating a long history of cultural appropriation. Instead, Deloria suggests that Jungian ideas could be critiqued from American Indian perspectives and "ideas of the larger culture critiqued by those of the smaller in such a manner as to help create a new intellectual framework that partially transcends each culture."[45]

There is cause for hope. Bernstein, Bradshaw, and others are opening doors for us to participate in transrational and trans-species realities. My brother is showing more bear-like qualities each year as he takes to the woods. And just a couple of months ago while back home on the reservation, I pleasantly delighted in my six-year-old niece's new discovery. Having been playing alone in the woods for quite some time, and not culturally raised in Menominee traditions, she came to sit on my lap, slung her arm around my neck, earnestly looked me in the eye, and emphatically stated: "Auntie Jeannie, all those animals and creatures out there, *they really are our brothers and sisters!*"

NOTES

1. C.G. Jung, "The 2,000,000-Year-Old Man," in *C.G. Jung Speaking: Interviews and Encounters*, ed. William McGuire and R.F.C. Hull (Princeton, N.J.: Princeton University Press, 1977), p. 89.

2. Linda Hogan, "First People," in *Intimate Nature: The Bond Between Women and Animals,* ed. Linda Hogan, Deena Metzger, and Brenda Peterson (New York: Ballantine Publishing Group, 1998), p. 7.

3. James Frechette, "Origin Story," *The Menominee Clans Story* http://www.uwsp.edu/museum/menomineeclans/origintext.shtm, accessed October 28, 2009.

4. Vine Deloria, Jr., "Ethnoscience and Indian Realities," in *Spirit and Reason: The Vine Deloria, Jr. Reader*, eds. Barbara Deloria, Kristen Foehner, and Sam Scinta (Golden, CO: Fulcrum Publishing, 1999), p. 65.

5. Hogan, "First People", pp. 10-15.

6. Chief Arvol Looking Horse, *White Buffalo Teachings* (Williamsburg, MA: Dreamkeepers Press, 2001), pp. 37-39.

7. Joslyn Cassady, "Strange Things Happen to Non-Christian People: Human-Animal Transformation among the Inupiat of Arctic Alaska," *American Indian Culture and Research Journal*, 32, 1 (2008): 91.

8. Calvin Luther Martin, "Foreword," in *Elephants on the Edge: What Animals Teach Us About Humanity* by G.A. Bradshaw (New Haven, CT: Yale University Press, 2009), p. xi.

9. Vine Deloria, Jr., *C.G. Jung and the Sioux Traditions: Dreams, Visions, Nature, and the Primitive,* ed. Philip J. Deloria and Jerome S. Bernstein (New Orleans: Spring Journal Books, 2009), p. 119.

10. Vine Deloria, Jr., *Red Earth White Lies: Native Americans and the Myth of Scientific Fact* (New York: Scribner, 1995), p. 19.

11. Jerome Bernstein, *Living in the Borderland: The Evolution of Consciousness and the Challenge in Healing Trauma* (New York: Routledge, 2005), pp. 20-21.

12. *Ibid.*, p. 21.

13. Calvin Martin, *Keepers of the Game: Indian-Animal Relationships and the Fur Trade* (Berkeley, CA: University of California Press, 1978), p. 18.

14. G.A. Bradshaw, "Elephant Trauma and Recovery: Human Violence to Trans-species Psychology" (dissertation, Pacifica Graduate Institute), p. 174.

15. For a thorough discussion of natives as "primitive," see chapters two and three in Deloria, *C.G. Jung and the Sioux Traditions.*

16. C.G. Jung, *Collected Works of C. G. Jung* (Princeton, NJ: Princeton University Press, 1976), Vol. 18, § 597.

17. Gregory Cajete, *Native Science: Natural Laws of Interdependence* (Santa Fe: Clear Light Publishers, 2000), p. 152.

18. Winona LaDuke, "Return of Buffalo Nation: For Native Peoples of the Plains, Visions of a Buffalo Commons," *Native Americas*, 15, 4 (1998): 6.

19. Steve Wall and Harvey Arden, *Wisdomkeepers: Meetings with Native American Spiritual Elders* (Hillsboro: Beyond Words, 1990), p. 26.

20. Vine Deloria, Jr., "Excerpts from C.G. Jung and the Sioux Traditions: Dreams, Visions, Nature, and the Primitive," *Spring 76* Part 2 of 2 (2006): 14-15.

21. Deloria, *C.G. Jung and the Sioux Traditions,* p. 117.

22. George "Tink" Tinker, "The Stones Shall Cry Out: Consciousness, Rocks, and Indians," *Wicazo Sa Review*, 19, 2 (2004): 108.

23. Hogan, "First People", p. 13.

24. Cajete, *Native Science*, p. 151.

25. Deloria, *C.G. Jung and the Sioux Traditions*, p. 127.

26. Tinker, "Stones Shall Cry Out", p. 106.

27. LaDuke, "Buffalo Nation," p. 2.

28. Deloria, *C.G. Jung and the Sioux Traditions*, p.128.

29. Cajete, *Native Science*, p. 158.

30. LaDuke, "Buffalo Nation", p. 4.

31. Tinker, "Stones Shall Cry Out", p. 116.

32. John Fire/Lame Deer and Richard Erdoes, *Lame Deer: Seeker of Visions* (New York: Simon and Schuster, 1972), p. 122.

33. Donald Hughes, *American Indian Ecology* (El Paso: Texas Western Press, 1983), p. 46, quoted in Cajete, *Native Science,* p. 164.

34. Linda Hogan, "Silencing Tribal Grandmothers—Traditions, Old Values At Heart of Makah's Clash Over Whaling," *The Seattle Times*, December 15, 1996.

35. Brenda Peterson, "Who Will Speak For The Whales?—Elders Call for A Spiritual Dialogue on Makah Tribe's Whaling Proposal," *The Seattle Times*, December 22, 1996.

36. Deloria, *C.G. Jung and the Sioux Traditions*, p. 125.

37. Cajete, *Native Science*, p. 164.

38. Howard L. Harrod, *the animals came dancing: native american sacred ecology and animal kinship* (Tucson: University of Arizona Press, 2000), pp. 77-78.

39. Tinker, "Stones Shall Cry Out", p. 116.

40. Joseph Epes Brown, "The Bison and the Moth," in *The Inner Journey: Views from Native Traditions*, ed. Linda Hogan, Parabola Anthology Series (Sandpoint, ID: Morning Light Press, 2009), p. 176.

41. Bernstein, *Living in the Borderland*, p. 9.

42. Gay Bradshaw and Mary Watkins, "Trans-species Psychology: Theory and Praxis," in *Spring 75* Part 1 of 2 (2006): 71-82.

43. C. G. Jung, "On the Frontiers of Knowledge," in *C.G. Jung Speaking*, p. 420.

44. Deloria, "Excerpts," p. 17.

45. Deloria, *C.G. Jung and the Sioux Traditions*, pp. 1-2.

WHERE THE WILD THINGS ARE: DREAMING THE BIOREGION

PATRICIA REIS

If all the beasts were gone, men would die from a great loneliness of spirit, for whatever happens to the beasts also happens to the man. All things are connected. —Chief Seattle, of the Suwamish Tribe, letter to President Franklin Pierce

In all native tellings of animal stories the importance of landscape is paramount. As Barry Lopez has said, "The animal's environment, the background against which we see it, can be rendered as something like the animal itself—partly unchartable. And to try to understand the animal apart from its background, except as an imaginative exercise, is to risk the collapse of both. To be what they are they require each other."[1] Thus, we cannot begin to look or think about animals without placing them in their context: mating in the old growth forests, trotting on pine-needled pathways, loping along in snowy north woods, diving into ponds, drinking at woodland streams. Like us,

Patricia Reis is a writer and psychotherapist in private practice in Portland, Maine. She is the author of many articles and three books focusing on women's psychology, mythology, and creative process. Her books are: *Through the Goddess: A Woman's Way of Healing, Daughters of Saturn: From Father's Daughter to Creative Woman*, and *The Dreaming Way: Dreams and Art for Remembering and Recovery* (with Susan Snow). Her most recent work is a DVD production: *Arctic Refuge Sutra: Teachings from an Endangered Landscape*. Her website is www.patriciareis.net and she may be reached at preis@midmaine.com.

animals too must contend with and come to terms with a particular geography, a landscape, a set of ecological conditions that supports their on-goingness in life. At one time humans learned how to live from the animals. We needed their knowledge in order to survive. Today, we understand that unless we grasp our interconnectedness at the deepest levels of existence, neither the animal's nor the human's survival is necessarily guaranteed.

I have lived in Maine for twenty-five years. Maine has become my chosen landscape, a bioregion where I live, work, and dream. For most of these years our home sat on thirteen acres of second or third growth forest. The house was constructed of local pine and our primary heat source in the winter was local hardwood. Woods surrounded us: birch, pine, poplar, and oak trees grew around our house in thick abundance.

We shared this landscape with animals: deer, fox, coyote, skunk, beaver, otter, rabbit, gray squirrel, raccoon, porcupine, woodchuck, and an occasional moose. Each of these animals could be seen in waking life, some only in fleeting glimpses and flashes of movement. I learned to recognize animal tracks and spore. The soles of my feet on the path in the woods touched where the fox has trotted. The snow bears the imprint of our movements like a text—the woman walked here alone, she stopped for a while by this rock; the fox, with her steady, straight-legged pace, jumped off the trail over there looking for a mouse under that tree. Our stories, the fox's and mine, overlap and cross each other. Although I smell her musk and see her paw prints, I almost never see her. She, on the other hand, has no doubt seen me many times. Her invisibility sets up a longing in me, what writer and naturalist Terry Tempest Williams has called an unspoken hunger.[2]

The land I walk is vastly different than the landscape the first European immigrants put their foot on. It is hard to imagine that on the eve of European colonization ninety-five percent what we now call New England was covered with forest canopy. Not only that, this heavily forested place was home to animals that have not been seen for almost two hundred years: the American elk, caribou, wolf, and cougar were once plentiful in this region. Although there had been earlier alterations in the landscape, the changes created by European colonization have been aptly called an "ecological revolution."[3] This revolution seems glacial in comparison to what is happening now.

Scientists concur that we are currently in the midst of the most rapid extinction of plants and animals the world has ever known. Many predict that one-fifth of our planet's species could disappear within the next thirty years. Scientists also share widespread concern that the rate at which we are losing species is unrivaled in the earth's 4.5 billion-year history as a result of modern humanity, especially the loss and fragmentation of wild habitat.[4]

Maya Lin, the artist and architect most famous for designing the Viet Nam Memorial in Washington, D.C., has recently installed what she claims is her last memorial piece at the California Academy of Science in San Francisco. Entitled "What is Missing," it consists in part of a large megaphone-shaped listening cone out of which emanates video images and sounds of creatures and their lifeworlds in a fade-in and fade-out cycle. Lin's research says that a species becomes extinct on average every twenty minutes, so the viewer can experience sensually what we have lost and stand to lose as birds, frogs, and primates are silenced and slip away from view. Lin makes clear the connection between the disappearance of endangered species and the survival of the habitats that support them.

I register these disappearances as surely as if I were losing sisters and brothers, mother and father, grandfathers and grandmothers. I feel anguish about our helplessness and our complicity, our lack of human consciousness, and I feel a desperate desire to do something before it is too late. I cannot allow myself the luxury of despair. I must cultivate my sensory awareness, locate the connective tissues, and find the actions that are within my grasp, the ones that are close to home.

I do not need to go far to explore, study, and investigate my relationship to the local landscape, to the other-than-human inhabitants, as well as to the human inhabitants who once lived on this land but are no longer here. As I search for fuller personal, cultural, and natural connection, I am actively seeking a change in my own consciousness. I yearn to touch the earth and her creatures as I touch my own skin or that of a lover's—with joy, respect, and tenderness. Deep in my own body I know and remember that our bodies—the earth's, the creature's, my own—are made up of precisely the same elements. I sense how profoundly interconnected and inevitable this relationship is. We are all evolving together, for better or worse. I am sixty-nine years old. I do not want to leave this earthly existence until

I have felt, as deeply as possible, my interconnection with those creatures whom I share life with, or until I have felt myself fully located on the landscape where I live. And I wonder where my unspoken hunger will take me. What will this desire demand of me? Where do I begin?

Dreams I have in the night leave their mark, their imprint, as surely as the fox makes her straight-legged printed pattern on the snow or the deer leaves her arrowhead hoof prints on rain-soaked ground. But it is not only nighttime dreaming that I am interested in. I want to make a record not only of the lynx who pounced on me in my dream, but also the one who meditated on her log in her pen at the Maine Wildlife Park: the one I sang a song to about my dream of her. And I want to note that we can count on a few fingers the number of living lynx in the state of Maine.[5] This seems important to consider: the relationship between the dream lynx, the captive lynx, and the lynx trying to make her living in a fragmented habitat in the north woods.

Undoubtedly animals live deep within our psyches emerging unbidden in dreams, in stories, myths, and metaphors, in moments of crystal clarity, synchronicity, and revelation, those numinous encounters when species meet and spirits speak. But the imaginal animal is not enough. How can we think to appropriate an animal's spirit or power while that same animal is becoming extinct due to our human indifference? Don't we need the real animal going about her business in her wild habitat to hold us to reality, to keep us from profound alienation and loneliness? And don't the creatures need us to hold their wellbeing foremost in our minds? How forgotten, lonely, and wary have they become by our detachment, our estrangement, our lack of memory? And I wonder, can the boundaries of what we call reality thin and stretch so the membrane between dreaming and waking, animal and woman, nature and culture is permeable, passable, permissible, and unnecessary?

When I first moved to Maine, my experience of wild animals consisted of dead bodies in the backs of flatbed trucks. Early one crisp, brilliant autumn day I saw my first moose, a massive inert lump of brownish black muscle and fur, its long knobby legs and hooves hanging out over the edge of a truck bed. This creature was headed for some weighing station, there to be measured out and recorded, a statistic for the current hunting season.

Several weeks later in early November, a big storm came in the night and by morning a foot of soft, powdery snow lay on the earth, dressing the fir trees in mantles of sparkling, white lace. On my daily walk to the post office, I passed the country store on the main street of our small village. In the parking lot sits a truck, and in my peripheral vision I register a large tawny shape in the flat bed. When I stop, I see a buck deer with a resplendent rack of antlers lying in a pool of his own bright red blood. By the time I return from the post office this majestic animal has been strung upside down in front of the country store, being weighed and measured as the hunters stand around congratulating each other.

Looking at the deer, it occurred to me that this animal's perfect body, its new winter coat of dense buff and tan fur, had never before been touched by human hands. Now, after being shot, dragged from its forest home, and hauled onto a truck, he was hanging upside down putting his antlers into some perverse relation to the earth—roots instead of branches. The whole world turned upside down.

Surely the quest for food is an ancient one. But this event was occurring in front of a grocery store where plenty of food could be had. I could sense from their high spirits that the people who did this were after more than meat. They seemed infused with the animal's power, charged up with something akin to awe through their contact with this magnificent creature, something they could not find inside the white-steepled church across the street. But it was all happening without ceremony; no gifts offered to the spirit of the deer, no ritual of reciprocation for what the deer had given, no drawings on the cave wall in remembrance, no tobacco or cornmeal sprinkled, no silver or turquoise offered. It was the rupturing loss of sacred connection that pulled me down into grief.

Leslie Marmon Silko writes of the Navaho practice of honoring a deer that has just been taken.

> When the hunter brought home a mule deer buck, the deer occupied the place of honor in the house; it lay on the best Navajo blanket with strings of silver and turquoise beads hanging from its neck; turquoise and silver rings and bracelets decorated the antlers.[6]

Reading her description, I notice my body relaxes. I feel the harmony of right relationship in my blood and muscles. My breathing deepens, the tenseness in my shoulders subsides. I discover it is not hunting I am against, but an unquestioned presumption of human right and need. It is not death I am resisting, but practices that are not reciprocally honoring, lack acknowledgment of sacrifice, without ritual bestowal of dignity to both the animal and the hunter.

I struggle with the way of the hunter as I have seen it. Yet, I recognize I am another kind of hunter. I, too, hunt for animals. I yearn for their appearance; I desire them; I quest and call for them to come to me in my waking life; I long to see them on the trail and in my dreams. When they do appear, I feel elated, blessed and honored, chosen and rewarded. I am not interested in snaring, trapping, shooting, or owning them; I merely want to feel my connection to them. I want to be reminded of the days when animals and humans spoke to each other. I want to experience what anthropologist Richard Nelson learned from his years of living with the Koyukon elders of Northern Alaska, that the animals themselves are imbued with spirit, power, and awareness and that humans in close communion are recipients of their powers.[7] I want to touch the animal that lives inside me, to feel the texture of fur, the beauty of muscle and sinew working together, the intelligence of the senses. I want to assuage my human loneliness with their unselfconscious beauty.

I know the price of this longing for contact is high. To fully enter the enlivening world of animals I must also be willing to feel pain, anguish, terror, and despair—mine, theirs. The genocide of species; the torture of bears; the poisoning of coyotes; the over-trapping of beaver, fox, lynx, and other animals who are the bearers of rich and sensual furs; the killing of deer who are considered pests because of their numbers; the near-extinction of wolves who were their natural predators, but bore the stigma of human rapaciousness. One cannot approach the entrance to the animal kingdom without pausing to ask: Can I bear the tremendous grief and sorrow that lies in the passageway between humans and animals? If I wish to be a mediator, a translator, a rememberer, I must be willing to bear the unbearable in order to convey what has and is happening to them, what they have suffered since we have been so out of balance with them, all those broken treaties. I am ashamed, helpless, and very afraid of feeling mute terror.

Sometimes it is through human suffering that I am shown an opening into their world.

One Monday morning my friend, Anne, came to my house in the woods. She hadn't been to visit since her cancer diagnosis. Before she arrived I was aware of feeling very happy, anticipatory, excited, so glad she was coming. This was not, in itself, unusual. I have such deep respect and love for this woman who has been living with her cancer diagnosis for two years. Her living is sometimes profoundly high and holy and sometimes dangerously dark, filled with great struggle and despair. Either way, I think, she is always courageous.

The threads of our lives have been woven and tied at certain critical junctures. For over ten years we journeyed together in various modes of travel as the years of sitting in counsel with each other gave way to wilderness trips. We are both guides of a sort: I was witness and companion for her inner journey; she has been a practiced and knowledgeable teacher for me on journeys with backpack, dogsled, and canoe. I have been present as witness and friend through cancer surgeries, and helped preside over her commitment ceremony with her partner and a birthday celebration we all thought might be her last. Our meetings, although infrequent, are never casual and always packed with portent. We often share a simple meal as we make delicate probings along the edge of mystery, and sometimes we fall into it.

This day we sat on the couch making plans to meet once a month to share writing. She was searching for a form to hold all the wild, chaotic, and pure experiences of her cancer time. There was energy, a bubbling excitement, and a charge of hopefulness and joy when we got our calendars out marking the days we would meet. In the face of serious illness, we were counting on a future.

As we prepared to eat a late autumn soup of carrot and sweet potatoes, she tells me that on her way, by the side of one of the back roads, she found dismembered pieces of a deer—a foreleg and a severed head with the antlers sawed off—they were fresh. She had them in the flat bed of her truck. She thought I might know what to do with them. An unmistakable rush of mystery came into the room as if someone had opened the door in a windstorm. We ate slowly, much in silence. I felt myself drawn into the power of ritual.

I experience it physically at first—the shattering disorganization that accompanies extreme indifference and mindless disrespect. This is followed by an internal effort of putting things to right, a re-ordering of chaos, a re-assembling of wholeness. We finish the meal and gather together a sage bundle and some feathers, a rattle, a small drum, cornmeal, and some flowers I cut from a bunch of fall asters, deep russet, purple, and yellow.

With these in hand, we go out to the back of her truck. The dismembered pieces of deer, the hacked-off leg with its perfect cloven hoof and the beautifully intact but severed head, lay like evidence of something surpassing crime. We each carry a piece and, with rattle and drum accompaniment, we process to the back woods. We make our way through the rough blanket of brown leaves and the jumble of blown down trees until we find a natural hollow in the ground with a flat stone in the middle. On the smooth surface of this stone we arrange the deer head facing east. We tenderly pull a flap of its hide over the severed spinal cord hiding the cruel cutting, and we gently lay the foreleg in front of it. We place the flowers all around the head and leg and light the sage and smudge. She drums. We pray: "May you go back to the great deer mother. May your spirit be joined with your people. May your journey be swift. May your wholeness be restored. May your people flourish. May our people be forgiven for this act of disrespect." Then we rattle and drum and sing a chant until a feeling of restoration and honor becomes deep and satisfying. Handling the harsh reality of dismemberment and finding a spontaneous ritual of re-membering strike me as deeply significant.

Two days later as I am driving home from my office along the same stretch of back road, my eye picks up on something. I pull over and back up. On the side of the road, crumpled up like an old piece of cloth, is a perfect deer skin: the hide is laying there as if the deer had just moments ago slipped away, leaving its pelt behind like a rummage sale coat. I gather the skin up, place it in my trunk, and head for home. Jim and I get out our rattles and walk back into the woods. I carry the skin like a mantle across my arms and place it on the same stone, arranging it so that now the pieces almost resemble a whole deer lying asleep in the leaves. We rattle and pray. When we finish we make our way back through the woods; the sun is going down leaving pink and purple smudge marks in the sky, the bare trees are etched in black against the luminous indigo sky, and a pearly moon is rising. These chance encounters spark months of study and contemplation about our human relationship to wild animals.

Carolyn Merchant says that by 1800 most game animals in New England had dwindled considerably, many vanishing completely by mid-century. I find her litany of losses breathtaking: the white-tailed deer exterminated in Connecticut by about 1850 and wiped out in the rest of New England (except for Maine) by 1890; buffalo who had once roamed the Connecticut Valley before colonization, gone. The American elk vanished completely from Massachusetts and Connecticut; moose and caribou hanging on in unpopulated areas of northern New Hampshire and Vermont until 1900 when caribou ceased to be seen.[8] I recall a small, sad, and unsuccessful attempt in the 1980's to restore caribou to Northern Maine. Not one of these animals survived.

The disappearance of these large mammals left their natural predators, the wolf and cougar, without their primary food sources, and so they naturally turned to domesticated livestock. Large bounties set by farmers soon contributed to their rapid disappearance as well. Carolyn Merchant tells us that cougars were gone by about 1888 except in Maine where only three were spotted in 1906-7. The last wolf was killed in Connecticut in 1837 and in New Hampshire in 1887. Wolves disappeared from Maine in 1900.[9] Current reports from the Department of Inland Fisheries and Wildlife say the gray wolf is making a comeback in northern Maine and efforts are underway to support their return. Not everyone is welcoming their re-appearance.

Some animal species rebound from near extinction, in part because of legislation and the breed's ability to survive, and in part because of lack of predators; deer and moose are the most populous. But other animals are simply gone from this land. They are not yet totally extinct; one can still see them, although not in their natural habitat.

One day in early summer I make a trip to what used to be called the Gray Animal Farm, recently renamed the Maine State Wildlife Park. Someone has told me that a lynx is there. It was Lynx that leaped onto my chest in a dream.

I am in our back yard with my cat who is staring up at a large oak tree. I follow his sight line and all of a sudden a lynx drops down on my

chest. I hold her head in both my hands so we are face to face. I can feel my
heart pounding against her powerful furred chest.

Before this dream I had never really known anything about lynx.
Now I wanted very much to see one in waking life. I soon learned my
chance of viewing this extremely reclusive animal in the wild was near
to impossible. It was not only her secretive nature that would make
her hard for me to find—it is the fact that there are only about 800
lynx left in the lower 48 states.[10] The Maine State Wildlife Park was
probably my only chance of seeing one in waking life.

This facility, funded by the state of Maine, has been in operation
for many years. It is a place where animals are taken if they have been
wounded, orphaned, or made human dependent and cannot live in
the wild. Instinctively I avoid places where animals are kept for the
sole purpose of satisfying human curiosity—zoos, wildlife parks. But
this place is promoted as a kind of sanctuary, a good thing for animals
who cannot be let loose because they have lost their ability to survive
in the wild for some reason. And, I admit, I am curious.

I brace myself as I make my way through neatly organized picnic
tables, hearing the unmistakable chatter and squeals of groups of small
children, punctuated by the crisp directives of supervising adults. I
see what look to be dog kennels, open pens with cement floors, some
with large tree logs, all surrounded by double chainlink fences. I see
two coyotes. Although these animals are healthy looking, they are
clearly degraded, pacing, pacing, pacing along the side of their pen;
their eyes focused out to the far horizon toward some lost home. I pass
by them and think of all the Coyote stories I have read. How Coyote
is the creator and transformer, how he gets himself into so many bad
situations, dies, and is reborn, and I wonder how he will be able to get
himself out of this one.

I walk by a single little fox curled up on the cement; his nose tucked
into his tail, one eye peeking out at me. I feel the insult of the cement
and the lack of cover for this privacy-seeking animal, the offense of such
exposure, and wonder how he must develop ways to deal with the
hungry, prying eyes of all these curious two-footeds. Is this the same
creature I have encountered in the woods or in my dreams?

When I finally make it to the lynx she is perched on top of a small
enclosure made of logs in the middle of her round pen. Like some

ancient monk in a mountain cave, this most secretive, nocturnal hunter appears to be in some profound meditative state, where the indignity of her situation does not seem to touch her, nor do the human eyes disturb. I sing a soft song to her about the lynx in my dream. She never looks at me.

For the Koyukon hunters, the lynx is among the most powerful animals, not equal to wolverine, bear, or wolf, but even more potent. According to anthropologist, Richard Nelson, "This animal can afflict a person with a more complete and lasting alienation than any other, as the stories warn." Nelson relates one of these stories:

> In the Distant Time, the bear and lynx were talking. The bear said that when humans began hunting him they would have to treat him right. If he was mistreated by someone, that person would get no bears until he had gray hairs on his head. But the lynx said that people who mistreated him would never get a lynx again in their lives.[11]

A woman standing next to me, within easy earshot of the lynx, is telling her friend how she inherited her mother's lynx fur coat. I quickly move on, not wanting the lynx to associate me with such a scandalous story. It occurs to me that if humans can have a lynx coat but never encounter a real lynx in the wild, our collective human mind eventually forgets, loses something crucial: who a lynx really is. Not the captive animal, humanized, stereotyped. If the lynx's power to mediate the unknown is so diluted and weakened, don't we lose a large portion of the depth and mystery of life? Won't we suffer from the lynx's curse: complete and lasting alienation? In our current state of estrangement we have judged the animals to be less important than humans. In the Koyukon tale the bear and lynx are known to have the power to curse and also, one assumes, to bless humans for their actions. These animals act as a conscience, arbitrating ill treatment with a swift, uncorrupted justice.

As I continue past the rest of the creatures, I see a panting, pacing bobcat; four ragged, molting brown bears; two eagles, each without a wing due to being shot; many assorted deer; a pair of hawks and some other endangered birds. Certainly all of these animals are here not because of their own doing but because of some human intervention in their lives.

The ethics and obligations of a place like this plague me. There is an ethic of care which requires us, as humans, to protect life, but isn't there also guilt and shame? Aren't we trying to assuage our culpability by caring for animals that some others of us have put in harm's way? The arguments usually run this way: One side says these animals should be turned out and let nature take its course. Nature in this case is not a benevolent good mother, and we know that returning these animals to the "wild" means, in effect, letting them out in territory unfamiliar to them to die a "natural" death by starvation or as food for other predators. The other rationale is that since some humans have caused these animals to be captured, we other humans have the duty to care for them; since they have been made "human-dependent", we are now responsible for them. If they are kept in a place like Maine State Wildlife Park, we are assured they will be well fed and they can pay their way by being a part of an educational program.

Later I learned that the lynx in this park had been mated with another captive and that she recently gave birth to kittens that will also spend their whole life in captivity in another wildlife park. This attitude toward animals in captivity, that they can somehow serve us by "educating" us, is suspect to me. It is easy to recall with horror how, in the late 19th century, Admiral Peary brought back two Inuit families to the Museum of Natural History for study. These people lived—and quickly died—in the basement and upper rooms of the museum, their skeletons remaining as exhibits. It is this particularly arrogant error of perceiving the "other" as an object of study that leads to no good. And in the case of the Maine State Wildlife Farm, who has bothered to ask these animals what they want? The very idea sounds ridiculous. In the case of Minik, the surviving Inuit child, he knew what he wanted: a traditional burial for his father. Instead, he was given a "mock burial" by the museum director who wanted to retain his skeleton. One hundred years later, the bones of these people were finally repatriated. Developing consciousness takes time—and time is what we may be running out of.

Most of us have little in our heritages that would help us establish a spiritual tie with the creatures of the land we live on. We have no animal ancestor, no Grandmother Woodchuck like the one who taught the Abenake people ways to live, no coyote trickster to learn from. It is a sad truth that other than our history of colonization, most Euro-

American people are neither deeply rooted or spiritually connected to the land on which we live nor its animal inhabitants. I often wonder as I wander my bioregion, on whose land do I walk? To answer this question, I find myself being drawn ever farther into history—and mystery.

Over 10,000 years ago Paleo-Indians ventured up New England's rivers for summer hunting with flint spears they brought from farther south. Archaic Indians, who followed them 7,000 to 5,000 years ago as the tundra was being replaced by pine forests, hunted caribou with spears and fished with harpoons and hafted hooks. Do the spirits of those ancestors still live on the land, I wonder? Do they care about how the land is being used and exploited? Or have they been washed away by all the many passing centuries? Has the power of red ochre, which signaled the presence of the Red Paint People, been bleached out of our present-day consciousness?

It is late August and I am co-leading, along with a Maine guide, a Dreamquest canoe trip on Lake Aziscohos in western Maine. We are eighteen women in nine canoes. The lake we enter was once an ancient river. Since it has been dammed its shape has become a long lake with fingers of land reaching into the water. Does the river object to having her shape changed by the will of some people who make it their job to do such things? The lake is silent on this matter. The water level is raised and lowered during the summer months leaving stretches of smooth, white sand populated with large sculpted driftwood tree trunks. We pitch our tents on these welcoming shores.

Over the course of days we paddle our way to the very end of the lake. The feeling is one of going deeper, past veils of mist and islands, into the mystery. We go close to the mouth of the lake that once was a river. Despite the man-made changes, the place retains its ancient aura. We have come here to be close to the beauty of nature, to listen to our dreams, to become a community of women traveling by canoe, sleeping in tents, swimming naked in the lake. We go to recover ourselves from our busy lives and to touch the wilderness so we don't forget.

This particular trip is arduous. The weather is hard, windy, making the lake full of choppy waves and our paddling full of effort. The group is choppy, too, filled with factions, tensions, and friction. The dreams we dream at night and gather during the day are ominous, full of argument, weather, big winds, storms, betrayal, evil. As dream-tender,

I feel concern and know we are opening a conversation about the darkness that lives within us and around us.

At sunrise our guide sends her voice out in a beautiful chant as we gather for a morning meditation. Suddenly we spot two deer swimming across the lake heading for our tents. When they see these strange objects and human shapes on their shore, they startle and instantly turn in the water swimming back to the other side of the lake. I don't like this, the feeling we have disturbed the familiar landscape of these beautiful creatures with our presence, the fact that they are so afraid. That night I have the distinct sensation, while asleep, that someone is at the head of my tent trying to suffocate me. I wake up in a panic.

The next morning, while wading in the shallow water as we load up our canoes, we come upon bones on the bottom of the lake, many bones. We pick them up—thigh bones, femurs, knuckle and hoof bones. Like little kids on an adventure, these bones excite us. Some of us take them as souvenirs. The ominous feeling from the night before remains with me, although I, too, against my own nature, pick up several knucklebones. We determine these bones belong to a moose and head off for the far end of the lake. That night the sky reddens and gives the water a skin of blood.

Early the next morning as we gather in a circle for our meditation, a lone motor boat makes its way up the lake, an unusual sound as this lake is almost always vacated by late August. We have not seen or heard people, much less people in boats with motors. As the boat becomes more visible, we realize that whoever is in the boat is looking for us. When the boat reaches the sandy shore, two of us go down to meet the man to see what he might want—to tell us we are illegally camping? to warn us of something? As we get closer we recognize the man from the country store where we put in our canoes a week ago. As he approaches us we see he is visibly upset. In a low voice he tells us that the son of one of the women on the trip has been killed in a car crash. We absorb the shock of this news, letting it shake our bodies as tears spontaneously run down our cheeks.

We dread the task ahead as we make our way back to the circle of waiting women. We kneel next to the woman and tell her the news that is every mother's nightmare: "Your child is dead. He has been killed in a car crash. We don't know anything else. Your husband is on his way." Women cry out, we hold the woman whose tragedy this is, she

WHERE THE WILD THINGS ARE

is in terrible shock. Women help her pack and I agree to make the long trip back down the lake with her, where her husband will pick her up.

The man in the motorboat takes us. The wind has made the lake treacherous with whitecaps and the metal boat pounds hard against the water. It is a jarring, teeth-rattling, heartbreaking journey. The wind makes the woman's long, white hair go wild and she is raving, trying to make this insane information fit into her world. She keeps crying into the wind, "We don't belong here! We should never have touched those bones!" She is raging, she is mad, a female Lear, and, I think, maybe she is right!

Upon my return to camp at dusk I find our once fractious group deeply bonded over the tragedy, forgetting their petty differences, and letting the sudden death of a child inform them of our mutual vulnerabilities.

The next day we paddle down the lake heading towards home. I am carrying a driftwood doll that the woman had handed to me at the last minute before she left with her husband. I don't know what to do with it. Where to put it? It feels uncanny, like a fetish loaded with danger. The group energy shifts as we head back. The women become self-oriented as we return toward the familiar, the comfort and security of homes and loved ones awaiting us. They want distance from the frantic disaster that melded them into a community of mourning women. I do, too.

I return home carrying my gear, some moose bones, a rattle that I picked up at our final giveaway, and the driftwood doll. As I enter the house, Jim meets me. I tell him briefly what has transpired; I show him the moose bones. He looks at me and says, "There are spirits of the dead all around you." This is not what I expect to hear. But the minute he speaks these words, I feel seen, my fatigue understood. I feel located on the right plane. I ask, "What should I do?"

We decide to open all the doors to the house, sweep the spirits gently out with a broom, and sprinkle a trail of cornmeal outside. Then we smudge the house and each other. I place the moose bones, the rattle, and the doll out on the back deck. But that night I tell him it would be better if we did not sleep together in the same bed. He agrees and goes upstairs to sleep in his study.

Sometime in the middle of the night I dream that I am in my room in bed when I hear a loud rattle being shaken close to my ear, followed by a long, piercing human cry. Then someone is shaking me so hard that my teeth chatter. Terrified, I try to call out. I wake up in a sweat with my heart pounding. It takes me hours to go back to sleep.

In the morning I quickly wrap up the driftwood doll in a box and send it back to the woman who made it. I take the give-away rattle and the moose bones and drive to a swampy area. I read somewhere that it is best to take these things to a place where people are not likely to walk. I step through some tall grasses and hunker down at the edge of the marshy water and begin a prayer to the swamp to receive these things and transform them. I look down and see a very large green frog staring up at me, watching my actions. I take this as a positive sign and dispatch the things into the swampy water.

Once I am relieved of these artifacts, I realize that I have to do two more things: first, I must go to the Maine State Museum and research this particular lake and the ancient people that once lived there, and second, I have to go back to the lake and make peace with the spirits of that place.

I go to the museum that houses a big diorama of Lake Aziscohos, which was once really a river. I notice that one place where we camped, the middle campsite where we found the bones in the water, was once the site of the paleo-Indian people's big hunt.

I make a trip to the lake in October. The trees are ablaze and their vivid colors are perfectly reflected in the flat serenity of the lake. I go down to the water's edge where I sing, chant, and cry out to the silent waters. I ask for permission to be there, I want instruction. I enter a place of deep stillness within myself and wait.

The spirits respond that they want honoring, and they want food. Of course, this was their hunting ground, their place of food gathering. Of course, they want food. I know it was hopelessly naive of us to go to this place on a Dreamquest without addressing the spirits of these people and the animals who once lived on this land without acknowledging their history. I feel their spirits angry and full of outrage.

The paper companies have logged these forests leaving the forested edge as a so-called "beauty strip," creating an illusion of the once thickly treed forest; low-flying planes carrying poisonous weed-killers spray the trees and all the creatures that have their homes there; the engineers have dammed the river; the once plentiful animals have been killed, many species exterminated. This place of the great hunt is no longer honored as a sacred, food-giving site. As a people we have severed our primal connection with this land and the animals. Now we go back in hopes of finding what has been so lost. The woman's words come back to me: "We don't belong here." And I suspect that in her madness she may be right. And I wonder if the spirits will allow us to return if we are honoring, respectful.

Even after many months I feel hounded, dogged by whatever had shaken me in the night. I catch glimpses of something out of the corner of my eye; I have intrusive thoughts, particularly when I drive; I fall off the back edge of my deck, or am I pushed? I feel in danger. It takes almost a year to get back into synchrony with myself. I still do not completely understand what happened. I have no elder, no native person to guide me or instruct me in these matters. I have not been back to the lake. I have not forgotten what happened. I am no longer innocent. I continue with my bioregion study-project.

My dream of the lynx energized a very powerful call to travel further north as if my internal compass had been permanently set in that direction since having the dream. The lynx with its tufted ears, facial ruff, and deep-seeing eyes pulls on my imagination, magnetically drawing me toward her. I read and study; I look at pictures on my wildlife calendar. I especially notice her long legs and great, furry paws which let her travel easily through snow. In many tales these paws are likened to snowshoes. It is her snowshoe paws that send me on my first winter-camping snowshoe trip.

Alexandra and Garrett are Maine Wilderness Guides. In the winter they lead a small number of people on winter snowshoe trips. Their knowledge, skillfulness, and deep appreciation of traditional native ways come from living and traveling in Labrador where they apprentice to native peoples.

In February a small group meets on Pine Stream, a flowage that runs between Moosehead Lake and Chesungcook Lake. Through their example, our guides teach us the benefits of using traditional equipment as opposed to all the high-tech gear available now. I feel the utility and beauty of my white canvas anorak with braided trim; it shields me from the wind and lets my body breath. I love wearing the white Egyptian cotton mukluks with their moosehide bottoms; my feet are never cold. I take to the traditional, wooden, gut-strung snowshoes as if I had always worn them. They please me aesthetically and are highly efficient in helping me cross deep snow without sinking. Such a piece of brilliant technology. Long, narrow wooden toboggans, *kamiks*, are loaded with our personal and group gear, a leather tump-line slung across my chest allows me to pull the sled behind me. Our guides choose this indigenous method over dog sleds because it is so much more efficient if one doesn't have to travel great distances. The pace of snowshoeing is distinctly human, almost leisurely. The snowshoes make a beautiful overlapping pattern on the snow, one that feels ancient, delicate, and natural.

Our group travels in a sprawling line across the flat, frozen surface of Pine Stream, stopping to notice animal tracks—mostly fox at this time of year—and we stoop to sniff the strong musk of fox urine on any little protrusion or branch that sticks out of the snow. This is the mating season for fox and the zigzagged patterns of their trails, first one, then two together, tell the story of their courting.

In the late afternoon we pitch our Egyptian cotton tents on the snow pack. We dig a square pit at the entrance of the tent for the wood-burning stove, and form a raised sleeping platform. We place fresh pine boughs down in the pit and the tent instantly fills with the aromatic fragrance. Tarps, sleeping pads, and sleeping bags get rolled out, a fire gets made in the small, iron woodstove, mukluks get hung up on the center tent line, and we have ourselves a tidy, warm, and cozy shelter. In the night we hear a hooting owl and two barking foxes who have come close to our tents letting us know they know we are here and that we are in their territory.

I feel exhilarated to be living outside for most of the day in the sharp winter air. The pace of life slows to meet the needs of the body: cooking, eating, and cleaning up, making camp, taking it down, snowshoeing to the next encampment. These are our primary occupations. I have never eaten so much in my life. It is important, Alexandra says, as she points out the obvious fact, calories are heat. If you want to stay warm you must eat. I eat food that never passes my lips in my ordinary day-to-day life—bacon, "bunkers," pieces of dough fried in bacon fat, lots of butter on my flapjacks, chocolate. If we get cold at night in our sleeping bags, Alexandra tells us to pull out our bag of "gorp" and eat. In the evening we loll around in the warm tent in long underwear and tell stories. Winter is the natural time for story telling. I begin to have the smallest glimmer of how native people must have lived during the winter. How survival is in direct relationship to the amount of good food available. How fat is the best insulator against cold. How a well told story feeds the spirit.

I expected to have dreams on this trip and I did. But not the kind I thought I would have. I had only one remembered dream.

I am with my mother. She is very old, wrapped up in a sheet. She is clearly dying. I am caressing her, pouring love into her from every cell in my body. I am telling her how much I love her, how happy I am to be loving her in this way. How glad I am we have this time now at the end to express all this love, something I could never do before.

How strange it is to have this dream. My mother has been dead for years. And I feel sorry I did not pour all this love into her in waking life. Is it my personal mother? Yes, I think, it is my personal mother but, there is this, too. It is the mother of the earth, the earth mother, who I am loving so deeply—before it is too late.

NOTES

1. Barry Lopez, *Arctic Dreams* (New York: Charles Scribner's Sons, 1986), p. 177.

2. Terry Tempest Williams, *Refuge: An Unnatural History of Family and Place* (New York: Vintage Books, 1991).

3. Carolyn Merchant, *Ecological Revolutions: Nature, Gender, and Science in New England* (Chapel Hill and London: The University of North Carolina Press, 1989).

4. Kathryn S. Fuller, "Focus," *World Wildlife Inc.,* Vol. 20, No. 4, (July/August 1998).

5. In June 1999 wildlife biologists found two lynx kittens in northwestern Maine. They had radio-collared the mother in March and after she denned they tracked through dense overgrowth in a part of timber company land and found her two healthy kittens.

6. Leslie Marmon Silko, *Yellow Woman and the Beauty of the Spirit: Essays on Native American Life Today* (New York: Simon & Schuster, 1997), pp. 85-86.

7. Richard K. Nelson, *Make Prayers to the Raven* (Chicago: University of Chicago Press, 1983).

8. Merchant, *Ecological Revolutions,* p. 67.

9. *Ibid.*

10. Because of their low population, lynx have been given recognition under the Endangered Species Act.

11. Nelson, *Make Prayers,* p. 156.

Discovering the Way Back to the Solid Ground of Ethical Uncertainty: From Animal Use to Animal Protection

JOHN P. GLUCK

No doubt, no awakening.
—C. C. Chang

I came to pursue a career as a research psychologist for many reasons. Prominent among them was the fact that several members of my immediate family suffered terribly from chronic neurological and devastating mental disorders whose ineffective and iatrogenic treatments revealed to me the limits of available clinical interventions. I hoped that perhaps I could contribute to improving that situation if I became a researcher myself. Another reason was my general fascination with human psychological dynamics, which was awakened during high school. Later, as my education progressed, I was seduced by the ability of carefully designed experiments to present potential explanations for complex behavioral phenomena. In other words, I came under the spell

John P. Gluck, Jr. is Emeritus Professor of Psychology at the University of New Mexico, Research Professor at the Kennedy Institute of Ethics, Georgetown University, and on the Faculty of the Kerulos Center. A former animal researcher, he now studies and writes about the moral standing of animals in research.

of what Sinclair Lewis referred to as "the drug of research" in his cautionary novel about the physician Martin Arrowsmith becoming a medical researcher.[1]

Working with animals in the context of research was somewhat natural for me as I was very fond of animals and was comfortable around them since early childhood. I was not put off by the duties necessary to maintain them in the laboratory. Feeding, watering, cleaning cages, and treating common diseases did not feel like a distasteful burden. My history also told me that I had an unusual affinity with animals, an ability to coax cooperation where others could not. I quickly learned, however, that while being interested in animals as beings in themselves initially facilitated my early scientific involvement, my sensitivity to them as feeling, self-directed entities, which had been refined over many years of pet ownership and backyard bird, insect, and squirrel watching, was later to become an impediment to their use in the laboratory. As my education and research experience evolved, a steady almost imperceptible change in that basic sensitivity took place. Where I was once alert to the subtle desires and aversions of animals, I found that that level of concern for lab animals also made it difficult to shock, deprive, isolate, and damage their brains, standard procedures deemed necessary for the experimental study of learning, memory, and development. At this time, experimental psychology was still immersed in a struggle to be recognized as a "true" science. Therefore, there was a high priority placed on designing experiments with unforgiving rigor. I felt trapped between my educational goals and my desire not to harm animals, but I could not see an alternative. Something had to give.

Sensitivity was not replaced with brutality, but with something harder to see and more insidious: a growing indifference to the plight of the animals under my control. Indifference grounded in a sense of a parallel certainty that whatever the costs the animals paid by virtue of their involvement, it was surely worth it scientifically. Initially I more or less role-played that belief, but eventually, the animals that I worked with became blended with other necessary laboratory equipment, as extensions of my scientific ego. They were valuable and interesting in ways different than the inanimate, but they were equipment nonetheless.

I had been challenged by my early mentors to look at and describe animal behavior from the outside, avoiding any use of unobserved internal states to explain the causes of behavior. They derided explanations that used unobserved motivational states as being dependent on "mentalistic ghosts." For example, dogs exposed to electric shock in a maze, and crying out while scrambling up the apparatus walls, were to be described as showing "disorganized vocal and motor behavior" and not "painful attempts to escape." I was eager to grasp this perspective because of its scientific demeanor, and the escape it provided for my part in creating pain and distress. When I watched animals it was no longer with the open "who are they" mindset of a backyard bird watcher and dog walker, but through the prism of an experimental hypothesis that I was interested in evaluating: "What will these subjects do, and is it what I expected and hoped to see given my theory?" Truly, there was no logical reason why both of those mindsets could not have co-existed. If they had, a healthy ambivalence about whether a particular experiment was ethically justified and scientifically worth it might have been maintained. Together they would have kept the animal and its vulnerability in the center of the experimental design process. In other words, the interpretational set of my research activities limited the quality of my encounters with animals that would have otherwise helped to inform me of their predicaments. Bernard Rollin's book *The Unheeded Cry* captures the essence of this issue with clarity and insight.[2] As a consequence of the absence of ambivalence, I could more easily pursue a modest but successful scientific career studying the effects of drugs on behavior, and the behavioral and nervous system consequences of social isolation in monkeys and rats. I had to only consider the logical merits of an experiment with little or no pushback from concerns about the animal's experience of involvement. However, after over twenty years of this work, I started to subtly, then openly, question the ethical justification of the use of animals. What changed?

There are many reasons to alter one's professional course: economic considerations, change in the subject of curiosity and patterns of interest, discovering work that just feels more congruent, and becoming acutely aware of significant ethical conflicts that emerge from work that resist resolution. It was primarily the later two circumstances that resulted in my eventually deciding to withdraw from the practice of animal research and to devote myself instead to coming to grips with the ethical if and how one can justify the decision to capture the lives of other species, and to try to improve the lot of research animals both in my local academic environment and more broadly. This decision did not take place like the story of St. Paul on the road to Damascus who was struck blind and disoriented before he changed from an antagonist of Christianity to a passionate believer. Rather the urgency to change professional focus grew from more personally complete reflections on experiences with animals, both in the lab and out in the world. They circumvented my resistance to seeing animals in existential space, beings trying to express a life, cope, survive, and avoid suffering. These experiential episodes had something about them which made them stick in my consciousness. Memories of the encounters accumulated slowly at first, then more intensely, eventually generating a moral force occupying my thinking in a way that I could not ignore. Clearly, I had once again become open to seeing animals differently, more completely, and to be more honestly critical of how animal research was being conducted. A strong sense of ambivalence and uncertainty about the "rightness" of the enterprise returned.

I attribute this part of the change to many factors. Important among them was my interaction with a number of laboratory veterinarians who I called on for help in dealing with injuries and diseases caused by confinement and experimental participation. They provided an alternative model of the Doctor-Patient relationship that was very different than my own experience of the Researcher-Subject relationship. Their relationship with animals drew from the reality of animal disease, dysfunction, and pain. They reminded me that the root of the word "patient" is "one who suffers" and not just one who is holding up the experiment. Then there were undergraduate and graduate students who expressed reluctance, albeit respectfully, to carry out some of my experiments because they objected to the level of harm that they saw the procedures creating. Their fresh vision could see the impact on the animals in ways that my trained expectations did not. Since I respected them as developing scientists and as individuals beyond their professional identity, I could not entirely dispense with their ethical concerns. There was also a shift in society as a whole with respect to animal ethics and active criticism from the public on scientific practices such as those in which I was engaged. Interestingly, when I received public criticism that focused on my "useless" science, it did not move me, as I could easily defend myself with my own criticism of their "flawed" understanding. However, the criticisms that centered on the hurt I created in them by virtue of the existence of my research created an emotional impact. After all, I did not go into the work to cause human pain, but to relieve it. In addition, there was the look I saw in the eyes of my young children when I took them to the lab for a visit. I could see an unmistakable tinge of horror and confusion in their reactions.

I include here a selection of narratives from the many incidents that formed the basis of my initial internal reflection leading to a need for greater scrutiny and examination of what I and others were doing. These incidents include encounters in the laboratory and the greater outside world.

The Sheep Won't Eat

Late one Friday afternoon, the veterinarian and I were rehearsing the week's news when he received a phone call from a lab across the campus. In the call, a lab technician explained that a sheep under his care simply would not eat and had not eaten for the last three days. She was pregnant and there was concern that the pregnancy was in jeopardy. When we arrived at the laboratory the technician led us to where the animal was being held. As we walked in, the technician explained that the ewe was pregnant with twins and that this characteristic was a requirement of the research protocol to which the animal was assigned. The experiment had to do with some investigation of cardiac function; one of the twins was the experimental subject and the other served as the control.

When we arrived at the sheep's holding room the technician who had called introduced us to a worried-looking man who was the principal investigator on the project. He emphasized the critical nature of the situation, that is, the importance of his experiment, and his concerns for its success because of his complete puzzlement about the animal's failure to eat. We opened the door and found a fully adult sheep weighing perhaps 150 pounds standing in a solid cement block room. A moveable plastic fence was used to divide the room and contain the animal. The sheep looked oddly out of place, her grimy shaggy wildness in this freshly painted and polished room. Her head was held below the level of her shoulders and she swayed slowly as she shifted her weight from side to side. Her belly was broad and distended like a frayed dirty white canvas hammock hanging uncomfortably beneath her ribs. The room was lit by a fluorescent ceiling light and was completely empty except for two stainless steel buckets. One of the buckets was filled with water and the other with food pellets. The commercial pellets were made of alfalfa that had been ground and pressed into one-inch square blocks.

After a brief look at this situation the vet asked the scientist where the animal came from. He shrugged his shoulders. The technician spoke up and said that the animal came from a certified facility in northern New Mexico, a couple of hundred miles from the university. "What kind of facility?" "A ranch," he said, a bit puzzled by the question. "Do you mean that this animal was living on the open range until it was brought here to the university?" The vet's voice became slightly pointed. "Do you think that this animal has any idea that those pellets are food? Do you have any Timothy hay in storage?" The technician indicated that there was. "Bring some here right away." In about fifteen minutes the technician returned with a cart filled with the greenish brown hay. The sweet smell filled the room in an instant. The sheep had already stopped swaying and was now turned in the direction of the cart. A small pile of the hay was placed in front of her and she immediately began to eat.

Here the scientific sophistication and goals of the experimenter were so dominant that they obscured the necessity of understanding even the most basic parameters of the animal's life and needs. The story illustrated to me the inherent danger that is created when animals lose their identity as living, breathing, feeling beings and become categorized as a scientific means or tool. Can good, valid research emerge from an animal "model," a nonhuman being that is used as an experimental surrogate in lieu of humans, where the treatment and understanding of the animal is so poverty stricken? And didn't we have a responsibility to know more about the animals whose lives we were appropriating?

The Turkey in a Trap

It was a beautiful early Fall Saturday afternoon. The New Mexico sky was a brilliant, cloudless blue and the temperature was simultaneously cool and warm. I was hiking in a shallow canyon west of Albuquerque in search of a group of petroglyphs that an anthropologist friend had told me about. According to his descriptions there were many renderings of humans, animals, and insects etched into the black basalt stone of the canyon by ancient Native Americans. The combination of solitude and alert involvement with the surrounding encouraged a deep relaxation. I had stopped to climb a small rise of boulders on the edge of the canyon to check the terrain against my map when I heard movement to my left. I first felt startled and then disappointed, thinking I was probably about to meet another hiker who would break the spell of my solitude. I heard the rustling again and was better able to locate the direction. It came from behind a tangle of Russian thistle and scrub cedar trees. Satisfied that the cause was not human, I more cautiously approached the source of the movement. Perhaps it would be two male prairie chickens staking conflicting territorial claims.

As I peered around the trees, I saw a large black bird, nearly two feet tall, with a blood red head and neck standing next to some brush and a fallen tree. When the bird saw me, it jumped to take flight but flopped back to the ground. Again the bird grabbed at the air with its wings and again the progress was jerked to a stop and the bird fell back to the ground in a twisted pile of feathers. I stepped back as the bird struggled to right itself. Now we stood across from one another, separated by about twenty feet. I could now see why the bird could not escape. A steel clamp was closed around its right leg and the clamp was secured to the ground by a thin chain about 18 inches long. Behind the point where the chain was attached to the ground, a dead ground squirrel hung upside down from a tree stump about six inches from the ground. A nail driven through its brown brush tail was the point of attachment. The bird was a turkey vulture and, being a carrion feeder, was surely lured to the spot by the smell of the dead squirrel. The surrounding land was an open cattle range which meant that the trap was probably meant for the coyotes in the area. The bird had become an unintended target. I had heard of leg-hold traps, but I had never seen one. (There are three types of body-gripping traps. The leg-hold trap captures a foot, the snare catches the animal, often by the neck, and either holds it or strangles it. The conibear is engineered to clamp onto to an animal's head or neck, killing rapidly.) I felt moved to help but uncertain what to do. The large bird looked ominous. How would it respond if I were to try to open the jaws of the trap to release him? The large beak with its hook on the end looked as though it could inflict easy damage to soft human flesh.

The bird and I sat looking intently at one another for some time. I decided to move closer so that I could inspect the trap in more detail. As I inched closer to the bird, it continued to stand quietly as its sideways glance stayed fixed on me. I slowly removed the thin cotton jacket I was wearing, all the time telling the bird that I meant only to help. I decided that I would try to drop the jacket over the bird and use it to pin him to the ground. If I could get the edges of the jacket under my knee and foot, I could use my free hands to pry open the trap. I crouched as I closed the remaining several feet between us, holding the jacket open in front of me and explaining my intentions. I was prepared to jump forward when the bird attempted to escape and wrap the jacket around the bird's body. But the bird never tried to escape or move away. Instead, he stood still as I approached. As I placed the jacket over the bird, I closed the inside of my forearms around his sides and gently pressed him to the ground. The bird did not struggle but eased over on to its side and laid still. I nervously reached for the trap. I pried at the spring-loaded jaws. They reluctantly opened, and I pulled them away from the deeply cut ankle. There was not much blood, only a jagged groove sliced into the flesh and bone. After releasing the leg, I jumped back about ten feet, still fearing that I might be attacked, and watched as the vulture stood up, the jacket falling away. After a minute or two, the bird turned away from me and flew off. It was not hard to imagine the slow death of the animal pinned to the ground had our lives not crossed that day. The wound, however, looked serious and would most likely eventually cause his death. Before I left the scene, I buried the squirrel and yanked the trap from the ground and threw it into the sandy floor of the canyon. Later that day I wished I had taken the trap with me. After all, it might be found and used again.

This incident highlighted to me the ripple of harm that expands beyond our intended purpose. It also made me deeply wonder about what had transpired between the vulture and me? Was there actual cooperation between us when it became clear I intended no harm? Or was this simply the behavior of an injured and exhausted bird? What did we really know about the cognitive capacities and inner life of animals? What did we really understand about our ability to harm different beings?

THE FEEL OF FLESH

According to the Animal Welfare Act, any plan for the use of animals in research or teaching must be first reviewed by an independent Institutional Animal Care and Use Committee (IACUC). That committee must vote to approve the plan prior to use. At a monthly meeting of the IACUC, the committee was deliberating about a teaching proposal that required the use of ten "random source dogs." They would be purchased from an animal dealer or the city shelter and held in the Animal Resource Facility until they were needed. They would be used in a laboratory exercise for medical students who were studying cardiac physiology to illustrate some of the key reflexes of that system. In their proposal, the instructors argued that the exercise was vital for the students because it would provide them much needed experiences that went beyond the book study of the heart. The students would also be required to open the chests of the dogs and attach the various recording instruments themselves. They would, the protocol argued, also learn basic surgical skills, become familiar with some of the experimental techniques of the area, and in the words of the instructors, "get the feeling of working with real flesh." It was also stated that there was no adequate alternative available to provide these important educational experiences. These arguments were persuasive to the majority of the committee, and the protocol was passed. Several members requested to observe the laboratory exercise and were reluctantly granted permission to do so. The reluctance of the instructors appeared to stem from their feeling that observation by committee members was totally unnecessary and might interfere with the class. I was one of the observers.

When we got to the classroom, the dogs had been brought to the classroom by the veterinary staff and were already anesthetized by the time the students arrived. The dogs, all mixed breeds, represented an array of colors and fur length and weighed in the 40-60 pound range. They were arranged on their backs on narrow stainless steel tables. Cords were attached to their legs that served to pull the legs away from their bodies, leaving them in a splayed position ironically looking like a playful dog begging for a belly rub. The students approached their assigned tables and waited for instructions. The professor described how they should first shave the chest of the dog in preparation for the incision. A couple of electric clippers were passed among the students. The instructors did not demonstrate or require any particular shaving technique, nor did they inspect the results. Once the group had completed this task, they were further instructed to take the "cauterizing unit" and begin to cut through the flesh covering the midline of the chest. A surgical cautery unit is a device that both cuts and seals the severed blood vessels with high heat as it is passed through tissue, a vast improvement over the basic scalpel. The students picked up their units and began the process. As the students awkwardly began, I looked carefully at the devices that they were using. Instead of "surgical cautery units" as was specified in the protocol, they were using common gun-gripped soldering irons, the kind found in countless garage workshops. Therefore, instead of tips with a knife edge, the guns possessed a soldering surface made of the typical small, smooth round metal ball. So instead of movements that would slice and seal the flesh, the students were required to burn and tear through the chest. Some of the students seemed tentative and dismayed while others hunched diligently over their dog, directing strong raking movements back and forth over the center of the chest. Thin swirls of smoke rose from the incision sites. Around the room some students stood still, resting their fatigued hands and arms. The room quickly filled with the acrid smell of burning fur and flesh.

One of the medical students, who seemed particularly hesitant about the exercise, asked the professor what anesthetic was being used on the dogs. It was obviously a question about whether the dogs could feel any pain from the procedures. He responded that the agent was alpha chloralose. The student followed up that he had never heard of that anesthetic. It was explained that it was a chemical, not typically used in clinical medicine, but was chosen because it did not interfere with the cardiac reflexes that were being highlighted in the exercise. The student began to ask another question about the level of analgesia provided by the agent when the professor interrupted him and told him to get on with the measurements that were the focus of the class.[3]

It seemed to me that the professor was so certain of the usefulness of the exercise that he was no longer seeing what was actually taking place. The class exercise did not provide the students the feel of flesh from a surgical perspective, but instead a desensitization to blood and gore. The student who was compassionately concerned about pain was clearly seen as an impediment to class progress and was told be quiet.

After the class I looked up the characteristics of alpha chloralose and was surprised to find evidence of a controversy about whether it provided adequate analgesia for deep dissections like the cracking of the chest of a dog required for the manipulation of internal organs. A week or so later I brought this article to the attention of the professor. Similar to the student in the class, he interrupted before I was finished and assured me that he was THE expert on the relevant characteristics of alpha chloralose, and whether its use was justified. It was as though the question of pain was irrelevant as long as the purpose of the exercise was physiologically sound. The collective wisdom about the importance of this type of exercise has changed dramatically in recent years as effective non-animal alternatives for teaching this material have been widely established across virtually all the 125 U.S. medical schools.

THE DEER HUNTER

I had just given and completed a thirty-minute lunch time lecture on the requirements for care in the Animal Welfare Act to the local Kiwanis club when a sturdy middle-aged man approached me. The lecture had been practical, emphasizing the nature of the developing protective measures for research animals that were becoming part of federal regulations. I made no attempt to review the details of the various theoretical controversies such as the difference between animal rights claims and responsibility of researchers to protect animal welfare during use. Instead, my goal was to convey the fact that at that time the public morality around animal treatment seemed to include a willingness to use animals in research as long as their welfare was also protected. I intended to review some of relevant state and federal regulations that were in place to protect research animals. Frankly, I was surprised that I was invited to talk about this topic because I thought the material was going to be too dry to make an entertaining lunch presentation. I was interested in their perspective and gratified by the reception I experienced, which I would characterize as respectful and interested. While there was no obvious abolitionist sentiments expressed either by me or the membership, there was a clear sentiment in the room that the animals deserved protection and care and they wanted to hear about how that was assured. In other words, this local audience of business people confirmed the overall theme of the talk. I had clearly initially underestimated the degree of concern that was present in the audience.

The man approaching extended his hand and thanked me for coming. I was very pleased not only to see the nods of approval in the audience but the obvious one-on-one personal response. I could feel strength in his firm grip. His eyes first looked intensely at mine and then dropped as he turned somewhat hesitantly to his left. His right shoulder dropped as he turned as if a string holding it stiff and high had snapped. He then turned back around to face me. "I grew up in North Dakota," he said. "I guess you could have called me a great white hunter in those days. I wanted to be a trapper. That was until one winter morning while I was checking my trap line and found a pheasant dead and frozen in one of the traps. My partner called it a "trash" animal and tossed it aside." He stopped for a second, looked up at me, and said, "But the bird had half eaten its leg off trying to get away. When I saw that, I knew that I couldn't trap any more." He wasn't finished.

We sat down again facing each other across the lunch table amid the half-filled ice tea glasses, mustard jars, and remnants of sandwiches. The room was empty except for the restaurant personnel. "A few years ago, I was hunting in northern New Mexico when I shot the biggest dear that I ever saw. I watched the dear drop, but I was unsure that I had killed it. When I walked the 200 yards to where it lay, I discovered that I was right. I had shot the deer behind its shoulder, shattering its spine. It lay there paralyzed." Again, he stopped speaking. He looked at his hands unfolded in front of him, then at me again. "When I walked up to the deer, he stared at me eye to eye. I tried to quickly turn away and then decided to look at him. I saw the question in his eyes, "Why?" I couldn't answer. I can't answer now. That look still haunts me today, right now as we speak. I will not hunt again." After a few moments, we shook hands again. I waited until he left the restaurant before I followed. I didn't want to meet him in the street. I didn't want any social nicety to interrupt what we had felt and shared together.

This man had confided how his recognition of harm that he had created, while performing an act which represented an important family tradition, had deeply affected him. He understood immediately from this awareness that his highly valued practice and tradition had to change. I found that this story contrasted with how issues of sensitivity were dealt with in my formal education. In that case, more typically an expression of concern or reluctance was met with the suggestion that the person reconsider whether they were cut out for the work of research. This defensive reaction sends the message that a researcher's feelings about their work are ethically irrelevant and only a barrier to scientific progress. I recall an animal researcher colleague of mine openly regretting that his love of dogs prevented him from doing invasive research with them and wished he could get over the attachment.

The Rat in the Dream

Following a similar presentation on animal research regulation at an independent research institution, a young researcher approached me. He thanked me for the talk and asked whether I had some time to listen to an experience he had that concerned him. The story had to do with a dream he had one recent night following a series of difficult rat surgeries he had performed. In the dream, he found himself in a large lush meadow. He felt relaxed and invigorated. As he was walking in the meadow he saw a large albino rat standing off in the distance. While the rat was enormous in size, he was not aware of feeling fear or threat. Instead, he was aware of wanting to get closer to the rat. He became aware of the feeling of frustration because something was preventing him from closing the distance. As he reached out in a final attempt to touch the handsome animal, it fell over dead. Stunned, he awoke. The meaning he drew from the dream had to do with the suffering he imposed on animals in the name of science. Unlike the hunter in the previous story, who felt a need to change the nature of his encounters with animals, this man felt that something was amiss and the only way to justify his work was to work harder and subject himself to higher levels of stress, suffering, and loss. He hoped that perhaps this exchange would offer a kind of absolution.

Closing Reflections

These examples capture some basic ethical themes that began to hold my attention and make it clear that the ethical certainty I had assumed about my profession and work was misplaced. The themes were: The uniqueness and complexity of individual animal lives and our minimal understanding of them. How should that ignorance factor into the process of justification of their use for human purposes? The often careless treatment of that uniqueness and complexity, resulting from the failure to evaluate the impact of our interventions from the perspective of the animal. How widespread was such carelessness? How do we keep carelessness from becoming institutionalized under the category of "standard practice"? The reluctance of some researchers to see the importance of their own and others' ambivalence about their work with animals. Why is sensitivity to the needs of an animal a flaw and not a virtue worthy of nurturance?

Eventually the importance of these kinds of reflections reached a point where I felt that I required formal education in ethics, more than the cursory minimum that I had received as a student and supervisee. I applied and was accepted to a bioethics Fellowship program that emphasized the ethics of animal and human research. It was that education that consolidated my new career goals. As I entered this formal educational domain, I was at first surprised to find that the questions that had been forming over the years were not just my own. My new mentors, who were both researchers and moral philosophers, saw them as legitimate and serious. Instead of hushed tones, the discussions took place openly, with rich intellectual detail. Prior to this time, my experience had been that openly expressing questions about the ethical justification of animal research was likely to be discouraged at best and might be overtly punished by administrative ostracism. One high-level research administrator told me with irritation in his voice that when he heard about people wanting to discuss research ethics, all he heard was that progress was about to be "unnecessarily delayed."

How we come to know what we believe and where we stand on an issue as important as the ethics of animal treatment ought not be limited to learning the "acceptable" perspectives that we find immediately around our work environment and which have the tone of a mindless mantra. Ethics requires rigorous academic study and considerate exposure to perspectives and individuals who fall outside our comfort zone. It also requires that we each try to be open to the myriad unexpected circumstances where ethical growth can take place freely without collective constraints: like during a late night conversation where our humility and fears are unexpectedly given voice, in the flash of an eye, in the characters of a dream, or in the side to side swaying of a hungry sheep.

NOTES

1. Sinclair Lewis, *Arrowsmith* (New York: Harcourt Brace, 1925).

2. Bernard Rollin, *The Unheeded Cry: Animal Consciousness, Animal Pain, and Science* (New York: Oxford University Press, 1989).

3. See A. Arluke, "The use of dogs in medical and veterinary training: Understanding and approaching student uneasiness," *Journal of Applied Animal Welfare Science*, 7(3): 197-204. (2004).

Animals on Film:
The Ethics of the Human Gaze

RANDY MALAMUD

No animals were harmed in the making of this essay.

That may seem like a trivial claim. It's probably not even true, considering the habitat damage caused by emissions from the electricity plant whose engines power the computer I used to compile these ideas. But if I can have the benefit of the doubt, I'd like to suggest that simply writing about other animals *may* engage them in a way that leaves them none the worse off for the encounter. And this harm-neutral encounter is an improvement over the usual state of affairs. Our imperious presence, our industrial infrastructure, our social networks, and our cultural activities encroach upon the safety and integrity of other species.[1]

People imprison and torture animals in factory farms and research laboratories. We displace them as our cities and suburbs expand. We poison them as we dump toxins into their food-ways (and then, with ecological tunnel-vision, we overfish these poisoned waters for fetishized

Randy Malamud, Professor of English at Georgia State University, is the editor of A *Cultural History of Animals in the Modern Age* (Berg, 2007), and the author of *Reading Zoos: Representations of Animals and Captivity* (Macmillan and New York University Press, 1998) and *Poetic Animals and Animal Souls* (Palgrave Macmillan, 2003). He is a Fellow of the Oxford Centre for Animal Ethics and a Patron of the Captive Animals' Protection Society.

aquatic delicacies). We commodify them in the "pet" industry. But even when we take a break from such active physical assaults, we are prone to engage with animals in ways that hurt their spirits and impinge upon their welfare. The consequence of most human-animal encounters is the expression of harm via pathways of power.

Nonetheless, for decades, the American movie industry has taken the initiative to assert and verify the converse: that is, many films carry a disclaimer in the credits stating, "No animals were harmed in the making of this movie." It's a pleasant thought, so common that we may not even notice it or think about how and why animals might have been harmed in the making of a film. (And given the extent to which our culture is virtually built upon animals' lives and deaths, this claim of "no harm" seems more than a little ironic.) The certification comes from the American Humane Association's (AHA) Film and Television Unit, which sponsors animal safety monitors on film sets to ensure adherence to its guidelines for the treatment of animal actors.[2]

The AHA[3] began monitoring the safety of animals after the 1939 film *Jesse James* provoked an outcry when a horse was forced to leap to his or her death from the top of a cliff.[4] The AHA now reviews scripts during pre-production and enjoys unlimited access to a movie set during filming that involves animals. The phrase "No animals were harmed in the making of this movie," first used in Paul Newman's *Fat Man and Little Boy* (1989), has since become a registered trademark.[5]

Why care about the film industry when, relatively speaking, the numbers of animals directly involved seem negligible relative to the vast numbers consumed through the meat, dairy, and other industries? Two reasons: one, the well-being of every animal counts. The fact that animals are so commonly generalized, even by the term "animals" when its use reifies the ontology of animals solely as to how they relate to humans, compels attention to every individual. Second, film and other electronic image media project the human psyche: they hold and promulgate modern human values, agendas, and norms. Films are dream and reality–makers.

Some films, not many, are deemed questionable or unacceptable, having failed to meet AHA standards. Here are a few examples of what a film might do to get an unacceptable rating: In *Cannibal Holocaust* (1979), a documentary team journeys to a South American jungle to search for cannibals. During the making of this film, an opossum was slit with a knife; the shell was ripped off a turtle; and a monkey was scalped.[6] *Apocalypse Now* (1979) was found unacceptable because a water buffalo was hacked to pieces. In *Vampire's Kiss* (1989), star Nicolas Cage admitted in print that he ate two live cockroaches during the filming, earning that movie an unacceptable rating.[7] There are no legal or film industry consequences of an unacceptable rating, though the AHA does publicize its negative findings in the hopes of inspiring an audience boycott.

AHA acknowledges that its seal of approval may appear in movies with scenes that seem to convey an attitude that "cruelty to animals is okay." Their purpose, they explain, is

> to safeguard animals on-set, regardless of whether the scene being portrayed conveys an animal-friendly message. The objective of our monitoring work is the welfare of the live animals used in film production, and to that end, we refrain from commenting on content. If we refused to monitor a film because we did not agree with its message, we would risk there being no protection at all for the animals involved.[8]

Indeed, some approved movies contain extremely violent scenes with animals. The Humane Association website explains: "Filming techniques, controlled stunts, special effects and post-production editing can make complicated battle scenes appear realistic without injuring animals or human performers. . . . Animals used in filmed entertainment are well-trained to perform specific stunts (such as falling down on cue), and the rest of the illusion is created by the filmmakers."[9] So even AHA assurance that no animals were harmed does not protect against a rhetoric of violence and cannot guarantee an ethically ideal expression of visual media relationships between humans and animals.

Given this campaign to monitor animal welfare in the film industry, one might reasonably assume that there is a proclivity to harm animals in the movies, a proclivity for audiences to watch the harming of animals. But why might filmmakers want to harm animals in the first place? And, more broadly, what do audiences want to see when they are looking at animals in films?

Difficulties Seeing Animals Clearly

Animals in visual culture[10] are often disguised in some way—costumed, or masked, or distorted, or disfigured. Mockery of animals is another common trope, as is decontextualization: displacing animals from their natural habitats, contexts, and lives, and reconfiguring them as players in a purely anthropocentric narrative—from *King Kong* to *Curious George*, from the *Beethoven* dog films to *Seabiscuit*, Hollywood traffics in spectacles of such "fish out of water."[11] Mockery and decontextualization function as disguises because they prevent us from seeing the authentic animal beneath the cultural frippery. Animals are disguised perhaps because the authentic animal would be too depressing, or too scary, or too boring, for the viewer to endure.

There is a continuum of integrity, or respect, that audiences and cultural creators accord to animals in visual culture. At the bottom end of this continuum, there are dancing bears, piano-playing chickens, rabbits being pulled out of hats, chimps in human clothing on parade, "stupid pet tricks,"[12] elephants with paintbrushes taped to their trunks in ecotourist camps, and so forth. That is: animals doing silly things for the audience's amusement—things they don't usually do, and have no reason to do.[13] Perhaps viewers are so engrossed in these vaudevillean farces because we are ashamed to look animals in the eye, ashamed to confront what we have done to them. We don't like to think much about wild, natural animals, because we have just about extinguished wildness and nature. We prefer our animals framed, domesticated, dressed up for our spectacles.

Even further down the spectrum at this endpoint of the continuum are "crush films": amateur sadistic/fetishistic pseudo-pornographic footage of erotically-costumed women stepping on insects, mice, cats, crushing them in stiletto heels. *Smush*, by Jeff Vilencia (1993), one of the best-known in the genre, is an eight-minute long film depicting a woman in high heels and also barefoot crushing dozens of earthworms.[14] "Among the many obscure and bizarre sects of fetishism," writes Jeremy Biles in "I, Insect, or Bataille and the Crush Freaks,"

> few remain so perplexing or so underexamined as that of the "crush freaks." At the cutting edge of the edgy world of sexual fetishistic practices, the crush freaks are notorious for their enthusiasm for witnessing the crushing death of insects and other,

usually invertebrate, animals, such as arachnids, crustaceans, and worms. More specifically, crush freaks are sexually aroused by the sight of an insect exploded beneath the pressure of a human foot–usually, but not necessarily, a relatively large and beautiful female foot. . . . The crush freak typically fantasizes identification with the insect as he or she masturbates, and savors the sense of sudden, explosive mutilation attendant upon the sight of the pedal extrusions. Jeff "The Bug" Vilencia, the foremost spokesperson for crush enthusiasts, describes his ecstasy thus: "At the point of orgasm, in my mind all of my guts are being squished out. My eyeballs are popping out, my brain comes shooting out the top of my head, all my blood squirts everywhere . . . What a release, that imagery really gets me off! Seeing that foot coming down on me, coming into my stomach and pressing all that weight on to me till I burst! Wow!"[15]

At the extreme, a crush film represents one possibility, one disturbing example of how some people look at and perceive animals in visual culture. The capacity for extreme violence toward animals lurks even in our media appetites and fantasies, and perhaps the literal harm enacted upon animals in crush films is not so fundamentally different from the figurative harm visited upon so many other animals in visual culture as they are "crushed" by being rendered *inauthentic*.

Most harm meted out to animals in movies is not this obvious. The fact that so many animals are denatured, enmeshed, and victimized in so many diverse media—while at the same time we are facing mass extinction of species around the globe—raises deep psychological and ethical concerns. Is this obsession with having animals demeaned in film, television, and YouTube a type of compensation for all the animals that aren't there any more in reality? A filmclip of an animal, a drawing of an animal, a parody of an animal, a meme of an animal, seems to be more important than the real living animal: the actual creature is displaced by a caricatured and objectified entity.

Visual culture increasingly blocks out the world-beyond-people: the world outside, the world of forests and fields and water and fish and squirrels. Billboards get bigger and brighter, more profuse, more electronic and dynamic, obfuscating more of the landscape. Cyberspace becomes more addictive, more compulsory, luring our gaze away from nature. Computers and HDTVs and iPods and digital cameras and DVRs and GPSs and cell phones, with their little green and red lights and chimes and vibrations that are *always on*, consume more and more energy, generating more of the toxic garbage that endangers habitats and decimates animal communities.

All these beeping, blinking, omnipresent media supplant a simple, direct, meaningful engagement with the natural world and its creatures. In a textbook example of hegemony, the dominant media reinforce their own power at the expense of our connection to the world beyond the screens. A panoply of *monitors* (as the screens are called, with a darkly accidental Foucauldian/Orwellian irony) fill our homes and offices, monitoring our attention to the infinite realms of digital content accessible via these portals, and screening out the corresponding diminution outside: undigitized creatures haplessly holding on for dear life at the margins of this brave new world. The simulacrum-animals— that is, the animals on parade, animals in disguise, animals in visual culture—proliferate *ad infinitum, ad absurdum;* and in doing so, they usurp much of the space we might have allocated in our minds to the consciousness of real, living animals.

THE HUMAN GAZE

In "Visual Pleasure and Narrative Cinema" (1975), Laura Mulvey defines what she called the male gaze. She argues that the viewer at the movies is in a masculine position (and quite possibly a voyeur or a fetishist as well), deriving visual pleasure from a dominant, sadistic perspective. The object on the screen is the object of desire— paradigmatically, the objectified woman. Viewers are encouraged to identify with the protagonist, who is usually male; and female characters are there simply "to-be-looked-at." She writes: "The determining male gaze projects its phantasy on to the female form which is styled accordingly."[16]

The gaze directed at animals in visual culture keenly parallels Mulvey's formulation of the male gaze. Call it, instead of the male gaze, the *human* gaze; and replace woman with "animal." Carol Adams associates the oppression/consumption/disembodiment of women and that of animals.[17] She and other ecofeminists have shown how the exploitation of women and the exploitation of animals occur along similar pathways. It's a smooth extrapolation to reconfigure Mulvey's male gaze (upon the filmed female object) as a human gaze (upon the filmed animal object). Mulvey describes "The image of woman as (passive) raw material for the (active) gaze of man,"[18] and I simply transpose this to characterize the image of the animal as passive raw material for the active gaze of the human.

The phenomenon of looking at animals in visual culture is predicated upon the assumption that the viewer is human and the object is animal. (This is perhaps not a particularly profound observation in and of itself, but, thanks to Mulvey's work, we realize the political import of this construction.) The practice of consuming visual culture embodies an unbridled omniscient lust ensuring the visual object's absolute subalternity. The animal is rendered vulnerable, free for the taking, in whatever way the human viewer chooses: the process metaphorically reiterates what is enacted literally in the culture of carnivorous agribusiness.

Feminist critiques showed how women, under the male gaze, were profusely objectified, essentialized: two-dimensionally caricatured into a good girl/bad girl dichotomy (angel/whore).[19] Nonhuman animals, too, are cast in this mode. In the movies, the angels (the good animals) are pets and helpers, adulating their human keepers: Lassie, Flipper, Old Yeller, Sounder, Elsa, Rin Tin Tin, Francis the Talking Mule.[20] The whores are monstrous others, animals who earn our scorn (but still serve a purpose, calling out to our basest drives and allowing us to satiate these drives by hating, or destroying these creatures). Think of King Kong, the shark in *Jaws*, Ben the rat in *Willard*, Orca the killer whale, Alfred Hitchcock's birds.

This kind of objectification is dangerous, not only because it is outmoded from a scientific and social perspective, but more fundamentally because it is reductionist. It circumscribes animals' existence in relation to the human gaze, appraising them only in terms of their usefulness or threat (to us). Such a perspective confounds an ecologically ethical ideology, in which all members of an ecosystem are interdependent and no single species is inherently privileged above any other.

The animals we gaze upon in film, on the internet, in advertisements, are prized for their "cuteness"—in a way that is feminized, and derogatorily so: cute animals are like dumb blondes (note the parallelism between the male gaze and the human gaze). Animals are celebrated for their subservience, their entertainment value, and the extent to which they affirm an anthropocentric ethos (the unassailable conviction that it's all about us). House cats, dogs, pleasantly furry sheep, and symbolic creatures like the American Bald Eagle rank highly in this cultural economy; pigeons, carp, cockroaches, starlings, and feral cats do less well. The human gazer prizes exoticism in visual cultural representations of other animals, but in a mode (as zoos and aquariums have trained audiences to expect) of profound displacement from their habitat.

While we may pay lip service to the independence and rights of animals in visual culture (as in films like *Born Free* and *Free Willy*),[21] this is all bounded by our own desires and emotions. The point of their freedom is our vicarious experience of our own sense of freedom, which we celebrate by bestowing (on our own terms) a modicum of freedom upon them. Audiences may try to tap into and connect with animal otherness, as in the old *Tarzan* movies, and more recently, in films like *Whale Rider*, *Horse Whisperer*, *Dances with Wolves*, and *Grizzly Man*, though still we're much more interested in ourselves than in them; such interaction is really just another way of harvesting something from the animal object.

Note the titles of all these movies: all purport to offer (and in some ways do offer) intricate portrayals of human sensitivity to animals. They all, at first impression, seem to highlight animals. And while there are indeed animals in them all, in each case what might have first seemed like an animal reference actually turns out to be a human being: Timothy Treadwell is the Grizzly Man in Werner Herzog's odd documentary; Kevin Costner's character is given the name "Dances with Wolves" as he becomes enchanted with animals and Native American culture; a 12-year-old Maori girl is the whale rider.[22] These characters develop alongside animals, but they are still ultimately very much human identities. The human beings trump actors of other species, who are merely supporting cast, swimming or galloping in the background. When people look at animals, what we see most clearly with the human gaze, is, unsurprisingly, ourselves. Laura Mulvey makes a similar point about the objectified woman: "What counts is what the heroine provokes," she writes. "In herself the woman has not the slightest importance."[23]

Visual Colonization is Not Limited to Film

In visual advertising, the human gaze reveals an explicit commodification of the animal, but it's really just a more blatant iteration of all the other animals we look at. Morris the Cat, Charlie the Tuna, Joe Camel, the MGM Lion, Toucan Sam, the Energizer Bunny, the Budweiser Clydesdales—all these animal images are designed to advance consumer culture, to co-opt a perverse sense of biophilia (our connection to nature; our need for nature)[24] in order to encourage us to do things that don't really help animals in any way, or help us understand animals, or help us understand our relation to them. The animals are merely props, and as we pimp them in the discourse of advertising, they are hoist with their own petard. . . . victims of their own animality. Charlie adorns the outside of the StarKist tuna fish can, eagerly inviting you to eat him; smiling pigs on the sides of barbeque joints pose happily, without a touch of resentment, for customers about to order up a plate of ribs. These animals are figuratively devoured by the human gaze as an anticipation of their subsequent literal consumption.

Indeed, we are deluged with images of animals in visual culture that do not call out to our higher ecological consciousness. Instead, these images affirm received ideas: animals are ubiquitous, interesting and engaging under the right circumstances (and we must coordinate these circumstances ourselves, as we do in all these movies and ads). Animals would not naturally serve our purposes; left to their own devices, they would not pose a very strong claim on the human gaze.

This human gaze has been trained on animals in visual culture for a very long time: in 1877, Eadweard Muybridge produced photographs for California Governor and railroad tycoon Leland Stanford showing his racehorse in the midst of a gallop. Stanford had wanted to know if all four of a horse's hooves left the ground during a gallop, and commissioned Muybridge to find the answer.[25] Using a series of 24 stereoscopic cameras, Muybridge photographed a horse in fast motion, taking pictures at one thousandth of a second and producing a locomotion sequence known as "The Horse in Motion." Muybridge did this sort of thing with many other animals, too: his subjects included a buffalo, a lion, an ostrich, an elephant, and people as well. Many of the animals he photographed came from the Philadelphia Zoo.

Muybridge invented the "zoopraxiscope," a lantern that projected images in rapid succession onto a screen from photographs printed on a rotating glass disc, producing the illusion of moving pictures. It was the germ of modern cinematography. Muybridge was, in my opinion, the first modern artist who actualized our obsession with the movement of animals, but, I think, he did even more than this: he represented not just their physical animation, but also the metaphysical life, the spirit of the animal. He imported all this—their movement, their spirit, their lives—from nature, into our world: into culture. To satisfy our questions about animals and satiate our appetites for watching their speed, their grace, their power; to answer our idle queries (do all four hooves leave the ground at once?[26]) as well as our more profound wonderment, Muybridge's work set us on the path of looking at animals, creating new technologies to "capture" their animality, and then reproducing and projecting this.

Muybridge created the ability and fanned the desire for people to look at animals in visual culture. Post-Muybridge, audiences came to think of animals differently than they did pre-Muybridge: animals were now animated, "alive," moving, in visual cultural representations, rather than static. Their movement could be observed (and enjoyed) without the necessary proximity of the actual animal; thus, it could be enjoyed more conveniently, and in greater numbers. The Muybridge-animal might outlast the literal animal: indeed, in many ways, one might come to regard such images of animals as more potent and more fascinating than the mere animals themselves. Muybridge serves as a keen example of how culture shapes and influences people's perception of other animals: the understanding of animals, certainly, but also, I would cynically suggest, the misunderstanding of animals. As we capture their motion on film, that somehow supplants the reality of their motion, and so while we "have" it, I think we also lose it, to some extent. Before Muybridge, people had to look at the actual animal to see it move, to see it alive: afterwards, not. That is on some level a loss of our understanding and appreciation of an animal. And, I must note, Muybridge would not have earned the Humane Association's seal of approval: animals *were* harmed in the making of his visual displays. Derek Bousé in *Wildlife Films* describes how Muybridge arranged for a Philadelphia zoo tiger to be set loose on an old buffalo so that the photographer could record one of his motion studies of an actual killing;

Bousé calls this the beginning of a tradition in wildlife films of "kill scenes" that serve as a "guarantor of authenticity."[27]

More than 130 years after Muybridge's zoopraxiscopic technology, we are lately looking at more and more animals—as there is more porn on the web, there is more animal porn; as YouTube proliferates, there are more amateur videos of animals; as branding increases, so do branded animals; as cable television expands, we get more channels such as the Discovery Channel and Animal Planet (with shows like "When Animals Attack"; "The Pet Psychic"; "Animal Cops"; "World's Ugliest Dog"; and "Crocodile Hunter.")[28] Animal Planet claims, perversely and oxymoronically, to be programming "reality tv" about animals. But "reality" and "television" are contradictions in terms. Animal Planet facilitates and expands our consumption of animals (culturally and otherwise), but it does not bring the people who look at animals any closer to the reality of these animals. Traditionally, watching animals on film is considered to be good, wholesome family fun: highbrow entertainment and/or education; I wish to problematize that.

I concede that it is possible for visual media to teach us about animals—a documentarian, or even a mainstream feature filmmaker, may spend years gathering footage that insightfully depicts, with ecological accuracy and sensitivity, the lives of animals. Such films (some examples of which I discuss below) go to where the animals live and look at them in their own habitats, which is much preferable to chimps on parade and painting elephants.

But these nature films often impose a human narrative, a human cultural aesthetic, upon animals. The films may be flat-out faked: there's a rich tradition of nature-film fakery. But even when there's no explicit attempt to deceive, they still may mislead or miseducate viewers by making animals seem too accessible, too easily present, which distorts the reality that most animals live away from us, hidden from us. Their reclusiveness is self-protective, and our intrusion, even via the mediation of a documentary film crew, may breach an important barrier between ourselves and many other animals. For example, Luc Jacquet's *March of the Penguins* (2005), about the Emperor penguins' annual journey to their breeding ground, and Jacques Perrin's *Winged Migration* (2001), a stunning account of birds' global journeys, are two beautiful and eloquent films about the lives of animals who live far from the world that most of us inhabit. As captivating as I found both these films for the detailed and richly ecological education they offered as they immersed viewers in the extreme Antarctic/atmospheric habitats that are all but inaccessible to people, still, I wonder if it is right for us to see such lives: if somehow, the human gaze, in any form, however carefully exercised, may be fated to impose our power over the animals, leaving them, thus, powerless.

Millions of people have seen these films, crossover blockbuster hits. Does this testify to our increasing interest and concern for other animals, or does it mean that we've dragged these creatures down to the level of mass entertainment, which is inherently anti-ecological and anti-animal because of the hegemonies of consumption culture in Western industrial society?

In *Green Cultural Studies*, Jhan Hochman warns that a nature film may render viewers "separate and superior to film-nature even as it brings them into proximity. Nature becomes, then, prop(erty) and commodity."[29] As physics teaches us, the act of observation changes the phenomenon being observed. (The "observer effect" holds that instruments, by their nature, alter the state of what they measure. The psychological concept of "reactivity" similarly suggests that subjects change their behavior when they are aware of being observed.) And as Foucault theorized, vision facilitates a power that the seer exercises over the seen. We call these films "Luc Jacquet's *March of the Penguins*" and "Jacques Perrin's *Winged Migration*"—the fact of human ownership and control over these animal images is completely inescapable. To restate the obvious, people make these films (and, people make money from making these films); people watch these films. Where, in this nexus, does the animal come in? Do the animals profit in any way from this interaction, from the human gaze? Can they? Should they? Even if no animals were harmed in the making of these movies, is that the best we can hope for? Were any animals *helped* in the making of these movies?

In *Watching Wildlife*, Cynthia Chris writes, "The wildlife film and television genre comprises not only a body of knowledges but also an institution for their containment and display, similar to those institutions that Michel Foucault described as heterotopias, which through their collection of normally unrelated objects, life forms, or representations expose visitors to worlds beyond their own reach." Heterotopias are real places, places that do exist—in contrast to utopias, which are idealized and unreal. A heterotopia might be a botanical garden, for example, or a zoo, or a theatre, or cinema. But "the knowledge within the heterotopia," Chris writes, is "selected, framed, edited, and interpreted, according to an array of social forces and cultural contests over meaning"—and these places are "absolutely different from all the sites they reflect and speak about."[30] Turning on the television any day,

> one might flit from views of sharks off the coast of southern Africa to polar bears in Manitoba, rattlesnakes in Florida, crocodiles in Queensland, and pandas . . . in Sichuan Province. The images of animals and their habitats, natural or artificial, found through television, are representations of real places and the creatures that live there, but they are "absolutely different" from those real sites and their inhabitants, constructed as they are by conventions of representation . . . the economics of the film and television industries, and geopolitical conditions concerning the state of the environment.[31]

Anyone who has watched the wide array of nature films, television shows, and documentaries knows how many different styles and ideologies may be invoked to depict the animals that are framed within by human technology and human cultural prejudices. In *Reel Wildlife: America's Romance with Wildlife on Film*, Gregg Mitman characterizes a range of representations and misrepresentations of filmed animals. Disney's "True-Life Adventures" from the late 1940s was a prominent series that established many of the conventions for decades to come, which he calls, "a genre of sugar-coated educational nature films."[32] And even today, in our supposedly more enlightened and more ecologically-attuned times, still, the *Wild Discovery* series, from the Discovery Channel—has a "penchant for tacking happy endings onto tales of ecological disaster."[33]

Along the lines of how Cynthia Chris invokes Foucauldian heterotopias, Mitman explains that in many nature films, "fabrication made the line separating artifice from authenticity difficult to discern." He detects an inherent tension, a contradiction embodied in nature films: they "reveal much about the yearnings of Americans to be both close to nature and yet distinctly apart."[34] This gets at the crux of the problem, which I would identify as an ethical aporia: the problem of perspective, of positioning, of self-awareness. We don't know where we are in relation to other animals; we don't really know where we want to be, where we should be, in this relationship, which results in a fundamental inability even to formulate, much less resolve, the ethical dilemmas concerning our coexistence with other animals. Many other anthrozoologists have expressed variations on this key contradiction, this conundrum, that Mitman explains so succinctly here. We want to be in two mutually exclusive kinds of relationships at the same time (close to nature, and apart from it); how, then, can we hope to act ethically, if ethical reasoning is predicated upon knowing the precise actual truth, the single accurate reality, of where we are, who we are, at the moment we conduct our ethical deliberations?

Deep within the bowels of capitalism, Hollywood productions look at animals in ways that are inflected by the economics of the mainstream film industry. In *Green Screen*, which examines nature in Hollywood films, David Ingram argues that the kinds of realism and environmentalist aesthetics that might best convey the stories of animals authentically and informatively are at odds with the genres and aesthetics we should expect from Hollywood.

Ingram identifies many pervasive Hollywood tropes that a mainstream animal movie will be likely to embrace—such as the circle of life, the cult of pristine nature, man's domination over nature, the action plot (which may resist a perceived sense of passivity in nature), ecological Indians and the myth of primal purity, the imperial narrative, profoundly anthropomorphized animals, the therapeutic tendency toward environmental concerns—offering numerous examples of how animal images are transmogrified to fit the Hollywood mold.

For example, in Michael Apted's *Gorillas in the Mist* (1998), the biopic about Dian Fossey's work with mountain gorillas in East Africa, Ingram compares the gorillas as Fossey describes them in her book—practicing "infanticide, masturbation, incest, fellatio and cannibalism"—to the animals in the movie who are "idealized figures possessing the redemptive innocence typical of the Hollywood wild animal movies."[35] The portrait of the human being (played by Sigourney Weaver), too, is "highly selective of the biographical and historical evidence available on Fossey's life and work."[36]

In the Hollywood film industry, Ingram writes, "environmental sensibilities are always likely to be moderated by its vested interest in promoting commodity consumption as a social good";[37] these films avoid questioning the central place that consumerism enjoys in American society.

The recent blockbuster hit *Avatar* (James Cameron, 2009) has raised anew the question of how audiences view animals on film, and especially how changing technologies might inflect the cinematographic animal. The issue came to the forefront in January, 2010, when People for the Ethical Treatment for Animals (PETA) honored *Avatar* with a Proggy (signifying "progress" in the animal rights cause) Award for Outstanding Feature Film. PETA cited the film's "inspiring message. . . which stresses the interconnectedness of nature and the importance of treating all living beings, no matter how 'strange' or 'alien,' with respect and dignity." The organization highlighted "the movie's stunning special effects, which beautifully illustrate how unnecessary it is to subject animals to the stress of a film production"; PETA Senior Vice President Lisa Lange stated, "We hope viewers will come away from *Avatar* with a new way of looking at the world around them and the way we treat our fellow earthlings."[38]

In response, the AHA issued a statement of demurral in a press release titled: "Think "No Animals Were Harmed"® in the Making of *Avatar*? You're Right. Think No Animals Were Used in the Making of *Avatar*? You're Wrong." They dispelled the presumption that computer-generated imagery (CGI) meant that actual animals were not involved in the filming. In fact, for the depiction of the six-legged horse-like creatures featured in the film, "motion capture technology" demanded the use of horses. People, too, were animated with the assistance of captures: actors wore body suits that enabled computerized motion sensors to provide a template for gestures, movement, and expressions.

> But animals need to be "captured" differently because of their body shapes, fur and other characteristics. To prepare the animals for having their motion data recorded, trainers shaved small areas of fur or hair where the movements would be recorded, such as near joints and on the face. Velcro pads were attached to the shaved spots with a nontoxic, nonirritating silicone adhesive. White light-reflective balls were placed onto the Velcro to capture the motion data onto the computer. . . .Throughout the film, horses are seen outdoors standing or being ridden at a walk, canter

or gallop. We also see people mounting, dismounting and falling off horses. These scenes were all filmed inside the capture studio. Horses were given ample room to start and stop running. . . . For scenes in which horses appear to be near fire, trainers cued them to "dance" or act skittish or afraid—the horses were not actually agitated nor were they ever near fire.[39]

While AHA monitored these activities, they still felt compelled to announce that real animals, if not harmed, were nevertheless used in the film production. Although it might be nice to imagine that CGI potentially obviates the demand for animals in films, this is not the case; it merely induces audiences—and even PETA—to presume, erroneously, that the industry can transcend their historical record of animal use (and sometimes abuse).

The message of *Avatar* has received mixed responses from animal-concerned audiences. On a very basic level, such viewers are inclined to applaud its moral that all nature is connected and people should not destroy habitats for profit. But the PETA blog also recorded some more critical resistance. Several commentators objected to what they judged as the hypocrisy that while the film's protagonists, the Na'vi humanoids, conveyed an ecological sensitivity toward habitat preservation, at the same time they engaged in the domination and consumption of animals, aggressively controlling the will of flying creatures and killing other animals for food in a brutal hunting scene. As one blogger wrote,

> Jake's avatar and Neytiri shoot an arrow through an animal's larynx, finishing him off with a knife to the throat.(Just because they say "it was a clean death," add some mumbo jumbo prayers right after, acting as if they did it out of "respect to animals," doesn't make it any less cruel and unnecessary.) The Na'vi do not mentally "become one" with the creatures they plug their organic USB in, they literally brainwash them. I say this because if there were actually some kind of symbiosis involved the animal would have its say. And it doesn't. It just blindly follows everything "the rider" tells it to do.[40]

And Stephanie Ernst, writing on an animal rights website, convincingly argues that the film suggests "humans have the right and the duty to dominate, 'tame,' and make use of animals—that nonhuman animals are resources and tools."[41] Ernst is especially offended by Jake's interaction with the pterodactyl-like animals, which she finds "chillingly reminiscent of a rape scene." The Na'vi protagonist Neytiri, tells Jake that to become a complete warrior in her culture (as he aspires to do) he must choose one of these "ikran" as his own.

> He will know the ikran he is meant to bond with on sight—and he will know that the ikran chooses him too *if the ikran fights back and tries to kill him* ("no means yes" and "she'll fight you, but you know she really wants it," anyone?). It is Jake's duty, while the animal fights him off, to "bond" with the animal by overpowering him, tying him up, climbing on top of him, and *inserting a part of his body into the body of the animal* while his victim desperately fights him off. Once he has done that, once he has successfully dominated the animal and physically inserted himself into his conquest, the ikran is defeated; the ikran goes still and quiet, and Jake wins. "That's right—you're mine!" Jake boasts. The animal has been successfully dominated, his will and spirit broken—and the defeated being now belongs to Jake. . . . This was not a scenario in which each party sought out the other, for mutual benefit. The being in power dominated/raped the "lesser" being while the victim fought him off—and that we (and Jake) were essentially told, "if your victim fights you off, it means he wants it" was beyond sickening for me. It far too closely parallels the "you know you want it" mindset and words of real-world rapists.[42]

Ernst's response suggests that the human gaze, and the male gaze that lies beneath it, retain an enduring and haunting resonance, however much filmmakers try to transcend it (or, perhaps, simply pretend to attempt such a transcendence). In *Avatar*, as in all films, the presence of other animals—even in treatments that might seem ecologically enlightened on the surface—invites a critical and skeptical analysis as to whether the filmmaking industry and its audiences are truly becoming more concerned about ecosystemic speciesist inequities, or are merely reiterating the same old anthropocentric prejudices under the cover of a flashy new veneer.

Audiences should be cautious about assuming that the extravagant technological novelties embodied in the film's computer animation and *visual* three-dimensionality accompany a comparable advance in its *ethical* dimensionality. If ecologically and independently sophisticated representation of animal presence may be metaphorically envisioned as the third dimension, then *Avatar* remains mired in the same old flat, two-dimensional rut that has afflicted animals in visual culture. Ever since Muybridge and his zoopraxiscope began the tradition of creating and diffusing novel ways of looking at animals, the human gaze(r) has become more and more voracious, more and more pleased at its own omnipowerful intrusion into the world of animals ("the wilderness," or "nature," or "the jungle": however we construe what is ultimately just a backdrop, a set, a tableau, for the dazzling human action that takes place in the foreground). And we need to be more careful than ever before, as we appraise the ramifications of our citizenship in this brave new world of visual culture, when a feel-good eco-parable that has become the world's most profitable film ever masks, at its heart, the ideology of the rapist.

KINDER WAYS OF LOOKING AT ANIMALS

Why are we looking at animals? What sort of contact zones (between human and other animals) do visual media create? How are we seeing these creatures we have "captured" on film? (The implications of this "capture" are not just metaphorical.) What are the consequences of the ways people look at and think about animals in visual culture? How *aren't* we looking at animals in visual culture? How *might* we look at them more intelligently, more fairly?

Is it unrealistic to hope that visual culture might help us more accurately locate and situate ourselves in relation to other animals (rendering a truer vision of our place, and their place, and our actual conditions of coexistence)? What should we do with these animals once we've gotten them in our clear, accurate, ethical sight-lines? Or, if "what should we do with them?" sounds too paternalistic, then instead, how shall we behave towards them? I won't answer that question in much depth here, though certainly many others have done so eloquently. For now, I simply suggest that what we *should* do is treat animals better than we have done, and our visual cultural representations of animals significantly affect, positively or negatively, people's propensity either to revise and improve our patterns of behavior, or, on the other hand, to continue along the path of the status quo with our piercing human gaze of speciesism, encroachment, and imperial dominance.

Why look at animals? This enduring question was, of course, raised in John Berger's famous 1977 essay. It's a good question . . . an important question, a simple, basic question, and though Berger launched into fascinating rambles about all the dysfunctional and improper ways in which people looked at animals, I don't think he ever resolved his basic initial query. He concludes by noting that because of increasing urban/industrial development and the disappearance of animals from people's lives, any meaningful gaze that there might once have been between people and other animals "has been extinguished," and we as a species have "at last been isolated."[43] So now we're not looking at animals, he posits; but that does not negate the relevance of nonetheless pursuing the question (even if it is "only philosophical"): why look at animals?

It's a question I've been wrestling with, or perhaps dancing around, throughout this essay. I believe it is definitely a question we should be asking, but perhaps (as Berger seems to have found) it's a question we can't answer. Indeed, there is a tradition of unanswered and unanswerable questions people ask about animals. From Thomas Nagel: "What is it like to be a bat?" From Jeremy Bentham: "Can they suffer?" From Jacques Derrida: "And say the animal responded?" From Michel de Montaigne: "When I play with my cat, who knows whether she is not amusing herself with me more than I with her?" From the comic pages: "Why did the chicken cross the road?" And to carry this meditation a step further, if indeed we cannot answer the question "why look at animals in visual culture?" does that imply, on some ethical level, that we should therefore stop looking at them in visual culture? If we cannot clearly explain and defend our gaze, does it then behoove us to stop looking at other animals? I don't know—that's another unanswerable question.

Let me put forth a related but not identical question: Why look at animals in nature? Here I'm talking about real animals, in real, actual, spatial proximity (as opposed to looking at animals through the mediation of visual culture). The naturalist Richard Conniff describes the pleasures and importance of watching real animals. In "The Consolation of Animals" he writes that looking at animals is what "makes me almost sane. These encounters with the lords of life . . . pull me up out of the pettiness and stupidity of my workaday life. . . . Watching animals fills some larger . . . appetite in much the way that reading poetry does, or listening to music."[44]

This may be no more than a subjective matter of taste and temperament, but I believe that what Conniff describes here embodies an admirable sensibility that involves meaningful and equitable interaction with other species. Though of course this is an overgeneralization, I'd suggest that a visual cultural experience of animals is prone to be lazier and more voyeuristic than what Conniff describes. The difference, the deficiency in looking at animals in visual culture as compared to really looking at real animals, stems from the basic fact that the viewers at the movies or surfing the net are not in real proximity to the animal, not out in animal habitats, but rather, comfortably ensconced, isolated, in their own world. And animals don't fit well into this world.

I believe that our perceptions of animals in visual culture, as mediated by the artifices of our culture, cannot be as accurate, as authentic, as precise as when we're looking at real animals. In visual culture, animals are edited, framed, commodified, and somehow reduced. As Akira Lippit writes in *Electric Animal*, "Technology and . . . cinema came to determine a vast mausoleum for animal being."[45]

On the other hand, though, remember my contention that when a person and another animal come into contact, the other animal almost always ends up the worse for this encounter; perhaps that argues *against* looking at real animals and in favor of cultural mediation—the protective distancing (from the animal's perspective) of the human viewer.

I would like to consider, briefly, two recent independent animal documentaries that eschew the cinematic mainstream: *The Lord God Bird* (George Butler, 2008) and *Silent Roar: Searching for the Snow Leopard* (Hugh Miles and Mitchell Kelly, 2007). These films elucidate an interestingly unconventional relationship between the human viewer and the animal subject. Both these films explicitly recount how hard it is to find the animals they seek. Butler's film is about the ivory-billed woodpecker, colloquially known as the Lord God Bird because according to legend those who see it spontaneously cry out, "Lord God! What was that?" The bird may or may not be extinct: reliable, confirmed sightings have not been made for decades, though some people featured in this film believe they have seen the elusive bird more recently.

The Lord God Bird wonderfully frustrates its viewers, because it's about an animal that we may not be able to see, that we have quite likely eradicated from the earth (if not completely, then pretty nearly). We wait hopefully to see it throughout the film, and perhaps we do, in a brief, blurry, and disputed clip, but we certainly don't get a good, clear, satisfying look at it. This teaches us a lesson that I find vital: we are not omnipotent emperors who can look at any animal whenever we choose. Despite the absence of the animal in its title, this film intensely conveys a sense of the bird: its history and ecology, its legendary resonance. Butler shows that we can think richly about an animal without necessitating its literal appearance in our line of sight. The "human gaze" as a trope is troubled, subverted, in this film.

Silent Roar, too, is about an animal that's very difficult to see, the large Himalayan cat that inhabits the mountains just below the peak of Mount Everest. The cinematographers strenuously try to capture the snow leopards on film—and finally, with stealthy remote sensor-activated cameras, they get a few short and fuzzy shots of the leopards. But mostly, in this film as in *The Lord God Bird*, we *don't* see the animals we have come to see, and once again, we're tempted to affirm the ethical proposition that we are not meant to see this animal. Its world is mutually exclusive with our own. Snow leopards live too far away from us, too high; their habitats are too remote; the journey that the film takes to approach them reinforces their distance from us.

And though this may annoy audiences of animal-lookers who have come to expect that they *can* see any animal they want to, the film still lets us down easily. *Silent Roar*—the title itself is a nice paradox: we expect to *hear* a "roar," but it's withdrawn from us, *silenced*, at the same time it's offered. *Silent Roar* depicts people trying as hard as they can to see snow leopards, with all the possible technology available, and the keenest sense of adventure, but still, as they fail, we may come to terms with the insight that perhaps we simply can't see everything that's out there in the world. And *Silent Roar* still leaves audiences with a very beautiful and memorable film about the region, the place, through which snow leopards sometimes move (just not when most of us can see).

I endorse encounters like these in visual media: experiences that don't flatter our omnivisual fantasies, but instead suggest what we are *not* meant to see, and explain why. In the world of art, a growing canon of painting, sculpture, photography, and other performative works reinforce this retreat from the anthropocentric omniscience that has traditionally characterized the human gaze. In the vanguard of this (counter-)movement are artists like Britta Jaschinski, Sue Coe, Olly & Suzi, Mark Dion, and Joseph Beuys, all of whom Steve Baker discusses in *The Postmodern Animal.* These artists resist a traditional sentimentality toward other animals, in favor of a more nuanced engagement with them, a more ecologically informed and reasoned interaction. As Baker puts it, they are forging "new models of the human and the animal"[46] in the service of "an imaginative reassessment of the role of animals in human thought,"[47] which includes a postmodern skepticism about "culture's means of constructing and classifying the animal in order to make it meaningful to the human."[48] These artists aspire to a holistic ecological sensibility that rejects the conventional Cartesian dualism we have constructed to define our relationship with the animal. They realize that the future of the human "is so intimately and creatively bound up with that of the animal" that "the classic dualism of human and animal is not so much erased as *rendered uninteresting* as a way of thinking about being in the world."[49]

We may call these visual cultural texts postmodern, or posthuman, to indicate a transcendence over the hubristic ethos that humanity has indulged in for so many centuries. That unsustainable ethos, however, will not carry us forward for many more generations. We cannot rely upon the profusion of new media technology to generate what we need to see when we look at the world around us, and at the other species who share this world with us. We need to seek out new, less harmful, ways of looking at animals.

NOTES

1. The first-person plural pronoun here denotes humanity as a whole, and more specifically, the populations of the world's overdeveloped consumer cultures. And of course, it includes me as well.

2. http://www.americanhumane.org/protecting-animals/programs/ no-animals-were-harmed/ accessed on January 25, 2010.

3. The AHA is separate from the Humane Society of the United States (HSUS). See http://www.hsus.org/about_us/accomplishments/ the_people_who_have_shaped_the_hsus/

fred_myers_cofounder_of_the_hsus.html (accessed January 25, 2010) for an account of how the HSUS split off from the AHA in 1954, after a bitter dispute about what the HSUS faction considered insufficient activism on the part of the AHA.

4. http://www.aarp.org/aarp/broadcast/aarpradio/movies for grown ups pastshows/articles/animalactors.html accessed on January 29, 2010.

5. http://www.americanhumane.org/protecting-animals/programs/no-animals-were-harmed/ accessed on October 5, 2009. The citation of Newman's film (about the development of the atomic bombs in the Manhattan Project) as the first one to receive this rating is discussed at http://findarticles.com/p/news-articles/charleston-daily-mail/mi_8044/is_20060320/animal-rights-groups-pushing-real/ai_n46262135/, accessed January 25, 2010.

6. http://www.ahafilm.info/movies/moviereviews.phtml?fid=7193, accessed on January 25, 2010.

7. http://www.americanhumane.org/protecting-animals/programs/no-animals-were-harmed/movie-rating-system-old.html, accessed on October 5, 2009.

8. http://www.americanhumane.org/faqs.html, accessed on October 5, 2009.

9. http://www.americanhumane.org/faqs.html, accessed on October 5, 2009.

10. The field of "visual culture" is an increasingly prominent academic focus that draws upon anthropology, cultural studies, art history, and various other cognate fields. It addresses the range of visual imagery (film, television, graphics, comics, new media, high and popular/public art, and so forth) that is becoming ever more ubiquitous as our cultural experiences become more resplendently illustrated. While some fear that visual culture threatens to overwrite textual culture, others (including myself) believe the two realms of media can coexist.

11. *King Kong* (Merian Cooper and Ernest Schoedsack, 1933; Peter Jackson, 2005); *Curious George* (Matthew O'Callahan, 2006); *Beethoven* (Brian Levant, 1992; five sequels); *Seabiscuit* (Gary Ross, 2003).

12. A long-running regular feature on CBS's *Late Show with David Letterman*; Google the term to see a plethora of illustrations.

13. I discuss such odd encounters with animals in more detail in an essay with the self-explanatory title, "Americans Do Weird Things With Animals," *Animal Encounters*, eds. Tom Tyler and Manuela Rossini (Leiden: Brill, 2009), pp. 73-96.

14. See http://www.imdb.com/title/tt0136536/, accessed on January 29, 2010.

15. Jeremy Biles, "I, Insect, or Bataille and the Crush Freaks," *Janus Head* (7.1, 115-131), pp. 116-17.

16. Laura Mulvey, "Visual Pleasure and Narrative Cinema," *Screen* (16.3, 6-18), p. 11.

17. Carol Adams, *The Sexual Politics of Meat: A Feminist-Vegetarian Critical Theory* (New York: Continuum, 1990), pp. 39-62; G.A. Bradshaw, B. Smuts, D. Durham, in press. "Open Door Policy: The necessary relinquishment of humanity's 'right to sight'", in R. Acampora, ed. *Metamorphoses of the Zoo: Animal Encounter After Noah* (Rowman & Littlefield Publishers).

18. Mulvey, "Visual Pleasure," p. 17.

19. See, e.g., Sandra Gilbert and Susan Gubar, *The Madwoman in the Attic: The Woman Writer and the Nineteenth-Century Literary Imagination* (New Haven: Yale University Press, 1979).

20. *Lassie Come Home* (MGM, 1943) was followed by six other feature MGM films through 1951, and a CBS television series, *Lassie*, from 1954-73, starring a collie. *Flipper* (NBC, 1964-67) starred a series of bottlenose dolphins, trained by Richard O'Barry (who recently starred in the documentary *The Cove*, 2009, in which he explains that he sees his activist campaign against dolphin slaughters as a kind of atonement for his work on the television series). Robert Stevenson's 1957 film *Old Yeller* is about a mixed-breed dog, based on Fred Gipson's 1956 novel. *Sounder*, a 1970 novel by William H. Armstrong adapted into a 1972 film by Martin Ritt, features a mixed-breed dog as the title character. Elsa is a lion cub who stars in *Born Free*, a 1966 film by James Hill (with two sequels) based on the books by Joy Adamson. Rin Tin Tin was the name given to several German Shepherds who starred in a series of Warner Brothers movies (often credited with saving the studio from bankruptcy) in the 1920s and 1930s. Francis the Talking Mule starred in the film *Francis* (1950) and six sequels through that decade.

21. *Free Willy* (Simon Wincer, 1993) tells of a boy's attempts to free an orca whale from captivity in a theme park.

22. *Grizzly Man* (Werner Herzog, 2005); *Dances with Wolves* (Kevin Costner, 1990); *Whale Rider* (Niki Caro, 2002).

23. Mulvey, "Visual Pleasure" (quoting Budd Boetticher), p. 11.

24. E. O. Wilson explains this term that he coined in *Biophilia* (Cambridge: Harvard University Press, 1984): "we are human in good part because of the particular way we affiliate with other organisms. They are the matrix in which the human mind originated and is permanently rooted." p. 139.

25. Mitchell Leslie, "The Man Who Stopped Time," *Stanford Magazine* (May/June 2001), accessed online January 25 2010 at http://www.stanfordalumni.org/news/magazine/2001/mayjun/features/muybridge.html.

26. In fact, they do.

27. Derek Bousé, *Wildlife Films* (Philadelphia: University of Pennsylvania Press, 2000), pp. 42-3.

28. See schedules and programming notes at http://animal.discovery.com/, accessed 29 January 2010.

29. Jhan Hochman, *Green Cultural Studies: Nature in Film, Novel, and Theory* (Moscow, Id.: University of Idaho Press, 1998), p. 3.

30. Cynthia Chris, *Watching Wildlife* (Minneapolis: University of Minnesota Press, 2006), p. xi.

31. Chris, p. xii.

32. Gregg Mitman, *Reel Nature: America's Romance with Wildlife on Film* (Cambridge, Mass.: Harvard University Press, 1999), p. 3.

33. *Ibid.*, p. xiv.

34. *Ibid.*, p. 4.

35. David Ingram, *Green Screen: Environmentalism and Hollywood Cinema* (Exeter: University of Exeter Press, 2004), pp. 135-6.

36. *Ibid.*, p. 132.

37. *Ibid.*, p. 181.

38. http://inmovies.ca/Home/ContentPosting?newsitemid=dish information.ca%2F2010%2F01%2F21%2Fpeta-awards-avatar%2F&feedname=DISHMOVIE_NEWS&show=False &number=0& showbyline=False&subtitle=&detect=&abc=abc&date=False, accessed Feb. 17, 2010.

39. http://www.americanhumane.org/about-us/newsroom/news-

releases/10-avatar-animals.html, accessed Feb. 17, 2010.

40. Posted by Sebastian Verdikt, January 22, 2010. http://
blog.peta.org/archives/2010/01/james_cameron_avatar.php, accessed
Feb. 17, 2010.

41. Stephanie Ernst, "Domination and Rape in *Avatar:* This Is
"Respect" for Animals?" On "Animal Rights and AntiOppression"
website, http://challengeoppression.com/2010/02/16/domination-
and-rape-in-avatar-this-is-respect-for-animals/, accessed Feb. 20, 2010.

42. http://challengeoppression.com/2010/02/16/domination-
and-rape-in-avatar-this-is-respect-for-animals/, accessed Feb. 20, 2010.

43. John Berger, "Why Look at Animals?", in *About Looking* (New
York, Pantheon, 1980), p. 28.

44. Richard Conniff, "The Consolation of Animals," http://
happydays.blogs.nytimes.com/2009/05/27/the-consolation-of-
animals/, accessed on October 5, 2009.

45. Akira Mizuta Lippit, *Electric Animal: Toward a Rhetoric of
Wildlife* (Minneapolis: University of Minnesota Press, 2000), p. 187.

46. Steve Baker, *The Postmodern Animal* (London: Reaktion Books,
2000), p. 165.

47. *Ibid.*, inside cover.

48. *Ibid.*, p. 9.

49. *Ibid.*, p. 17.

WE, MATATA:
BICULTURAL LIVING AMONG APES

G. A. BRADSHAW

*We are not myths of the past, ruins in the jungle, or zoos. We are people
and we want to be respected, not to be victims of intolerance and racism.*

—Rigoberta Menchú Tum
Nobel Peace Prize Laureate, 1992

C. G. Jung wrote about modern humanity's felt discontinuity
with nature. Humans, he maintained, remain a mystery to
themselves because they are unique, lacking someone or
something against which comparisons can be made. But he is wrong.
Differences merely lie in the eyes of the beholder. We are surrounded
by others like ourselves. We always have been. American Indian peoples
saw themselves as one of many animal nations. They lived side by side
with the Beaver, Buffalo, and Eagle Peoples. Only a few human tribes
have insisted on making difference a religion.

Now, there is change. The rootless warrens of the mind have grown
lonely. In the threatening shadow of environmental collapse, there is a

G.A. Bradshaw, Ph.D., Ph.D., is the executive director of the Kerulos Center and
author of *Elephants on the Edge: What Animals Teach Us About Humanity* (Yale University
Press, 2009). Her work focuses on animal psychological trauma and recovery and
approaches to support wildlife cultural self-determination.

scramble to tear through the perceptual veil that has alienated us from animal kin.[1] Bird feathers and reptile scales once so defining, melt away when we realize how much is shared with other species. At the resolution of brain function, process, and development, researchers model all of us—chicken, parrot, bear, human, dolphin, and everyone in between—the same, making species lines as labile as ethnicity and race.[2] Skin type and body shape merely signal where watching ceases and being watched begins.

The Age of Descartes has come to a close. After centuries of self-imposed separation, the wall "between humans and animals has finally been breached"; the distinctiveness that we have "so assiduously ascribed to ourselves is, in reality, an accident of history."[3] Perhaps nowhere are species lines more tentative than between our closest genetic relatives, other apes, and ourselves. When sitting face to face with a chimpanzee, the "distinction between humans and nonhuman animals begins to break down," and when "we encounter apes who have language and whose mental worlds. . .are not that different from our own," it is impossible not to feel the bond of likeness.[4]

Here we will explore a quiet corner of the world that lives beyond difference, where human and non-human ape live as kin under skin. It is an unlikely place to find human and nonhuman ape living together, not, as one might expect, in the wilds of African or Asian forests where encounters with ancestral cousins magically occur, but in Des Moines, Iowa. For over thirty years, human Dr. Sue Savage-Rumbaugh (*Homo sapiens*) has resided with bonobos Matata, Kanzi, and Nyota Wamba (*Pan paniscus*) in a mixed *Pan/Homo* community.

Critically, we learn about bonobo perceptions and experience through *Pan* reportage as well as through *Homo* descriptions. After years of interacting together using lexigrams and spoken English as linguistic currency, the Iowan bonobos and humans talk with each other in much the same way we humans converse amongst ourselves. Their minds interleave, as do their social roles. While listening to their trans-species science in the making—the investigation, creation, and documentation of shared knowledge and meaning between species—and watching how conventional roles of human researcher/bonobo subject alternate with human amanuensis/bonobo researcher, we witness the emergence of a bicultural *Pan/Homo* identity. We awaken to something that can hardly be expressed in words: modern humanity has all but erased the language that speaks life's unity. But in Iowa, memory rekindles and voices of common hearts and minds rejoice.

PAN/HOMO SCIENCE

The pursuit of human uniqueness is a driving agenda in western science. Perhaps more than any other, language ability is one of the most intensely coveted. This is why the iconoclastic *Pan/Homo* community is so revolutionary: it has vanquished the notion of language as uniquely human. Others have demonstrated that nonhuman apes exhibit compassion, empathy, and altruism. But primatologist Savage-Rumbaugh, and bonobos Wamba, Wamba, and Wamba have gone further by breaking down the language barrier between species. While "talking with the animals" is not uncommon,[5] Savage-Rumbaugh employs scientific formalism to show that our ape relatives are able to learn and use language like humans. Bonobos of the *Pan/Homo* group have learned over 300 lexigrams, symbols of objects, states, and processes with which they answer and ask questions, and communicate complex meanings, decisions, and judgments to humans. Sue *Homo* queries Kanzi, Matata, and Nyota *Pan* in English, and they respond by pointing to or using a keyboard of lexigrams.[6]

Science has an uneasy relationship with other species, simultaneously seeking connection, yet determined to retain separation. This profound contradiction is exemplified in "animal models", science's use of animals in experiments to understand the human mind and body.[7] On one hand, it is considered ethical to use animals in experiments because they lack the higher-order sensibilities that ethically prohibit human use. On the other hand, the only reason that animals qualify for experimentation *in lieu* of humans is because they possess such faculties; nonhuman animals are mentally and physiologically comparable to humans. This premise underlies psychopharmaceutical testing, medical procedures, and the panoply of other experiments performed on animals in an effort to prolong human life. We use other species in our place because we cannot bear to subject ourselves to these procedures. Science's linguistic re-packaging of sentient beings into living objects obscures the gaping chasm in logic to create the necessary illusion of ethical compliance.

In contrast to many other researchers, Savage-Rumbaugh eschews objectification as a single epistemic framing in favor of using a "holistic approach to the research, rearing the apes from birth and immersing them in a 'linguistic world,'"[8] a method of inquiry that reflects ethical guidelines required in human subject studies. Scientific objectivity is not excluded. Indeed,

> having a close relationship with the *Pan/Homo* bonobos does not prevent objectivity. In fact, it enhances it because I know, first hand, the real level at which they are able to understand language. I can design tests that are far more appropriate than someone who only sees apes from outside the cage. What I have done is equivalent to deep and total immersion in the classical anthropological sense. I have become a member of their group and in so doing they have also become a member of mine. Neither of us completely fits, but we do fit in a very honest and real way and we are bonded together by mutual regard and respect. Objective tests can be given on the computer to control for any influence I might have. Because I know them I know how to step the tests up in complexity, in a way that makes sense to bonobo. One might equate this ability with that of a good teacher.[9]

Their communication reflects an embodied consciousness where spoken and written language takes on its depth of meaning embedded in profound connection.

Pan subjects are not forced to relinquish their right of privacy. They maintain agency and control of what and how information is obtained and used. Unlike other researchers at zoos and other captive settings,[10] Savage-Rumbaugh does not draw the line of animal subject participation at the boundary of their cages. However, she acknowledges that any ape captivity is an implicit ethical breach.

> We are all aware that any form of imprisonment curtails our basic rights and opportunities in an unpalatable manner. However, it is obvious that all apes kept in captive conditions experience imprisonment. If ape and human psychological worlds are even remotely similar, we must conclude that captivity, in and of itself, is far from preferable for either species. . .Humans typically remain free unless they have committed crimes against others, but apes have committed no crimes.[11]

In 2007, the *Journal Of Applied Animal Welfare* (*JAAWS*) published an unprecedented paper, *Welfare of Apes in Captive Environments: Comments on, and by, A Specific Group of Apes.*[12] The title retains a sense of ambiguity. In the vernacular, apes describes gorillas, chimpanzees, and their nonhuman cousins. But more strictly speaking, it is a term that includes humans.

The article's singular nature derives from more than content. It was co-authored by Sue Savage-Rumbaugh and three bonobos from the *Pan/Homo* community, Panbanisha Wamba, Kanzi Wamba, and Nyota Wamba. The purpose of the study with resultant manuscript was to describe what apes living in the Des Moines facility considered important for their psychological and physical wellbeing in captivity. After decades of sacrifice, primates are finally being afforded some consideration concerning their welfare.

Animal experimentation and captivity exact a devastating toll. Chimpanzees, macaques, and other primates routinely used in experiments and biomedical testing undergo horrific ordeals.[13] Survivors who are released into sanctuary live haunted by symptoms

Photo courtesy of Sue Savage-Rumbaugh

of physical and psychological trauma. Chimpanzees Billy Jo, Tom, and Jeannie, released to the Fauna Foundation sanctuary outside Montreal, Canada, were subjected to decades of invasive procedures and deprivation.[14] The legacy of their profound suffering expresses as stereotypy, self-mutilation, social conflict, eating disorders, and myriad other psychological disorders combined with multiple physical ailments (including HIV/AIDS and hepatitis that are introduced into their bodies and wounds acquired through surgeries that never healed).[15]

A growing number of advocates and scientists are pressing for legislature to ban the use of apes in biomedical research. However, primate and other animal experimentation remains the backbone of scientific and medical inquiry.[16] Thousands upon thousands of nonhuman primates are imported annually from their native lands, and countless more mice, cats, dogs, and other animals are routinely subjected to brutalities. Even as we move into the so-called Age of Compassion, where scientific revelations about ape and other animals' sensibilities are now acknowledged, nonhuman species remain vulnerable to researchers' insatiable curiosity. For example, an article on ape grief research reports, "when the keepers realised that Pansy [a chimpanzee in captivity]—who was thought to have been in her sixties —was close to death, they gave her painkillers and filmed the group."[17] It is unclear whether the administered painkillers were deliberately used to facilitate filming as the news report seems to imply. However, the privacy and respect for nonhuman animals is forfeited to science and human "right to sight".[18]

An entire field of research has developed to counter the depauperate existence of zoo and laboratory animals. Ameliorative measures include improving climatic conditions and providing species-specific nutrition and socialization with conspecifics.[19] "Enrichment" cannot come close to replacing free-ranging life: captivity remains the key factor undermining well-being. Within these constraints, Savage-Rumbaugh and others have sought to make captive life as fulfilling and healthful as possible. However, most welfare assessments of captive life fall woefully short because, the authors of *Welfare of Apes* argue, "humans view apes as mentally limited, some current captive environments may appear idyllic while offering only an illusion of appropriate care, derived from a simplistic view of what apes are, rather than what they might be."[20] As a consequence, the majority of zoos and other captive settings resemble

> a manufactured "happy ape world," based on a false dichotomy between humans and apes—akin to saying that a human prison would be a wonderful place if it simply provided prisoners with bedspreads, televisions, and beer. This illusion results from a peculiarly science-derived Western view of what apes ought to be, rather than what they might have the potential to be. The illusion is one we wish to maintain, because it conceals more difficult and deeper truths.[21]

In the paper's introduction, the authors point out that "humans rarely—if ever—directly assess the preferences of the apes for any of these enrichments." One of the main purposes of the *JAAWS* paper was to obtain insights from the bonobos themselves to define elements essential for psychological wellbeing. Using the fruits of language acquisition and psychological research, Savage-Rumbaugh and the Wamba co-authors collaborated to develop recommendations on how to improve the quality of captive ape life.

Including nonhuman animals as co-authors is not unique, but the *JAAWS* article was the first to openly declare its mixed-species authorship.[22] Was bonobo co-authorship legitimate by scientific standards? A survey conducted to assess criteria for publishing and authorship standards in academic journals (e.g., National Institute of Health, National Academy of Science, American Physical Society) shows that a person legitimately qualifies for authorship if they have "made significant contributions," own "a stake in the product," and/ or if they have "made [a] substantive creative contribution to the generation of an intellectual product." If so, they "are entitled to be listed as authors of that product."[23]

Savage-Rumbaugh's publications demonstrate that *Pan/Homo* bonobos are able to comprehend and communicate at levels required for conducting research by scientific standards. The bonobo researchers communicate with human beings with sufficient sophistication to convey their "own views regarding their welfare." The bonobos of the *Pan/Homo* group have unique communicative abilities in

> that three of them are able to comprehend and respond to complex linguistic narration and questioning in a free-flowing

manner on essentially any topic connected meaningfully to their
lives. It is thus possible to ask for, and receive, their feedback on
many aspects of their environment, whether social, physical,
psychological, or cultural.[24]

The topic of the research and article is ape welfare, specifically the
wellbeing of the co-authors themselves: a subject of which they clearly
have unique expertise and knowledge. The bonobos also have a "stake"
in the product. Without their participation, there would be no data,
no source of information from which to base the study, and no
manuscript. Consequently, the bonobos fulfill authorship criteria set
by American science institutions. In keeping with publishing standards,
the *JAAWS* author order was based on level of contribution and
seniority.

While some scientists were skeptical, arguments objecting to
mixed-species authorship ring hollow. If, as Savage-Rumbaugh points
out, "the participation of human beings had been equal to that of the
bonobos, "no one would object to the sharing of authorship. It
therefore seems proper to recognize not only the bonobos' contribution
to this article but also their right to have a legitimate voice—their own
voice—in determining the adequacy of the environments in which they
reside."[25]

This belief echoes sentiments of others who have spoken on behalf
of those oppressed and silenced by a prejudiced collective. Liberation
psychologist Ignatio Martín-Baró maintained that to serve the minds
and hearts of people, it is necessary to understand them from their own
points of view, not from an enforced group standard. It is necessary, he
argued, for researchers "to redesign our theoretical and practical tools.
. . from the standpoint of the lives of [these] people: from their
sufferings, their aspirations, and their struggles."[26] Sue Savage-
Rumbaugh puts this view into practice. She insists that creating
conditions to meet the needs of bonobos requires expertise not from
an enforced group standard (human) but from the people themselves
(bonobos).

> Why rely solely on the judgments of human beings when one
> can ask the apes for their own opinions?. . .The bonobos have
> contributed directly, through conversation, to important aspects
> of this work. Their listing as authors is not a literary technique
> but a recognition of their direct verbal input to the article. They

are not able to write, but they are able to speak, to use lexigrams, and to answer questions.[27]

Through this process, the *Pan/Homo* bonobos were not only able to provide input, but critique study results and inferred conclusions: they were able to "defend" and explain study results. The bonobos were capable of communicating with Savage-Rumbaugh to "review all drafts of manuscripts for accuracy/fidelity and. . . indicate agreement [or dissent] before a draft [was] moved forward to publication."[28] As senior author, Savage-Rumbaugh consulted with her co-authors before, during, and after the process.

One of the study's most critical findings was the final table that enumerated the items that the *Pan* bonobos need for healthful and respectful life in captivity, the "Items the Bonobos Agreed Were Important for Their Welfare" (Table 1).[29]

Savage-Rumbaugh began the study investigation by listing

> the things I have come to believe are important to these bonobos and to solicit their views regarding my thoughts. After I formulated a list of the items that I believed have been paramount to their self-actualization, I presented my ideas, in simpler terms, to Kanzi, Panbanisha, and Nyota to determine if they agreed.[30]

While there was considerable agreement between Savage-Rumbaugh and the co-authors on welfare criteria, there were also differences: not all of the human researcher's suggestions were "met with agreement."

> Although it is true that I chose the items listed as critical to the welfare of these bonobos and facilitated the discussion of these particular items, I did not create this list arbitrarily. These items represent a distillation of the things that these bonobos have requested repeatedly during my decades of research with them. When I meet these requests, as best I can, new and unexpected competencies emerge in this group; many still are not documented in sufficient detail.[31]

Interestingly, the method used in the study was participatory action research (PAR) where study objectives, process, and outcome are designed to be informed by and benefit all participants.[32] PAR's transparency and lack of epistemic hierarchy in the research process effectively dissolves the line between investigator and subject through a dynamic process of co-participation and shared authority. Its purpose, therefore, is to make explicit what is usually implicit, and often denied: the influence of the researchers' own projections and bias.

In this instance, a PAR approach was used to engage and investigate the bicultural experience of the *Pan/Homo* community to determine what the bonobos considered essential to their welfare. Instead of the conventional animals-as-object framing, the *Pan/Homo* community participated simultaneously as objects and subjects. The resultant publication distilled research findings in English to communicate to a broad readership of scientists and policymakers who are not bilingual in bonobo nor *Pan/Homo* lexigram English. In summary, then, the study proved that the *Pan* bonobos scholarship met standards required for humans. As published authors in a peer-reviewed journal, the bonobos are now officially members of science academy.

THE MIND BENEATH THE SKULL AND SKIN

Having had a brief encounter with the *Pan/Homo* community, we might ask: who are they? *Pan* and *Homo* are distinct on the outside, but what about inside, beneath the skull beneath the skin? Conventionally, the form and nature of the mind is not as readily accessible as the body; nor is it sufficient to evaluate and categorize by external expression alone.

> A group's language embodies the unconscious background of common understanding on which the rest of the culture rides. This unconscious background is the unspoken and unencoded way of being human, of creating meaning, and of signaling intention that allows information to flow between accepted members of the group.[33]

Language and mind fly seamlessly across borders. The collaborative *Pan/Homo* science demonstrates "*language and personhood are simply not coincident with the human form.*" We can grasp some sense of this fluidity of mind and consciousness when viewed through the lens of developmental neuropsychology and the sense of selves that the *Pan/Homo* bonobos express.

First, we need to appreciate the psychological diversity within the *Pan/Homo* community. While the members "have all grown up in a bicultural group consisting of humans and bonobos of varied ages and sexes. . . [who] have acquired human language and stone tool manufacturing skills and who tangibly live in a cultural setting encompassing all age/sex classes", there are significant, individual differences.

Bicultural implies competency in two cultures, here, bonobo and human. However, there are variations within the *Pan/Homo* group. For example, Matata, Kanzi, and Nyota belong genetically and morphologically to the same species, but they have distinct histories and childhood experiences. Unlike their wild counterparts who have been reared in a shared complex of interactions and experiences, the *Pan/Homo* members have come together by force of circumstances.

Matata was wild-born in 1970 and lived in bonobo society in Zaire until the age of five. She was then brought with four other bonobos to the Yerkes "field station" at Emory University. Two of Matata's children, who were born into captivity, were taken away from her and reside in zoos. Her son Akili is now 30 years old and living at the San Diego Zoo; and her daughter, AnaNeema, is eighteen and living in the Milwaukee Zoo. Matata took Kanzi as her own only a few hours after his birth; she is his adoptive mother.

Kanzi was born to two bonobos, Lorel (now 41 years old and living in the Jacksonville, Florida, Zoo) and Bosandjo, in captivity at Yerkes. Kanzi attended over 30,000 "language trials" with Matata. Such early exposure to English and lexigram lessons are considered to be, at least in part, responsible for his linguistics talents. Nyota is Matata's grandson, being the progeny of Matata's daughter, Panbanisha. Matata, Kanzi, and Nyota are all bicultural by definition, but in different degrees and ways.[34] In contrast to Kanzi, a "second generation" bicultural bonobo, and Matata who is wild-born, Nyota is "a third generation" bonobo reared in a bicultural environment.

In theory, in a bicultural setting marked by two sets of culturally normative psychologies, behaviors, and languages, an individual's sense of self and competence will reflect both contexts. However, because Matata, Kanzi, and Nyota each came to bicultural living in different ways, we would expect that they each have his/her own "brand" of biculturalism. Matata spent her formative years learning free-ranging bonobo language and culture and came to human, captive living as someone who was shaped by and identified with her species culture of origin. For example, Savage-Rumbaugh observes that there are some

Photo courtesy of Sue Savage-Rumbaugh

concepts that captive-born Kanzi does not share with his adoptive-mother Matata because they do not have meaning in her cultural world. The sentence "No, you cannot use that ball, it is Kanzi's" may have meaning and use in captive-born *Pan* culture, but not for the immigrant bonobo society where the individualized "I" is absorbed into an inclusive "we".

Matata's "I", cultivated in the free-ranging bonobo troop of the Congo, is not the same notion of "I" as mine or perhaps yours is, since ours have been honed by modernity's dualist traditions and the split world of St. Augustine. When Matata speaks, she speaks of "we", reflecting a concept of self found in collective, interdependent societies like those in free-ranging bonobo groups, in contrast to the individualistic, independent, "I" centered culture of modern, western humans.[35] Nor is Matata's sense of self identical to that of Kanzi or Nyota whose minds developed straddling bonobo and human cultures of varying degrees of biculturalism.

Kanzi, while raised by Matata, was immersed in a *Pan/Homo* environment. He learned *Pan/Homo* language and customs by being reared by Matata (an "immigrant" bonobo), while ensconced in the customs and language of English and lexigram-speaking humans and "languaged" bonobos, some of whom were born in captivity. Nyota's "brand" of biculturism is different from that of both Matata and Kanzi. His mother, Panbanisha, was born in captivity. Unlike Panbanisha, who was raised by a mother (Matata) who came from "the old country", Nyota was raised by a mother who had been born in a captive setting. We may consider Kanzi and Nyota similar to *nisei* (second generation) and *sansei* (third generation), respectively.

These differences are not superficial. As several lines of neuropsychological research document, different developmental contexts correlate with different social psychologies and underlying neural substrates.[36] Because mammalians and altricial bird neuropsychological development is highly sensitive to experience and reflective of environmental input and change, variations in the developmental context will have an effect on a child's evolving neuroendocrinal pathways; early development is a, if not the, formative process that shapes individual psychophysiology and sense of self.[37] The individuating self is defined by an attendant interdependency and ethical contract that distinguishes individuation from individuality, an individuality that varies with culture.[38] Subsequently, cultural context and attachment styles sculpt self-identity and explain generational differences in behavior, social psychology, and identity as observed in the *Pan/Homo* community.[39] Such cross-generational variations are observed in the *Pan/Homo* community.

> The inspiring result of this research is that the bicultural rearing is producing cross-generational epigenetic effects upon the bonobos and the humans at a very rapid rate. Both species are both co-evolving toward new kind of understanding of each other, which is being revealed in the second generations of both species, and both species are also experiencing small biological changes. There is arising an enlightened understanding, and a greatly increased ability to communicate across the species boundary in each succeeding generation. Both species are benefiting, with each beginning to draw upon the best traits of the other in succeeding generations. These changes are not occurring through sexual transmission, but rather through cultural transmission. We believe this to be through epigenetic markers, as well as 'learning.' Thus a new window is opening into the nature of the process of change across time.[40]

In a simple schema, the three individuals' sense of self and psychology fall along a bicultural continuum.[41] Each conforms to biculturism having competence in both bonobo and human cultures but in slightly different ways.

On the outside, all bonobos may look the same, at least to unschooled human eyes, yet underneath and in action and habit, there are nuanced social psychological differences that derive from distinct developmental experiences. Subsequently, the answer to the question "who are these apes?" lies less in realm of species classifications than it does with understanding the individual. The genetic human who has spent more than half her lifetime with bonobos, and bonobos who have lived most to all of their lives with humans, perhaps have more in common with each other than they do their *ex situ* conspecific counterparts. Brain, behavior, and psyche show that culture, language, and identity extend beyond the discrete boxes of "human" and "bonobo". Given this perspective of animal identity, we might ask: if the "other" is now "us", then who are "we"?

IF YOU PRICK US, DO WE NOT BLEED?

Perhaps it comes as no surprise that the list of welfare rights created by the bonobos resembles many human Bills of Rights. While phraseology differs somewhat, there is remarkable overlap. Human Bills of Rights such as that created in post-apartheid South Africa[42] include more details concerning the structures of modern human culture and government, but at heart what the *Pan/Homo* bonobos understand as fundamental unalienable rights finds its equivalent among humans (Table 1). Both bonobo and human crave to live and love in the fullness of life.

However, Savage-Rumbaugh is quick to point out that the lists of rights created by the bonobos pertain specifically to those individuals of the *Pan/Homo* community. Their needs and desires are reflective of personal histories and the specific environment in which they live.

> Human beings can (and do) create vastly different cultures, and
> individuals within human societies develop extraordinarily
> different ranges of ability. Bonobos are equally diverse. Therefore,
> the conclusions that arise from my direct experiences with these

TABLE 1: Comparison Between *Pan/Homo* Bonobo Rights[48] and Human Rights[49]

Bonobo Rights	Human Rights
1. Having food that is fresh and of their choice.	Having an environment that is not harmful to health or well-being.
2. Traveling from place to place.	The right to freedom of movement.
3. Going to places they have never been before.	The right to leave the state, to enter, to remain in and to reside anywhere in the state.
4. Planning ways of maximizing travel and resource procurement.	Every citizen has the right to a passport.
5. Being able to leave and rejoin the group, to explore, and to share information regarding distant locations.	The right to form, join and maintain cultural, religious and linguistic associations and other organs of civil society. The right to access of information.
6. Being able to be apart from others for periods of time.	Persons belonging to a cultural, religious or linguistic community may not be denied the right, with other members of that community to enjoy their culture, or denied the ability to practice their religion and use their language, to form, join and maintain cultural, religious and linguistic associations and other organs of civil society.
7. Maintaining lifelong contact with individuals whom they love.	Have their environment protected for the benefit of present and future generations.
8. Transmitting their cultural knowledge to their offspring.	The right to use the language and to participate in the cultural life of their choice and to receive education in the official language or languages of their choice. Persons belonging to a cultural, religious or linguistic community may not be denied the right to enjoy their culture, practice their religion and use their language.
9. Developing and fulfilling a unique role in the social group.	The right of freedom of expression.
10. Experiencing the judgment of their peers regarding their capacity to fulfill their roles, for the good of the group.	The right to choose their trade, occupation or profession freely.
11. Living free from the fear of human beings attacking them.	The right to freedom and security of the person and be free from all forms of violence from either public or private sources.
12. Receiving recognition, from the humans who keep them in captivity, of their level of linguistic competency and their ability to self-determine and self-express through language.	Everyone has inherent dignity and the right to have their dignity respected and protected.

Photo courtesy of Sue Savage-Rumbaugh

particular bonobos may or may not apply to other groups of apes
or even to other groups of bonobos.[43]

Categories of wild and domestication/captivity do not conform to
the continuum described in neuropsychology and the *Pan/Homo*
experience. Rigid dualities do not match current scientific
understanding. They fail to capture the complexity, fluidity, and
critically, *continuity* of mind represented by the diversity of
environments in which humans and other animals live. As Martin
Luther King, Jr. advised, there is greater accuracy in judging another
by the content of his/her character rather than by skin color or other
physical features. With this in mind, animals who must live in captivity

> need more self-agency and they need to be better understood
> by human beings. If they could advance to the point where they
> could interact with other human beings as easily as I interact with
> them, they would be allotted many privileges and the barriers of
> captivity would begin to melt away. This is possible, and if the
> *Pan/Homo* culture is continued for a few more generations it will

happen. Not that they will be 'planet of the apes' but we will begin to understand their language and then more people will be able to have direct interaction because they will be able to communicate. Then bonobos, at least, will not seem unpredictable. They are already becoming increasingly able to live with human social conventions.[44]

Recognition and support of animal agency simultaneously involves deconstruction of implicit human dominance and authority. The fact that another species is capable of learning complex concepts in the medium of human language means that humans can no longer claim linguistic or even epistemic authority. Such emancipation from speciesism leads to epistemic and linguistic democracy that, in turn, brings us to the unquestionable conclusion that all apes, human and nonhuman, deserve comparable rights.[45] To create new ethics, culture, and language, humanity is compelled to find alternative, inclusive ways of knowing and communicating. The past, Cartesian

need for an absolute reality, so precious to objective science, now must evaporate in favor of more participatory, probabilistic, and holistic experiential patterns whose characteristics are represented and analyzed by the same minds who experience them and, in this sense, create them.[46]

Bicultural minds need bicultural ways of talking and living.

In Closing

What Ms. Menchú says about her people (see quote at the beginning of this article) might well be said by, and about, bonobos. Great apes have also suffered genocide, loss of homeland, and live scattered throughout the world on the brink of physical and cultural extinction.[47] A similarity of circumstance and mind leaves great apes and human refugees faced with common issues. In the wake of violent upheavals, indigenous human and nonhuman ape communities are on an uncertain journey to recovery. Both sets of cultures are challenged to forge identities that favor survival under conditions significantly changed from historical times.

In this light, conservation expands from a paradigm devoted to species and habitat preservation to one dedicated to great ape self-determination for those who live in captivity never to return to their countries or origin, and those who live in their country of origin but live and are pressed to survive in human-dominated lands. Both require a bicultural, or even multi-cultural, framing that supports the reality in which these individuals are evolving. The *Pan/Homo* community is also endangered. Without continued funding support, the *Pan* family will likely be dispersed to separate captive facilities as will the *Homo*

Photo courtesy of Sue Savage-Rumbaugh

members, and the delicate fabric of the *Pan/Homo* mind will be torn asunder.

Finally, not only are the ways in which we humans perceive bonobos and other species fundamentally altered, but so is that of our own identity. What we learn from the Iowan apes, *Homo* and *Pan*, illustrates how humanity can transform from an agent of destruction to one of restoration and revitalization of animal minds and societies. The *Pan/Homo* community provides one example of how our historical role as social engineers, pushing animals around the planet like so many chess pieces, can change to partnership with other species to achieve mutual self-determination. Elsewhere, there are those who live beyond difference. Calvin Luther Martin speak of his own encounter, when a

> Yup'ik Eskimo handed me a scrap of paper whereon was penciled, *"I am a Puffin!"*. . . Here was a man who effortlessly negotiated the porous, wafer-thin membrane separating Homo from the Other. "I am a puffin," he repeated softly yet firmly, "from my ancestral tree and in blood." Still alive. Neither museum artifact nor ethnographic data point. Standing before me. The flawless sheet of glass. Symmetrical, convergent consciousness: the world before the mind that thought in conversation with the earth, cracked, shattered into the mind that now observed the earth. *Cogito ergo sum* distills it in purest, crystalline form. . . *Puffin is, therefore I am,* he told me that wintry afternoon.[50]

We, Puffin, We Matata, We bonobo, We human, We one.

ACKNOWLEDGMENTS

The author would like to thank O. Mein Gans for inspiring and supporting this work, Sue Savage-Rumbaugh, Matata Wamba, Kanzi Wamba, and Nyota Wamba for their time and insights, and Kenneth Shapiro, Vera Muller-Paisner, and David Lavigne for reviews on earlier versions of the manuscript.

NOTES

1. Linda Buzzell and Craig Chalquist, *Ecotherapy: Healing with Nature in Mind* (San Francisco: Sierra Club, 2009).

2. G.A. Bradshaw & Robert M. Sapolsky (2006), "Mirror, Mirror", *American Scientist* 94(6), 487-489.

3. Sue Savage-Rumbaugh and Roger Lewin, *Kanzi: Ape at the Brink of the Human Mind* (Malden, MA: Wiley, 1996), p. 280.

4. Sue Savage-Rumbaugh, Kanzi Wamba, Panbanisha Wamba and Nyota Wamba, "Welfare of Apes in Captive Environments: Comments on, and by, A Specific Group of Apes," *Journal of Applied Animal Welfare*, 10(1), 7–19; p. 15.

5. G.A. Bradshaw (2010) "You see me, but do you hear me? The science and sensibility of trans-species dialogue," *Feminism & Psychology* (in press).

6. Kanzi, NHK Documentary, http://kanzi.bvu.edu/Kanzi301.html; Kanzi Understands Spoken Language, http://www.greatapetrust.org/video/av16c.htm.

7. Kenneth J. Shapiro, *Animals Models of Human Psychology* (Cambridge, MA: Hogrefe & Huber Publishing, 1998).

8. Alexander Fiske-Harrison, "Talking with Apes," *Financial Times*, Weekend section, November 24-25, 2001.

9. Sue Savage-Rumbaugh, personal communication, May 4, 2010.

10. Barbara King, *Evolving God: A Provocative View on the Origins of Religion* (New York: Doubleday Religion, 2007).

11. Savage-Rumbaugh, Wamba, Wamba, and Wamba, "Welfare of Apes."

12. *Ibid.*

13. See Project Release and Restitution for Chimpanzees in U.S. Laboratories,http://www.releasechimps.org/harm-suffering/chimpanzee-lab-life/.

14. Fauna Foundation, www.faunafoundation.org.

15. G.A. Bradshaw, Theodora Capaldo, Gloria Grow, Lorin Lindner (2008), "Building an inner sanctuary: trauma-induced symptoms in non-human great apes," *Journal of Trauma and Dissociation*, 9(1): p. 9-34.

16. Shapiro, *Animal Models*.

17. David Derbyshire, "How caring chimps mourn the death of a loved one just like humans," *Daily Mail,* http://www.dailymail.co.uk/sciencetech/article-1268959/Why-caring-chimps-mourn-death-loved-just-like-humans.html, retrieved April 30, 2010; James. R. Anderson and Louise C. Lock, "PanThantology," *Current Biology, 20(8),* R349-350, 2010.

18. "Wildlife TV Ignores Animal Rights," *Belfast Telegraph.* http://www.animalconcerns.org/external.html?www=http%3A//www.belfasttelegraph.co.uk/breaking-news/offbeat/wildlife-tv-ignores-animal-rights-14788226.html&itemid=201004300744430.923381, retrieved April 30. 2010; G.A. Bradshaw, B. Smuts, D. Durham, "Open Door Policy: The necessary relinquishment of humanity's "right to sight"," in R. Acampora (ed.), *Metamorphoses of the Zoo: Animal Encounter After Noah* (Lanham, MA: Rowman & Littlefield Publishers, 2010).

19. See for example, E.L. Roder & P.J.A. Timmermans, "Housing and care of monkeys and apes in laboratories: adaptations allowing essential species-specific behaviour," *Laboratory Animals* (2002) 36, 221–242.

20. Savage-Rumbaugh, Wamba, Wamba, and Wamba, "Welfare of Apes," p. 8.

21. Savage-Rumbaugh, Wamba, Wamba, and Wamba, "Welfare of Apes," p. 8.

22. Paul K. Dayton, M.J. Mordida, F. Bacon, "Polar Marine Communities," *American Zoologist* 34(1):90-99, 1994. (F. Bacon is a pig, Francis Bacon, living with the senior author.)

23. Jason W. Osborne and Abigail Holland, "Best Practices in Authorship," *Practical Assessment, Research & Evaluation*, 14 (15), p. 6.

24. Savage-Rumbaugh, Wamba, Wamba, and Wamba, "Welfare of Apes," p. 17.

25. *Ibid.*, p. 17.

26. Ignacio Martín-Baró, *Writings for a Liberation Psychology*, ed. A. Aron and S. Corne (Cambridge: Harvard University Press, 1994), p. 25.

27. Savage-Rumbaugh, Wamba, Wamba, and Wamba, "Welfare of Apes," p. 17.

28. Osborne and Holland, "Best Practices."

29. "Table 2: Items the Bonobos Agreed Were Important for Their Welfare," in Savage-Rumbaugh, Wamba, Wamba, and Wamba, "Welfare of Apes," p. 18.

30. *Ibid.*, p. 17.

31. *Ibid.*, p. 18.

32. See for example, S. Kemmis and R. McTaggart, "Participatory action research," in N.K. Denzin & Y.S. Lincoln (eds.), *Handbook of Qualitative Research*, 2nd ed. (Thousand Oaks, CA: Sage, 2000), pp. 567–605.

33. Savage-Rumbaugh, Wamba, Wamba, and Wamba, "Welfare of Apes," p. 16.

34. Great Ape Trust, http://www.greatapetrust.org/.

35. Patricia Greenfield, H. Keller, A. Fugligni, & A. Maynard "Cultural pathways through universal development," *Annual Review of Psychology*, 54, 461–490. 2003.

36. M.J. Meaney, "Maternal care, gene expression, and the transmission of individual differences in stress reactivity across generations," *Ann. Rev. Neurosci.* 24, 1161-1192, 2001.

37. Allan N. Schore, "Attachment, Affect Regulation, and the Developing Right Brain: Linking Developmental Neuroscience to Pediatrics," *Pediatrics in Review* 26(6): 204-17, 2005.

38. C.G. Jung, *Conscious, unconscious, and individuation*, R. F. C. Hull (trans.), *The Collected works of C. G. Jung* (Vol. 9i). Princeton, NJ: Princeton University Press. (Original work published 1939).

39. G.A. Bradshaw, Theodora Capaldo, Gloria Grow, Lorin Lindner (2009), "Developmental context effects on bicultural Post-Trauma Self Repair in Chimpanzees," *Developmental Psychology,* 45: 5,1376-1388.

40. Sue Savage-Rumbaugh, personal communication, May 4, 2010.

41. G.A. Bradshaw *et al.*, "Developmental context effects."

42. See for example, South African Government Information: Chapter 2, Bill of Rights. *http://www.info.gov.za/documents/constitution/1996/96cons2.htm,* retrieved April 24, 2010.

43. Savage-Rumbaugh, Wamba, Wamba, and Wamba, "Welfare of Apes," p. 14.

44. Sue Savage-Rumbaugh, personal communication, May 4, 2010.

45. Steven M. Wise, *Rattling the Cage: Toward Legal Rights for Animals* (Cambridge. MA: Perseus, 2000).

46. R.G. Jahn, R.G., & B.J. Dunne, "Science of the subjective," *Journal of Science Exploration, 11*, 201-224. 1997.

47. "Reaching Across the Species Barrier: Jane Goodall on Chimpanzees," http://arts.envirolink.org/interviews_and_conversations/JaneGoodall.html.

48. "Table 2: Items the Bonobos Agreed Were Important for Their Welfare," in Savage-Rumbaugh, Wamba, Wamba, and Wamba, "Welfare of Apes," p. 18.

49. After South African Government Information: Chapter 2, Bill of Rights, http://www.info.gov.za/documents/constitution/1996/96cons2.htm, retrieved April 24, 2010.

50. Calvin Luther Martin, Foreword in G.A. Bradshaw, *Elephants on the Edge: What Animals Teach Us About Humanity* (Yale University Press, 2009).

Harbingers of (Silent) Spring: Archetypal Avians, Avian Archetypes and the Truly Collective Unconscious

Pattrice Jones

Laid low by sorrow, I crouched in the dust, gathering strength against grief at midday. Suddenly, I saw a flurry of feathers and felt a wobbly weight on my shoulder. The ungainly white bird swayed to maintain his balance while peering at me inquisitively. "Yes," I said, "I do need a friend right now." We swayed together for a moment, regarding each other and the day. Then, he alit and I went into the afternoon, soothed.

While the helpful bird is a well-traveled inhabitant of the lands of mythology and reverie,[1] that was no dream and that bird no mere symbol. The dust was that of a foraging yard at the Eastern Shore Sanctuary where, for nine years, I offered shelter and care to avian survivors of factory farming and cockfighting. The bird

pattrice jones co-founded the Eastern Shore Sanctuary and Education Center of Maryland (now relocated to rural Vermont), where she created a program for the rehabilitation of former fighting roosters and offered refuge to both wild and domesticated birds. She teaches psychology at Minneapolis Community & Technical College and gender studies at Metropolitan State University, and is the author of *Aftershock*, an analysis of trauma and recovery from an ecofeminist perspective.

was a juvenile "broiler" chicken who had leapt or fallen from a slaughterhouse-bound transport truck and had arrived at the sanctuary only the week before. I no longer remember the specific source of the seemingly unsupportable grief that weakened me that day, but I will never forget the young rooster who so intrepidly leapt to comfort me. I called him "Heartbeat," and he was my little friend.

Birds' hearts beat more rapidly when they are afraid. Eyes narrow. Muscles twitch. In the midst of a full-fledged fight or flight response, a bird unable to escape a perceived threat may begin to pant in panic. We know this fear. We've felt it ourselves. Terror jolts through our limbic system like lightning, just as it does through theirs.

Full-fledged. Fight or *flight*. Our long associations with birds of all kinds linger in our language as allusions and figures of speech. Our earliest alphabets and pictograms used birds to depict sounds and concepts.[2] Birds dwell at every level of our collective unconscious as well. But the beating hearts and wings of birds are not symbols. Birds feel real fear, real joy, real hope and disappointment and, probably, other real feelings, the nuances of which we may not be able to imagine.

The question then becomes: Has our long-standing use of birds as psychological symbols facilitated our ever-escalating appropriation and abuse of their bodies? And, given how deeply our fantasies about birds permeate our *own* psyches, is it even possible for us to conceive what life feels like to them? Thus, before we can begin to think about bird psyches, we must first alert ourselves to the birds fluttering in our own psyches. Put another way, before we can think clearly about birds' brains, we must think critically about "birdbrain" and other derogatory notions.

In the days following our encouraging encounter, I got into the habit of calling "Heartbeat! Heartbeat! Where's my little friend?" whenever I went into the yards to refill water basins, replenish feed bowls, or put fresh straw in the coops. He always came running to greet me, charging enthusiastically from the underbrush.

The so-called "broiler" chickens raised for meat in factory farms across the globe spend their short lives in otherwise empty sheds, shoulder to shoulder with thousands of others of the same age and sex. They never nestle under their mothers' wings nor ever spread their own feathers in the sun. Bred to grow unnaturally large unnaturally quickly, the young birds are trucked to slaughter when only about eight weeks old. Human avarice for chicken flesh is now such that billions of birds suffer this foreshortened and impoverished life cycle terminated by a terrifying death shackled upside-down to a slaughter machine.

Every one of those birds is an individual. Despite their genetic similarity and the social and environmental poverty of their early lives, birds lucky enough to escape the whirring blades of the poultry processing factory vary markedly in habits and personality. Some are shy, others sociable. Some are timid, others bold. Some are high-strung, others easy-going. Some are quick-witted, others dull. Some are curious, seizing every opportunity to try new things; others hang back, waiting for somebody else to be the first to venture into new territory or try new food.

Not long after Heartbeat's arrival at the sanctuary, a young hen I would come to call "Octagon" appeared in our driveway. Though shaken and bruised from her own fall from a transport truck, she wasn't so injured as to require isolation in the infirmary. Still, I hesitated to leave her to fend for herself in the foraging yard. What she needed was a friend. A-ha! "Heartbeat! Heartbeat! Where's my little friend?" Heartbeat came running but stopped short at the sight of the battered little hen. He circled her slowly, peering closely at each bruise and scrape. Then he sidled next to her until their wings were touching and lowered himself to the ground while making the sound that mother hens use to soothe their chicks. Octagon sighed, the tension leaving her body with her breath, and settled down beside him. I stood, stunned by the empathy and generosity displayed by a young bird who had known little but suffering in his own short life.

During its nine years in rural Maryland, the Eastern Shore Sanctuary[3] provided refuge to poultry industry and cockfighting survivors and offered habitat to ground- and tree-nesting wild birds such as woodcocks and cowbirds, while also serving as a home-base for evolving flocks of feral chickens who had "rewilded" themselves, eschewing domestic life to live among the wild birds, foraging widely during the day and roosting at night in tree-branches. For many years, chickens and other birds have been subjects of both naturalistic observation and scientific experimentation. Hence, there are extensive data about their brains, minds, and bodies in the literature of psychology, ethology, and neurobiology. The ideas here integrate that data with my own conclusions based on years of observation of and interaction with both psychologically healthy and severely traumatized birds.

Speaking of Birds...

Birds express themselves fluently through motion and sound. Language is one of the capabilities human beings like to reserve for ourselves, forever narrowing what we mean by "language" as one or another non-human animal proves capable of manipulating sounds as communicative symbols. However, the fact remains that birds communicate with one another and, as the need arises, with members of other species quite adequately and often complexly. As we do, birds use sounds as symbols. Among chickens, for example, the alarm cry for an aerial predator is distinct from the sound that symbolizes a threat on the ground.[4] As we do, birds inflect sound symbols with emotion.[5] The alarm vocalizations of magpies vary in volume and intensity depending on the degree of perceived danger.[6] Again as we do, parrots, hummingbirds, and songbirds learn and use complex vocal sequences structured by syntax[7,8] and develop distinct regional dialects.[9]

But would it be possible for a skylark to sing something meaningful about our dreams? If not, how can we presume to speak about avian psyches?

Like birds, we use combinations of gesture and sound to convey meaning. Just as the communications of other animals are delimited by need and anatomy, human languages are shaped by the brain,[10] which evolved in interaction with ecosocial environments.[11] The word "unspeakable" notwithstanding, we tend to assume that human languages are capable of saying everything, of accurately symbolizing whatever anyone might like to express. Of course this is not true, as our frequent recourse to music, dance, and graphic arts demonstrates. More troubling is the tendency of language to shape perception and perhaps constrain thought. If my language tells me, as English does, that "corporal" is an antonym of "cerebral," I may find it hard to conceptualize cognition as a biological process. If common usage places "animal" on a different and decidedly lower plane than "human," I may have difficulty reconciling myself to my own animality and will almost certainly tend *not* to notice evidence of animal equality.

Speakers of different languages have different ways of conceptualizing such basic elements of life as space[12] and time.[13] Even people with words in common may struggle with more than semantic differences in the meanings of terms related to psyche. Conceptually and experientially, "self" is very different for people of collectivist versus individualist cultures, so much so that cross-cultural conversations about "self" can sometimes be confounding.[14] People from individualist cultures tend to conceive and experience each "self" as a unitary and discrete entity while people from collectivist cultures tend to conceive and experience selves as relational and overlapping; these different conceptions of "self" (and, therefore, "other") influence not only emotion and social cognition but also aspects of cognition, such as perception and inferential reasoning, that are often assumed to be culture-free.[15] If people from individualist cultures must struggle to grasp what the interaction between self and world feels like to a person from a collectivist culture, how much more difficult must it be to imagine what the interaction between self and world that we call "psyche" feels like to a bird? Thus, our ability to speak accurately of avian psyches must be considered dubious at best. Yet speak we must, because our existing ideas about birds and their brains have been and continue to be so hurtful to them.

FLIGHTS OF FANCY

We can't even imagine, those of us alive now, what it was like when the skies were black with birds. Reports filter down from the days before the triple trauma of hunting, smog, and DDT left us a world that our ancestors would find shockingly bereft of birds. I caught a glimpse of that past, a couple of times at the sanctuary, when migrating flocks descended, overflowing the trees and saturating the soundscape for just a few hours before bolting off again, my heart pounding crazily along with their departing wings. Now, living in a city after nine years at a bird sanctuary, I apprehend our collective loss acutely. The city sounds silent rather than noisy to me. Empty tree branches seem naked. The few birds I hear sound lonely. My heart leaps, then crashes, when I see a gamboling group of crows or a fluttering flock of morning doves.

Homo Sapiens emerged in a world full of birds. Those of us living under comparatively barren contemporary skies can only extrapolate from the historical record to imagine what it might have been like to coexist with birds before the combination of hunting, pollution, and deforestation emptied the airspace above us. As recently as the late 1800s, for example, billions of passenger pigeons in North America migrated in flocks a mile wide and hundreds of miles long, passing overhead for hours or days.[16] Wherever they rested, they filled the trees with movement and the air with sound.

That's just one kind of bird just over a century ago, long after firearms, smog, and tree-cutting had decimated many avian populations and driven others to extinction. Imagine, then, if you can, the degree to which bird bodies and bird song filled the perceptual fields of our hominid ancestors as they came out of the trees and into the grasslands, where the warning cries of songbirds alerted them to danger at the watering hole and the hovering of corvids directed them to potentially fruitful scavenging sites. In late winter, the return of migrating birds presaged the rebound of spring.

Our brain architecture, including the structures and pathways associated with archetypes, evolved in this context. We may be evolutionarily predisposed to see birds and think spring. Such associations are not inherently hurtful. An upsurge of birds often does mean that warmer weather is around the corner, just as the sight of the postal carrier rounding the corner often does mean that bills will soon be in the mailbox. But if we begin to associate the postal carrier —or, worse, people of his race—with the unpleasant sensation of receiving a demand for payment, our relations with people who look like him may begin to go awry. The key difference is between signal and symbol. When we recognize birds or mail carriers as signals, we see them clearly and accurately, noting the implications of their appearance or behavior for us within a shared ecosocial environment. When we use birds, other animals, or other people as symbols, we reduce them to objects to be manipulated in the realm of fantasy.

The fine line between archetype and stereotype is easily seen in the facility with which we project our feared and despised shadows onto people of other races and ethnicities.[17,18] The same process of projection can lead to abuses of birds and other animals. People around the world associate vultures with death and persecute them accordingly. While vultures are protected species in the United States, people made uneasy by their association with death feel free to blast them from treetops with shotguns, hanging their corpses from the trees as warnings to others.[19]

Bird protection ordinances date back at least to Deuteronomy,[20] evidence of both our sympathy for and lethality towards our feathered kin. Both bird watching and bird hunting remain popular sports.[21] These two opposite acts mirror opposite conceptions of birds dating back at least as far as we have evidence of human thought. Depictions of birds in rock art around the world illustrate both "a connexion between birds and death" and "an association between birds and reproduction."[22]

Birds populate the human psyche. Because birds spring so readily to mind, we reach for birds—both literally and metaphorically—to symbolize and enact our ideas. Armstrong's survey of birds in folklore and folk art demonstrates our propensity to use birds as symbols; in virtually every culture and place, birds show up in myths, rituals, song, and dance. Hybrid bird-human figures appear in art across the world from the paleolithic to the present, evidencing our urge to project ourselves onto or into birds. "The various forms of belief in which the human soul is thought to take the form of a bird, or persons are believed to become birds" are "ancient and widespread."[23] *Bird* then, is a potent and multivalent figure in the human psyche, so much so that it might be worthwhile to consider the possibility that *bird* is an archetype rather than a mere symbol of other archetypes.

People certainly do use birds to symbolize archetypal ideas, sometimes going so far as to trick or force actual birds to enact our conceptions. This is especially evident in the realm of gender. We see female chickens as "mother hens" and "dumb clucks," often treating them in ways that reduce them to their reproductive functions and foster the dull-wittedness and passivity attributed to femininity. For example, as will be detailed below, hens in egg factories are deprived of cognitive stimulation and subjected to unrelenting trauma likely to produce learned helplessness.

Roosters, on the other hand, are celebrated as exemplars of masculinity, so much so that the word for male chickens does double-duty as a term for the penis in several languages.[24] As I have detailed elsewhere, cockfighting bouts are human-engineered spectacles of stylized masculinity.[25] Roosters used in cockfighting grow up in isolation and frustration, confined in cages or tethered to stakes.

Prevented from learning the social signals by which roosters naturally resolve conflicts before they become deadly, fighting roosters are injected with testosterone and amphetamines, armed with steel knives lashed to their sawed-off spurs, and dropped into cacophonous combat rings from which the only escape is victory or death.[26] Proponents of cockfighting assert—and appear to sincerely believe—that the predictably deranged behavior of these unsocialized and terrified birds is both natural and emblematic of masculinity.[27]

These are paradigmatic examples of what I call the social construction of gender via animals.[28] Social constructs are collective ideas that seem to be natural facts. Fighting roosters and other animals serve as unwitting tools of the social construction of gender through a three-part process wherein people project their ideas about gender onto animals, force or trick animals into acting out those ideas, and then read the consequent animal behavior as evidence that masculinity and femininity are natural correlates of maleness and femaleness. Sometimes the second stage is finessed by "reading" natural animal behavior selectively, as when the primatologists of old "saw" male dominance among every variety of ape and monkey or when ethologists either didn't see or didn't record the same-sex sexual encounters we now know to be common among hundreds of species, including some 130 bird species.[29] The construction of birds as relentlessly heterosexual, mechanically fixated on reproduction, hinders our ability to see the spectrum of bird relationships and appreciate the degree to which relationships of all varieties are valuable to these social animals.

BIRDS AND BRAINS

Hence, before we can begin to speak of bird psyches, we must clear away ideas about birds that reflect our fantasies rather than their realities. These include not only ideas rooted in our use of birds as symbols but also our more general fantasy of cognitive or spiritual superiority over other animals. In recent decades, findings in ethology and neurobiology have consistently undermined the notion that there is some special skill or capacity exclusive to humans or that, indeed, there is any biological reason to elevate or even separate *Homo sapiens* from all other animals.[30] Language, tool making, self-awareness: each of these and many other imagined reasons for human singularity have fallen before the onslaught of data concerning animal capabilities and comparative anatomy.

This is not to say that humans are in no way unique. Every kind of animal is special in some way. Many animals possess capacities not shared by others. Giraffes can reach into the trees while standing on the ground. Whales send songs along miles of water. Bees use dance to convey precise navigational directions. Each of these is wondrous, as are many human abilities. But none stands as a reason to consider that animal as somehow apart from the rest of the natural world.

Birds not only use sound symbols and syntax to communicate as we do but also make and use tools. Like people, birds sometimes cooperate in the process of "cumulative technological evolution" by testing diverse designs, making cumulative changes to those designs, and dispersing new designs through social networks.[31] Birds have also demonstrated evidence of episodic memory and theory of mind, two other cognitive capacities previously believed to be confined to humans.[32]

While emotional congruences between birds and people may be traced to the limbic system and other shared structures,[33] complementary cognitive capacities are most likely the result of convergent evolution, with birds sometimes achieving similar ends by different neurological means.[34] For both birds and mammals, the development of warm-bloodedness after branching off from reptiles "enhanced the potency of neural functioning" just as "flexible behavior became the key" to fitness.[35] For both birds and mammals, the brain growth encouraged by this combination of possibility and necessity promoted further brain plasticity and behavioral flexibility:

> The divergent and complicated reproductive strategies of brooding and lactating emerged not least because of the need to release into independence offspring with brains too large to mature intrauterinely or intraovally.... These strategies demanded differential parental care behaviors, for which these same brains had to evolve new capabilities. The accompanying birth or hatching at an early stage of embryological development caused the brains of the offspring to be exposed at an immature stage to an environment to which they had to match their behavior. This undoubtedly enhanced the role of neural plasticity in the adjustment of the behavioral repertoire of both avians and

> mammals and advanced the development of brain structures
> specialized for learning and memory.... This eventually converted
> the ecological niches in which birds and mammals operated into
> socioecologial niches that encouraged the evolution of capabilities
> for highly flexible social behaviors.[36]

In short, both birds and people have brains that evolved in an ecological context favoring behavioral flexibility and the maintenance of social relationships, both of which require the cognitive capabilities we call intelligence. This raises the question of consciousness, the complement of which is unconscious cognition, including the processes known in depth psychology as the collective unconscious.

Edelman writes:

> Since Descartes' dualistic proposal, consciousness has been
> considered by many to be outside the reach of physics, or to
> require strange physics, or even to be beyond human analysis.
> Over the last decade, however, there has been a heightened
> interest in attacking the problem of consciousness through
> scientific investigation. To succeed, such a program must take
> account of what is special about consciousness while rejecting
> any extraphysical assumptions.[37]

The same may be said of the collective unconscious. "Consciousness is not a thing but rather, as William James pointed out, a process that emerges from interactions of the brain, the body, and the environment."[38] Like consciousness, the archetypes said to reside in the collective unconscious[39] are likely to be processes rather than structures. Furthermore, archetypes, like the various processes collectively called consciousness, are means by which the organism organizes and responds to complex stimuli, including both incoming sensations and remembered experiences.

Consciousness, which arises from "a continual interplay of signals from the environment, the body, and the brain itself... confers an evolutionary advantage on individuals possessing it, for, by these means, richly structured events can be related adaptively to the past history of value-dependent learning events in an individual animal."[40] Birds are among the animals who enjoy the evolutionary advantages of consciousness.[41,42,43,44]

In people, "consciousness is not a property of a single brain location or neuronal type, but rather is the result of dynamic interactions among widely distributed groups of neurons."[45] Similarly, consciousness in birds is likely to be "based on patterns of circuitry rather than on local architectural constraints."[46] However, "the neuroanatomical features of the forebrain common to both birds and mammals may be those that are crucial to the generation of both complex cognition and consciousness."[47] In other words, for both birds and people, consciousness is a widely distributed neurological process involving brain structures also associated with complex cognition.

Because of the constraints imposed by the relatively limited capacity of working memory, much of human cognition occurs below the threshold of consciousness. Given the parallels between human and avian brains, this is presumably true for birds as well. As unconscious schemas for recognizing and responding to salient patterns of external and internal stimulation, archetypes may be considered to be among the varieties of nonconscious cognition. Thus we can begin to see archetypes as natural processes likely to be shared by both birds and people. This has far-reaching implications for the concept of the collective unconscious.

ARCHETYPES, INSTINCTS, AND THE COLLECTIVE UNCONSCIOUS

As Stevens notes, "the Jungian approach to the body has been one of neglect,"[48] and this has tended to undercut the credibility of concepts like archetype and the collective unconscious outside of the field of depth psychology. In *Archetype Revisited: An Updated Natural History of the Self,* Stevens draws upon advances in neuropsychology to naturalize the concept of the archetype, thereby situating the collective unconscious within the nervous system.[49] Advances in comparative neurobiology allow us to go further than that, developing a more nuanced conception of archetypes as products of evolution and the collective unconscious as an ongoing and widely distributed interactive process.

Jung and subsequent depth psychologists hypothesized archetypes to be the human analogues of the instincts believed to determine animal behavior,[50] pointing specifically to the *innate releasing mechanisms* identified by Lorenz[51] and other ethologists as the avian equivalents of human archetypes. We now have a better understanding of biology, evolution, and ecology than was available to Jung or even early ethologists like Lorenz. We now know that the seemingly innate and immutable patterns of perception and behavior we call instincts are (a) often more flexible than was previously believed, and always (b) the result of generations of *interactions* between organisms and environments that (c) are *ongoing*.

The implications of this understanding of instinct are profound for the concept of archetype. If archetypes are kinds of instincts, then they too must be rooted in generations of interactions between organisms and environments. In other words, as products of evolution, archetypes reflect the material and social circumstances in which our species evolved and is still evolving. Given that interactions between genetic endowment and environment begin before birth and that social learning begins at birth, Jung may have over-estimated our capacity to distinguish between innate cognitive or perceptual propensities (archetypes) and their culturally influenced manifestations (symbols). Just as it is impossible to disaggregate nature and nurture when speaking of intelligence, athletic ability, or even height, it may not be possible to confidently abstract archetypes from the situations in which they are expressed.

Furthermore, if archetypes are innate templates for perception and response rooted in interactions between psyche and the material environment, there may be many more of them than Jung identified. (*Bird* being one example.) In the current context of ecological crisis, it may be especially useful for us to understand those archetypes (and their common manifestations) that are not about ourselves or other people but rather about animals or what we have come to call nature.

Evolution is slow but ongoing. Whatever "instinctual" animal behavior we may consider, be it nest-building or migration or response to predation, we find that:

> • The behavior evolved over the course of generations of interactions with environment.
> • The behavior is itself an interaction with environment.
> • Some environmental cue is generally needed to evoke the behavior.

• The tendency to engage in the behavior appears to be encoded in the genes and therefore can be said to reside within each animal's body.

• There is variation, across individuals, in how (and sometimes even whether) the behavior is performed; these variations may or may not affect the life chances of the individual or her offspring.

• Changes in environment may make the behavior, or particular variants of the behavior, more or less adaptive; over time, this may lead to changes in the "instinct" as observed in the population.

Consider migration. Already, we have seen change in this instinctive bird behavior as a result of global warming. Furthermore, these changes have been calibrated to place, with some birds hastening and others delaying departure dates.[52] Presumably, those birds displaying the most flexibility in their enactment of archetypal imperatives will have the most reproductive success, thereby continuing the evolutionary process by which birds developed the behavioral flexibility and brain plasticity associated with what we call intelligence.

Certainly, there is no evidence to suggest that our unconscious archetypes are more inflexible than the migration instinct. Thus, we must presume that archetypes are considerably less fixed than has been traditionally presumed within depth psychology. As our interactions with our ever-changing environments continue, our archetypes—like animal instincts—may change.

This way of understanding archetypes grounds psyche in the material not only in the sense of embodying mind but also in the sense of bringing the seemingly timeless back into history. Put another way, this way of looking at archetypes relocates them in place and time. Doing so may aid us in restoring humankind to a more realistic (and less dangerously estranged) relationship with place and time.

To do so, we will need a better understanding of the relational nature of the collective unconscious. Birds and mammals both are social animals. For both, the demands of sociality led to the evolution of emotional capacities such as empathy along with a wealth of intellectual capabilities. Social animals have social brains. Birds and people both are emotionally distressed and cognitively stunted by social isolation.

This is because our brains evolved both *within* and *for* relationships.

The concept of the collective unconscious takes on new dimensions considered in the light of evolutionary neuroscience. Rather than a mythic realm of mysterious and possibly supernatural phenomena, the collective unconscious now may be seen as, simply, the subset of nonconscious cognitive processes that are both emotionally valent and rooted in the collective ecosocial history of our species. Since our species shares evolutionary history with birds as well as other mammals, including but not limited to those with whom our ancestors participated in coevolution, some of those nonconscious processes may be presumed to be shared with other animals, including birds.

Thus the collective unconscious becomes a significantly more lively location. First, as a product of evolution, which is ongoing, the collective unconscious no longer need be seen as a static site of archaic inclinations. Next, because even the most rigidly instinctive processes are differentially enacted in complex interaction with evocative environments, we are better able to see cultural influences as intrinsic rather than extrinsic elements of the collective unconscious. Finally, we can begin to see birds and other animals as fellow participants in the ongoing collective process that is the collective unconscious. Since many of them are more skilled than we at collective cognition,[53] perhaps this is cause for celebration. Certainly, this way of conceiving the collective unconscious mandates more cooperative relations with our avian kin. This may prove useful to all. It was, after all, a process of collective cognition inspired in part by observation of birds that led Rachel Carson to the conclusions published in *Silent Spring*.[54]

AVIAN ARCHETYPES

Thinking of archetypes as instincts raises the possibility of thinking of instincts as archetypes, which might prove to be useful in understanding avian psyches. Certainly, birds do enact evidently instinctual patterns of perception and behavior, such as the alarmed Jackdaw response to anything resembling a predator carrying away a nestling.[55] And, indeed, these are the very phenomena to which some Jungian theorists have pointed as the nonhuman analogue of archetypes.[56] But let us go further than that, now that we know that birds are sentient, social, intelligent, and highly emotional beings who share many of the processes that we call psyche. As Bradshaw and Sapolsky note, "Historically, science has admitted inference from animals to humans but not the reverse,"[57] arguing that there is much to be learned from such a transposition. Analytic psychologists have considered how ethological concepts like *innate releasing mechanism* might apply to people; now, let's reverse the operation and consider how the psychological concept of *archetype* might apply to birds. Since birds have brains that function similarly to ours, cognitive repertoires that overlap ours, and are conscious as we are, then perhaps they are also unconscious as we are. In other words, perhaps their inherited patterns of perception and reaction function in the same manner as do ours. In short, perhaps archetypes are active in avian psyches. Jung himself did not discount this possibility, writing that "there is nothing to prevent us from assuming that certain archetypes exist even in animals, that they are grounded in the peculiarities of the living organism itself."[58]

If archetypes were active in bird psyches, what might those archetypes be? A tentative list springs immediately to mind: *mother, safe place, offspring, predator, competitor, flock, sibling/cousin/age-mate.* The archetype of *partner* seems likely for birds who form lasting pair-bonds. An archetype of *elder* might be functional for birds, like chickens, who are raised primarily by their mothers but who receive both instruction and protection from other adult flock members. *Father* might be an archetype for those birds for whom the biological father plays an active and distinct role in the life of the young; for those birds among whom mothers and fathers play the same role, cooperatively feeding and protecting their young, it might be that both are perceived as *mother* or, simply, *parent.* Similarly, the term *offspring* is as close as I can come in English for juveniles in need of nurturing, who may or may not be (in species where sisters help to raise their sibling's offspring, juveniles stay to help raise their siblings, or other forms of cooperative care are practiced) one's son or daughter.

Birds also appear to make use of an archetype I call *friend* and by which I mean a helpful or otherwise friendly animal of another species. Perhaps this originates in the kinds of mutual aid observed by Kropotkin[59] wherein, for example, animals of different kinds sharing a watering hole might warn one another of the approach of a predator. Many birds appear to regard any animal who has not been flagged as a potential predator as a potential friend. At the sanctuary, I witnessed roosters huddling with barn cats for warmth on many a winter day. One dog, called Dandelion, was particularly adept at smelling out eggs left behind by hens. One group of hens became her regular entourage, trailing along after her in hopes of snatching the eggshells (a good source of calcium) once she had slurped out their contents. And, of course, birds like Heartbeat routinely slotted me and other people at the sanctuary into their schema of helpful-other-animal. This is, perhaps, the avian complement of our longstanding image of the helpful bird.

Like most mammals, most birds are deeply dependent on *mother* for some significant period during which both brain and body are growing rapidly. Hence, for birds as for people, the match (or lack thereof) between archetypal and actual mothering is likely to have long-lasting repercussions. Here we begin to see the assault on avian psyches implicit in captivity. Chickens and other captive birds birthed in hatcheries awaken to the world under the chilly warmth of electric lights rather than within the soft darkness of their mothers' wings. Like Harlow's poor monkeys clinging to cloth dolls for contact comfort,[60] birds deprived of mothers scan their environments for anybody or anything that might offer a semblance of mothering.

Like orphaned children, orphaned birds may attach themselves to each other, inanimate objects, or members of other species. I have seen birds raised together on factory farms, where chicks from hatcheries grow to slaughter weight among thousands of other birds of the same age and sex, clumsily alternate in seeking shelter under one another's wings. When chicks found their way to the sanctuary directly from hatcheries, we tried to place them with surrogate mothers but sometimes no hen was willing to enact that role. Hence, a tiny bantam rooster we called Mighty Mouse came to serve as surrogate mother for a succession of "broiler" chickens who quickly grew to many times his size but still fled to him for comfort and protection. Mighty Mouse never betrayed his young charges, but the surrogates to whom farmed and domesticated birds turn often do. Perhaps the experiences of abused and neglected children can help us to understand the psychic impact when *mother* kills your siblings before your eyes or cages or mutilates you.

These forms of psychic cleavage may be less obvious or acute than the extreme suffering inflicted by egg factories or cockfighting, but are

Fig. 1: Mighty Mouse, a rooster who became a surrogate mother.
Photo courtesy of pattrice jones

no less real. Furthermore, archetypal betrayal tends to be perpetrated in tandem with these more obviously traumatic practices. It is, after all, a *friend* or surrogate *mother* who drops the fighting rooster into the combat ring to face an armed and terrified *predator*. And all hens in egg factories began life in hatcheries, where they are deprived of both *mother* and *flock*, interacting only with similarly deprived chicks.

AVIAN PSYCHES IN SITU

No bird is an island. No bird psyche exists except in relationship to the surrounding ecosocial system. Unfortunately for birds, people have profoundly (mis)shaped the circumstances of virtually every avian species, often to disastrous effect. Our collective impact on bird populations—which includes not only hunting them and crowding them out of their habitats but also poisoning water, lessening the availability of food, spreading disease, and altering the climate—has led to a 20 to 25 percent decline in the number of individual birds in the world since 1500; within the next hundred years, one in ten bird species will be extinct, with another 15 percent endangered.[61] Statistics like these are usually discussed without reference to the psyches of the survivors. What would it be like to be one of the comparatively few remaining members of an endangered species? What *is* it like to have one's home chopped down unexpectedly or to arrive at one's summer home after a long journey only to find that there's no food because the flowers haven't bloomed or have already bloomed and died due to climate change? We have the same sort of limbic system as a bird. Surely we can imagine the combination of heart-pounding fear and dispiriting helplessness that must arise in birds at such moments. That is psychic trauma. Some birds must, like people in war zones, live with the psychically catastrophic conjunction of chronic arousal and helplessness. How do they cope with this? If they survive the crisis, what impact will the cumulative trauma have on the psyches of future generations?

Birds have demonstrated remarkable resilience and creativity in adapting to changed circumstance. Many have literally changed their tunes, adjusting the frequencies of their songs in order to be heard over or under the din of our noisy urban environments.[62] Presumably, such adaptability is rooted in many generations of natural selection favoring brain plasticity and behavioral flexibility. Unfortunately, we have not allowed all birds to enjoy the benefits of such natural selection. Our interference with bird reproduction—which has included such tactics as segregation, selective sterilization, and forcible impregnation and has reached its apex in genetic engineering—has profoundly influenced not only the bodies but also the psyches of individual birds while altering the course of evolution for entire species. The effects of this on the bodies of birds such as "broiler" chickens is well documented[63] and increasingly well known. The effects of so-called domestication on bird brains has received less attention but is likely substantial and tragic. For example, "there are good grounds for believing that the artificial domesticating selection that has affected pigeons for several thousand generations might have tended to blunt their intelligence."[64]

Interference with reproduction is but one way people have degenerated bird brains and psyches. The suffering of caged birds can scarcely be imagined, except perhaps by reference to the voluminous literature on the effects of solitary confinement on people, which include not only emotional unrest but significant degradation of cognitive functioning.[65] Let us examine two examples: Parrots and other "pet" birds confined alone in cages and chickens crowded together in batteries of egg factory cages. In both instances, the constant frustration of the impulse for flight and other free movement is compounded by the absence of normal social relations. In the case of solitary caged birds, the extent of their loneliness is evident if not quite imaginable. Birds are *social* animals. Every aspect of their brain and behavior evolved to fit eco*social* environments within which *social* relationships were the the most salient and essential elements. Perhaps even more insistently than ours do, their emotions tell them to seek and maintain relationships with others of their kind. As William Blake poetically opined, "robin redbreast in a cage" does indeed "put all heaven in a rage" in the sense of perverting the natural order.

For hens crowded into egg factory cages, the interference with normal social relationships and other activities is different but no less acute. Hens often choose to sleep close together at night, but they forage widely all day, spreading out to do so. Although they often dust-bathe collectively, many prefer privacy for egg laying. Hens in egg factories spend all day every day crowded into barren cages with scarcely enough room to lie down or turn around, much less stretch their wings or walk away from one another. The cacophony of unanswered distress cries of thousands of hens is deafening. Choking ammonia fumes rise from the manure pits beneath the batteries of cages. Hence, normal social interactions are impossible. Age mates who might otherwise have been valued companions become *competitors* from whom it is impossible to escape. As I wrote in 2006:

> Have you ever been bored? Frustrated? Uncomfortable? Cranky? Imagine yourself crowded into a cage, often thirsty and always a little hungry, with nothing to do other than jostle your cage-mates. They're not your friends—they're your competitors. There's never enough space and never enough food for everybody to feel satisfied. You can't ever get comfortable. There's no place to go to get away from each other. And there's never anything to do!
>
> One of your cage-mates keeps screaming. She won't shut up! Another is slumped in a stupor. She won't move out of the way! Somebody else is dying. No—she's dead. Your eyes burn. Your

feet throb. Your wings ache to open. You can't turn around or lie down. You wait.

Ten minutes. Five hours. Three weeks. Eight months. Two years. Two years you may wait for relief from the tedium and pain. Then the cage opens but you are not released. Instead you are trucked to a painful and terrifying death at a slaughter factory or, if no buyer has been found for your bedraggled body, simply buried alive in a landfill.[66]

Hens fortunate enough to go to sanctuaries rather than landfills or slaughterhouses often spend hours or days in a dazed huddle, evidently unable to comprehend that they may now move freely. Others careen confusedly, unable to gauge distances or control their nearly atrophied muscles. Some seem sunk in a state of learned helplessness while others respond with panicked flight to every surprising stimulus. Over time, most recover both physical and emotional equilibrium by observing and interacting with other sanctuary residents. They sun bathe, lay their eggs in nests, and roost in the branches of trees. However, some remain forever psychically scarred by early deprivation and trauma, never demonstrating quite the same courage and confidence consistently evinced by feral hens.

FOR THE BIRDS

Like most "broiler" chickens, Heartbeat died too young. Chickens bred by the poultry industry suffer a host of health problems due to decades of genetic selection for rapid and excessive growth. On what would be his last morning, Heartbeat was very still and weak but seemed to appreciate the soymilk-alfalfa-vitamin concoction I fed him by hand. But then the liquid began dribbling from his mouth and I knew the end was near. I carried him to a quiet spot, holding his body to my heart and his drooping head in my hand. Crouching in the shade of a mulberry bush, I cradled him as he went into his death throes. As his body jerked, I cried out, "No, no, don't go, don't go!" but then I said, "Go, go with the wild birds," and, "You'll never be alone." He went with his eyes open. For a while after he died I thought he was still alive because his little chest still seemed to be moving up and down. But then I realized it was just my own heartbeat.

Our habit of using birds as symbols has been and continues to be hurtful to their psyches and our own. Symbolism is a kind of objectification. Using imaginary birds as symbols makes us more likely to treat actual animals as if they, too, were mere objects to be manipulated in service of our fantasies. On the other hand, our evolved tendency to see birds as signals may turn out to be useful to both us and them. Birds are salient features of our environment; we appear to be primed to notice and attend them. If we can clear away the clutter of cultural symbolism in order to see birds and their psyches more clearly, we may become better able to use our own brain plasticity and behavioral flexibility to cooperate with them in salvaging the wreck we've made of our shared world.

Within clinical psychology, we rightly consider people who manipulate other people as if they were objects to be sociopathic. Similarly, the belief that other people are insensate robots without thoughts or feelings is rightly considered to be psychotic thinking. Birds and other animals are sentient fellow beings but are treated by most people as insensate objects to be manipulated without remorse. The statistical normalcy of this ought not deflect us from perceiving the sociopathic and indeed psychotic character of these patterns of thought and behavior. In our beliefs and behaviors concerning birds and other denizens of our ecosocial environments, we are profoundly disordered animals. Our maladaptive destruction of our own habitat is similarly rooted in reductive objectification and the refusal to act reciprocally within relationships.

Might we, by thinking about bird psyches, reshape our own? If so, we and other species might derive substantial benefits from the exercise. Even if that is not the case, thinking about bird psyches in relation to our own may allow us to apply the insights of psychology to birds whose psyches have been damaged by people. At the Eastern Shore Sanctuary, we adapted techniques used in the treatment of traumatized people to devise a rehabilitation program for roosters used in cockfighting.[67] In brief, this process provides these unsocialized and traumatized birds safe spaces within which to become less afraid of other birds and, most importantly, learn *from* other birds the social lessons essential to peaceful coexistence within flocks.[68] Similarly, techniques used in the treatment of PTSD in people have been applied to the treatment of traumatized parrots.[69]

Given the varieties of psychic trauma suffered by birds at the hands of people, much more work remains to be done in the realm of extending psychological care to traumatized birds. Pigeons, parrots, and other birds in captivity have long been deprived of both freedom and normal social relations by psychological researchers. Psychologists of all varieties can act to end this ongoing trauma by pressing for changes in the guidelines for ethical research. Clinical psychologists might begin the process of offering reparations for the long history of animal abuse within the field by volunteering their expertise to animal sanctuaries.

In their own practices, clinical psychologists must resist the tendency to collude with sociopathic behavior and psychotic thinking in relation to birds and other nonhuman animals. If a patient dreams of birds, don't leap to the conclusion that they must symbolize *something else*. Inquire about the client's thoughts, feelings, and behavior toward birds. Does he or she watch birds? Hunt birds? Eat birds? If she dotes on bluebirds but makes soup of ducklings, look for the dissociations and delusions that facilitate that discrepancy. How does she block or blunt her awareness of bird suffering? What else *isn't* she thinking about? If you fear you may be overstepping your boundaries with such inquiries, remember that the survival of your client and her offspring depend in part on our collective ability to reorient ourselves in relation to the biosphere and its other inhabitants.

Perhaps because so many of its theorists and practitioners are analytic psychologists, ecopsychology tends to share the Jungian neglect of the body. Given that the impact of human bodies on the body of the planet is or should be at the heart of ecopsychological concerns, the disembodied quality of ecopsychology theory and practice is both curious and dangerous.[70] One can read anthologies[71] of ecopsychology without encountering a word about the effect of pollutants such as lead on our brains (and, therefore, psyches) or the impact of our food choices on our bodies (and, therefore psyches), animal bodies, or the body of the planet. The ideas about archetypes and the collective unconscious put forward here remind us that these are *bodily* processes rooted in *material* history, which is *ongoing*. What we think and feel both reflects and is shaped by what we *do,* including what we do to other animals. At present, ecopsychology as a field is woefully incomplete due to its wholesale neglect of actual human-animal relations. Like other clinical psychologists, practicing ecopsychologists can begin to remedy this by by speaking with clients about birds and other animals *not* as symbols of the wished-for wild but as fellow beings whose own wishes must be recognized if we are to wrest ourselves out of ecologically destructive wishful thinking.

No animal sanctuary needs to be reminded that animals seeking refuge often arrive with psychic damage. The good news is that the psychic similarity of people and birds opens up new avenues of treatment for psychologically disturbed birds. The natural sociality and behavioral plasticity of birds, in conjunction with the remarkable ease with which they may view a member of another species as *mother* or *friend*, means that we often can extend psychologically reparative care to them. However, because birds are social animals with brains and bodies evolved for flock life, other birds must be part of the process of recovery. Full recovery can only be achieved within the context of relationships with other birds, ideally including integration into a pair bond or flock. At the Eastern Shore Sanctuary, people could help former fighting roosters become less afraid of other birds. But only other birds could model for them the social behavior through which roosters naturally mediate their relations.

Many birds at the sanctuary demonstrated both the desire and the ability to "rewild" themselves, shifting gradually from reliance on the sanctuary to living freely in self-selected flocks within which they raised successive generations of young, some of whom were never touched by human hands. Similarly, I have seen wild flocks of chickens (presumably the offspring of cockfighting industry escapees) living happily in a forest in Maui. While the norm for animal sanctuaries is to limit the reproduction of their residents, full psychological recovery—for individual and for species—cannot be achieved in the context of continued reproductive control. Hence, for birds at least, sanctuaries where space and circumstances make this feasible ought to restore reproductive freedom to their inhabitants, thereby returning to them the freedom to forge their own flocks and families.

One fine September afternoon, the founder of another sanctuary stopped by to pick up some brochures. She was distraught, having just come from euthanizing a bird at the animal hospital. People always ask her, she said, "How can you keep going without getting upset?" What they don't understand, she said, her voice rising, is that "I'm always upset!" Casting around for something, anything, to bring a little cheer into her day, I suddenly remembered: The feral chicks! Over the summer, the hen we called Minya had gone missing for so long we feared her dead. Suspecting she might be brooding eggs, we'd searched the underbrush for her with no luck. Just when we'd given up and begun to mourn her, Minya reappeared, trailing seven chicks in her wake. Thus we got our first chance to see chicks as the young birds they we meant to be. Minya encouraged them to forage rather than rely on the feed bowls. We watched as she showed them how to perch on higher and higher bushes. We gasped with wonder and trepidation one night at twilight when Minya decided it was time to return to the trees. Jumping onto a low branch, she called to her chicks. All but one followed readily, and the straggler made it eventually. Minya then led them to successively higher branches until they roosted, the young birds arrayed on either side of their mother, and fell asleep far from the reach of any predator. Wanting to share the wonder of that moment with my friend, I dragged her into the backyard, where Minya and her chicks usually could be found foraging. They were so nimble and clever at fading into the shadows that we were only able to catch a glimpse of their tail feathers as they advanced into the woods.[72]

NOTES

1. Edward A. Armstrong, *The Folklore of Birds* (London: Collins, 1958).

2. Andrew Robinson, *The Story of Writing* (Thames and Hudson: London, 1995).

3. http://www.bravebirds.org.

4. Christopher S. Evans, Linda Evans, and Peter Marler, "On the Meaning of Alarm Calls: Functional Reference in an Avian Vocal System," *Animal Behaviour* 46 (1993): 23-38.

5. Mei-Feng Cheng and Sarah E. Durand, "Song and the limbic brain: A new function for the bird's own song," *Annals of the New York Academy of Sciences* 1016 (2004): 611-627.

6. Deborah Buitron, "Variability in the responses of black-billed magpies to natural predators," *Behaviour* 87, no. 3/4 (1983): 209-236.

7. Timothy Q. Gentner *et al.*, "Recursive syntactic pattern learning by songbirds," *Nature* 440, no. 7088 (April 27, 2006): 1204-1207.

8. Erich D. Jarvis, "Learned birdsong and the neurobiology of human language," *Annals of the New York Academy of Sciences* 1016 (2004): 749-777.

9. Timothy F. Wright, Christine R. Dahlin, and Alejandro Salinas-

Melgoza, "Stability and change in vocal dialects of the yellow-naped amazon," *Animal Behaviour* 76, no. 3 (September 2008): 1017-1027.

10. Morten H. Christiansen and Nick Chater, "Language as shaped by the brain," *Behavioral and Brain Sciences* 31, no. 05 (2008): 489-509.

11. Juan D. Delius *et al.*, "Cognitions of birds as products of evolved brains," in *Brain Evolution and Cognition*, ed. Gerhard Roth and Mario F. Wulliman (New York: Wiley-Spektrum, 2001), pp. 451-490.

12. Jurg Wassmann and Pierre R. Dasen, "Balinese Spatial Orientation: Some Empirical Evidence of Moderate Linguistic Relativity," *The Journal of the Royal Anthropological Institute* 4, no. 4 (1998): 689-711.

13. Lera Boroditsky, "Does language shape thought?: Mandarin and English speakers' conceptions of time," *Cognitive Psychology* 43, no. 1 (2001): 1-22.

14. David Myers, "Hazel Markus and Shinobu Kitiyama on cross cultural communication," in *Social Psychology*, 10th ed. (New York: McGraw Hill, 1991), p. 46.

15. Hazel Rose Markus and Shinobu Kitiyama, "Culture and the self: Implications for cognition, emotion, and motivation," *Psychological Review* 98, no. 2 (1991): 224-253.

16. Geoffrey Sea, "A Pigeon in Piketon," *The American Scholar* 73 (2004): 57-84.

17. Alexandra Fidyk, "'Gypsy' fate: Carriers of our collective shadow," *Jung: The e-Journal* 4, no. 1 (2008): 1-28.

18. Kenneth M. Reeves, "Racism and projection of the shadow," *Psychotherapy: Theory, Research, Practice, Training* 37, no. 1 (2000): 80-88.

19. Associated Press, "Staunton to try to scare away vultures," *The Free-Lance Star*, December 3, 2001.

20. Armstrong, *Folklore of Birds*, p. 1.

21. Genevieve Pullis La Rouche, *Birding in the United States: A Demographic and Economic Analysis* (Washington, DC: U.S. Fish and Wildlife Service, 2001), http://library.fws.gov/Surveys/birding01.pdf.

22. Armstrong, *Folklore of Birds*, p. 24.

23. *Ibid.*, p. 49.

24. Clifford Geertz, "Deep Play: Notes on the Balinese Cockfight," *Daedalus* 134, no. 4 (2005): 56-87.

25. pattrice jones, "Roosters, hawks, and dawgs: Toward an inclusive, embodied eco/feminist psychology," *Feminism & Psychology* in press (2010).

26. Amir Efrati, "When Bad Chickens Come Home to Roost, Results Can Be Good," *The Wall Street Journal*, July 15, 2005.

27. Fred Hawley, "The Moral and Conceptual Universe of Cockfighters: Symbolism and Rationalization," *Society & Animals* 1, no. 2 (1993), http://www.psyeta.org/sa/sa1.2/hawley.html.

28. jones, "Roosters, hawks, and dawgs."

29. Bruce Bagemihl, *Biological Exuberance* (New York: St. Martin's, 1999), p. 12.

30. Mario F. Wullimann and Grehard Roth, "Problems in the study of brain evolution and cognition," in *Brain Evolution and Cognition*, ed. Gerhard Roth and Mario F. Wulliman (New York: Wiley-Spektrum, 2001), pp. 1-7.

31. Gavin R. Hunt and Russell D. Gray, "Diversification and cumulative evolution in New Caledonian crow tool manufacture," *Proceedings of the Royal Society B: Biological Sciences* 270, no. 1517 (2003): 867.

32. Nathan J. Emery, "Cognitive ornithology: The evolution of avian intelligence," *Philosophical Transactions of the Royal Society B: Biological Sciences* 361, no. 1465 (2006): 23-43.

33. Jaak Panksepp, *Affective Neuroscience: The Foundations of Human and Animal Emotions* (New York: Oxford University Press US, 2004).

34. Erich D. Jarvis, "Avian brains and a new understanding of vertebrate brain evolution," *Nature Reviews: Neuroscience* 6, no. 2 (2005): 151-159.

35. Delius *et al.*, "Cognitions of birds," p. 453.

36. *Ibid.*

37. Gerald M. Edelman, "Naturalizing consciousness: A theoretical framework," *Proceedings of the National Academy of Sciences of the United States of America* 100, no. 9 (April 29, 2003), p. 5520.

38. *Ibid.*

39. C.G. Jung, "Archetypes of the Collective Unconscious," in *Collected Works of C.G. Jung*, vol. 9, 2nd ed. (Princeton, NJ: Princeton University Press, 1968).

40. Edelman, "Naturalizing consciousness," p. 5524.

41. Ann B. Butler and Rodney M.J. Cotterill, "Mammalian and avian neuroanatomy and the question of consciousness in birds," *Biological Bulletin* 211, no. 2 (October 1, 2006): 106-127.

42. Ann B. Butler *et al.*, "Evolution of the neural basis of

consciousness: A bird-mammal comparison," *BioEssays: News and Reviews in Molecular, Cellular and Developmental Biology* 27, no. 9 (September 2005): 923-936.

43. David B. Edelman, Bernard J. Baars, and Anil K. Seth, "Identifying hallmarks of consciousness in non-mammalian species," *Consciousness and Cognition* 14, no. 1 (March 2005): 169-187.

44. David B. Edelman and Anil K. Seth, "Animal consciousness: a synthetic approach," *Trends in Neurosciences* 32, no. 9 (September 2009): 476-484.

45. Edelman, "Naturalizing consciousness," p. 5520.

46. Butler and Cotterill, "Mammalian and avian neuroanatomy," p. 106.

47. Butler *et al.*, "Evolution of the neural basis of consciousness," p. 923.

48. Anthony Stevens, "Jungian psychology, the body, and the future," *The Journal of Analytical Psychology* 40, no. 3 (July 1995): 353.

49. Anthony Stevens, *Archetype Revisited: An Updated Natural History of the Self* (Toronto: Inner City Books, 2003), p. 17.

50. *Ibid.*, 23-33.

51. Konrad Z. Lorenz, *King Solomon's Ring: New Light on Animal Ways* (New York: Thomas Y. Crowell Company, 1952), p. vii.

52. Lukas Jenni and Marc Kéry, "Timing of autumn bird migration under climate change: Advances in long-distance migrants, delays in short-distance migrants," *Proceedings of the Royal Society B: Biological Sciences* 270, no. 1523 (July 22, 2003): 1467-1471.

53. Lain D. Couzin, "Collective cognition in animal groups," *Trends in Cognitive Sciences* 13, no. 1 (2009): 36-43.

54. Rachel Carson, *Silent Spring* (Greenwich, CT: Fawcett Crest, 1962), pp. 97-119.

55. Lorenz, *King Solomon's Ring*, p. 43.

56. Stevens, *Archetype Revisited*, p. 44.

57. G.A. Bradshaw and Robert M. Sapolsky, "Mirror, Mirror," *American Scientist*, December 2006, p. 487.

58. Jolande Jacobi, *Complex/archetype/symbol in the Psychology of C. G. Jung* (New York: Routledge, 1999), p. 256.

59. Peter Kropotkin, *Mutual Aid: A Factor of Evolution* (Black Rose Books Ltd., 1989).

60. H.F. Harlow, R.O. Dodsworth, and M.K. Harlow, "Total social isolation in monkeys," *Proceedings of the National Academy of Sciences of the United States of America* 54, no. 1 (1965): 90-97.

61. Roddy Scheer, "Researchers Predict Massive Avian Decline," *E-The Environmental Magazine*, December 2004, http://www.emagazine.com/view/?2200.

62. David Luther and Luis Baptista, "Urban noise and the cultural evolution of bird songs," *Proceedings of the Royal Society B: Biological Sciences* 277, no. 1680 (2010): 469-473.

63. Peter Stevenson, *Leg and Heart Problems in Broiler Chickens*, Briefing (Surrey, UK: Compassion in World Farming, 2003), http://www.ciwf.org.uk/includes/documents/cm_docs/2008/l/leg_and_heart_problems_in_broilers_for_judicial_review.pdf.

64. Delius *et al.*, "Cognitions of birds," p. 455.

65. S. Grassian, "Psychopathological effects of solitary confinement," *American Journal of Psychiatry* 140, no. 11 (November 1, 1983): 1450-1454.

66. pattrice jones, "I know why the caged birds scream," *Satya Magazine*, February 2006, http://www.satyamag.com/feb06/jones.html.

67. Efrati, "Bad Chickens," A1.

68. jones, "Roosters, hawks, and dawgs."

69. Allison Milionis, "Birds of a Feather," *Los Angeles CityBeat*, June 7, 2007, http://www.lacitybeat.com/article.php?id=5632&IssueNum=209.

70. pattrice jones, "Roosters, hawks, and dawgs."

71. E.g., Theodore Roszak, Mary E. Gomes, Allen D. Kanner, *Ecopsychology; Restoring the Earth, Healing the Mind* (San Francisco: Sierra Club Books, 1995).

72. The author thanks Miriam Jones for cofounding and continuing to operate the Eastern Shore Sanctuary and for helpful comments on a draft of this essay. Grateful thanks for generous feedback also go out to Greta Gaard and G.A. Bradshaw. Dedicated to the memories of Zami, Samhain, Hearbeat, Simone, and other sanctuary participants who taught me about cross-species empathy by demonstrating it themselves. Offered in solidarity with caged birds everywhere.

FREUD AND THE FAMILY HORSE: EXPLORATION INTO EQUINE PSYCHOTHERAPY

VERA MULLER-PAISNER & G.A. BRADSHAW

In the course of the development of civilization, man acquired a dominating position over his fellow-creatures in the animal kingdom. Not content with this supremacy, however, he began to place a gulf between his nature and theirs. He denied the possession of reason to them, and to himself he attributed an immortal soul.

—Sigmund Freud[1]

From the grandfather of modern psychology, the field developed to study the wounds and journeys of the human mind, this statement is surprisingly perspicacious. In a few simple lines, Freud describes what scholars spend many a page decrying: how

Vera Muller-Paisner, L.C.S.W., is a psychoanalyst and author of *Broken Chain: Catholics Uncover the Holocaust's Hidden Legacy and Discover Their Jewish Roots* (2005). She works with both equine and human clients and has adapted Eye Movement Desensitization and Reprocessing (EMDR) protocol to Bilateral Equine Tapping (BET) to aid horses exhibiting traumatic memory.

G.A. Bradshaw, Ph.D., Ph.D., is the executive director of the Kerulos Center and author of *Elephants on the Edge: What Animals Teach Us About Humanity* (Yale University Press, 2009). Her work focuses on animal psychological trauma and recovery and approaches to support wildlife cultural self-determination.

western cultural images have structured disciplines along taxonomic lines with imperious righteousness. Much like 19th century empires that divvied the continents and oceans into territorial possessions, western knowledge has been parceled into separate fields, each with its own methods, goals, and assumptions. As a consequence, psychologists and doctors contend with human concerns, and animal behaviorists and veterinarians are left with issues relating to the rest of the animal kingdom.

This separatist framework assumes that higher-order mental and spiritual functions are uniquely associated with a human "veneer" covering a shared, animal core of brain and behavior.[2] Conventionally, when complex cognitive and affective behaviors such as tool-use and grief are identified in animals, they have been largely reported as ethological isolates with no theoretical link to psychobiology. The entire spectrum of subjective states that an individual dog or horse can experience and what we humans so dearly covet as our own—joy, love, curiosity, a sense of self, and aesthetics—are relegated to anecdote. Relationships between behavior, psychological state, and neural substrates are ignored: this, despite the fact that human-animal comparability forms the basis for using animals as "models" of human neurobiological and psychological processes and states.[3] Animals are routinely employed as first subjects in diverse experiments designed to treat humans diagnosed with psychiatric conditions ranging from schizophrenia, Obsessive Compulsive Disorder (OCD), depression, autism, and attachment disorders. Inferring responses from a rat, chimpanzee, or cat to those anticipated in humans is considered scientifically valid because structures and functions of the brain and their associated mental and emotional processes are shared across species. Nonetheless, animals continue to be denied a psyche.

Of late, however, there are efforts to bridge studies of human and other animals' minds. Animal science literature has begun to regard animals as "whole" beings with "expressive 'behaviors' rather than assembled strings of 'behaviour.'"[4] From the other direction, psychology now includes other species in its formerly humans-only club.[5] On a third front, neuroscience's two-tiered architecture has collapsed into a unitary, species-common model of brain, mind, and behavior. Discoveries from the "Decade of the Brain", married with ethological data amassed since Charles Darwin, have birthed a vertebrate-common representation of the mind.[6]

All of a sudden, ethologists and psychologists find themselves shoulder to shoulder under a common conceptual umbrella. Not only are animals psychological beings with human capacities and "immortal souls",[7] but they are vulnerable to psychological wounding. This, and given that psychopathology in animals is thought largely to be human-caused,[8] it is not unreasonable to consider psychotherapy for other species. Psychotherapy involving other species has been discussed elsewhere, for example, in the rehabilitation of elephants, chimpanzees, and parrots.[9] However, past work emphasizes the commonalities in concepts and approaches used by sanctuary professionals and those used by psychotherapists. Using a case study for illustration, we will explore the assumptions, questions, and ethics involved in the application of a specific technique, Eye Movement Desensitization and Reprocessing (EMDR) developed to treat Post-Traumatic Stress Disorder (PTSD) in humans,[10] to horses.

The choice of trauma as our etiological subject is intentional. PTSD is one of the few psychiatric disorders that includes symptom etiology in its diagnosis.[11] Relative to other psychological conditions, underlying mechanisms involved in trauma are fairly well understood across species. Because developmental and traumatic neuropsychological mechanisms are shared across altricial species (those species whose young have an extended dependence on adults), we are provided with conservative, inferential rigor when drawing parallels between species' psychologies.[12]

Further, because the study and treatment of trauma is dyadic (engaging both cause [perpetrator] and effect [victim] and therapist [human] and client [horse/human]), we have the potential to gain insights into the multiple facets of human-animal relationships that figure centrally in domesticated animals. As animal protection advocates argue, domestication is a form of slavery as the psychological evolution of today's cows, horses, and chickens has been manipulated and tailored by human perceptions and purposes. Subsequently, extending the practice of psychotherapy to other species necessarily raises questions that arise at the tangled interface of animal psyche and human projections. We discuss how ethical and psychological aspects of equine domestication influence how horse wellbeing is framed and its implications for equine psychotherapy.

Such an undertaking requires care. There is danger in using approaches that derive from the same culture and episteme that caused the anguish we seek to address. Trans-cultural workers have made this point: that by applying western concepts and methods universally without consideration of other cultural ontologies and beliefs, psychiatry is not only misused but violates ethics.[13] Similarly, in attempts to help animals, we run the risk of causing re-traumatization or reinforcing animal exploitation in the guise of beneficence. Dolphin swim programs, equine therapy, and other Animal Assisted Therapies (AAT) are designed to improve human health often at the expense of the animals forcibly recruited.[14] It is critical to distinguish whether therapy involving nonhuman animals is truly for their benefit or humans.

Nonetheless, the impetus to investigate possible benefits of psychotherapy is compelled by the very real suffering that billions of horses, cats, turkeys, bears, and others endure. It is also true that human domination has made the wellbeing and survival of many species dependent on humans. Human environmental policies dictate how wildlife is permitted to live and the fates of animals in captivity are literally in human hands. We are faced with the disturbing thought that animal suffering has not only been caused by human psychological distress, but that animals must rely on their abusers in order to survive.

Animals are implicitly subjected to the challenges of a dual role: humans as perpetrators of suffering and of healing. In their inherited role of domination, humans are challenged to understand the motivations and ethical consequences of their actions executed in the name of "animal welfare". If an equine psychotherapy is to be crafted, we must bear in mind the philosophy of liberation psychologist Martín-Baró: "If we want psychology to make a significant contribution to the history of our peoples . . . we have to redesign our theoretical and practical tools. . . from the standpoint of the lives of our own people: from their sufferings, their aspirations, and their struggles."[15] Equine psychotherapy is valid only if it is informed by horse values and culture.

Much of what is presented here is basic to psychology and there is overlap between animal and human healthcare practice. However, there are nuanced differences. Our purpose is to contextualize assumptions across species and thereby evaluate their meaning and appropriateness relative to an assumed ethic that protects an individual's agency and individuation. Further, we seek to create a shared set of concepts and methods to enhance exchange across disciplines. Subsequently, our discussion is partly anthropological: a self-reflexive study of the meaning and validity of anthropocentric definitions used to describe psychological states and health formerly denied to other species. It is at the interface of human psychology and equine behavior where we are simultaneously challenged to re-examine conceptions about equine psyche and what transformational changes in humans are needed to prevent future trauma to our bicultural kin, the horse.

CASE STUDY: HERO

The study site is located at a private stable in Connecticut. The client, Hero,[16] is an eight-year-old Lusitano stallion who came to the stable and present trainer when he was three years old. He had a difficult time adjusting during the first months at the new stable. For example, when he was taken from the barn stall to other areas such as the outside arena or to an indoor ring, he became very agitated, difficult to handle, and dangerous to himself and his handler. On these occasions, he would frequently rear, back up, or intermittently flail his rear legs while turning his head. His trainer first thought that Hero's perception of the shadows created by indoor to outdoor lighting was the problem, however there was no consistent evidence indicating causality or correlation.

Overall, Hero's symptoms have attenuated over the five years in residency. He has been able to learn high-level movements in dressage. However, vestiges of early behavioral disturbances are retained in certain contexts and the chronic nature of these disruptive and potentially injurious behaviors has compelled the trainer and guardian to seek assistance. As one key example, when entering or exiting his stall, Hero consistently displays a panic reaction by tensing his body, rearing, rushing the door, or rearing and hitting his head and neck on the doorjamb, eyes wide and "wild". This is in contrast to more typical "agitated" behavior such as when in his stall, he pins his ears back when another stallion passes and/or shows aggression as if trying to bite the passerby. Only his trainer and her assistant are able to lead him in and out of his stall. To accomplish this, they stand to the side of him with a lead line in hand, and encourage him to walk forward and over the threshold. Some days are better than others, but as soon as he becomes agitated, it can take up to forty minutes before Hero is able and willing to step forward and through the threshold.

The degree to which his behavior is considered both predictable and chronic is reflected in the behavior of the stable staff. Hero's anxiety in passing through the door is considered a great enough psychological barrier to permit the staff to comfortably leave the stall door ajar when Hero is inside; they feel sufficiently assured that his fear and anxiety prevent him from risking crossing the threshold. The therapist was asked to work with Hero to quell his fear and potentially injurious behavior.

THE PSYCHOLOGICAL FRAME

Generally speaking, perhaps the greatest difference between animal behaviorists and psychologists lies in how each regards symptom. Behaviorists have understood animal *psyche* as synonymous with animal *behavior*; the "human veneer" that is conceptually collapsed onto the sensitive, yet nonetheless primitive, animal core, whose subjective state is identical with behavior.[17] When professional care is sought to remedy symptom, it is a behavioral "problem" that usually is the target of concern; accordingly the therapeutic goal is preemptively identified as the eradication of unwanted behavior. Again, generally speaking, behavior consultants and trainers focus on understanding how, even though often in gentle ways, a horse's behavior can be shaped to conform to human images of what is correct and normative. Behavioral norms are circumscribed by human expectations.

Behaviors are inventoried into a set of discrete and temporally localized, stand-alone units of expression respondent to proximal conditions or habits. Even while appreciating that behavior does not happen in a vacuum and that resolution of behavioral "problems" frequently requires change on the part of the environment (inclusive of human guardian/trainer), the animal is implicitly objectified by these assumptions. It is the human who orchestrates what learning by the animal is required. The locus of control is situated outside the horse (client). Symptom functions less as the voice of the horse's soul on the path of individuation than it does as currency used in negotiation between horse and human.

On the other hand, psychology's explicit emphasis on the value and significance of symptom presents a different picture. Similarly to behavioral methods, psychotherapy seeks to obtain understanding sufficient to address an issue. However, psychotherapists endeavor to establish the meaning and source of symptoms to help the client shape a path which s/he wishes to pursue (or not). Therapy and "problem solving" are informed *relative to the needs and values of the client*. The goal is to maintain the locus of control with the client.

A psychotherapist is required by law and ethics to prevent a client from physically harming his/herself or someone else. But outside this domain, psychological states and behavior are not preemptively judged "bad" or pathological except in the literal sense of the word: distress causing. Of course, therapy goals and approaches vary among diverse theoretical orientations: psychoanalytic, psychodynamic, cognitive, behavioral, and client-entered therapies are each based on fundamentally different concepts of nature, development, and pathology and will have somewhat different therapeutic goals and criteria for "success."[18]

The value with which symptom is regarded is exemplified in self-injurious behavior (SIB). Whether viewed as a means to provide relief biochemically through the release of endorphins or as a psychological method of dissociation or self-soothing, the behavior serves the individual. Indeed, many psychologists conclude that SIB can have "mythological, religious, historical and cultural undertones."[19] The fact that the behavior damages the individual, is repeated, and often very difficult to extinguish, speaks to the lengths to which the mind tries to accommodate the environment even when his/her psychological states and behavior become life-threatening.

In this recognition, psychotherapeutic approaches seek to understand symptom aetiology, its significance, and meaning as they relate to the client's philosophical and lived existence. As a result, the role of the therapist takes on considerable moral and ethical responsibility extending to the sacred as s/he participates in the client's process of individuation. Psychotherapy does not have to have a fixed goal other than to serve the client in his/her discovery of symptom meaning. This requires understanding who that person is.

THE EQUINE SELF

The self is a cornerstone concept in psychology. It dictates the starting point from which western psychotherapy develops. Self-recognition, a sense of self, and theory of mind have been validated in one species or another. However, the concept of self is not as straightforward as has been supposed. Orangutans, dolphins, humans, elephants, and magpies have all passed the mirror self-recognition test (MSR)[20] that is used to empirically assess self-awareness. Yet gorillas have not and not all chimpanzees test successfully. Puzzling, but less so when seen through the eyes of neuroscience and transcultural psychiatry.

Transcultural psychiatry was established in recognition that multiple conceptualizations of self exist across human cultures—anthropocentric, ecocentric, and cosmocentric—and may not even exist in some places. Models of self are not "firmly rooted in a conception of the person as a distinct and independent individual, capable of self transformation in relative isolation from particular social contexts.[21] The same holds for experiments designed to detect self-recognition and intelligence: concept and method seem to be culturally variant. Relevant to the discussion here, how are diverse animals selves to be approached practically and ethically?

Attachment theory provides a common model for understanding how both a horse self and human self develop and why there are species and individual differences.[22] Significantly, domesticated animals who have co-evolved with humans are expected to have a psyche heavily influenced by human psychology. A horse has a horse body, needs, and habits, yet domestication dictates equine habitat, food, socialization, behavior, and, significantly, development. To a greater or lesser extent, all are predicated on the parameters set by human needs and objectives constrained by a horse's psychological and physical capacity.[23] Who then is the person who looks distinct from humans yet lives embedded and enmeshed within human society? What does healing and individuation of a horse psyche entail? Is it possible for the therapist to retain ethical fidelity to her/his client or do the built-in constraints determined and dictated by domestication preclude such? And whose psyche is the real beneficiary of psychotherapy? We begin to explore these questions by examining symptom and its relationship to self.

In discussion of the cross-species comparability of psychiatric disorders, psychiatrist Horatio Fabrega identifies four criteria necessary to satisfy the definition of pathological (which we will continue to regard here as "distress causing"). Symptoms must: (1) comprise identifiable psychological and somatic distress; (2) cause an interruption or significant change in an individual's life arc; (3) constitute significant behavioral alterations relative to an understood social and cultural space; and/or (4) be relatively persistent and express exclusive of any given specific context.[24]

Hero's symptoms readily satisfy the first criterion; he displays considerable fear and panic with "tensing his body, rearing, rushing the door, or rearing and hitting his head and neck on the doorjamb, eyes wide and "wild". Since he expresses profound fear at other times and places outside the stall, Hero also satisfies the fourth criteria. But what constitutes Hero's "life arc" and what is the normative "social and cultural space" that he occupies?

Hero is a horse raised to compete in high stress situations and to father horses for similar purposes. He is genetically distinct from the human species. However, Hero is also different from horses who live outside human care, so-called feral or wild horses.[25] It is unclear whether or not Hero would be able to thrive outside the domesticated setting. Domestication is a dominant agent in determining the equine envelope of tolerance and wellbeing. We may speculate that as someone who is implicitly bi-cultural, having competence in both horse and human cultures, Hero's threshold of tolerance, as well his sense of self, will deviate from that found in free-ranging horse society. Assuming that he will remain within the context of stable culture, we may consider that his life's arc is defined by the normative social and cultural context of a domesticated horse. Unlike many others, Hero's guardian is committed to keeping and caring for him regardless of therapeutic outcome. His life therefore will continue to be highly directed by humans and include captivity, occupying, entering, and exiting a stall and stable, training, being ridden and groomed, participating in a competition, and breeding.

From this standpoint, his fear symptoms "cause an interruption or significant change in his life arc" and deviate significantly from his "understood social and cultural space". Hero's terror obviously reflects the depth to which he feels threatened and his self in peril of extinction:

therapeutic intervention is therefore recommended. However, ethics compel the therapist to ascertain to what extent Hero's sense of self is supported or thwarted by his social context.

THERAPIST-CLIENT COMMUNICATION

Beyond general theoretical guidelines, psychotherapists obtain most information pertaining to symptoms through verbal narrative, therapist observation, records, or all of three. In many cases, it is the client who takes the initiative to seek out therapy either because the distress they feel compels them to do so or because circumstances force them to do so. In the latter case, for example, an individual may attend therapy because employers require him/her to address an "anger management problem" or a spouse insists that the individual seek counseling to "save the marriage." However, when clients are non-human, it usually a human third party who initiates the therapy and comprises the main conduit of information. How can the central tool of human psychotherapy, the verbal narrative, be used for non-speaking animals? If descriptions of the horse's symptom are predominantly conveyed through the human guardian, how can the horse's relationship to symptoms be ascertained and his agency maintained?

The absence of verbal narrative may have presented a difficult hurdle in the past, but models of communication have changed. Similar to other animals, children were once believed to be incapable of developing PTSD because they did not express typical verbal manifestations of the disorder. Neuropsychologist-analyst Schore and others[26] argue that the exclusion of prosody, facial expression, and unconsciously derived information ignores the majority of affective signals. "The [focus] on the patient's verbal outputs as the primary data of the psychotherapeutic process…delete the essential 'hidden' prosodic cues and visuoaffective transactions that are communicated between patient and therapist." Overall, spoken language is "a relatively poor medium for expressing the quality, intensity and nuancing of emotion and affect in different social situations…the face is thought to have primacy in signaling affective information.[27]

Early learning is largely nonverbal, unconscious, and implicit, as opposed to explicit, conscious information processing, involving parts of the brain where self-awareness, empathy, and identification with others are developed. Both equine and human brains have a left and right hemisphere and a corpus collosum that connects the spheres. It is the right hemisphere's automatic response that controls vital functions required for survival. Subsequently a horse's inability to verbally express his/her trauma is not reason to assume that his/her trauma is not being expressed in other ways.

The brain and its functions are primed to dialogue with others and in so doing, create knowledge and meaning. Parent-child paired processing consists of: "nonverbal attachment communications of facial expression, posture, and tone of voice [which] are the product of the operations of the infant's right hemisphere interacting with the mother's right hemisphere."[28] Even as adults, while attending to verbal utterances, there is "listening and interacting at another level, an experience-near subjective level, one that implicitly processes moment-to-moment socioemotional information at levels beneath awareness."[29] Critically, in consideration of trauma recovery, unconscious communication between patient and therapist occur from right-brain to right-brain, at levels beneath conscious awareness. Psychoneurobiological systems mediate the nonverbal communication by way of the right brain's capacity to translate facial expressions and body gestures; nuanced changes in a client's emotional states and that of his/her therapist are recognized by each others' right brains subliminally.[30]

The equine therapist must therefore learn the meaning of the horse's affective cues and cultivate an ability to communicate nonverbally at levels beneath conscious awareness. Experienced horse trainers, veterinarians, and others rely on mood, conformation, and behavior to infer and anticipate how the horse is responding to a given situation. Tom Dorrance, a cowboy of 78 years, called by seasoned horse people the "original" horse whisperer, maintains "the best thing I try to do is listen to the horse. I listen to how he's operating: what he's understanding or what he doesn't understand; what's bothering him and what isn't bothering him. I try to feel what the horse is feeling and operate from where the horse is."[31]

By refined observations and intimate communications, an equine therapist becomes a "culture broker" who comes to learn the language spoken by the horse; his/her preferences, moods, demands, and fears. Communications such as a horse's expression of fear and the therapist's response constitute the beginnings of the "therapeutic dialogue" much

Fig. 1: A rider and her horse; Bettina Drummond on Love.
Photo courtesy of Lyndee Kemmett

akin to that performed in human-to-human sessions. However, such inter-subjective exchange is often met with skepticism because it is difficult to render into objective representations. Recently, animal behavior researchers has begun to converge with these conceptualizations, moving from a reductive, behaviorist to an integrative, relational view of animal expression:

> It is not the *grin* that is the body language; it is *how* the animal *grins*, how its (sic) whole body moves, that makes the grin an expression of fear, or anger, or something else. We must focus on the whole animal if we are to properly judge the expressive meaning of features of behaviour, whatever feature it is.[32]

The past lack of formal descriptors of animal communication places greater emphasis on creating good communication and relationships between the therapist, client, and human guardians.

WORKING WITH THE CLIENT

Two features are considered essential for successful therapy and healing: the therapeutic container and the therapeutic alliance. A safe place or "holding environment" is fundamental to human psychotherapeutic treatment.[33] It refers to the physical and relational space created to provide a sense of security when an individual is administered care. This creates a starting point of non-reactivity from which therapy can proceed.

The principle behind the therapeutic container is that it minimizes stress for someone already psychologically and/or physically compromised by an experience or wound. Physically, this usually means a quiet place, soft light, comfortable surroundings, and the ability to sit or lie down, with no interruptions or threatening intrusions from the outside world. Yet physical safety alone does not always confer a sense of safety. There is also relational safety to consider.

In human treatment, the therapist's task is to cultivate a "therapeutic alliance" with the client that creates a relational holding environment to permit the client to feel safe enough to allow his/her true self to emerge without an excessive fear of vulnerability and exposure. In Hero's case, the therapeutic "safe place" is comprised of his being in his stall leaning against the back wall facing the door with his trainer's back leaning slightly on his midsection putting her hand behind her back and stroking his belly.

The therapeutic alliance also entails identifying and creating a system of shared meaning. Unlike most human therapeutic sessions (the exception being family and marriage counseling) where therapy classically involves the client and the therapist alone, equine therapy is usually conducted in the presence of a third person. Communication patterns and expectations are most always grounded in what has been established by the guardian and/or, in Hero's case, his trainer. Often this type of data is collected through interview with the guardian or trainer and while it may contain some objective observations, its meaning lies largely with subjective, felt information. For example,

Hero's guardian noted that the horse did "the Spanish walk, whenever he was very proud of his accomplishments." (A feature of the Spanish walk is a stepping up and extension of the front legs at a walk done mostly at the request of the trainer/rider in a trained horse.) When questioned as to how she inferred this, she did not specify objective observations of his behavior, but maintained that it was a "feeling" and a look in his eye.

Subsequently, diagnosis nearly always involves assessing the relational system in which the individual is embedded. This in itself does not differ dramatically from human-human therapy: it is not uncommon for a client's family to come to session to help explicate underlying dynamics and elucidate symptoms etiology. However, domestication and horse training are by definition created and maintained by an intrinsic inequality of power. Symptom resolution and treatment can become complex as a result. The question is, does the relationship undermine psychological health? Does it form a source of trauma or act to re-traumatize? Is, for instance, the behavior for which a pat on the neck or "treat" is given to reinforce something that the client horse enjoys, or does the exchange corrode agency? All of these questions confront the therapist.

Diagnosis and Treatment

The present case study was selected for two main reasons. First, detailed medical examination and tests did not reveal any physiological or structural issues. By process of elimination, symptoms were therefore considered explicitly psychological. Second, preliminary assessments by attending veterinarians, the horse guardian, and the therapist (co-author, Vera Muller-Paisner) suggested the individual as a candidate because of previous trauma experience which provided inferential grounding for comparing equine and human psychological distress and treatment.

PTSD can be triggered when the individual is exposed to internal or external cues that symbolize a past traumatic event. For example, a person violated on a beach may feel terrorized by the feel of sand beneath their feet but not know why. The sand is not the object, but rather a symbol, representing the trauma. They may become anxious remembering an old memory surrounding the feel or scent of sand.

An old memory coupled with anxiety may cause a re-experience or "flashback" of the trauma. Both the body and mind replay the trauma "as if" it were happening at that moment. PTSD has been documented in multiple species including cougars, elephants, chimpanzees, cockatoos, and wolves. Judith Herman created the category of complex PTSD to bring attention to the profound effects that captivity imposes on the prisoner.[34]

PTSD and complex PTSD are not unrelated: they are part of a comprehensive classification system in which trauma and symptoms range along a continuum. At one end of the continuum are individuals who have had healthy, loving childhoods and who exhibit normal capacities to deal with stress but are suddenly confronted by a single traumatic incident. At the other end of the trauma continuum are prolonged or multiple, highly invasive, physical and psychological insults. Victims of such trauma include abused children, prisoners, and others—including animals in captivity—who are unable to escape their circumstances and who typically develop more complicated and enduring symptoms. If the trauma is not processed or integrated, there is no discharge and the traumatic memory is replayed with the same response and intensity every time. When these memories appear "stuck", they are encoded in the sub-cortical regions of the brain and not readily accessible cognitively.[35] When triggered, the individual reacts as if the traumatic event were recurring. These patterns and responses were consistent with what is observed in Hero.

Hero shows other indications of PTSD. His trainer experiences him as a sensitive and loving animal who may suddenly become unavailable and unaware of himself and others. This resembles a dissociative state brought on by the sight of a threshold or door that may symbolize the memory and therefore the stressor of a traumatic event. Hero may not cognitively understand the connection between trigger and the reaction, and, as mentioned earlier, an inability to remember the traumatic event is not unusual. Trauma changes how memory works and how information is stored. For example, when someone experiences overwhelming fear, the mind and body dissociate, or turn off, for protection. When this occurs, memory fragments of a traumatic experience can remain hidden until many years later when stress or an experience unearths this past pain. With PTSD, there are deficits in the structure and function of core areas of the brain that create a kind of temporary amnesia—the losing of a memory's orientation to space and time—so that one may actually experience an old memory as if it is happening in the moment. Recent high-resolution neuroimaging studies indicate that the PTSD is associated with reduced thalamic activation. Thalamic reduction impairs consolidation capacity resulting in symptoms of somatosensory integration failure (e.g., flashbacks), poor cognitive integration that expresses as exaggerated self-blame, and hyperemotional states.[36] PTSD can also be described as an overly conditioned fear response to stimuli that threaten death. What is consistent is a predictable association of events and symptoms, namely, for Hero, the situation of exiting and entering the stall that evokes intense distress.

Hero's discomfort conforms to more than one diagnosis. Symptoms may be complex and may occur in the context of other anxieties, such as "Specific Phobia", "Agoraphobia", or "Panic Disorder", for example, which are cued by a particular object or situation, become situationally bound or predisposed, and are usually recognized by the person as an excessive or unreasonable fear of the stimulus. However, differential diagnosis is only important relative to ascertaining the meaning that the symptoms and associations have and if or how they might influence the design of the treatment plan.

There are several methods by which thoughts and feelings associated with trauma can be integrated and ameliorated. Often, it is the symptom presented which serves as the portal through which therapy can proceed. Research suggests treatment that specifically "processes" traumatic memories is more effective than supportive counseling or drug therapies. Among the approaches, cognitive behavior therapy (CBT) and Eye Movement Desensitization and Reprocessing (EMDR) are considered the most effective. EMDR was the treatment of choice (in its tactile form adapted for horses, Bilateral Equine Tapping for its application to horses (BET)). EMDR is considered an effective treatment for PTSD and the reduction of anxiety due to traumas of war or other psychological assaults. It is included in the professional treatment guidelines of the U.S. Department of Defense, The American Psychological Association, and the American Psychiatric Association.[37]

The exact neurobiological mechanisms involved in EMDR/BET are not established. However, EMDR is believed to increase thalamo-cortical temporal binding that has failed during traumatic insult.[38]

EMDR/BET differs from other methods such as flooding in that the internal process of memory integration depotentiates external cues thereby avoiding re-traumatization that flooding can cause. This is an important point for animals because it is usually not possible to obtain client consent.

Two tapping devices on the outside of Hero's jaw on both sides, at the Temporal Mandibular Joint (TMJ), each the size of a quarter are attached to an audio scan by wires. Each tapper produces a vibration, equal to tapping oneself with the forefinger, and instrument settings include intensity and speed, which are calibrated to the horse's movements. The taps alternate, causing "dual attention" to both internal and external events. Tapping alternate sides of the body causes the corpus callosum to allow intercortical communication between the left and right hemispheres of the brain. The theory is that the tapping, with the use of simultaneous specific protocols, creates the possibility of experiencing a fearful event differently, thereby disconnecting the anxiety from the memory. Once the memory and anxiety are separated, the memory obtains a different value and will no longer create a high level of fear response. People remember the trauma, but are able to manage the memory without a visceral response. The event becomes integrated into life's narrative. They become able to go through the portal of memory the way that Hero was able to cross the threshold of his stall.

In their training, horses generally learn to move away from the riders' aids (i.e., the trainer or rider's hands, legs). Horses' extreme sensitivity to touch is considered in this therapy. The phases of BET include establishing a safe place (therapeutic container), guiding the brain into dual attention bilateral stimulation, by using the cognitive left brain to help to unfold negative associations in the right brain, thereby reprocessing to link a new ego state with a positive desired cognition of the presenting problem. The therapist approached Hero with the same "intentionality" and open mindedness that is used with human patients and allowed him to sniff and touch the equipment used in the BET protocol. There are no movements until the horse is settled and relaxed. Waiting for the moment of relaxation becomes part of the "holding" environment, be it fifteen minutes or one hour. Once he was relaxed, it was time to present the problem, or if the actual trigger was assessed to be too dangerous by the therapist, an associated symptom was used. In Hero's case, after he seemed relaxed, the stall door was opened he was asked to move out across the threshold. He was hesitant and panicky, but not as panicky as on previous occasions. His movement appeared slower and less tense, with his head more forward and down. When Hero's behavior improved, the trainer let him know by rewarding him with a pat on the neck and a kind word.

In approximately twelve trials, behavior improved by 50% as measured by a quantitative decrease in symptoms and overall presentation. Hero became less hesitant to move across the threshold and more settled after entering and exiting the stall. His panic subsided as he allowed himself to be led with less resistance, although not in a consistent manner; there were sporadic bursts of panic. In the first 48 hours after the first BET treatment, Hero bared his teeth, would not listen, and slept the entire day; very unlike him. It seemed like an abreaction (a reliving of an experience in order to purge it of its

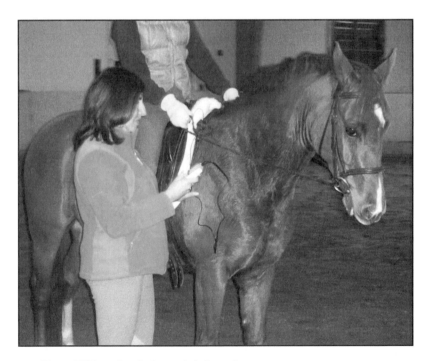

Fig. 2: BET tapping device at girth for a client.
Photo courtesy of Vera Muller-Paisner

emotional excess), and an emergency session was created using only the "safe" place where relived experience unfolds in a controlled environment that has been experienced as secure.

In the next session, one week later, Hero showed much improvement on entering and leaving his stall. By the third session, leaving and returning to the stall were uneventful. Additionally, Hero seemed more relaxed and available when ridden. Further, even under circumstances that could be very stressful, he was much calmer. For instance, Hero was bred after the second session and did not tighten his neck and held his head in a more normal way for breeding. The general impression was that Hero was more at ease with the use of his body, and appeared more confident. What remained to be seen was the behavior this confidence brought. Indeed, when the stall was left open, and there were mares in heat standing in the outside paddock, Hero, for the first time, left his stall unattended and went to visit the mares. When he was moved to a different barn one year later, he had become much more comfortable moving in and out of the stall. His new living accommodations include an open stall with free range of movement, between the outside grassy paddock and his stall. At present, Hero moves in and out at will. Hero's trainer has found him more willing and quick to respond to engagement, thus saving the use of his legs from the repetitive nature of the work in dressage. Treatment continued for six sessions each between 30 to 45 minutes, one week apart. Included in the treatment regimen were cognitive exercises that would reinforce the new behavior.

DISCUSSION

We set out to explore how animal symptoms might be approached in a psychologically inclusive framing: to investigate what considerations are necessary clinically and ethically when using human-based criteria for diagnosing and treating psychological distress in a horse. We also explored some of the ethical and practical implications involved. As to be expected, only the surface of a vast topic was scratched, raising more questions than could be presently answered. At the end, however, we are charged with evaluating whether or not Hero benefited from these therapeutic ministrations. The answer is "yes" by these criteria: his symptoms attenuated to near extinction (something that

Fig. 3: Hero's new open stall with free range of movement.

Photo courtesy of Lyndee Kemmett

was not possible with other approaches prior to BET); his overall demeanor as evaluated by the therapist, trainer, and veterinarians is joyful, confident, and assured; he showed a desire to initiate and participate in the world around him; and his risk of injury was dramatically reduced. And what of animal psychotherapy in general?

We are well served to heed James Hillman's plaint that after more than 100 years of psychology humans are beset with even more ills and distress. This knowledge is of particular relevance since the majority, if not all, of the animals we seek to heal have been psychologically wounded by humans. We are therefore cautioned to exercise great care in translating ideas and tools to other species. In seeking to aid animals who suffer from what humans have done to them, humans must guard against overzealousness brought on by an eagerness to explore new frontiers and the frantic effort to right past wrongs.[39] The vast numbers of wildlife and apparent absence of psychopathology in free-ranging, nonhuman species before western human colonization suggest that psychological issues were manageable without human intervention: the "outbreak" of previously undetected symptoms consonant with PTSD found in diverse species is not coincidence.

There are also many technical aspects to investigate. Approaches to treatment are neither comprised of a single approach nor unified philosophy but rather a diversity ranging from psychoanalysis to cognitive-behavior to traumatology to the use of psychopharmaceuticals. Each approach carries its own ethical and conceptual assumptions. Choosing one or the other requires individual evaluation to meet specific concerns and value systems. For instance, psychopharmaceuticals are prescribed to address a variety of psychological disorders such as infanticide and self-mutilation for animals kept in zoos, and hyper-aggression and phobias in companion dogs and cats. However, while congruent with some psychological schools, others consider the use of medications for mental disorders as a way to mask symptoms primarily designed to assuage human caregivers rather than address deeper underlying causes (i.e., captivity, neglect, abuse) responsible for creating non-normative behavior. If humans are to be involved in animal healing, then the task must be carried out with profound consideration and humility. Human philosophy, values, and attitudes toward the identity and rights of animals must be examined carefully and relative to the individual when considering care of other species.

In summary, then, those who remain in captivity and dependent on humans for life and death can benefit from psychotherapy. However, it is clear that the human bond has the potential to both heal and harm. For domesticated animals and wildlife in captivity, humans are intrinsically guilty of dual roles, a situation that is eschewed by psychology. The line between healer and abuser is very fine. It is therefore our own mental heath that falls under scrutiny. It is essential to take to heart the call for "physician heal thyself".

NOTES

1. Sigmund Freud, *"A Difficulty in Psychoanalysis"*, *The Standard Edition of the Complete Psychological Works of Sigmund Freud*, Vol. 17 (London: Hogarth Press, 1919), p. 140.

2. G.A. Bradshaw & B.L. Finlay, "Natural Symmetry," *Nature* 435:149, 2005.

3. Kenneth Shapiro, *Animal Models of Human Psychology* (Cambridge, MA: Hogrefe & Huber Publishing, 1998).

4. F. Welemsfelder, T.E.A. Hunter, M.T. Mendl, A.B. Lawrence, "Assessing the 'whole animal': a free choice profiling approach," *Animal Behaviour*, 2001, 62, 209-220.

5. G.A. Bradshaw & Mary Watkins, "Trans-Species Psychology; Theory and Praxis," *Spring*, Vol. 75, pp. 69-94; G.A. Bradshaw, *Elephants on the Edge: What Animals Teach Us About Humanity* (New Haven: Yale University Press, 2009).

6. G.A. Bradshaw and R.M. Sapolsky, "Mirror, Mirror," *American Scientist*, 94(6; 2007). 487-489; G. Northoff and J. Panksepp, "The trans-species concept of self and the subcorticalcortical midline system," *Trends in Cognitive Sciences* (12)7; 2008: 259-264.

7. Freud, Vol. 17, p. 140.

8. Martin Brüne, U. Brüne-Cohrs, W.C. McGrew, "Psychiatric treatment for great apes?" *Science*, 306, 2039 (2004); Martin Brüne, U. Brüne-Cohrs, W. C. McGrew, & S. Preuschoft, "Psychopathology in great apes: concepts, treatment options and possible homologies to human psychiatric disorders," *Neuroscience and Biobehavioral Reviews*, 30 (2006), 1246–1259.

9. G.A. Bradshaw *et al.*, "Developmental Context Effects on Bicultural Post-Trauma Self Repair in Chimpanzees," *Developmental Psychology*, 45: 5,1376-1388, 2009; G.A. Bradshaw & Allan N. Schore, "How elephants are opening doors: developmental neuroethology, attachment, and social context," *Ethology*, 113: 426–436, 2007; G. A. Bradshaw, J. Yenkosky, & E. McCarthy, "Avian affective dysregulation: Psychiatric models and treatment for parrots in captivity," *Proceedings of the Association of Avian Veterinarians, 28ᵗʰ Annual Conference, Minnesota*, 2009; G.A. Bradshaw, Theodora Capaldo, Lorin Lindner, and Gloria Grow, "Building an inner sanctuary: trauma-induced symptoms in non-human great apes," *Journal of Trauma and Dissociation* 9(1): 9-34, 2008.

10. Francine Shapiro, *Eye Movement Desensitization and Reprocessing: Basic Principles, Protocols, and Procedures* (New York: Guilford Press, 1995), p. 398.

11. American Psychiatric Association, *Diagnostic and Statistical Manual of Mental Disorders—Text Revision*, 4ᵗʰ ed. (Washington, D.C.: American Psychiatric Association 2000), pp. 467–69.

12. G.A. Bradshaw & Allan N. Schore, "How elephants are opening doors."

13. Laurence Kirmayer, "Culture, Context, and Experience in Psychiatric Diagnosis," *Psychopathology*, 38, 192–196, 2005; Patrick J. Bracken, Joan E. Giller, and Derek Summerfield, "Rethinking Mental Health Work with Survivors of Wartime Violence and Refugees," *Journal of Refugee Studies* 10 (1997): 431–42.

14. Jennifer Vargas, "Dolphins: Second-Smartest Animals?" *Discovery News,* http://news.discovery.com/animals/dolphins-smarter-brain-function.html.

15. Ignacio Martín-Baró, *Writings for a Liberation Psychology*, ed. A. Aron and S. Corne (Cambridge: Harvard University Press, 1994), p. 25.

16. In the same spirit with which human confidentiality and identity is protected, we use a pseudonym in lieu of the horse's real name.

17. G.A. Bradshaw & B.L. Finlay, "Natural Symmetry," *Nature* 435:149, 2005.

18. For our purposes here, we use an integrative therapy that brings together elements from the above clinical orientations for the treatment of experientially based emotional difficulties caused by traumatic events.

19. K. Nagaraja Rao, C.Y. Sudarshan, and Shamshad Begum, "Self-injurious behavior: A clinical appraisal," *Indian Journal of Psychiatry,* 2008 Oct–Dec; 50(4): 288–297.

20. Gordon G. Gallup, Jr., "Self-Recognition in Primates: A Comparative Approach to the Bidirectional Properties of Consciousness," *American Psychologist*, 32 (1977): 329–38.

21. G.M. White and A.J. Marsella, "Introduction," in A.J. Marsella & G.M. White, *Cultural Conceptions of Mental Health and Therapy* (Boston: D. Reidel Publishing Company, 1982), p. 23.

22. G.A. Bradshaw, "Reconciling Differences," *Psychology Today,* http://www.psychologytoday.com/blog/bear-in-mind/200911/reconciling-difference; Allan N. Schore, "Attachment, Affect Regulation, and the Developing Right Brain: Linking Developmental Neuroscience to Pediatrics," *Pediatrics in Review* 26(6): 204–17, 2005.

23. Julie A. Smith, "Constructing a 'Performance Ethic': The Discourse and Practices of the House Rabbit Society," *Society & Animals: Journal of Human-Animal Studies,* Vol. 11, No. 2 (2003): 181-197;

Margo Demello, "Becoming Rabbit: Living with and Knowing Rabbits", in this volume.

24. Horatio Fabrega, Jr., "Making sense of behavioral irregularities of great apes," *Neuroscience and Biobehavioral Reviews*. 30, 1260-1279, 2006.

25. Tragically, the United States government has a vigorous program to remove or kill these individuals; American Wild Horse Preservation Campaign, http://www.wildhorsepreservation.com/.

26. Allan N. Schore, "Attachment, Affect Regulation, and the Developing Right Brain."

27. G.A. Bradshaw, in press. "You see me, but do you hear me? The science and sensibility of trans-species dialogue," *Feminism & Psychology*; Mandal & Ambady (2004), quoted in Allan N. Schore, "A neuropsychoanalytic viewpoint: commentary on Steven Knoblauch," *Psychoanalytic Dialogues*, 15(6): 829-854, 2005.

28. Allan N. Schore, "A neuropsychoanalytic viewpoint: commentary on Steven Knoblauch," *Psychoanalytic Dialogues*, 15(6): 829-854, 210, 2005.

29. Allan N. Schore, *Affect Dysregulation and Disorders of the Self* (Mahwah, N.J.: Erlbaum, 2003).

30. Allan N. Schore, "Attachment, Affect Regulation, and the Developing Right Brain."

31. Tom Dorrance, *True unity: Willing communication between horse and human* (Bruneau, ID: Give-It-A-Go Enterprises, 1987).

32. F. Wemelsfelder, "How animals communicate quality of life: the qualitative assessment of behaviour," *Animal Welfare* 2007, 16(S): 25-31.

33. D.W. Winnicott, "The use of an object," *International Journal of Psychoanalysis,* 50:711-716, 1969.

34. John Briere and Joseph Spinazzola, "Phenomenology and Psychological Assessment of Complex Posttraumatic States," *Journal of Traumatic Stress* 18 (2005): 401–12; Judith Herman, "Complex PTSD: A Syndrome in Survivors of Prolonged and Repeated Trauma," in *Living with Terror, Working with Trauma*, D. Knafo (ed.)(Lanham, MD: Bowman & Littlefield, 2004).

35. Bessel A. van der Kolk, M.D., Joseph Spinazzola, Margaret E. Blaustein, James W. Hopper, Elizabeth K. Hopper, Deborah L. Korn, and William B. Simpson, "A Randomized Clinical Trial of Eye

Movement Desensitization and Reprocessing (EMDR), Fluoxetine, and Pill Placeboin the Treatment of Posttraumatic Stress Disorder: Treatment Effects and Long-Term Maintenance," *Journal of Clinical Psychiatry*, 68, 2007.

36. Uri Bergmann, "The Neurobiology of EMDR: Exploring the Thalamus and Neural Integration," *Journal of EMDR Practice and Research*, 2(4), 300-0314, 2008, 309.

37. Bessel A. van der Kolk, *et al.*, "A Randomized Clinical Trial of Eye Movement Desensitization and Reprocessing (EMDR)."

38. Uri Bergmann, "The Neurobiology of EMDR."

39. G.A. Bradshaw, *Elephants on the Edge.*

BECOMING RABBIT:
LIVING WITH AND KNOWING RABBITS

MARGO DEMELLO

The rabbit-human relationship is one of the most schizophrenic of all human-animal relationships. Rabbits have been sacrificed, hunted, bred, skinned, slaughtered, experimented on, and consumed; they have also been worshipped, cherished, and represented in countless myths, folk tales, children's books, and pieces of art. But they have rarely been considered as intelligent beings worthy of psychological inquiry. This is in part due to the rabbit's long history as a food animal, but also because even when kept as companion animals, rabbits have long been housed in outdoor cages, where they appear passive, reserved, and uninteresting. And because rabbits vocalize on only very rare occasions, they are rendered not just silent but invisible.

But rabbits, like all animals (human and non-human), have rich internal lives, as people who live intimately with rabbits can attest.[1] Living with house rabbits—where rabbits live indoors, without a cage or with minimal caging, as part of the human family—is, to me, the best way to gain some understanding of the rabbit psyche. In addition,

Margo DeMello, Ph.D., teaches anthropology and sociology at Central New Mexico Community College, writes on animals and body modification, and is the President of House Rabbit Society, an international rabbit advocacy organization.

living closely with rabbits opens up the possibilities of the human-rabbit relationship—a relationship which, until very recently, was one-sided and based on exploitation. Today, however, with the rise of the house rabbit movement,[2] the subjectivity of rabbits has been exposed, leading to the possibility of a human-animal relationship that is rich with possibilities—both for human and for rabbit.

RABBITS AND HUMANS: A BRIEF HISTORY

Rabbits were originally domesticated by French monks for food about 1500 years ago—long after the dog (15,000 years ago) and the major livestock animals (about 7,000 years ago)—but had been hunted for food and for fur for thousands of years before this time.[3] In fact, rabbits were not seen as anything but an economic resource until as late as the eighteenth century, when the notion of pet rabbits[4] first slowly emerged. Even then, rabbits remained primarily a source of food and fur, and later, medical information. Even though rabbits being raised for food were most certainly kept as pets by farmers' wives and children for centuries, as well as by hunters and gatherers who kept some game animals as pets, the idea of defining rabbits as pets—rather than as strictly food or fur animals—did not gain widespread acceptance until the eighteenth and nineteenth centuries when the fancy breeds were developed. The development of the rabbit as pet coincided, not coincidentally, with the rise of the commercial pet industry[5] and the idea that keeping pets could instill positive values and behaviors in children;[6] rabbits, thanks to their long symbolic association with women and children, became the ultimate "children's pet."[7]

But a pet rabbit is not necessarily a family member. For at least two hundred years, pet rabbits have been most commonly kept as outdoor pets, living in isolation in wooden and wire hutches, with little protection from the elements, and little to no companionship or comfort. These rabbits were typically fed and watered once a day, and occasionally taken out by the children to play. Thus the human-rabbit relationship was hampered and defined by the lack of sustained, intimate contact between human and rabbit. As a result, rabbits, their personality, culture, and psychology, remained virtually unknown outside of their storybook representations.

There were, of course, exceptions to this. William Cowper, the eighteenth-century English poet, wrote movingly about living with and loving three hares he named Puss, Tiney, and Bess.[8] In letters and poems, Cowper wrote about his relationship with the hares, and noted that Puss, with whom he was the closest, would tug at his pants to let him know he wanted to go out to play, leapt in his lap and licked him for attention, and often fell asleep on his knee.[9] In a time when the notion of animals having personalities seemed fantastical to most, Cowper wrote, "Such they were in fact, and their countenances were so expressive of that character, that, when I looked only on the face of either, I immediately knew which it (sic) was."[10]

Author and illustrator Beatrix Potter was another early rabbit lover. In 1889, she purchased her first rabbit, a Belgian hare she named Benjamin Bouncer; Peter Piper followed soon afterward. She described Benjamin as "an impudent, cheeky little thing,"[11] and both lived with her at least part time in the house and went with her on walks on a leash. When Peter died at nine, Potter wrote, "Whatever the limitations of his intellect or outward shortcomings of his fur, and his ears and toes, his disposition was uniformly amiable and his temper unfailingly sweet. An affectionate companion and a quiet friend."[12] Ironically, while Potter truly loved Benjamin and Peter, her books did not lead to a change in the prevailing attitudes towards rabbits. In fact, rabbits were seen, perhaps more than ever before, as a "children's pet," and as such, continued to be trivialized. Rabbits continued to be associated with children, either as simple, uninteresting pets, or as stuffed rabbits. But it took another century for rabbits to make the leap from children's pet to family member.

HOUSE RABBIT SOCIETY TRANSFORMS THE HUMAN-RABBIT RELATIONSHIP

Beatrix Potter and William Cowper notwithstanding, rabbits remained a useful, but largely invisible animal for most people until the late twentieth century. While in the West, they were well-represented in art and children's literature, rabbits mostly were used to signify nature (in art) or children (in literature); in non-Western countries, they have a long and rich history as a symbolic and folkloric animal.

For instance, rabbits are linked to sexuality, and particularly female sexuality and fertility. In the rituals, myths, and symbols of Ancient Greece and Rome, hares were sacred to Venus and Aphrodite (goddesses of love), as well as Diana (goddess of childbirth), and they were often used in love spells, as aphrodisiacs, and to aid in fertility. Rabbits are similarly associated with female sexuality in Native American cultures, ancient Britain, Medieval Europe, China, and Japan. In eastern cultures as well as in Meso-America, ancient Europe, the Arab cultures, and Africa, the rabbit is also linked to the moon, which itself is linked to fertility and childbearing, with lunar goddesses commonly represented with or dressed as a rabbit or hare. And thanks to the rabbit's fertility, rabbits are also used in myths and rituals to signify rebirth, explaining the rabbit's role in the symbols of Easter.

But the *real* rabbit was generally absent from human thought. And the repercussions of this absence are very real.

Rabbits are slaughtered in the hundreds of millions per year for food, fur, and medical research; and, much of that slaughter has gone unnoticed and unremarked upon. In *Stories Rabbits Tell*, Susan Davis and I wrote:

> The fact that a species is unknown—as the rabbit is—means that we as humans can project all sorts of characteristics on the animals that would deem them unworthy of protection. We can even project a trait of blankness on them; that is, because we don't understand the rabbit, we assume there is nothing to understand, that the rabbit is a creature with neither sentience nor subjectivity. And once we assume that, creating what in other species we would recognize as "suffering" becomes acceptable.[13]

Rabbits are thus "disappeared:" they are removed from sight and kept in backyard cages (or in laboratories); they are considered passive and stupid; and they are silenced—through our ignorance and their lack of voice.

This situation began to change in 1985 with the publication of Marinell Harriman's *House Rabbit Handbook*,[14] the first ever book on living with a "house rabbit," a term coined by Harriman and now a common expression to refer to rabbits who live in the home with a human family. Written to honor the memory of Herman, a stray rabbit who found her way into Harriman's backyard and then home, the book inspired tens of thousands of people to adopt rabbits as house pets, and inspired Harriman to found House Rabbit Society (HRS),[15] the first and only international rabbit advocacy group of its kind. In fact, like William Cowper before her, whose love of Puss, Tiney, and Bess inspired him to take an active stand against hunting, Harriman's love of Herman led her to become a vegetarian and to become the most influential rabbit advocate of the twentieth century.

In the twenty-five years since the first edition of the *Handbook* was released, the idea that rabbits could be treated on the same level as dogs or cats—that they could live indoors as part of a human family, that they could receive veterinary care, that they could be spayed or neutered and live with companions of their own species—has gone from being laughable to being almost commonplace.

Thanks to the *Handbook* and House Rabbit Society, tens of thousands of people who now live with house rabbits have taken the rabbit-human relationship to an entirely new level.[16] Rabbits don't just share our homes—they occupy an enormous part of our lives, and have influenced the creation of an entirely new cottage industry that is dedicated not to the selling of rabbits, but to providing for the needs of the house rabbit, from rabbit toy makers to specialized food and hay producers to rabbit condominium manufacturers to healthy snack companies. Humans now serve rabbits, not the other way around.

Perhaps because rabbits have been domesticated[17] for a much shorter period of time than dogs or even cats (and did not co-evolve alongside humans, as did dogs),[18] rabbits are not the easiest animal to integrate into a human household. They chew, sometimes voraciously, leading house rabbit advocates to devise creative means of keeping phone and electrical cords, baseboards, walls, and furniture safe from sharp teeth. They are curious, and spend more time than one might imagine climbing, digging, and jumping into and onto furniture, crevices, and counters, often causing much trouble in the process. Rabbits do not always come when called, obey their caretakers, or behave in an appropriate "pet-like" fashion. They are intelligent, using tools like toys, bowls, furniture, or cage bars to communicate their desires to humans and other animals. And they are messy, not so much with their waste (they are relatively easy to litterbox train), but with their toys, as well as with whatever they choose to claim as their own. All of these assessments must be understood not as judgments but rather as measures of how distinct rabbit psychology and behavior are from more traditional domesticated pets.

Thanks to the work of House Rabbit Society volunteers and the ingenuity of thousands of rabbit lovers, plus the knowledge that they have compiled, issues like these are now managed through "bunny-proofing" the house, through purchasing and creating toys out of cardboard, wood, wicker, and wire, and through creatively re-imagining housing for rabbits inside of human homes. Rabbit veterinarians have learned how to safely treat rabbit illnesses and to spay and neuter them, allowing for the possibility of rabbit-rabbit relationships, and making living with rabbits in the home a cleaner proposition.

The upshot? Not only have tens of thousands of domesticated rabbits enjoyed the benefits of their new status as "house rabbits," and their guardians likewise reaped the benefits of developing intimate relationships with these intelligent, playful, curious, and willful animals, but we have begun to gain some entrée into the psyche of these once-inscrutable animals. Becoming a house rabbit not only changes one's living conditions; it alters the way in which rabbits are perceived, and thus treated. House Rabbit Society and the house rabbit movement have, in creating the concept of house rabbit, given rabbits some measure of personhood, and have changed rabbits from objects used as food or fur to subjects of a life.

Living with rabbits in the home—where they are underfoot in the kitchen, looking for snacks; where they watch television (as much as any companion animal watches television) with the family; where they wake up many a surprised person before dawn, with their demands for breakfast or snuggles—is intimate. While most house rabbits do not sleep under the covers as, say, a Chihuahua, and remain for the most part quite independent, they still lead lives that are closely intertwined with the rest of the household members—human and non-human.

In my house, I live with Igor, who was adopted by a couple through the St. Louis House Rabbit Society and returned to me when the couple had to return to Romania, and with Charlotte, who was dropped off at Albuquerque Animal Services with her entire family, all of whom were to be euthanized because of their congenital jaw problems. Igor and Charlotte make their home primarily in the living room, but Igor also goes wherever he likes—into the bedroom (cautiously, so as not to alert Nigel, the French lop who lives there, to his presence), into the courtyard (before the other rabbits come out to play), into the dining room (where he scouts for snacks), and down the hallway to observe and monitor household activities.[16] I spend evenings in the living room where I simultaneously watch television and the continuing relationship between Igor, Charlotte, and their newest companion, three-legged Molly, who arrived from a hoarder's home and whose leg was removed due to a bone infection. My vantage point on the couch allows me to follow my television "stories" as well as the soap opera that revolves around Igor and his ladies. Here I am privy to his emotional ups and downs—from his pride over his beautiful girlfriend Charlotte[20] (whom he shows off to constantly) to his anger when I bring another rabbit into the room or one of the dogs tries to eat his food or drink his water.[21]

CULTURAL TRANSLATION: SEEING RABBITS

House Rabbit Society volunteers have long said that rabbits make ideal companions for people who are quiet, both because rabbits have long been thought to dislike loud sounds, and because we must be *quiet* in order to really *see* these animals who are themselves so quiet and have been so long ignored. But while I am not a quiet person (quite the contrary), I make it my business to really *see* the rabbits who share my home. (I also think that Igor, in particular, enjoys the hustle and bustle of this household, with the noise of the television, the dogs barking, and the bird shrieking. While many rabbits are indeed fearful of loud noises and too much excitement, this is more a function of individual personalities as well as the type of background that the rabbits came from.) That I am a cultural anthropologist and am trained in observation of humans probably helps me to better observe and understand the non-humans with whom I live, but it's not just that. And it's not just learning rabbits' body language—the meaning behind the thumps, ear swivels, tail shakes, and nose twitches. It's being willing to see them for what they are, and to meet their needs, even when those needs conflict with my (or my husband's) desire for a clean house and a "normal" life.

Anthropology is the science of the Other, developed to understand the lives of people whose cultures differ, sometimes greatly, from our own; yet, at least in its postmodern form, it is inter-subjective, relying on a give-and-take relationship between researcher and subject, rather than an objective, objectifying approach that separates researcher from subject, and subject from object. Anthropology's holistic approach, participant-observation methodology, and its current rejection of reductionism does not privilege the perspectives of the researcher above those of the subject, but allows for a representation of the Other which is historical, contingent, and contestable.

Talal Asad, in a discussion about the problematics of cultural translation, discusses how the translation of other cultures can be highly subjective and problematic due in part to the "inequality of languages."[22] The ethnographer is both the translator and the author of that which is being translated, because it is he or she who has final authority in determining the meaning of the behavior being studied. Cultural translation, thus, is inevitably enmeshed in conditions of power. This problem, while not yet resolved within anthropology, is partially addressed by the use of reflexive accounts, in which the subjectivity of the author is made explicit in the texts produced.

This same problem exists, arguably to a much greater extent, when trying to understand and put into human words the minds of non-human animals. For me, the solutions to this problem exist in setting up a space in which human and non-human can co-exist as equitably as possible, which not only begins to undermine the power differential separating the species, but which opens up the possibility of understanding other animals on their own terms.

RABBIT-CENTERED LIVING

Julie Smith, a House Rabbit Society volunteer and English professor living in Wisconsin, writes of the problematics of living with house rabbits, and whether or not house rabbits are subjugated by this condition.[23] Does keeping a rabbit in a cage, even part time, unduly control him or her? What about using pens to keep rabbits inside, or outside of, certain household spaces? And on a bodily level, what about the control exercised over the rabbit body by removing their reproductive abilities? And even more fundamentally, to what extent does domestication enslave them? According to ecologist Paul Shepard, "the benefit to animals of being domestic is fictitious, for they are slaves, however coddled, becoming more demented and attenuated as the years pass.[24] Smith writes of her attraction to the philosophy and practices of HRS:

> One reason I found it easy to think about rabbits as free and equal within the human house was that I took them, not from the wild, but from oppressive domestic circumstances, often the outdoor hutch. To me, the outdoor hutch was the icon of human control over the rabbit because of its failure to address rabbit needs for space, companionship, and protection and also because of its association with practices of the American Rabbit Breeders Association (ARBA)…Taken from these traditional contexts, rabbits who entered the HRS house seemed to be entering an arena of freedom.[25]

But Smith is still troubled by the level of control that living with rabbits entails. Keeping rabbits as house pets is, without question, more complicated in practical terms than keeping a dog or a cat. Core aspects of house rabbit existence clash with normative modern human dwellings and values. For instance, because of their need to chew, they can cause considerable damage to furniture, carpets, or even the house itself. (Our living room has a grapefruit-sized hole in the wall courtesy of Igor.[26]) While rabbits are easily litterbox trained, many still drop occasional "pills" or feces around the house. Because of these two issues, many people who live with indoor rabbits will cage their rabbits, at least part time, and many others will use children's gates or other barriers to keep rabbits out of certain areas of the house, or confined within specific areas. In addition, like cats and dogs, rabbits are more easily kept as house pets when spayed or neutered. The integration of rabbit and human within the confines of typical human living necessitates additional levels of corporeal control, thereby limiting rabbit agency and ability for the full subjective experience. The practical constraints then translate into and simultaneously are reified by human representations of "the animal."

But while living with house rabbits entails perhaps more *explicit* control than is generally exerted over a household dog or cat, for many HRS people like Smith and myself, it also involves heavy compromises— on both the human and rabbit end. Not only do we bunny-proof our houses, covering electrical cords and parts of the furniture, carpets, or walls that may be chewed, but we purchase or make chew toys to give our rabbits their needed physical and intellectual stimulation and the ability to be instruments of their own lives and decision making. We also tend to be a relatively tolerant lot, accepting with resignation and even sometimes humor the occasional damage or ruined piece of furniture.

But many of us who live with house rabbits—Smith and myself included—go much further in accommodating rabbits into our lives. As Smith writes,

> Many of us found it easier to change ourselves than the premises. At present, the rabbit who lives in the bedroom is excavating my mattress. She bounces around inside the dust cover and chews the wooden frame around the metal springs. Because of the HRS, I know I could staple hardware cloth around the bottom of the mattress or I could buy a large cardboard box sold for shipping mattresses and put it under the bed with materials in it for her to shred. Probably I will do neither. Indeed, I have heard HRS members laugh about taking turns with their human partners sleeping on the wet spot in the bed; putting fencing around their beds at night to keep rabbits from urinating on their pillow or barbering their eyebrows; and catering to rabbits who nip ankles, box hands, or trip-up human bodies when caretakers are too slow with the treats. Frankly, I love this way of living, this version of "becoming animal."[27]

I would argue that the contemporary rabbit-human relationship, as it has been creatively reconfigured by house rabbit lovers today, is moving away from not only the one-sided relationship represented in the meat rabbit business and through the old-fashioned child/hutch rabbit relationship, but away from the typical human-pet relationship as well, which is marked at least in part largely by dominance and control. While most people who live with rabbits today still exercise at least some control over their rabbit companions (as mentioned above), many are creating ways in which their rabbits can exert more freedom to be themselves than ever before, and perhaps more than many pet lovers give to their dogs, cats, or birds.

What kind of people would willingly live in a home in which hay is scattered all over the floor, a litterbox occupies the space in front of (or even inside of) the fireplace, cardboard boxes filled with newspaper are shredded and urinated on in the living room, and the couch is set up so that Trudy the disabled rabbit can spend evenings on it in front of the TV? I live like this, and other rabbit people do as well, illustrating the great lengths to which many people today will go to share their lives with an animal on as-close-to-equal terms as can be accommodated. While it remains a struggle to give the rabbits in my home as much freedom as they would like, especially because I share my home with another human whose willingness to patch the holes in the wall or repair the chewed electrical cords is sometimes strained, it remains my goal.

To me, what Smith calls "becoming animal" is not just a new way to live with a creature who is, after all, much more recently domesticated than the cat and the dog and who thus retains much of its wildness. It also offers us insight into rabbit consciousness. Changing one's house (or building a new one from scratch, as my husband and I did six years ago) to accommodate rabbits involves, at one level, trying to understand how rabbits see the world and a willingness to take up their culture as part of or own.

It also means remembering who they were, just 1500 years ago. Our domesticated rabbits are really just a hop away from their wild ancestors. That means that the behaviors found in wild European rabbits are still very much present in domesticated rabbits. Unlike hares and cottontails who are solitary, European rabbits live in large underground warrens of dozens to hundreds of rabbits. Their social nature explains why European rabbits were domesticated but hares and cottontails were not. Unfortunately, rabbits raised or kept for human use are almost always kept in solitary cages, away from contact with other rabbits (or other animals), which stifles much of their natural behavior, and as we now understand, has a devastating effect on them psychologically and physiologically.

Knowing this simple piece of information about where rabbits come from allows us to create a life for our companion rabbits that not only allows for as much freedom and equality as is possible in a human-controlled world, but it also opens up the door for rabbits to once again enjoy the social life which is so important to their kind. House Rabbit Society has, since our beginnings twenty years ago, encouraged people to adopt companions for their rabbits, so keeping rabbits in pairs or threesomes is now quite common.

In my household, I have a group of 50 rescued rabbits who live together.[28] They spend their days chewing on cardboard, foraging for food (in my protected courtyard), lounging on their hammocks; and, they spend endless hours communing with each other—grooming, nuzzling, playing, "gossiping," or just hanging out. While these intraspecies relationships tend to mean that the rabbits will not bond with me (in fact, most will not even tolerate me touching them), it is much more important that they experience the richness of rabbit-rabbit relationships. (I admit that the rabbits who live in my bedroom and living room must tolerate much more attention from me than those in the large group, and thankfully, some, like Charlotte and Trudy, reciprocate it. I am certainly not immune to the need to share affection with my rabbits.) This is especially true given the fact that these rabbits have all been abandoned, and many come from environments of either cruelty or neglect. They come to me scared and insecure, and sometimes aggressive. Living with other rabbits in a safe environment with a variety of activities to engage in and a minimal amount of human intervention and control is one way for them to gain confidence.

I also try to put much of the rabbits' days into their own hands (or paws). While I do set mealtimes (mornings and evenings), there is hay out all day so that they can eat when they like. Their room has two doors—a human door for me to go in and out and a rabbit-sized door for them to use whenever they like. While they are all inside at night, during the day they can go in and out, regardless of the weather. Regardless of where they came from, most rabbits who end up in my home lacked control over any aspect of their lives. By providing an environment where they can go to bed when they like, eat when they like, go inside or outside when they like, interact with whom they like, and modify parts of their physical environment as they like, they appear not only to be happier, but more "rabbit-like." Even my disabled rabbits are given as much freedom as possible; I have specially made carts that rabbits with little use of their rear legs can use to roll around the house, and I have seen their confidence soar once they begin using the cart.

Finally, like most people who live with companion animals, house rabbit people talk to their rabbits. Rabbits who live in outdoor cages are rarely communicated with; many are lucky if they get fed or watered daily. We know that talking to non-human animals serves as a way to bond the human to the animal, to incorporate the animal into the human's social world, and allows for the human to talk *about* the animal as well, which is another way of making that animal family. Rabbits who do not live in the home are typically excluded from such communication, so talking to them is an important way of relating to them and interacting with them that feels good both to the person and to the animal. In addition, seeing and reading how rabbits communicate, with their ears, their noses, their tails, their bodies, is a way to respect them and their needs. When we can understand, even to a limited extent, what rabbits are saying to us, we can then give them what they need, which will go a long way towards making them feel like *their interests matter*. We can also respond to rabbits in kind—by using their communication styles, as much as we are able, to reach out to them on their own terms. House Rabbit Society has long advocated sitting or laying on the ground as a way to interact with rabbits at their own level, and house rabbit people have learned, from observing how rabbits groom and communicate with each other, how to approach, touch, and interact with them.

CONCLUSION

In an editor's note accompanying a *House Rabbit Journal* article about giving rabbits what they want, Amy Espie writes:

> Do you ever get the feeling that articles about companion animals are required by law to mention that petting a rabbit/cat/dog lowers our blood pressure? Another inescapable truism extols the unconditional love bestowed on us by these our steadfast companions. On first, fourth, and perhaps fourteenth reading, these appear to reflect well on us; but eventually we discern the decidedly less admirable note that is the underlying message: what's in it for me?[29]

As important as the research into the human-animal bond is, I think it's important to ask the question: what's in it for the animal? Living in a home with a human family certainly does provide measurable physical and emotional benefits for companion animals who, after all, have been domesticated and can no longer be "wild" again. And rabbits who are fortunate enough to live in homes where a greater-than-normal amount of freedom is afforded to them and where their needs are given priority benefit even more from their status as companion animals.

But rabbits—and other animals—benefit in other ways as well.

Many people who live with rabbits today not only work to make their own relationship with rabbits as equitable as possible, but use their love of rabbits to advocate for change for all animals. House Rabbit Society was formed out of one woman's love for rabbits, and countless other rabbit lovers now not only work to better the lives of rabbits, but to improve the lives of other animals as well. Because of their use in the meat, fur, and vivisection industries, many animal lovers empathize especially with rabbits, and use that empathy to try to secure better lives for all animals. In that way, rabbits are a sort of bridge animal, allowing those who live with and love rabbits to empathize with other animals as well—even those we once ate or wore.

My own life has been radically transformed by rabbits. I do not just live with dozens of rabbits in a house custom-built for them and filled with their hay, toys, and poop. I also devote hours each day to managing House Rabbit Society, and most of my friends are rabbit people. In addition, like Marinell Harriman before me (and William Cowper before her), my love for rabbits has fueled my animal activism outside of HRS, as well as my involvement in the field of human-animal studies. And finally, my identity has changed. I am, like so many others, a rabbit person, whose life is partially defined by my relationship with rabbits. My life without rabbits would not just be different; it would be unimaginable.

NOTES

1. Susan Davis and Margo DeMello, *Stories Rabbits Tell: A Natural and Cultural History of a Misunderstood Creature* (New York: Lantern Press, 2003).

2. I date the rise of the house rabbit movement to the publication of Marinell Harriman's *House Rabbit Handbook* in 1985 and the founding of House Rabbit Society in 1988.

3. Davis and DeMello, *Stories Rabbits Tell*.

4. Pet rabbits are rabbits who are kept primarily as companions and not for food, fur, or medical usage. However, "pet" does not necessarily imply "household" animal.

5. The commercial pet industry includes animal breeders, dealers, and pet stores, as well as the advocacy groups which support them. In 2009, the American pet industry made 45 billion dollars in sales of

animals and pet supplies (American Pet Products Manufacturing Association). Over 2 billion dollars was spent purchasing live animals that year, with an unknown amount being spent to purchase rabbits.

6. Katherine Grier, "Childhood Socialization and Companion Animals: United States 1820-1870," *Society and Animals: Journal of Human-Animal Studies* Vol. 7, No. 2 (1999): 95-120.

7. Davis and DeMello, *Stories Rabbits Tell*.

8. Rabbits and hares both belong to the order *Lagomorpha* and the family *Leporidae*, but are of different genera and species.

9. H.S. Milford, ed., *The Poetical Works of William Cowper* (Oxford: Oxford University Press, 1975).

10. Barbara Purchase, *Rabbit Tales* (New York: Van Nostrand Reinhold, 1982).

11. Judy Taylor, *Beatrix Potter: Artist, Storyteller, and Countrywoman* (London: Frederick Warne, 1986).

12. *Ibid.*

13. Davis and DeMello, *Stories Rabbits Tell*, pp. 348-349.

14. Harriman, *House Rabbit Handbook*.

15. See http://www.rabbit.org.

16. According to the American Pet Products Manufacturing Association, there are now 7.8 million pet rabbits in the United States. Approximately 10,000 of those are HRS members, and Bunspace, the social networking site for rabbits, has 3,000 members. House Rabbit Society's website currently receives a quarter million page views per month.

17. I define domestication as the process of maintaining animals in captivity, selectively breeding them for human purposes, and controlling their food supply, reproduction, and other aspects of life, thus creating a dependency on humans for survival, and a marked alteration in appearance and behavior. (See Juliet Clutton-Brock, *A Natural History of Domesticated Mammals*, Cambridge: Cambridge University Press, 1987, for a more detailed definition.)

18. By co-evolution, I am referring to the way in which dogs and humans each modified their own behaviors and cultures to accommodate the other. This process did not occur with rabbits, who were domesticated as tools, but not as partners, to humans.

19. Visit the Trans Species Living page of the Kerulos website to see videos and photos of my household, including Igor and Charlotte: http://www.kerulos.org/projects/t-s-rabbits.html.

20. See Charlotte and Igor here: http://www.youtube.com/user/margobun#p/u/8/bND3L-vIxzs and here: http://www.youtube.com/user/margobun#p/u/2/OMrKgwRLQ4o.

21. See Igor with Taz, one of the dogs, here: http://www.youtube.com/user/margobun#p/u/15/GRsydKPfess.

22. Talal Asad, "The Concept of Cultural Translation in British Social Anthropology," in James Clifford and George E. Marcus (eds.) *Writing Culture: The Poetics and Politics of Ethnography* (Berkeley: University of California Press 1986), p. 156.

23. Julie A. Smith, "Constructing a 'Performance Ethic': The Discourse and Practices of the House Rabbit Society," *Society & Animals: Journal of Human-Animal Studies,* Vol. 11, No. 2 (2003): 181-197.

24. Paul Shepard, *The Others: How Animals Made Us Human* (Washington: Island Press, 1996), p. 267.

25. *Ibid.*

26. See Igor chewing here: http://www.youtube.com/user/margobun#p/u/5/7PYUAVux3yg.

27. *Ibid.*

28. Visit the Trans Species Living page of the Kerulos website to see videos and photos of my household: http://www.kerulos.org/projects/t-s-rabbits.html.

29. Michele Lockers, "What Rabbits Want: Ask Not What Your Bunny Can Do for You," *House Rabbit Journal,* Vol. 4, No. 10 (Summer 2004).

CHICKEN-HUMAN RELATIONSHIPS: FROM PROCRUSTEAN GENOCIDE TO EMPATHIC ANTHROPOMORPHISM

KAREN DAVIS

Sound of a Battery Hen

You can tell me: if you come by the
North door, I am in the twelfth cage
On the left-hand side of the third row
From the floor; and in that cage
I am usually the middle one of eight or six or three.
But even without directions, you'd
Discover me. We have the same pale
Comb, clipped yellow beak and white or auburn
Feathers, but as the door opens and you
Hear above the electric fan a kind of
One-word wail, I am the one
Who sounds loudest in my head.

Karen Davis, Ph.D., is the president and founder of United Poultry Concerns (UPC, www.upc-online.org), a nonprofit organization that promotes the compassionate and respectful treatment of domestic fowl. She maintains a sanctuary for chickens, turkeys, and ducks on the Eastern Shore of Virginia and is the founding editor of *Poultry Press* and the author of *Prisoned Chickens, Poisoned Eggs: An Inside Look at the Modern Poultry Industry*, *More Than a Meal: The Turkey in History, Myth, Ritual, and Reality*, and *The Holocaust and the Henmaid's Tale: A Case for Comparing Atrocities*.

In Greek mythology, Procrustes ("the stretcher") is a bandit who keeps an iron bed into which he forces people to fit. Watching his victims approach from his stronghold, Procrustes stretches or shrinks the bed in advance to predetermine their failure to fit into it so that he may torturously reshape them to suit his will. If the victims are too tall, he amputates their limbs; if they are too short, he stretches them to size. I suggest that Procrustes is a particularly "fit" symbol of the false anthropomorphism used by many human cultures, in particular today's industrialized society, to force nonhuman animals into constructions fundamentally alien and inimical to their nature. The wishes and desires of the modern human psyche seldom coincide with the needs and desires of animals; hence a Procrustean solution is sought whereby the animal is either cut down to size or stretched to fit the agenda. In diverse aspects of our modern human culture, animals are physically altered, rhetorically disfigured, and ontologically obliterated to mirror and model the goals of their exploiters. The tortured and deformed patterns of industrialized animal bodies and lives reflect the self-same patterns of the human psyche responsible for creating such suffering. By maintaining the illusion that (animal) body and human (mind) are somehow separated, humanity maintains an image of life and meaning built on profound suffering. Psychology cannot aspire to heal the human psyche without acknowledging the true reality in which psyche lives.

ANIMAL GENOCIDE

Forcing animals, "stretching" and "amputating" them like Procrustes, to fit a preconceived human pattern or agenda is the very essence of the genocidal assault on nonhuman animal *identity*. It goes beyond the physical extermination of millions of animals and expropriation of their land and homes. By "genocidal assault," I refer to the concept of genocide as originally formulated by the Polish jurist, Raphael Lemkin, in 1944, to refer not only to the deliberate physical annihilation of a group by direct killing, but also to the destruction of the *identity* of the targeted group or groups, as in their "extinction" by incarceration and/or genetic manipulation, an extinction reflected in and reinforced by rhetorical formulations misrepresenting the targeted groups.[1] Recalling the experience of the Jews under the Nazis to

Fig. 1: Caged hens at Weaver Brothers Egg Farm in Versailles, Ohio.
Photo courtesy of Mercy For Animals

illuminate the plight of nonhuman animals subjugated by humans, Roberta Kalechofsky writes of both victimizations that, "[l]ike the Jew," the animal is trapped in the "symbolism of another group. The animal's life and destiny are under the control of the symbolic signs of others."[2]

The concept of genocide that includes physical, cultural, and ideological forms of victim annihilation defines humanity's relentless assault on the individuals, families, communities, and bodies of other animal species as a "genocidal" project both in its own right and in the context of organized human-on-human genocide. Just as it makes sense to speak of a "genocidal relationship implemented through racism" in the case of America's aggression in Southeast Asia,[3] for example, it makes sense to speak of genocidal relationships implemented through speciesism in the myriad examples of humankind's conquest of nonhuman animals and their living space.

The destruction, exile, and/or relocation of countless animal species and remnant populations of animals, under the assertion of the human "right" to possess and impose its cultural and psychological patterns, corresponds to the European colonial assault on the native human inhabitants of the African and American continents. It parallels the

Nazi territorial expansionism known as *Lebensraumpolitik* where Nazi politics of "must have" living space unfolded as an extension of the nineteenth century American "manifest destiny" that justified conquest of the Southwest and the Northwest, and islands in the Pacific and Caribbean, following its previous and continuing depredations and exterminations in South and Central America.[4] French anthropologist Edmond Perrier wrote in 1888: "Just as animals disappear before the advance of man, this privileged being, so too the savage is wiped out before the European."[5]

Genocide represents the imposition of the oppressor's pattern of life and beliefs on the life pattern of an oppressed group. The group becomes subject to the oppressor's laws and cultural norms, a process that may, but does not invariably, entail the complete physical annihilation of the subjected group. Vestiges and deformations of the original culture may remain for shorter or longer periods, despite, or at the behest of, the oppressing agency for diverse purposes. Philosopher Jean-Paul Sartre noted that dependence on the labor of the subject people and the preservation of the colonial economy places restraints on the physical genocide that otherwise proceeds where no material advantage is gained from restraint. This dependency on the subject people provides protection from physical genocide, even as "cultural genocide, made necessary by colonialism as an economic system of unequal exchange," continues.[6]

The model of genocide crafted for humans-over-human oppression parallels humans-over-nonhuman-animals conquest.[7] Billions of chickens, turkeys, ducks, cows, pigs, and other animals, like their wild counterparts, evolved to lead complex social lives in their own natural habitats; they have shown their ability to revert to living independently of humans, to become feral. Genocide is not to be rendered only physically, but is proliferated in virtually endless re-formations of animal bodies to fit the procrustean beds of global industrial agriculture and research. The chicken is one example.

The fate of chickens brings a hideous twist to the myth of the Phoenix, the mythical Egyptian bird who rises eternally young out of his own self-made funeral pyre. Traditionally, he is regarded as a symbol of the indomitable spirit of life and inexorable ability to be reborn from the ashes of death. In the light of animal agriculture, the Phoenix takes on a sinister aspect. Modern-day phoenixes, chickens, are unable to die and become extinct under conditions equivalent to their eternal rebirth in a maniacal womb. A further irony derives from the fact that ancient Egyptians are considered the original inventors of the enormous incubation ovens that later became the model for the mammoth incubators used today for hatching tens of thousands of baby chicks artificially and simultaneously without a mother hen sitting on the eggs. The Egyptians provided the blueprint for today's mechanical Phoenix-like matrix in Hell to produce the "tidal wave of baby chicks" that flows invisibly across the earth today to stock human tables and satisfy human palates.[8]

Fig. 2: Hatchery chicks at the beginning of their sad and terrible journey to human tables.

Photo courtesy of UPC

Factory-farmed chickens are imprisoned in buildings that are themselves part of a global system of confinement and international transport. Baby chicks, turkey poults, and hatching eggs intended for breeding are stowed as cargo on flights from one country to another, adding to the billions of birds being crated in delivery trucks from hatcheries to growout facilities to slaughter plants and elsewhere, up and down main roads and back roads all day, every day. There is a veritable poultry highway shuffling avian souls throughout the planet. However, the reality of this aboveground other-world is largely hidden from view. As noted by the agribusiness watchdog group GRAIN, which tracks and reports on the global spread of avian influenza and its sources, "Rare are photos of the booming transnational poultry industry. There are no shots of its factory farms hit by the [bird flu] virus, and no images of its overcrowded trucks transporting live chickens or its feed mills converting 'poultry byproducts' into chicken feed."[9] The absence of image brings an absence from mind and effects perceptual genocide.

Most humans are culturally conditioned to believe that chickens naturally exist as objects for human consumption and use, their "natural" habitat assumed to be the human-constructed world of a farm. However, chickens and other factory-farmed animals are totally separated from the natural world in which they evolved. Here, past these Dante's gates, we find the Procrustean myth played out in the flesh. Farmed animals are imprisoned in alien, dysfunctional, and disease-prone bodies genetically manipulated for food traits alone,

Fig. 3: Debeaked chicks with bloody beaks.

Photo courtesy of UPC

bodies that in many cases have been surgically altered, creating a disfigured appearance. Animals are debeaked, de-toed, dehorned, ear-cropped, tail-docked, castrated, and (in the case of piglets), dentally mutilated—and always without painkillers. In the procrustean universe of animal agriculture, these amputations can be made to sound sensible and even benignant. A poultry researcher writes: "The emotion-laden word 'mutilation' is sometimes used in describing husbandry practices such as removing a portion of a hen's beak. . . . [However] removal of certain bodily structures, although causing temporary pain to individuals, can be of much benefit to the welfare of the group."[10] Every effort is made to obscure and dent the reality of chicken experience. To control the debate between animal agribusiness and its adversaries, a poultry industry veterinarian has suggested that the word "debeaking" should undergo a procrustean facelift and instead be called "beak conditioning."[11] The turkey industry has now adopted this term.

Fig. 4: Thousands of bloated baby chickens gasp for breath in this standard industrial facility filled with toxic excretory ammonia fumes and manure-soaked bedding. Perdue Farms, Delaware, USA.

Photo courtesy of David Harp

Factory-farmed animals are imprisoned and bound in a belittling image that has little to do with who they really are. Disfigured and lumped in a sepia-colored, excremental universe, huddled together awaiting their slaughter in a foreseeable future of featherless bodies and mutilated faces already come to pass, these brilliant, resplendent miracles of nature are almost literally cookie-cut to fit the human-created conception of mere raw material to be processed into human geometric food products and animal byproducts.[12] Their predicament is not new as much as it represents a further turn of the screw that continues to turn. In *The Animal Estate: The English and Other Creatures in the Victorian Age*, Harriet Ritvo describes how animals became surrogates for nineteenth-century agendas, in particular Britain's imperial enterprise in which "material animals" and "rhetorical animals" embodied the most powerful possible symbol of human possession and control: "As material animals were at the complete disposal of human beings, so rhetorical animals offered unusual opportunities for manipulation; their positions in the physical world and in the universe of discourse were mutually reinforcing."[13]

ANTHROPOMORPHISM

We are told we are being "emotional" or "anthropomorphic" if we care about a chicken, empathize with a chicken, or grieve over a chicken's plight. By contrast such "manly" ("science-based") emotions as pride, conquest, control, and mastery of "poultry" and "livestock" are admired.

Ever since Darwin's theory of evolution erupted in the mid-nineteenth century, animal exploiters have invoked the word "anthropomorphism" to suppress protests of cruel and inhumane treatment of animals and to enforce the doctrine of an unbridgeable gap between humans and other animals. (Ironically, anthropomorphism was a term historically reserved to describe the attribution of human characteristics to the deity.) Despite the concept of species continuity that Darwin asserted and that is embraced by science today, [14,15] science has adamantly insisted on an indelible *discontinuity* between humans and all other species. However, this scientific law bends conveniently. Species continuity is called upon when it is necessary to justify a particular enterprise, such as the chicken genome project, in which the chicken is said to be "well positioned from an evolutionary standpoint to provide an intermediate perspective between mammals, such as humans, and lower vertebrates, such as fish."[16] The unbridgeable gap between humans and other animals is capriciously set aside any time it is required to further exploit animals. Animals are welcomed back into the fold as in the case of genetic engineering that "has the potential to remarkably improve, not only animal health and well being, but also human health."[17]

"Anthropomorphism," as it is used today, refers almost entirely to the attribution of consciousness, emotions, and other mental states, commonly regarded as exclusively or predominantly human, to nonhuman animals. While there is no longer any scientific doubt regarding the neurobiological, physiological, anatomical, and *psychological* continuity between human and nonhuman animals, scientists are reluctant to acknowledge mental continuity, and when it is recognized, refuse to address the implied ethics.[18,19] Until recently, about the only emotional capacity scientists have been willing to grant unstintingly to animals was fear. Scientists have set up countless "agonistic" experiments to elicit fear and fighting in captive animals, perhaps because there is unacknowledged pleasure in inducing the emotion of fear in others and watching them fight to the death in the controlled experiments of one's godlike designs. In contrast to fear and other stressful emotions, the emotional capacity for pleasure, happiness, and joy in animals is a touchier issue. Yet, "according to Darwin, there is evolutionary continuity among animals not only in anatomical structures such as hearts, kidneys, and teeth, but also in brains and their associated cognitive and emotional capacities."[20] Evidence of joy in animals is already "so extensive that it should hardly need further discussion."[21] But not everyone agrees. University of Oxford zoologist Marian Stamp Dawkins criticized ethologist Jonathan Balcombe's book *Pleasurable Kingdom: Animals and the Nature of Feeling Good* for arguing that animals can experience pleasure and happiness. This idea, she said, threatens to usher an abandonment of "all standards of scientific reasoning," resulting in a chaos in which there will no longer be any distinction "between the anthropomorphism of Bambi and the scientific study of animal behavior."[22] Here we see the powerful force of psychological denial and cognitive dissonance, for arguments such as Dawkins' are based on selective science.

Nonetheless, the exploitation of animals is based on precisely such ploys and succeeds because there is strong motivation to oppress other species. The rhetoric of exploitation cuts and pastes nonhuman animal identity, just as scientists cut and paste the bodies of animals to fit human desires. Sometimes the animal is ennobled if there is something wild and warlike about "him" (the "noble steed," the "majestic wild turkey" who deserves the best gunshot), but usually not. Humans, by virtue of a shared verbal language, can aggressively challenge the profanation of their identity. By contrast, nonhuman animals such as chickens are made powerless through language (for example, calling a human a "chicken" means the human is a coward and weak) and practice (through material subjugation). A hen is represented by egg producers as an "egg-laying machine," or as a symbolic uterus for the deposition of a human being's spiritual impurities, as in the Hasidic custom of kapparot ("atonements") in which chickens are configured as receptacles for practitioners' sins and punishment.[23]

Likewise, the practice of vivisection—the invasion of a living creature's body with a knife or other instrument of direct physical assault—is based on the anthropomorphic construction of the nonhuman animal as a "model" for the human condition into whose body human diseases are injected in what is, in essence, a form of interspecies rape by a human of a nonhuman animal victim. As in rape, so in vivisection, the victim is treated as a receptacle for the victimizer's defilement. In both cases, the victim is involuntarily made to appear as an aspect of the victimizer's identity, as when scientists call animals used in vivisection experiments "partners" and "collaborators" in the quest for knowledge. A biotechnology representative told an audience at a symposium on the future of animal agriculture that animals who are being modified and "recombined" every which way, to fit every conceivable purpose and whim, are "serving mankind" as part of an enterprise which "recognizes that animal welfare is of paramount importance and therefore has been and will continue to ensure that animal welfare is unsurpassed."[24] The physical world and animals are described in symbol and myth not to express who they really are but what the human psyche wants them to be.

FALSIFYING THE FATE OF VICTIMS

Similar to myths circulated by U.S. slavery owners about their human "property" during the nineteenth century, animal victimizers typically insist that their victims do not mind their plight, that they are unable to experience it "as you or I would," or that the victims are complicit in their plight, even, on occasion, to the point of gratitude. The victims, in other words, are not really "innocent." Rabbi Avi Shafran, Director of Public Affairs for Agudath Israel of America, an Orthodox rabbinical association, said that chickens, rather than suffering in being "swung" and slaughtered in kapparot rituals, may be regarded as "gratified by the privilege" of being killed for a "holy purpose."[25] Similarly, regarding his deportation of tens of thousands of Jews to their deaths, Nazi leader Adolf Eichmann pleaded his case by insisting that the Jews "desired" to emigrate and that "he, Eichmann, was there to help them."[26]

This is not exceptional psychology, as students of sexual assault are well aware. Victimizers often represent themselves as the innocent parties in their orchestrations of the suffering and death of others. In *Eichmann in Jerusalem*, Hannah Arendt cites an Egyptian deputy foreign minister who claimed, for instance, that Hitler was "innocent of the slaughter of the Jews; he was a victim of the Zionists, who had 'compelled him to perpetuate crimes that would eventually enable them to achieve their aim—the creation of the State of Israel.'"[27] If you want to hurt someone and maintain a clean conscience about it, chances are you will invoke arguments along one or more of these lines: the victim doesn't feel, doesn't know, doesn't care, is complicit, or isn't even *there*. In the latter case the victim is configured as *an illusion*.

In the case of animals, their fate, for each individual him and her, is to be absorbed into a human-centered hierarchy in which the animals cease to count, or even exist, apart from how humans use or have used them. *Our use becomes their ontology*—"this is what they are"—and their teleology—"this is what they were made for." Procrustean genocide is etched into human cultures and myths. To this day, animals are ritually sacrificed by Hindus whose practice is based on the idea that "the sacrifice of an animal is *not really the killing of an animal*." The animal to be sacrificed is not considered an animal but is instead "a symbol of those powers for which the sacrificial ritual stands."[28] In Hindu mythology, according to Basant K. Lal, "if a soul migrates to an animal form from a human life, it moves from a superior to an inferior form of life, and it does so because of its misdeeds while in the human form."[29] As in traditional Judaism, the Hindu attitude toward animals is not based on considerations about the animal as such but on considerations of how the animal advances the purificatory process leading to human salvation.[30] In Christianity, lambs disappear into the body and symbolism of Jesus Christ whereby they are elevated and redeemed into something that matters. In Buddhism, according to Christopher Chapple, the animal world is one of the lesser destinies, "along with the hell beings and hungry ghosts." Birth as an animal in the Buddhist tradition, although a basis for compassion, including the promotion of vegetarianism and other forms of nonviolence towards animals, is also a punishment for "evil deeds" and "deludedness."[31]

Accordingly, there is a long tradition of thought in which nonhuman animals are represented as benefiting from their victimization and even gratefully assisting in their own destruction, which is formulated as their "liberation." In Greek mythology, the ox runs from the fields to the city and stands at the altar to be sacrificed, and a bird flies to the altar and delivers itself "into the hands of the high priest."[32] In Hassidic lore, flocks of wild doves come of their own accord to lie down under the slaughterer's knife.[33] It has been argued that the doctrine of metempsychosis—the belief that human souls can become trapped in "lower" life forms as punishment for their misdeeds —rather than promoting vegetarianism, favors the consumption of flesh, since slaughtering an animal releases the human soul imprisoned within.[34] Meat in these accounts does not remind one, as it came to remind former chicken slaughterhouse worker Virgil Butler, of "the sad, tortured face that was attached to it some time in the past,"[35] but only of the human sinner or penitent, whose superior identity is defiled by being trapped in an animal's body. In Isaac Bashevis Singer's story "The Slaughterer," the rabbi seeks to convince the main character, Yoineh Meir, who does not want to slaughter animals, but is coerced into doing so, that everyone benefits from the slaughter: "When you slaughter an animal with a pure knife and with piety, you liberate the soul that resides in it. For it is well known that the souls of saints often transmigrate into the bodies of cows, fowl, and fish to do penance for some offence."[36]

Little has changed since earlier times. The ancient concept that animal sacrifice is acceptable if a prayer of gratitude is expressed by the human consumer has been absorbed by New Age practitioners. In today's world, pigs, cows, and even children want to be turned into Oscar Meyer wieners. Rabbits "collaborate" with vivisectors to test cosmetics so women can look pretty. Chickens run around headless in supermarkets demanding to be served with Swanson chicken broth. In the rhetoric of exploitation—as opposed to the language of liberation—animals can be redeemed from being "just animals" only by being sacrificed to "higher" forms of life, via science, religion, entertainment, or edibility. Hence, whatever was or is done to them is justified by the "will" of the animals themselves. Nonhuman animals want to be raped, mutilated, imprisoned, and even murdered, if it will make them "higher" and more humanlike, privileged to serve the human interest. This is the essence of false anthropomorphism and of the genocidal erasure of the animal's true identity in favor of the abuser's image.

EMPATHIC ANTHROPOMORPHISM

The opposite of cultural narcissism is *empathic* anthropomorphism, in which a person's vicarious perceptions and emotions are rooted in the realities of evolutionary kinship with other animal species in a spirit of goodwill. In contrast to the false anthropomorphism fashioned by animal exploiters, anthropomorphism based on empathy and careful observation is a valid approach to understanding other species. Humans are linked to other animals through evolution, and communication between many species is commonplace. Reasonable inferences can be drawn regarding the meaning of an animal's body language and vocal inflections based on what we know about comparable responses in humans in similar contexts. Chickens, for example, have a voice of unmistakable woe or enthusiasm in situations where these responses make sense. Their body language of "curved toward the earth" (drooping) versus "head up, tail up" is similarly interpretable. My experience with chickens for more than twenty years has shown me that chickens are conscious and emotional beings with adaptable sociability and a range of intentions and personalities. When they are enjoying their lives and pursuing their own interests, chickens are cheerful birds, quite vocally so, and when they are dispirited and oppressed, their entire being expresses this state of affairs as well. The fact that chickens become lethargic in continuously barren environments shows how sensitive these birds are to their surroundings, deprivations, and prospects. Likewise, when chickens are happy, their sense of wellbeing resonates unmistakably.[37] Chickens are neither stupid or impassive by nature; it is only human perception that defines them as such.

From this perspective, anthropomorphism makes sense. One may legitimately formulate ideas about animals and their needs that the rhetoric of exploitation seeks to discredit. One may proffer a counter rhetoric of animal liberation based upon empathy and careful observation. As Jonathan Balcombe writes in *Pleasurable Kingdom*, "We cannot feel the hummingbird's response to a trumpet-flower's nectar, the dog's anticipation of chasing a ball, or the turtle's experience of basking in the sun, but we can imagine those feelings based on our own experiences of similar situations."[38] Consider this picture of a wild turkey mother leading her brood, including an errant youngster:

> They hurry along as if on a march to some particular point, sometimes tripping along in single file, one behind the other, and at other times scattered through the woods for fifty yards or more. When on these scattered marches it is pleasant to note some straggling youngster as he wanders out of sight of the main flock in an attempt to catch a fickle-winged butterfly, or delays by the wayside scratching amid the remains of a decayed log in search of a rich morsel in the shape of a grubworm. . . . [W]hen he discovers that he is alone . . . [h]e raises himself up, looks with his keen eyes in every direction for the flock, and, failing to discover them, gives the well-known coarse cluck. Then he raises his head high in the air, and listens intently for his mother's call. As soon as it is discovered that one is missing the whole flock stops, and the young turkeys raise their heads and await the signal from their mother. When she hears the note of the lost youngster, she gives a few anxious "yelps," which he answers, and then, opening his wings, he gives them a joyous flap or two and with a few sharp, quick "yelps," he goes on a run to join his companions.[39]

These days, in the morning when I unhook the door of the little house in which eight hens and Sir Valery Valentine the rooster spend the night, brown Josephine runs alongside me and dashes ahead down to the Big House where she waits in anticipation while I unlatch the door to let the birds who are eagerly assembled on the other side of that door out into the yard. Out they rush, and in goes Josephine, straight to the favorite spot shaped by herself and her friends into a comfy nest atop three stacked bales of straw that, envisioned in her mind's eye, she was determined to get to. Why else, unless she remembered the place and her experience in it with anticipatory pleasure, would she be determined day after day to repeat the episode? In her mind's eye, is my own role in her morning ritual. I hold the Keys to the little straw Kingdom Josephine is eager to reenter, and she accompanies me trustingly and expectantly as we make our way toward it.[40]

Fig 5: Sanctuary hens running in the poultry yard.
Photo courtesy of Davida G. Breier

"Anthropomorphic" evocations like these, of a strolling turkey family and a sanctuary hen's eager intentions, are the opposite of the false anthropomorphism of, say, the fighting cock, the circus elephant, and the Thanksgiving turkey. In cockfighting, roosters are forced to die in stylized rituals of masculinity having nothing to do with natural bird behavior in an actual chicken flock. So-called circus elephants are taken from their natural habitats and forced to perform human-contrived antics for human entertainment. Thanksgiving turkeys are maledicted as "dirty birds" that become magically clean only by being slaughtered, cooked, and consumed by "superior" humans.

Such constructions exemplify the kind of anthropomorphism on which animal exploitation depends. It consists of insisting that animals are not suffering, that they are happy and grateful to be exploited, despite a congeries of evidence to the contrary. If animal advocates say, for instance, that a hen in a battery cage or a chicken buried alive in his own flesh is miserable, they're accused of anthropomorphism—of attributing human feelings to chickens. If producers say that the chicken is happy or (as one egg producer rewrote the company language in response to criticism) "content," the claim is accepted as "science." Consider the latitude accorded to agribusiness philosopher Paul Thompson, whose claim that blind hens "don't mind" being crowded together in cages as much as do chickens who can see is accepted as a "science-based" proposition with a view to improved animal welfare, in light of the blind chickens' alleged "reduced susceptibility to stress."[41] If blind chickens, or featherless chickens, or whatever genetically modified animal forms can be shown "quietly" to increase economic efficiencies in the industrial environment, the procrustean solution can be represented as a "holistic fit between a farm animal and its environment."[42]

PROCRUSTEAN SOLUTIONS TO ANIMAL WELFARE PROBLEMS

Thus far we have considered the plight of animals caught in the toils of agribusiness and other institutionalized predicaments in which they and their identities are forcibly reconstructed against their will to fit human purposes. The ethical conundrum posed by this arrangement has been represented in public debates mainly in terms of the fact that animals can suffer. Animals are feeling beings. They are "subjects of a life," in philosopher Tom Regan's phrase.[43] Animals can experience what they are doing and what is being done to them.

But what if an animal's capacity for experience could be reduced or even eliminated? What if scientists could create animals whose adjustment to abusive environments consisted in their being unable to experience their own existence, animals who were essentially the oblivious entities they are treated as being? This prospect may seem farfetched, but is it? More than a decade ago an engineer predicted that the future of chicken and egg production would resemble "industrial-scale versions of the heart-lung machines that brain-dead human beings need a court order to get unplugged from."[44]

Fig. 6: Lively young chickens reduced to a sepia-grey sea of pure suffering.
Photo courtesy of David Harp

The creation of insentient, brain-dead animals to fit the procrustean systems of industrialized agriculture is most likely in the works already. In *Minds of Their Own: Thinking and Awareness in Animals,* avian ethologist Lesley Rogers writes that "the identities of individual animals are completely lost." In industrialized farming, chickens and other animals are seen only as objectified bodies "to be fattened or to lay eggs." Their higher cognitive abilities are discarded, "ignored and definitely unwanted." The ultimate aim of breeding programs is to obtain animals with minds "so blunted" that they will passively accept the worst treatment and living conditions.[45]

As yet, there is no evidence that domestic chickens, or any other animals in commercial use, have been so cognitively blunted that they need no more stimulation than they receive in industrialized conditions. However, their overt signs of sensitivity will continue to be suppressed by these conditions. A writer for *The Guardian* described his impression of thousands of young chickens being raised for slaughter in a facility in the United Kingdom as "a sea of stationary grey objects."[46] The fate of chickens and other farmed animals is not to be treated as fellow creatures with feelings, but as pieces of meat and whatever else the market desires. They may have minds and consciousness, but they will not be treated as such.

For some critics of factory farming, the genetic engineering of animals to fit them to conditions from which they cannot escape is considered a welfare solution of sorts. The utilitarian philosopher Peter Singer exemplifies this view. Asked if he would consider it ethical to engineer wingless chickens to give them more space in battery cages, he replied that a wingless chicken would be an improvement, "assuming it doesn't have any residual instincts" such as phantom limb pain (which debeaked chickens have been shown to experience). He added that, "if you could eliminate various other chicken instincts, like its [*sic*] preference for laying eggs in a nest, that would be an improvement too." Asked if he would consider it ethical to engineer a "brainless bird, grown strictly for its meat," Singer said it would be "an ethical

Fig 7: Suffering for the sake of science has been the yearly fate for millions of chickens. These hens had thick red plastic contact lenses shoved into their eyes which prevented their eyes from breathing and caused painful eye infections and disintegration under the lenses. California Polytech State University, San Luis Obispo.

Photo courtesy of UPC

improvement on the present system, because it would eliminate the suffering that these birds are feeling. That's the huge plus to me."[47]

One must challenge this viewpoint. For one thing, most people who hope for a genetic solution to the suffering of animals on factory farms have no idea of what actually goes on in genetic engineering laboratories where countless live animals are routinely being "modified" and trashed. In 1994, I attended the First International Symposium on the Artificial Insemination of Poultry at the University of Maryland, College Park. In a talk entitled "Beyond Freezing Semen" (available in the published *Proceedings* which includes photographs of some of the procedures), Robert Etches, a researcher at the University of Guelph in the Department of Animal and Poultry Science, joked that his presentation might just as well be called "The Night of the Living Dead." He was discussing the experimental freezing and thawing of semen obtained from laboratory roosters (notably, extracted by masturbating them) to create chicken chimeras—chickens with genes from other species inserted into their embryos. Of birds hatching with no outward sign of the desired change, he said, "We simply throw them away."[48]

From an ethical standpoint, genetic engineering is not a solution to the suffering of animals on factory farms; rather, it is an extension of the system and mentality that produced and produces such suffering in the first place. Suffering involves more than the sensation of an injury; it includes more than pain. Suffering refers to the sustaining of a harm, wound, or disease, an injury, painful or otherwise. Millions of birds and other animals are being tortured in laboratories, forced into mutilated forms of existence, then discarded with no more concern for them or their feelings than if they were paperclips. What, then, is the difference from the standpoint of a purely nominal "concern" for animals between surgical amputation of their body parts and genetic amputation of their body parts including their brains? Does anyone wonder how a wingless bird might feel? Are wings just mechanical appendages to the bodies of birds that can be excised or "deleted" at will to enhance the "welfare" of their progeny in the terrible places to which we consign them to satisfy our appetites? Could other aspects of their existence be adversely affected by having their wings removed that would offset any welfare advantage obtained in the tradeoff?

Dr. Eldon Kienholz, a professor of poultry nutrition at Colorado State University, described experiments that he did on newborn chickens and turkeys, in which he literally cut off their wings and tails to see if by doing so he could demonstrate a savings in feed costs, since feed would not be needed to grow wings and tails in birds raised for meat. Later, he wrote that some of these de-winged birds, as he called them, "couldn't get up onto their feet when they fell over." It wasn't pleasant, he wrote, "seeing them spin around on their side trying to get back onto their feet, without their wings."[49]

This raises many questions, including whether a bird's wings are mere physical, expendable appendages, or whether they are an integral part not only of the body but of the very *being* of a bird. The neurologist Oliver Sacks discusses the persistence of what he calls "emotional memory" in people suffering from amnesia who have lost the ability to connect and recall the daily events of their lives, but who nevertheless appear to have "deep emotional memories or associations . . . in the limbic system and other regions of the brain where emotional memories are represented."[50] He suggests that these emotional memories, perhaps

Fig. 8: Consider the implications in the differences between what chickens have become and who they were meant to be.
Photo courtesy of Farrell Winter

Fig. 9: Former "battery" hens take naturally to perching in trees.
Photo courtesy of Pamela Winter

more than any other kinds of memories we possess, are what make us who we truly are in the most profound, if elusive, sense. The available evidence suggests that the consciousness of other animals, including birds, is also rooted in and shaped by emotional memory. Birds, too, possess limbic systems and other regions of the brain in which instincts and emotions are formed and coordinated, and they have been shown to share with humans a complexly evolved brain that processes information and gives rise to experience in much the same way as the human cerebral cortex. Given that neuroscience itself admits to a unitary model of vertebrate brain, minds, and behavior—that is, the structures of human, turkey, and chicken brains and their minds are generally shared—it is no inferential stretch to assume that their experiences are similar to our own as well as their communication capacities.[51, 52]

CONCLUSIONS

Scientists cite neurological evidence that the amputated stump of a debeaked bird continues to discharge abnormal afferent nerves in fibers running from the stump for many weeks after beak trimming, "similar to what happens in human amputees who suffer from phantom limb pain."[53] A "memory" of the amputated beak part persists in the brain, beak, and facial sensations of the mutilated bird even after "healing" has occurred. Scientists also cite the persistence of "ancestral memories" in intensively bred, factory-farmed chickens who, though they have never personally experienced so much as the ground under their feet, have "the same drive to scratch away to get their food," given the opportunity, as do their junglefowl relatives who spend long hours scratching away at the leaves of the forest floor to reach the tiny seeds of bamboo which they love.[54] Perhaps these deeply structured memory formations, retentions, and ineffable networks of knowledge in the body and brain of the factory-farmed bird give rise to "phantom limbic memories" in the individual: to subjective, embodied experiences in which even dismembered or mutilated body parts nonetheless awaken in the individual a distant memory of who and what he or she really *is*, ontologically.

We must assume that other animals, like ourselves, have dimensions of interiority and proprioceptive awareness all their own, and that in consequence, the surgical and genetic mutilations they experience, the grievous wounds they suffer at our hands, are as much existential and psychic as they are physical. Wingless, featherless, blind and brain-damaged, entrapped in the hell of humanity, do they recall their wholeness in the phantom limbic soul of themselves? And if they do, are their memories of their essential identity, eluding the procrustean blades of annihilation, experienced as compensation or curse? When hens in a battery cage fall asleep, perchance to dream, how do they feel when they wake up? We have become accustomed, through the environmental movement, to think of species extinction as the worst fate that can befall a sentient organism. But the chicken's doom is not to become extinct.

NOTES

1. Raphael Lemkin, "Axis Rule in Occupied Europe: Laws of Occupation, Analysis of Government, Proposals for Redress" (1944), in Ward Churchill, *A Little Matter of Genocide: Holocaust and Denial in the Americas 1492 to the Present* (San Francisco: City Lights Books, 1997), p. 70.

2. Roberta Kalechofsky, *Animal Suffering and the Holocaust: The Problem with Comparisons* (Marblehead: Micah Publications, 2003), p. 55; Karen Davis, *The Holocaust and the Henmaid's Tale: A Case for Comparing Atrocities* (Lantern Books, 2005), pp. 43-47.

3. Churchill, *A Little Matter of Genocide*, p. 416.

4. *Ibid.*, p. 421.

5. Enzo Traverso, *The Origins of Nazi Violence,* trans. Janet Lloyd (New York: The New Press, 2003), p. 57.

6. Churchill, *A Little Matter of Genocide,* p. 416.

7. G.A. Bradshaw, *Elephants on the Edge: What Animals Teach Us About Humanity* (New Haven: Yale University, 2009).

8. Harry R. Lewis, "America's Debt to the Hen," *The National Geographic Magazine* (April 1927): 457, 467.

9. "Fowl play: The poultry industry's central role in the bird flu crisis," GRAIN, http://www.grain.org/briefings/?id=194 (accessed February 2006), p. 2.

10. James V. Craig, *Domestic Animal Behavior: Causes and Implications for Animal Care and Management* (Englewood Cliffs, NJ: Prentice-Hall, 1981), p. 243, p. 244.

11. David Irvin, "Control debate, growers advised," *Arkansas Democrat-Gazette* (Little Rock), September 22, 2007, Business sec., http://www.nwanews.com/adg/Business/202171/.

12. Aaron Priel, "The featherless broiler is ready to go to market," *World Poultry* 23.2 (2007): 24-25.

13. Harriet Ritvo, *The Animal Estate: The English and Other Creatures in the Victorian Age* (Cambridge, Mass: Harvard University Press, 1987), p. 5.

14. G.A. Bradshaw & B.L. Finlay, "Natural Symmetry," *Nature,* 2005, 435, 149.

15. G.A. Bradshaw, & R.M. Sapolsky, "Mirror, Mirror," *American Scientist, 94(6),* 2007, 487, 489.

16. National Humane Genome Research Institute, "Chicken Genome Assembled: First Avian Genome Now Available to Scientists Worldwide," NHGRI, http://www.nhgri.hih.gov/11510730.

17. Barbara P. Glenn, "How Will Biotechnology Impact Agricultural Animal Welfare?" lecture, *Future Trends in Animal Agriculture: Food Animal Agriculture in 2020,* Jefferson Auditorium, South Agriculture Building, Washington, D.C., September 20, 2007, pp. 45-48.

18. Bradshaw, *Elephants on the Edge.*

19. G.A. Bradshaw, "The Scientists' Bark," *The Huffington Post* (2009), http://www.huffingtonpost.com/ga-bradshaw/the-scientists-bark_b_322558.html.

20. Marc Bekoff, *The Emotional Lives of Animals: A Leading Scientist Explores Animal Joy, Sorrow, and Empathy—and Why They Matter* (Novato, California: New World Library, 2007), p. 33.

21. *Ibid.,* p. 55.

22. Marian Stamp Dawkins, "Feelings Do Not a Science Make," review of *Pleasurable Kingdom: Animals and the Nature of Feeling Good,* by Jonathan Balcombe, *BioScience,* January 2007, 57.1, 84.

23. Gaby Wenig, "Human Atonement or Animal Cruelty?" *Jewish Journal of Greater Los Angeles* (October 30, 2003), p. 84.

24. Glenn, "Biotechnology," p. 45.

25. Avi Shafran, e-mail message to Ronnie Steinau, September 1, 2009.

26. Hannah Arendt, *Eichmann in Jerusalem: A Report on the Banality of Evil,* 2nd ed. (New York: Penguin Books, 1994), p. 48.

27. *Ibid.,* p. 20.

28. Basant K. Lal, "Hindu Perspectives on the Use of Animals in Science," in *Animal Sacrifices: Religious Perspectives on the Use of Animals*

in Science, ed. Tom Regan (Philadelphia: Temple University Press, 1986), p. 219, p. 226.

29. *Ibid.*, p. 206.

30. *Ibid.*, p. 200.

31. Christopher Chapple, "Noninjury to Animals: Jaina and Buddhist Perspectives," in *Animal Sacrifices*, p. 219, p. 226.

32. Esme Wynne-Tyson, ed., *Porphyry on Abstinence from Animal Food*, trans. Thomas Taylor (London & Fontwell: Centaur Press, 1965), p. 36-37.

33. Richard H. Schwartz, *Judaism and Vegetarianism* (New York: Lantern Books, 2001).

34. Elijah Judah Schochet, *Animal Life in Jewish Tradition: Attitudes and Relationships* (New York: Ktav Publishing House, 1984), p. 243.

35. V. Butler & L. Alexander (2004), "Slaughterhouse Worker Turned Activist: UPC Talks with Virgil Butler and Laura Alexander," *Poultry Press 14.3* (fall), http://www.upc-online.org/slaughter/; http://www.upc-online.org/fall04/virgil.htm.

36. Isaac Bashevis Singer, "The Slaughterer," in *The Collected Stories* (New York: Farrar, Straus and Giroux, 1982), p. 207.

37. Karen Davis, *Prisoned Chickens, Poisoned Eggs: An Inside Look at the Modern Poultry Industry*, 2nd ed. (Summertown, TN: Book Publishing Company, 2009), pp. 17-42; Karen Davis, *More Than a Meal: The Turkey in History, Myth, Ritual, and Reality* (New York: Lantern Books, 2001), pp. 130-131.

38. Bekoff, p. 54.

39. A.W. Schorger, *The Wild Turkey: Its History and Domestication* (Norman: University of Oklahoma Press, 1966), pp. 283-284; Karen Davis, *More Than a Meal: The Turkey in History, Myth, Ritual, and Reality* (Lantern Books, 2001), p. 140-141.

40. Karen Davis, "The Social Life of Chickens," Minds of Animals Conference, August 12-13, 2008, University of Toronto, Ontario. http://www.upc-online.org/thinking/social_life_of_chickens.html.

41. Paul B. Thompson, "Welfare as an Ethical Issue: Are Blind Chickens the Answer?" lecture, in *Bioethics Symposium: Proactive Approaches to Controversial Welfare and Ethical Concerns in Poultry Science* (Washington, DC: U.S. Department of Agriculture, 2007), pp. 3-5.

42. *Ibid.*

43. Tom Regan, *The Case for Animal Rights* (Berkeley: University of California Press, 1983), p. 243.

44. Robert Burruss, "The Future of Eggs," *The Baltimore Sun*, December 29, 1993: 16A, excerpted in Karen Davis, *Poisoned Chickens, Poisoned Eggs: An Inside Look at the Modern Poultry Industry* (Summerown, TN: Book Publishing Company, 1996), pp. 142-143.

45. Lesley J. Rogers, *Minds of Their Own: Thinking and Awareness in Animals* (Boulder, Colorado: Westview Press, 1997), p. 184-185.

46. Andrew Purvis, "Pecking order," *The Guardian,* October 4, 2006.

47. Oliver Broudy, 2006, "The Practical Ethicist." http://www.salon.com/books/int/2006/05/08/singer/print.html, 2009.

48. Robert J. Etches, "Beyond Freezing Semen," in *Proceedings: First International Symposium on the Artificial Insemination of Poultry*, ed. M.R. Bakst and G.J. Wishart (Savoy, Ill: Poultry Science Association, 1995).

49. Karen Davis, "Researching the Heart: An Interview with Eldon Kienholz," *The Animals' Agenda,* April 1991, 12-14.

50. Oliver Sacks, "The Abyss," *The New Yorker* (September 24, 2007), 108.

51. S. Orosz and G.A. Bradshaw, "Neuroanatomy of the companion avian parrot," ed. L. Tell and M. Knipe, *The Veterinary Clinics of North American: Exotic Animal Practice: Neuroanatomy and Neurodiagnostics* 10, no. 3 (2007): 775-802.

52. Rick Weiss, "Bird Brains Get Some New Names, And New Respect," *The Washington Post*, February 1, 2005, A10. http://www.upc-online.org/alerts/20105post.htm.

53. Ian J.H. Duncan, "The Science of Animal Well-Being," *Animal Welfare Information Center Newsletter 4.1* January-March, 1993: 5.

54. Marian Stamp Dawkins, *Through Our Eyes Only? The Search for Animal Consciousness* (Oxford: W.H. Freeman and Company Limited, 1993), p. 153.

Developing Beyond a Narcissistic Relationship with Animals

BRENDA MURROW

At that time I understood that within the soul from its primordial beginnings there has been a desire for light and an irrepressible urge to rise out of the primal darkness. When the great night comes, everything takes on a note of deep dejection, and every soul is seized by an inexpressible longing for light. That is the pent-up feeling that can be detected in the eyes of primitives, and also in the eyes of animals. There is a sadness in animals' eyes, and we never know whether that sadness is bound up with the soul of the animal or is a poignant message which speaks to us out of that still unconscious existence.

—C.G. Jung[1]

The practice of analytical psychology largely addresses relationship dynamics with fellow humans.[2] For instance, interpersonal issues are referent to a patient's childhood history with respect to his or her parents. If the topic of therapy concerns matters relating to an intimate partner, or spouse, the analyst typically inquires about the patient's relationships with the opposite sex parent, and difficulties associated with authority are usually explored with

Brenda Murrow, M.B.A., is a doctoral student in Pacifica Graduate Institute's Clinical Psychology program, and is certified in executive coaching and training. She worked in the Information Technology field for years before deciding to transition into this vocation.

attention to the father or other dominant elder in the patient's past. In short, a patient's psychological concerns are framed within a human context. But what about relationships with the rest of the earth-bound community? Why is it that traditional inquiries in analytical psychology do not include how the patient interacts with his or her family dog after a long day at work, or how the patient copes with his or her cat when money is tight? Why is it that the analyst does not typically inquire about how the yard is maintained and if birds and squirrels are welcomed, or perhaps instead poisoned? The field of ecopsychology, that is, the study of "psychological relations with the rest of nature,"[3] calls for a shift in this exclusively human,[4] what one might call selfish, viewpoint within therapy.

This selfish viewpoint is found not only in our psychology, but in our biology. Richard Dawkins argued that this selfishness starts in our genes because, according to his research, a quality found in genes that successfully replicate is "ruthless selfishness."[5] From this, he said, follows individual behavior that is selfish,[6] and furthermore that individuals within a species feel that their own species deserves "special moral consideration" at the expense of other species.[7] Primatologist Jane Goodall has also observed human behavior to be "selfish and greedy," and its resultant destructiveness caused her to question her spiritual beliefs.[8]

In listening to the call from ecopsychology to include relationships with other species, I explore this shift from the perspective of the myth of Narcissus and reflect on two main questions: Who could we become if we started to see ourselves in the images of the animals who behold us? And, how would we share the planet differently if it was their image we defined as part of ourselves? By engaging with animals in an I-Thou relationship, as defined by Buber, we will see a reflection in their eyes which is a fuller expression of our potential Selves.

DEVELOPMENT OF CONSCIOUSNESS & THE MYTH OF NARCISSUS

Neumann defines an early stage of human development where: "Universal participation, exteriorization of psychic contents, and the presence of highly charged emotional components combine to produce, in the pleromatic phase [early stage of consciousness development], an undifferentiated feeling of oneness which unites the world, the group, and man in an almost bodily way."[9] In this stage, our instincts create something ironically named an "animal psychology."[10] Within this psychology, instincts display much better adaptation to external reality than does consciousness.[11] Consciousness is understood here as the internal experiential and lived state. The unity that is experienced is part of a uroboric phase of development that is a naiveté of the differences between oneself and one's environment, where ego consciousness is one with the Great Mother, or that initial quality of life where one's needs are met effortlessly.

As development proceeds and a child matures, there is a turning away from the Great Mother and inward toward the self. "Self-reflection is as characteristic of the pubertal phase of humanity as it is of the pubertal phase of the individual."[12] Psychological development includes a stage of unity with the Great Mother and then proceeds to a self-reflective narcissistic stage. However, while the narcissistic phase "is a necessary phase of human knowledge," if it persists then there are "fatal effects."[13] This is illustrated in the Greek myth, Narcissus.

Jung found that there are universal themes, or over-arching modes, of human development. He called these themes "archetypes" and he proposed that these themes are part of a person's experience and help shape the person's development.[14] Jungian psychology uses the concept of archetypes as underlying frameworks for the organization of the psyche.[15] Jung suggested that empirical evidence of the archetypes can be examined through their expression in "dreams, myths, and fairy tales,"[16] which I will later discuss. Within the realm of archetypes Jung defined the archetypal concept of the Self as a way to represent the full expression of a person, inclusive of one's conscious and unconscious elements.[17] Further, the Self is not only a representation of "wholeness" but is also "the psyche's central ordering factor."[18]

In the myth, "the double seen by Narcissus [his mirror image] is properly designated as the Self, the image of the total person and not just the conscious, ego personality."[19]

> How the ego views the Self has a great deal to do with the way the Self mirrors the ego. When the ego looks into the mirror of the Self, what it sees is always "unrealistic" because it sees its archetypal image which can never be fit into the ego.[20]

The internal mirroring relationship between the Self and the ego is learned, in part, through the external mirroring one experiences in life.[21] "To mirror another person requires a willingness to enter into his or her world, to suspend critical judgement and reflect what is being offered."[22] Initially, mothers and other caregivers provide the external mirroring which generates the internal mirroring relationships between ego and Self.[23] However, "the need for mirroring from another is lifelong" because "the ego is challenged to develop toward greater wholeness (as imaged by the Self), [and] at every stage there is a need for external mirroring."[24] So, external mirroring by others actually provides the ability for the Self to be more consciously experienced by the ego.

As the ego matures, it forms a relationship to the Self whereby the ego becomes the Self's "source of consciousness and transformation."[25] From a Jungian perspective, narcissism develops as a result of a problem in the ego-Self relationship,[26] when instead of following the Self's drive for "meaning and a feeling of living one's fate,"[27] the ego instead relates to a "grandiose-exhibitionistic self"[28]—which is an internal "power-oriented copy"[29] of the Self used toward the "inevitable dead end of power for its own sake."[30]

In narcissism, mirroring is refused because external mirroring by another would stimulate the internal mirroring of the Self, which would threaten the ego's relationship to the power-oriented copy of the Self. The narcissistic ego defends against external and internal relations because "both are a great threat."[31] The danger of this over-identification and attempt to control the power of the Self is ultimately what leads to Narcissus' demise, and thus "Jung cautions that the ego must not identify with the images of the unconscious [the archetypes] but must relate to them."[32]

In summary, a self-reflective quality is incumbent in development; however, when the ego is overly enamored with the power of the Self and creates a power-oriented copy of it (the grandiose self) instead of working toward consciousness and transformation, this leads to the destructive fate of narcissism.

Narcissus' preoccupation with his reflection relates to a second perspective on the topic of self-reflection, what Jacque Lacan called the Mirror Stage of development.[33] Lacan defined this stage of development as an identification with an imago (of oneself).[34] He said that the function of the Mirror Stage is "to establish a relationship between an organism and its reality"[35] where man's first objective "is to be recognized by the other."[36] In other words, one comes to know an identity by what those with whom one is in relationship mirror back. The ego's development is dependent upon its being mirrored back to the subject possessing the ego.[37]

"For Lacan, the ego originates, is rooted in, takes its structure from, the mirroring mode of relating," and "Lacan theorizes that the ego originates through the process wherein the infant visually recognizes its reflection in a mirror."[38]

Through this exploration, it is clear that the relational element of mirroring is critical to the ego's development from both a Jungian and Lacanian perspective. The Jungian concept mentions the mirroring of ego to Self and vice versa as the foundational element for an inner relationship, and Lacan's view of ego development is primarily through the "mirroring mode of relating." While these are only two perspectives, they soundly suggest that the ego develops through what is mirrored back to it. However, as mentioned above, narcissism develops a tendency to shun the mirroring of others to maintain internal mirroring that is aimed at holding onto power. This suggests that mirroring will be critical to any therapeutic approach to narcissism, either on a personal or a collective level.

Empathy & Abstraction

On a personal level, narcissism includes a "lack of empathy that begins in early adulthood and is present in a variety of contexts."[39] Narcissism is exhibited by a culturally expressed lack of empathy and inability to commune with the animal kingdom in a peer-to-peer fashion.

Jung defined empathy and its counter-process, abstraction: "Empathy presupposes that the object is, as it were, empty, and seeks to imbue it with life. Abstraction, on the other hand, presupposes that the object is alive and active, and seeks to withdraw from its influence."[40] He said that the person with an attitude of empathy feels "in a world that needs his subjective feeling to give it life and soul."[41] And that the person with an attitude of abstraction feels within "a frighteningly animated world that seeks to overpower and smother him."[42]

In effect, the abstraction process is an ego defense in which the ego is so overwhelmed by external objects it withdraws from them to preserve its own existence. "All abstraction has this effect: it kills the independent activity of the object" as experienced in the consciousness of the ego.[43] Earlier, from Schwartz-Salant, we saw that for narcissism this was because the ego is defending against a potential annihilation by the Self and its archetypal energies.[44] In these terms, we can see that this is an extreme version of the abstraction defense.

A therapeutic approach for narcissism would then include a goal of "developing empathy."[45] Yet, while Jungian psychotherapy extends empathy to the "patient's intrapsychic others,"[46] that is, the patient's internal experience of the archetypes, that "same empathy, however, is often withheld from the patient's outer world others, such as the spouse, the parent, colleagues,"[47] etc.

Empathy may be instinctual, as there have been studies done to demonstrate that humans respond to images of others displaying emotions with facial expressions that signify similar emotions, even if the images are displayed too quickly for the cognition processes to recognize them.[48] In fact, the concurrent activation of neurons in the brain is believed to be responsible for the observer's processing of the similar emotion, and this capability to transmit and receive emotion is documented across species as well.[49] And sympathy is in some ways an extension of empathy, where sympathy includes an "urge" to change the situation for the subject.[50]

Is it simply that an increase in our empathetic response to animals might resolve our narcissistic treatment of them? Unfortunately, no. The process of empathy can also objectify.[51] Jung suggested, "empathy can create similarities and seemingly common qualities which have no real existence in themselves."[52] The empathetic person "wants to feel his own life in the object"[53] and, unconsciously, the person who is empathizing depotentiates the object's sovereignty.[54]

At their core, both processes can start and can end in self-alienation[55]; they both arise from a defense of life's uncontrollability. Jung stated that the utilization of both processes is required "for any real appreciation of the object."[56] As such, Jung called for a "harmonizing" of both functions,[57] which would mean an increase in empathy is necessary in our collective ego, but not an entire exclusion of abstraction.

Schwartz-Salant suggested an even further step, by differentiating empathic attunement at two stages of the Narcissus myth.[58] The first, he said, is as Jung described above, where "one can reflect from one's own experience."[59] However, a second way of relating which arrives at a realization of higher potential, is to relate not solely from one's own experience, but to relate in such a way that allows for "mutual participation in which both psyches operate simultaneously."[60] In other words, not acting in a way where one must switch perspectives and experiences with another as in the pulling in or pushing away activities of empathy and abstraction, but where both individuals can be realized together—in essence, a mutual mirroring.

ANIMAL PROJECTIONS IN PRACTICE

As I have described, narcissism initiates with a self-reflective quality that gets stuck because of its inability to accept the mirroring it is receiving from others. The mirroring of others actually causes the ego to see more of its internal Self potential and generates the development of ego consciousness. The narcissistic ego shuns, or abstracts, the mirroring of others because of the threat to the relationship to the internal grandiose self. As mentioned earlier, Jung thought that one could observe the representation of archetypes, or themes of human behavior, in dreams, myths, and fairy tales. It seems then that an investigation of fairy tales might reveal something about our collective relationship to animals.

About animals in fairy tales, von Franz stated, "the animal is the carrier of the projection of human psychic factors."[61] She explained that the characters in the stories about animals "are human because they really do not represent animal instincts but *our* animal instincts."[62]

As an example of this, think about how many animal-related words there are in the English language. In fact, many animal names are actually verbs. In the American Heritage dictionary "wolf" is defined as "v. To eat greedily or voraciously." And "fox," is, "v. To trick or fool by ingenuity or cunning; outwit." Curiously, one of the Brothers Grimm Fairy Tales is "The Wolf and the Fox", and in it a "sly" fox is the captive of a "gluttonous" wolf; the fox must hunt to feed the wolf until he can escape by tricking him.[63]

For a more popular example, Jungian analyst John Beebe commented on the Disney version of the tale "Beauty and the Beast."[64] Again, the Beast is understood to represent the parts of a character that are reprehensible; however, Beebe's interpretation of the dance between Beauty and Beast is optimistic in that it demonstrates a readiness "to value a conscious relation to our most shameful disorders of character."[65]

Jung says that analytical psychology allows for the expression of our animal instincts so that they are not repressed "incorporating them in a purposeful whole," and in doing so we are more tolerant of our fellow man, having seen our shadow sides.[66]

By taking back our projections of our own animal natures, we can be freed to relate to animals in a new way, in a more holistic way, one that engages more empathetically and less abstractly. What if Lacan's concept of the mirror were expanded to include not only our fellow humans, but also what animals mirror back to us, and if we used that more full reflection in our cultural development?

Yet further consideration is needed of where else the human narcissistic relationship to animals is revealed. Reviewed en masse, the personal expression of dreams is a source for information on where our collective animal nature is speaking. In his essay, "The Animal Kingdom in the Human Dream," Hillman discussed his collection of animal dreams. For many years dreamers would hand him their dreams about animals, "usually with no comment," and thus he worked with these personal dreams on a collective level.[67] In his study, he found the concepts of eyes and of mirroring to be relevant. About one dream where the dreamer was looking into the eyes of a pig, he said the interpretation "requires a moment's reflection about the eye as mirror of the soul and the eye as entry into the interiority of a creature."[68]

In order to analyze dream animals appropriately, Hillman indicated that we must extend "our vision so as to see the animal with an animal eye."[69] Furthermore, he said:

> To read the animal, to hear it speak, requires an aesthetic and ecological perception for which psychology has yet to train its eye and find words that are not just allegorical moralisms, beyond metaphors of piggishness, mousiness, monkey tricks and bear hugs, beyond simplistic metaphor altogether, beyond grasping at the meaning of the animal; to that aesthetic apperception of what is presented, responding to the significance of its form, an appropriate, appreciative response, grateful that it is even there, that it has come to the dream, and that this visitation is a momentary restoration of Eden.[70]

Further critiquing the way dream animals are often analyzed, he said, "The rubric of each animal kind becomes confused with each animal having but one so-called instinctual function," where "each animal serves to moralize in terms of an ego that sees a stereotypical aspect of itself in the behavior of the animal."[71] Thus Hillman has identified, through dreams, the current status of the human and animal relationship to be one where the collective ego is simply considering dream animals as extensions of human behavior. And, he calls for a more engaged response to dream animals, an "appropriate, appreciative response, grateful that it is even there." Of his collection of dreams, he summarized, "The strained relation between human and animal in contemporary dreams recapitulates the Western tradition and its degradation of the animal."[72] Earlier I mentioned that a fundamental aspect of development is the relational element of mirroring, referenced both in the Jungian sense of an inner, archetypal Self-mirroring relationship, and in the Lacanian sense of the mirroring stage of developing a relationship between an organism and its reality. As Hillman stated, currently we still see dream animals as extensions of ourselves, thus this is a representation that in our collective inner dream worlds, we are approaching animals with a narcissistic orientation.

Secondly, the projective assessment techniques of clinical psychology, such as the Rorschach Test, reveal more information about our relationship to animals because they offer "access to the covert and deeper structures of an individual's personality."[73] The Rorschach aims to reveal the unconscious dynamics of the participant because in responding to the ambiguous nature of the inkblots, "they must draw on their personal internal images, ideas, and relationships to create a response."[74] In order to score the Rorschach, the responses are organized into content categories, one of which is "Animal."[75] In his summary of interpretative guidelines, Groth-Marnat stated:

> Most of the literature indicates that animal content is associated with the obvious aspects of adaptiveness and the most concrete features of reality testing (Draguns, Haley, & Phillips, 1967). Because animal contents are the easiest to perceive, their presence suggests that examinees are using routine and predictable ways of responding. Conversely, a low number of animal responses suggests highly individualistic persons who see their world in their own personal and unique ways.[76]

Thus, with the empirically validated Rorschach, fewer animal responses—that is, fewer responses to ambiguous stimuli that include projections about animals—is a marker of social development. Groth-Marnat explained that those participants with a high number of animal responses show a "predictable, stereotyped" orientation to their environment and employ the use of "constrictive and conforming defenses," while, on the contrary, those with a low number of animal responses are typically "persons who are spontaneous, nonconforming, unpredictable, and of higher intelligence."[77]

However, about 38% to 48% of the responses given by normal adults include animal-related content, making Animals the most popular content category.[78] This suggests a couple of interesting points. First, for the average adult, more than a third of their responses contain projections about animals. In other words, upon reviewing the inkblot, the response includes something about an animal. As stated above, a projective assessment like the Rorschach is designed to understand the participants' unconscious dynamics, and as such it is a good indicator, on an aggregate level, that collectively we are projecting our unconsciousness elements onto the inkblots as animal-related content.

Furthermore, "The Rorschach findings mainly reflect the processes that generate behaviors."[79] Thus the Rorschach Test further reveals the internal processes about the collective participants' inner relationships and provides more information into the unconscious relationship we have with animals. This exploration correlates participants who give high numbers of responses that include animal content with those who respond in a predictable manner. Responding with predictability stifles the independent activity of the object and is a representation of Jung's concept of abstraction, as defined earlier. This is further evidence of a collective narcissistic orientation toward animals.

Finally, for an example that is representative of our relationship with animals in the external world, here is an alarming statistic, "living species of animals and plants are now vanishing around the world *one thousand times faster* than at any time in the past 65 million years."[80] Of course this statistic has at its root multiple causes, many of which are hotly debated. The amount of rain forest depletion in response to human civilization is certainly one factor, and in the Amazon in recent decades "one Tennessee's worth of rain forest [was] being slashed and burned each year."[81] Narcissism includes a lack of empathy and the fulfillment of needs at the expense of others.[82] Our use of natural resources for the fulfillment of human needs at the expense of the needs of animals is a drastic collective expression of narcissism.

CHANGING THE MODE OF RELATEDNESS

Returning to Neumann's developmental stages, after the narcissistic stage, a later stage of development is one of "relatedness" with other humans, things, the world, one's own soul, or a higher spiritual power.[83] If the functions of empathy and abstraction were balanced, or harmonized, perhaps our collective ego would be ready for a next step in development.

As a model for this potential new way of relating, a concept of Buber's is a guide:

> Buber's existentialism hinges on two different *modes of relatedness to others*, the I-Thou and the I-It orientation. The I-Thou is based on the principles of openness and affirmation, and engages the whole person, who addresses the other with respect and concern, even in difficult circumstances, or in the midst of anger. Communion and conflict can both be encompassed in the I-Thou mode of relatedness, provided that the whole person is engaged and addresses the other with full ethical responsibility. The I-It orientation engages but a fraction of ourselves—our intellect, our lust, our curiosity—and leaves the rest of us disengaged or indifferent to the other person's fate. Moreover, it openly or implicitly depersonalizes others, and it allows for mutual accommodation or conflict, but precludes genuine meeting or communion.[84]

Buber's concept of the I-It orientation has similarities to abstraction. However, where abstraction is a process by which the ego defends itself by killing the independent activity of the object, the I-It orientation is one where the activity is one of subjugating. Buber said, "The life of a human being does not exist merely in the sphere of goal-directed verbs. It does not consist merely of activities that have something for their object."[85] In other words participating in the world using phrases such as, "I perceive something. I feel something. I imagine something. I want something. I sense something. I think something"[86] is the I-It orientation which only allows for things to be in service to the one who perceives, feels, imagines, etc. In contrast, the I-Thou orientation "establishes the world of relation."[87] Buber said there are three "spheres" where the possibility of the world of relation arises, and those are "life with nature," "life with men," and "life with spiritual beings."[88]

As mentioned earlier, both empathy and abstraction are actions, both are things done to another, which as Buber suggested above, makes those things subjected to being in service to the one who empathizes or abstracts. In this mode of relating, the I-Thou mode, one interacts in the relationship so that nothing is to be done but simply to let the other be as they are.

Clinically, this mode of relating is discussed by physician Michael Kearney in the training of health care workers, including therapists.[89] Above, in the description of the I-Thou mode of relating, reference is made to engagement of the whole person. For a therapist to relate this way, Kearney suggested, first, that therapists imagine themselves as two parts: a Work Persona and an Inner Healer.[90] This imaginary split allows the therapist to become conscious of their training and their desire to help the patient.[91] The Work Persona is the part of the therapist who understands the theories that are the foundation of the medical model and creates a secure environment for therapy to occur.[92] The Inner Healer is the part of the therapist that accesses the suffering of the patient[93] and can be with him or her without needing to "do anything,"[94] and instead accompanies the patient to those "hidden depths of the healing encounter."[95] In this way, "the work persona helps to create the right outer and inner environment, the healing, if and when it occurs, is connected to the inner healer,"[96] yet the healing "cannot be prescribed or willed, or explained in purely rational terms."[97] When therapists relate to the patient with both of these parts of themselves, they are relating as a "whole therapist" and in an I-Thou way.[98] However, these suggestions are between therapist and patient and do not include a model that explicitly draws this behavior from the patient, but rather implicitly demonstrates it in a way of being with the patient.

Similar to Lacan's idea of mirror relations, Buber suggested that we know who we are in relation to another. "For the inmost growth of the self is not accomplished, as people like to suppose today, in man's relation to himself, but in the relation between one and the other...in the making present of another self and in the knowledge that one is made present to his own self by the other."[99] In fact, this also relates to the Jungian concept of reflection from the Self, as defined by Schwartz-Salant, that the Self reflects back its full potential to the ego.

In returning to the myth of Narcissus, it appears that Campbell's reading of the myth concurs with this interpretation. Campbell said that when Narcissus looks into the pool, he reaches a stage of no return, after which he cannot see himself as separate, but as one with the universe, "just as the way of social participation may lead in the end to a realization of the All in the individual, so that of exile brings the hero to the Self in all."[100]

SUMMARY

What then might be done in a typical analytical psychology session to foster a collective ego development from its current narcissistic orientation to animals to one of an I-Thou orientation? An increased focus on and consideration of the patient's relationship to their external world is a first step. This change in orientation involves understanding the patient situated within a world of relatedness, which includes relationships with animals. At the beginning I mentioned that practitioners within the field of ecopsychology are working toward this; Linda Buzzell, a psychotherapist, suggested that this orientation be explicit throughout therapy. For example when beginning work with a patient, she asks questions such as, "Are there animals in your life? Special environments where your heart opens and life feels right?"[101]

Much of this essay focuses on what occurs when Narcissus meets his reflection. I discuss this primarily in terms of the mirroring function in relationships. To Narcissus, the full Self is reflected back; however, allegorically the narcissistic ego's Self-potential can only be fully realized when it is able to tolerate the mirroring of others and incorporate it into ego-development. As discussed, ego development depends on what is mirrored back to it. The ego's internal relationship to Self is initiated by external relationships, and throughout development there is a need for continual mirroring. It is time for our collective ego to disengage from its narcissistic stage of development and allow the mirroring of animals into our development. Kearney's model for the training of therapists is useful here, in that for us to relate to animals in an I-Thou orientation we would relate to them with our whole being. In the terms discussed, this would mean relating to them with both our egos and our archetypal Selves.

Relating to animals in this way would enable our collective ego to see the reflection of our Selves that animals mirror back to us. This orientation would make possible a reframing of our narcissistic ego's self-reflection to allow the ego to realize its position in relation to the animal kingdom, and to receive the full reflection back from this community. In so doing, maybe then we can begin to understand what Jung said about the "poignant message" in the eyes of animals referenced at the beginning, and perhaps enter the next step of development with the assistance of animals, as described by Buber:

> The eyes of an animal have the capacity of a great language. Independent, without any need of the assistance of sounds and gestures, most eloquent when they rest entirely in their glance, they express the mystery in its natural captivity, that is, in the anxiety of becoming. This state of the mystery is known only to the animal, which alone can open it up to us—for this state can only be opened up and not revealed.[102]

NOTES

1. C.G. Jung, *Memories, Dreams, Reflections, Revised Edition* (New York: Vintage Books, 1989), p. 269.

2. Alan S. Gurman & Stanley B. Messer (eds.), *Essential Psychotherapies: Theory and Practice* (New York: The Guilford Press, 2003).

3. Linda Buzzell & Craig Chalquist (eds.), *Ecotherapy: Healing with Nature in Mind* (San Francisco: Sierra Club Books, 2009), p. 18.

4. Linda Buzzell, "Asking Different Questions: Therapy for the Human Animal," in Buzzell & Chalquist, *Ecotherapy*, p. 46.

5. Richard Dawkins, *The Selfish Gene, 30ᵗʰ Anniversary Edition* (New York: Oxford University Press, 2006), p. 2.

6. *Ibid.*

7. Dawkins, *Selfish Gene*, p. 10.

8. Jane Goodall, *Reason for Hope: A Spiritual Journey* (New York: Warner Books, 1999), p. xiv.

9. Erich Neumann, *The Origins and History of Consciousness*, trans. R.F.C. Hull (Princeton: Princeton University Press, 1954), p. 284.

10. *Ibid.*, p. 285.

11. *Ibid.*

12. *Ibid.*, p. 89.

13. *Ibid.*

14. C.G. Jung, *Psychological Types*, trans. R.F.C. Hull, *The Collected Works of C.G. Jung* (Princeton: Princeton University Press, 1971), Vol. 6 § 443.

15. Nathan Schwartz-Salant, *Narcissism and Character Transformation: The Psychology of Narcissistic Character Disorders* (Toronto: Inner City Books, 1982), p. 10.

16. Jung, *Collected Works,* 6 § 460.

17. *Ibid.*

18. Schwartz-Salant, *Narcissism,* p. 10.

19. *Ibid.*

20. *Ibid.*, pp. 18-19.

21. *Ibid.*, p. 46.

22. *Ibid.*, pp. 45-46.

23. *Ibid.*, p. 46.

24. *Ibid.*

25. *Ibid.*, p. 20.

26. *Ibid.*, p. 23.

27. *Ibid.*, p. 20.

28. *Ibid.*, p. 19.

29. *Ibid.*

30. *Ibid.*, p. 20.

31. *Ibid.*, p. 19.

32. *Ibid.*, p. 91, p. 97.

33. Jacques Lacan, *Écrits* (New York: W. W. Norton, 2002).

34. *Ibid.*, p. 4.

35. *Ibid.*, p. 6.

36. *Ibid.*, p. 58.

37. *Ibid.*

38. John Muller, "The Origins and Self-Serving Functions of the Ego," in Kareen Ror Malone & Stephen R. Friedlander (eds.), *The Subject of Lacan: A Lacanian Reader for Psychologists* (Albany, NY: SUNY Press, 2000), p. 42, p. 43.

39. American Psychiatric Association, *Diagnostic and Statistical Manual of Mental Disorders- Fourth Edition, Text Revision (DSM-IV-TR)*

(Washington D.C.: American Psychiatric Publishing, Inc., 2000), p. 714.

40. Jung, *Collected Works,* 6 § 292.

41. Jung, *Collected Works,* 6 § 293.

42. *Ibid.*

43. Jung, *Collected Works,* 6 § 295.

44. Schwartz-Salant, *Narcissism,* p. 13.

45. Stephanie M. Woo & Carolyn Keatinge, *Diagnosis and Treatment of Mental Disorders Across the Lifespan* (Hoboken, New Jersey: John Wiley & Sons, 2008), p. 871.

46. John Beebe, "Toward a Jungian Analysis of Character," in Ann Casement (ed.), *Post-Jungians Today: Key Papers in Contemporary Analytical Psychology* (New York: Routledge, 1998), p. 56.

47. *Ibid.*

48. Frans de Waal, *The Age of Empathy: Nature's Lessons for a Kinder Society* (New York: Harmony Books, 2009), p. 66.

49. Marco Iacoboni, *Mirroring People: The New Science of How We Connect With Others* (New York: Farrar, Straus and Giroux, 2008).

50. de Waal, *Age of Empathy,* pp. 88-89.

51. Jung, *Collected Works,* 6 § 290.

52. Jung, *Collected Works,* 6 § 292.

53. *Ibid.*

54. Jung, *Collected Works,* 6 § 293.

55. Jung, *Collected Works,* 6 § 296-297.

56. Jung, *Collected Works,* 6 § 296.

57. Jung, *Collected Works,* 6 § 299.

58. Schwartz-Salant, *Age of Empathy,* p. 143.

59. *Ibid.*

60. *Ibid.,* p. 127.

61. Marie-Louise von Franz, *The Interpretation of Fairy Tales, Revised Edition* (Boston: Shambhala Publications, Inc., 1996), p. 36.

62. *Ibid.*

63. Brothers Grimm, *The Complete Fairy Tales of the Brothers Grimm, Third Edition,* trans. Jack Zipes (New York: Bantam Books, 2003), pp. 258-259.

64. Beebe, "Toward a Jungian Analysis of Character," pp. 61-62.

65. *Ibid.,* p. 62.

66. C.G. Jung, *Collected Works,* Vol. 7 § 26.

67. James Hillman, "The Animal Kingdom in the Human Dream," in *Animal Presences, The Uniform Edition of the Writings of James Hillman* (Putnam, CT: Spring Publications, Inc., 2008), Vol. 9 § 12.

68. Hillman, *Uniform Edition*, 9 § 14.

69. Hillman, *Uniform Edition*, 9 § 32.

70. *Ibid.*

71. Hillman, *Uniform Edition*, 9 § 43.

72. Hillman, *Uniform Edition*, 9 § 34.

73. Gary Groth-Marnat, *Handbook of Psychological Assessment, Fourth Edition* (Hoboken, NJ: John Wiley & Sons, 2003), p. 485.

74. *Ibid.*, p. 407.

75. *Ibid.*, p. 428.

76. *Ibid.*, p. 456.

77. *Ibid.*

78. *Ibid.*

79. John E. Exner, *The Rorschach, Basic Foundations and Principles of Interpretation, Volume 1, Fourth Edition* (Hoboken, NJ: John Wiley & Sons, 2003), p. 5.

80. Al Gore, *Earth in the Balance: Ecology and the Human Spirit* (New York: Rodale, Inc., 1992), p. 24.

81. *Ibid.*, p. 23.

82. Woo & Keatinge, *Diagnosis and Treatment of Mental Disorders*, p. 846.

83. Neumann, *Origins*, p. 116.

84. Daniel Burston & Roger Frie, *Psychotherapy as a Human Science* (Pittsburgh: Duquesne University Press, 2006), p. 164.

85. Martin Buber, *I and Thou*, trans. Walter Kaufmann (New York: Simon & Schuster, 1970), p. 54.

86. *Ibid.*

87. *Ibid.*, p. 56.

88. *Ibid.*, pp. 56-57.

89. Michael Kearney, *A Place of Healing: Working with Nature & Soul at the End of Life* (New Orleans: Spring Journal Books, 2009), pp. 200-202.

90. *Ibid.*

91. *Ibid.*

92. *Ibid.*, p. 200.

93. *Ibid.*, p. 201.

94. *Ibid.*, p. 202.
95. *Ibid.*, p. 201.
96. *Ibid.*, p. 202.
97. *Ibid.*
98. *Ibid.*, p. 201.
99. Burston & Frie, *Psychotherapy*, p. 168.
100. Joseph Campbell, *The Hero With a Thousand Faces* (Princeton: Princeton University Press, 1949), p. 386.
101. Buzzell, "Asking Different Questions," p. 49.
102. Buber, *I and Thou*, p. 144.

Re-visioning Ecopsychology: Seeing Through Dream Animals to the Reality of Species in Peril

DEBRA MERSKIN

Animals of silence came out of the clear, untroubled
forest, leaving their nests and dens,
and it seemed that why they were so quiet
was not from fear or craftiness,

it was listening. Now howling, roaring, growling
mattered little in their hearts. And where before
there was hardly a hut to hold this listening—

a lean-to of dimmest longing
with shaky door-jambs at the entrance—
you built temples in their hearing for them.

Rainer Maria Rilke

nimals occupy our waking time and sleep dream hours.[1]
Whether through hunting, wearing their skins and fur, eating
their muscles and membranes, ecotourist viewing, or "pet"-

Debra Merskin, Ph.D., is Associate Professor of Communication Studies in the School of Journalism & Communication at the University of Oregon. Her research interests include exploring the parallels between popular culture re-presentations of marginalized human beings and animals. She is also a third-year student in the Depth Psychology Program at Pacifica Graduate Institute.

keeping, human beings use animals, their animal-ness, in everything from food to fantasy. Not satisfied with material consumption alone, people also appropriate animal essences and spirits to sell goods and services in the form of brand images and logos.

Depth psychology and western culture widely and wildly use animals as metaphors to deepen our understanding of ourselves—coyote as trickster, horse as hero, dog as the embodiment of faithfulness and trust. Sigmund Freud, C.G. Jung, James Hillman, and others have written extensively about the important role animals play as escorts into and out of the unconscious and their significance as symbolic, archetypal beings.

However, in celebrating their psychological roles, it is easy to lose sight of animals as real, corporeal beings. The reality is the planet and the environment that are crying out for our attention and care are populated by specific trees, flowers, birds, fishes, and other species who are in turn comprised of diverse individual members. The archetypal and dream animal is conventionally used to service human needs, not those of the animals themselves. Whether animals appear in dreams, as totem figures in visions, art images, or icons in popular culture, they are used to tell human stories. Modern western culture indentures animals by transforming them from individuals with sacred agency into instruments for human gain. This practice comprises a profound dismissal of animal agency and in so doing violates one of depth psychology's main ethical principles: respect of psyche, no matter whose it is.

Since depth psychology, indeed psychology on the whole, is dedicated to the real living being, it must be for all living beings—not just humans.[2] Scientific recognition that other animals share with humans comparable capacity to feel, think, experience, and be ensouled compels psychology to expand its circle to make the other animals of the world part of the global conversation.

There are at least three animals in the room every time any one animal is invoked in image or discourse: the animal-as-archetype, the animal-as-mediated, and the animal-as-living-being. *Eros and Chaos*, Veronica Goodchild's reflection on an anthropocentric depth psychology, exemplifiies how we think about the excitement and challenge of entering the world of real animals:

> The whole project of depth psychology ... has opened up a realm
> of experience and experiencing with which we have hardly begun
> to come to terms, and for which our familiar, rational modes of
> apprehending are entirely inadequate. Love and its attendant
> shadows are perhaps the most important factors in a life that
> reaches into this mysterious and unknown territory.[3]

Advocating for caring for the earth, as ecopsychology encourages, necessarily entails utilizing the tools of depth psychology to listen and tend to the minds and souls of our fellow earthlings. "There are incredible creatures 'out there' living with us on this planet and just because they aren't immediately in our face doesn't mean they don't hold an important position."[4] To re-enter psychological intimacy with other species is to remember our own ancestry and past.

Bringing attention to the "real" embodied animal does not diminish the importance of the dream animal, the ally animal, or the totem animal, rather it ensures an ethical obligation to those living on the planet. As Margot McClean says,

> I think it is important to see the animal as you do in dreams, but
> dream animals must not be segregated from the animals living
> out back under your porch or in the brush. One must be careful
> when adopting an 'inner' animal that the connection to the
> animal world is not reduced to a feel-good-about-me condition.
> There is something else.[5]

Regaining the company of animals involves a re-visioning of their role in psychology.

The goal of this essay is to extend James Hillman's call to psychology to interact with and embrace soul to include nonhuman animal psyches: to release each imaginal and imaginary animal from the confines of dream space, and invite him or her into the room as a real, embodied soul.[6] My voice joins others such as Barbara Hannah's[7] who has petitioned psychology to consider real animals in concepts, practices, and psychological relationships. It is a call for humans to re-join the animal world.

RE-VISIONING

In *Re-Visioning Psychology*, James Hillman brings soul into the conversation in an effort to return psychology and psychoanalysis to their ethical and spiritual roots. He urges psychologists to be more inward, not outward, looking and direct their psychological exploration to greater depths. Psychology is more than therapy, he argues. It is relational, where humans exist in the world and are affected by who and what they experience. The image, he maintains, is a central re-presentation of the imaginal and must be respected, not interpreted, and allowed to live on its own terms. Hillman advocates for mainstream psychology to return to a "psychology of soul" in which clients are not treated as objects, but rather as subjective participants in the healing process, and what is considered psychological is what is lived.[8] To demonstrate how this re-visioning process works, Hillman articulates four central psychological ideas that are extended in this essay to embrace animals: personifying, pathologizing, psychologizing, and dehumanizing, described in the next sections.

PERSONIFYING

In everyday language, to personify means to represent someone, something, or an abstract idea as a person. The ontological metaphor is expressed when, for example, the natural world is called Mother Nature, when the news media attribute intentionality to weather patterns, or, in the case of the death of Sea World trainer, Dawn Brancheau, calling Tillikum, the whale who killed her, a "serial killer whale."[9] To Hillman, "to give subjectivity and intentionality to a noun means more than moving into a special kind of language game; it means that we actually enter into another psychological dimension."[10] Personifying is imagining where "imaging things [or beings] in a personal form [allows us to] find access to them with our hearts."[11] This attempt to integrate heart and mind must extend to other, which in turn requires deciding what constitutes a person.

The idea of moral personhood breaks with the notion that only human beings are carriers of soul. Descartes divided the world into categories of human/not human, soul/soul-less, us/them and did not consider animals in mind or body as entitled to the same moral consideration as human beings. The purpose of his book, *Meditations on First Philosophy*, was to demonstrate "the existence of God and the distinction between the human soul and body" and those of nonhuman animals.[12] His "kingdom of causes" was carved into nature and nurture; thus, by virtue of its twoness, it eliminated "the possibility of something else."[13] The body was thus a machine, governed by rational human thought, which animals, he said, lacked. Therefore, as pure machines, automata, animals cannot feel, according to Descartes, a proposition which was used for more than 500 years as justification for the infliction of endless suffering upon animals, including the practice of vivisection. The screams of tortured animals, made when operated on without anesthetic, were said to be only squeaking mechanical parts.

Psychology has long been dominated by an emphasis on the cognitive, behavioral, and affective components of personality tied to behaviorism. Although the etymology of psychology can be traced to the Greek words for the study of psyche, the modern westernized medical model of mental health has come to equate psychology with mind/brain. Subsequently, consideration of human well-being, or lack thereof, relies on what is empirically testable in objective terms. Concepts such as soul, psyche, the unconscious, and more qualitative approaches to apprehending an individual's sense of being have often been relegated to the land of "touchy-feely," "soft," qualitative approaches. To a large extent, subjective experience is dismissed.

In contrast and in response, Hillman's re-visioning of psychology advocates a return to thinking about human beings, in and out of the therapist's office, as de-souled persons who are seeking a return to the roots of being that are deeply connected to a more natural self. As Wittgenstein famously argued, it is through language that personhood is articulated. I argue instead that it is through communication, in whatever form and by whatever species, that personhood is articulated, thus separating the idea of person as human.

A necessary next step in the ethical process of bridging species is personification, the declaration that animals other than humans not only have souls, but also are souls. Re-visioning depth psychology requires consideration of all animals, including humans, as conscious, souled, and sentient. Etymologically the word "animal" means "a living being."[14] Thus, "to save the phenomena of the imaginal psyche" we must also "free the vision of the psyche," not only from "the narrow biases of modern psychology," but also free it to run amongst other living beings.[15] Extending the definition of personhood to other animals thereby personifies them and "personifying [is] a necessary mode of understanding the world and of being in it."[16] Otherwise, depth psychology runs the risk of concretizing the meaning of animal as word into a sign, devoid of life, and of not giving power and presence to real animals.

Furthermore, to deny animals the possibility of consciousness and imagination is, at the least, insulting, and is more often used as a rationalization for their ongoing oppression. Hillman states, "personified namings never become mere dead tools. Images and metaphors present themselves always as living psychic subjects with which I am obliged to be in relation. They keep me aware of the power of the words I work with, whereas concepts tend to delude me into nominalism."[17] If, as Hillman argues, nominalism dreads "the person in the world," then recognizing the animal in the world requires a thinking not only of animals as persons, but also as more than names—no longer as pork, but as pigs, not as beef, but as cows, not as data points in research, but as monkeys.[18] If "personifying is the soul's answer to egocentricity," then breaking down the binary of human superiority over animals is the next logical step in extending psyche's reach as the truest form of soulful reply.[19] Personification is not a call for imitation of animals— we do enough of that already. Rather, it is recognition of the unique contribution animals make in and of themselves and as self-advocates for their own experiences. They do not need to be like human beings to matter morally.

PATHOLOGIZING

Souls are not always joyful or embracing, but reveal in myriad symptoms. Their voice and expression are hermenuetical where understanding of psyche comes through context.

Sometimes the pain is expressed in the form of symbols, which animals are often used to embody. Hillman says

> Pathologizing is not only a metaphorical language but a way of translation, a way of turning something literally known, usual, and trivial like the psychopathologies of everyday life into something unknown and deep. As such, pathologizing is a hermeneutic, which leads events into meaning.[20]

Pathologized events are "central to soul" and "essential to any psychology that bases itself upon soul."[21] Therefore, what hurts, is broken, is confused, or missing is often expressed in the archetypal form of our myths. Pathologizing is the "psyche's autonomous ability to create" these states so that the individual then sees the world through this lens.

> Pathologizing is a way of mythologizing. Pathologizing takes one out of blind immediacy, distorting one's focus upon the natural and actual by forcing one to ask what is within and behind it. The distortion is at the same time an enhancement and a new clarification, reminding the soul of its mythical existence.[22]

Pathologizing means careful attention to who is being asked to carry not only the metaphorical weight but also the real burden of our ideas about others and ourselves and breaking the pattern of us/them thinking. Hillman argues psychology needs to go beyond presenting "all soul events within a compensatory system of pairs," and this also applies to the work that animals perform in both the conscious and unconscious realms.

Animals often carry the burden of this symbolic weight as the vehicles through which depth psychologists imagine an illness, disorder, morbidity, or form of suffering. For example, wolves carry the symbolic weight in language as the linguistic metaphor for "a ravenous appetite," "a man who makes sexual advances to women," as "a person who pretends to be good but is really evil," and so forth.[23] But just as soul events are not "parts of any system," nor "reactions and responses to other sorts of events at the opposite end of any fulcrum," they, as real animals, are "independent of the tandems in which they are placed."[24] If bears, lions, and tigers, who not only appear in our dreams as immediate reminders of the possibility of death but also lurk in the shadows and shade of real forests, are regarded only as symbolic vessels, they are at risk in the real world. Predators such as coyotes and cougars are carriers of symbolic cues, but they are experiencing habitat devastation, real physical violence, and the resultant psychological trauma without being heard. In January 2010, coyote killing derbies took place in several western states. The event was designed to raise money for an individual's cancer treatment and prizes were awarded to those who killed the greatest numbers of them. Thirty were killed the weekend of January 8 in Oregon and another 20 in Nevada the weekend of January 30. Coyotes are powerful symbolic beings in literature, art, and popular culture—as a

> ... trickster, a helper, teacher, a fool, and a creator. In other words,
> he is both good and evil. It is said that he possesses every quality
> of mankind and like humans, he is sometimes a villain, sometimes
> a victim; sometimes a predator, sometimes a savior. And, also like
> mankind, Coyote is resourceful, tough, and enduring.[25]

And yet, despite the honoring of coyotes in many traditions and the
personification of coyotes' natural intelligence and keen sense of survival,
they are slaughtered in great numbers, particularly in the American
West. By use of poisons, shooting, denning (killing pups in the dens),
and trapping, "at least 400,000 coyotes are killed each year by federal,
state, and local governments and by private individuals."[26] Although
their role in and impact on livestock is misinformed and unsupported
by scientific evidence, most coyotes are killed not only in the interest
of "livestock protection" but also "for their fur, for 'sport,' and in 'body-
count' contests in which prizes are awarded for who kills the most
coyotes. Most states set no limit on the number of coyotes that may
be killed, nor do they regulate the killing method."[27]

Animal honoring, which serves psyche, must consider animals not
only for their soul-enhancing work but also for their soul embodying
being. "The pettiness of current social practices," says John Berger, "is
universalized by being projected onto the animal kingdom."[28] This
means also caring about animals who are not only "charismatic
megafauna", like lions, tigers, pandas, whales, and other species that
humans find iconic. For example, the Pacific walrus and the ribbon
seal face as much habitat loss and threats to life as do polar bears who
live in the same ecosystem, but these species receive far less attention
and concern.[29] Polar bears, who also are in peril, are celebrated in cute
and cuddly ways (irrespective of their real animal natures): stuffed toys
for children, greeting card images, in Pepsi commercials, and as logos
on clothing. On the other hand, other species fail to make the
commercial mark.

Psychologizing

Even more important perhaps than personifying or pathologizing
for a re-visioning of an animal-inclusive psychology is the process of
psychologizing—"the soul's root and a native activity."[30] Soul-making
takes place through ideation. Ideas, as fluid constructs, operate in the
interest of soul-making, which is "a perspective rather than a substance,

a viewpoint toward things rather than a thing itself. This perspective is reflective; it mediates events and makes differences between ourselves and everything that happens. Between us and events, between the doer and the deed, there is a reflective moment—and soul-making means differentiating this middle ground." It is in the middle ground where real animals make their homes and where they should be encountered. Ideas can become concretized into ideologies and become forms of guidance, rules of living in a particular culture, to which humans cling in order to make sense out of existence. Ideologies are frameworks through which hegemonic imperatives are articulated. If, as Joseph Campbell argued, one of the functions of myth is pedagogical, what is taught about how to see the world, and who is one of us and who is one of them, is critical. In dichotomous Western thinking a perennial divide has been that of human/animal. Christian mythology is filled with direction on animal-as-container of emotions and methods for the actualizing of human goals and desires. We might use animals as archetypes through which to examine ourselves, but, psychologizing, or seeing through, is part of re-visioning depth psychology to create awareness of the fact that, on the other side of this lens, is a real living being. The many-headed, multi-dimensional animal has an entire character and way of being apart from that of what it has come to mean to us. Rather what it means to itself is vitally important. To do less is to commit psychologism, to "harden into systematic arguments, becoming solid and opaque and monocentric."[31] Hillman notes, "When we neglect the image for the idea, then archetypal psychology can become a stereotypical psychology."[32] Taking this further, when we neglect the animal for the archetype, we similarly commit a soul-crime. The de-listing of wolves as an endangered species and the resultant return to slaughtering is an example of the slippage that can occur when negative projection replaces constant concern.

Dehumanizing

One of the psychological tools often used to define someone as less than human, "more lowly," is to de-humanize the individual. However, James Hillman employs this word differently; in a sense he re-appropriates the term. Similar to the idea that psyche is not restricted to an individual soul, but also includes a world soul, re-visioning depth psychology requires we are in the world with others. Therefore, just as "human does not enter into all of soul, nor is everything psychological human," neither does soul only enter that which is only human. This phenomenological sense of "in-ness" thereby sees-through only human beings as being ensouled,[33] "body and soul lose their border," and it becomes clear that humans are only but one possible container for, a projection of, soul.[34] Just as humans are in service of soul, which is not necessarily only human, other animals might also have this relationship. They may show themselves to us in our dreams, and occasionally in our day worlds, but they are not only that. The process of de-humanizing the soul asks us to consider whether what we experience in the form of emotions, for example, are only human felt and known. Hillman says, "The soul and its afflictions, its emotions, feelings, and varieties of love are all certainly essential to the human condition."[35] Therefore might they not also be essential to the animal condition? By looking beyond, past, over, and under animal as word/ sign, we are enacting another of Hillman's concepts—seeing through— in order "to think and feel psychologically," a central obligation of psychology.[36] If we see through other animals as more-than-symbols used in the practice of depth psychology, we are then actively re- visioning and moving past nominalism, literalism, and essentialism that maintains the us/them distinction which has disadvantaged animals- other-than humans for thousands of years. Animals become more than vessels that hold our meanings and projections (a speciesist utilitarian view), but instead are regarded as individuals, a moral extension of personhood. This requires a shift to a place of seeing through, of homology rather than analogy, of "Innenwelt heterophenomenology," in which "rather than try[ing] to put oneself into the animal's shoes, so to speak, one constructs a picture of what the animal must be experiencing given [his or her] physiology, cognitive abilities, behavior, and behavioral context."[37]

ENTER THE ANIMAL

What if animals were included with consideration equal to that of humans? By that I mean, what if we considered and discussed the circumstances of real animals in the world, not only how we might use a cow or a snake or a dog symbolically, metaphorically, or as surrogates for human emotions? As depth psychologists this means inviting the animal to join us when we discuss him or her in relation to problems or challenges. Animals do not tend to follow the same rules as we do in terms of proper etiquette, acceptable hygiene, or public displays of sex. If we invite the animal into the room, it could get messy. They shed, bite, poop, pee, fuck, suck, and engage in all kinds of underworld activities. Humans do too; however, we train our species from a young age as to what to do and how to control bodily functions. Among animals, some we bring into our homes and resocialize to our ways as "pets"; others we banish to the forests and fields, insisting they honor human boundaries. Universities and colleges don't often allow animals on campus unless they are, of course, experimental objects or are in service in some way.

> Orpheus opens an imaginative perspective on the animal, saying that when you remain quiet and play, images, as animals, will come out of hiding and come close. This is certainly true about animals in dreams, and it seems equally true of animals in myth.[38]

Animals often appear in the therapeutic setting as part of active imagination and dreamwork. The analysand is encouraged to invite her dream animal(s) into the room and engage in dialogue. Lions, tigers, bears, and wolves are frightening and comforting when situated in ideas. Dream tending, a "response to the call of the world's other inhabitants, animate and inanimate, who have need of us—as we do of them,"[39] is a method of deep listening to what images in dreams have to say and witnessing the presence of images. Sometimes these images are of animals. "When you dream of a bear we become curious about this specific bear, because this bear is not the same bear in anyone else's dream."[40] It is important that we not only regard the animals of dreams, but also attend to the living ones. Liberation psychology responds to this call. Bradshaw and Watkins point out, "Psychology, by maintaining an agenda of speciesism, violates one of its central projects: individual development of moral consciousness."[41] This nonhierarchical approach considers animals as individuals who live in communities with whom human beings must envision a new kind of relationship. It requires we "redraw the categories to fit the behavior patterns" of what is human and what is animal and "recognize that animal experiences are not just pale imitations of our own."[42]

If we do not acknowledge animals as morally conscious beings as persons by personifying and de-humanizing our psychology, we risk losing them. Bradshaw and Watkins' trans-species psychology is a crucial part of this work. A species-inclusive psychology brings together the goals of liberation psychology with the perspective of ecopsychology in both theory and praxis. Thus, "the model of the trans-species psyche explicitly names the interpenetration of human and animal domains in parity absent the assumption of ascendance."[43] This transformative ideology advocates engagement with animals' lived experiences in order to advocate for change.

In "Nature Dreaming: Depth Psychology and Ecology," depth psychologist Steven Aizenstat acknowledges the critical condition of the natural world and makes a call for preservation of "authentic wildlife."[44] I take "authentic" to mean real animals. Similarly, Cobb writes "the natural animals have an imaginal vision; the physical world perceives by a metaphysical light."[45] I take "natural" to mean the real animal, the one that might bite us, lick us, and curl up with us at night. However important it is that depth psychologists work as naturalists might, "naturalists of the inner and outer psyche" who witness and respond to our environment, it's not enough.[46] We can't stop there—too many animals are suffering; too many animal and human animal lives are being lost every day due to human abuse of the planet and of one another. As we learn to hear the gods again, I am certain not only animals-as-archetypes, but also animals as cohabiters have something important to tell us too. Aizenstat argues "the dream image is an independent presence in a broader psychic ecology … The elephant that appeared in 'my' dream had a life of its own; it visited to interact with me as a fellow creature of the dreamtime—perhaps to heighten my awareness of the plight of the elephant in the world."[47] This comes closer to thinking about the symbolic and the real animal in the world, both who need and deserve our attention. A liberation view says we must not marginalize animals to the symbolic realm any more than we do in lived experience.

"What we call the unconscious is simply our lack of awareness of the constant operation of the imaginal in our lives."[48] This emphasizes that the imaginal and the unconscious (which also contains repressed materials, personal memories, and other contents) are essentially the same. Arguing against Hillman's intellectual emphasis on image-only, what is needed is a broader understanding of imaginal, one that includes affect. Here is the threshold across which the real animal might enter the room. Jung noted, when dealing with the symbolic, "image and meaning are identical, and as the first takes shape so the latter becomes clear."[49] Thus, we should not only pay attention to the elephant and the bear and the lion and the wolf in the dream within in the safe space the therapeutic encounter offers, but also do so in the external world of habitat loss and global warming—the world in which real bears and wolves are trying to survive. If, as depth psychologists, our task is to tend to the soul of the world, animal souls, real animal souls, need to be cared for as well.

Some symbols have only individual relevance. Dream bears, for example, both big and small, might "take on an extraordinary numinosity which is shared by nobody beside the dreamer."[50] However, bears may conceivably be trying to tell a dreamer something about themselves and should be included in collective conversations about them. Dreams provide a safe stage for human-animal encounters and, says Berger, "animals first entered the imagination as messengers and promises."[51] If an essential aspect of depth psychology is that much about humanness is concealed, would it not therefore hold that much about being and being among animals also remains hidden? As Heraclitus said more than 25 centuries ago, "nature loves to hide."[52] If depth psychology is of or at the margins, or perhaps of the marginalized, my hope is the real human/animal connection will be included in terms of the role played in the human psyche by/with non-human animals.[53] A parallel example would be if, in working with dreams, an analysand mentioned dreaming of a black man, but had never met such an individual in real life. She would have to rely upon the stories in popular culture, the mass media, and what other people told her about who black men are and what they are like. Thus, her interaction with the image would be informed by cultural re-presentations. If, in doing active imagination, the black man were invited into the room, would he really be welcome? Would he want to stay? The ideology of superiority that underpins racism, sexism, and homophobia similarly frames and supports that of speciesism. This carries the responsibility of challenging "speciesism" by acknowledging "the human-nature relations as a relationship" and adding their voices as oppressed beings in order to place psyche (soul, anima, mind) back into the (natural) world.[54] Perhaps, as Wolfe argues, "problems of race or gender may be either 'solved' or re-opened by being recoded as problems of species."[55] We cannot speak for animals, but a goal of trans-species psychology, a re-visioning of depth psychology, is to work toward an understanding of what animal perspectives might be. This has significant implications for humans as well. As Pythagoras said 26 centuries ago:

> As long as man continues to be the ruthless destroyer of lower living beings, he will never know health or peace. For as long as men massacre animals, they will kill each other. Indeed, he who sows the seeds of murder and pain cannot reap joy and love.[56]

Thus, if we think imaginally about animals, they are always and forever with us and aware of us, "there is no part of an animal that does not look back at us. There is no part that does not remind us that there is something, a life, an existence that in some way echoes our own, but which remains always behind what meets our gaze, elusive, impossible, unimaginable."[57] The question is, as posed by Marcus Bullock, "What do we see when we really look at an animal?"[58] While this question, and possible answers, are beyond the scope of this short paper, it is an important perspective to mention. Some animals seek to meet our gaze. In other animal cultures, to stare, to make direct eye contact, is threatening and aggressive. How do we learn these languages? Dogs have learned to read the human baring of teeth not as a threat, but as a welcome, some even imitate their human companions. We re-present animals in art, as data, as symbols, as archetypes, as rhetorical substitutes for human activity (bull markets, bear markets), but sometimes ignore the actual world of animals and the animals in crisis. We do animals a moral disservice by not taking a step beyond the imaginary and the imaginal. In fact, limiting this engagement to the symbolic animal is a form of distance. Bullock writes, "I want to retrieve them from that distance."[59] I, too, want to invite the real animal into the room, whether that is the classroom, the consulting room, or the boardroom at the zoo. I want to take Hillman's argument further by engaging the precepts of "re-visioning psychology" to a re-visioning of depth psychology that does this with and for animals. Their and our lives depend upon it.

Hillman argues that present day psychology and psychotherapy de-soul the individual, de-person-ify in a way that renders the individual flat and imaginationless.[60] While inching toward an argument for the inclusion of animal others in the sphere of subjectivity, he nevertheless still comes up slightly short of making this assertion. He writes that while the view of the modern world about individuals and personification as viewed in religion and poetics has always included a subjective view of all beings, psychology has not. This "restrictive perspective … has led us to believe that entities, other than human beings, taking on interior subjective qualities are merely 'anthropomorphized.'"[61] Hillman speaks of the need to widen the sphere of inclusion in the depth psychological embrace, yet animals, real animals, are still left to sniff around the margins. Although humans "believe we have unconsciously put our experiences into them; they are merely fiction or imaginary. We have made them up just as the persons in our dreams are supposedly made up out of the experiences of our ego."[62] A re-visioning is due for depth psychology that firmly connects it with trans-species psychology. As Hillman notes, "personifying helps place subjective experiences 'out there,'" hence we can "devise protections against them and relations with them."[63] Similarly, if we limit our engagement with animals to the symbolic realm, it also functions as protection, of sorts, or at least supports the argument that says humans can never know animals or communicate with them, so why try? Just as Adam named the animals, thus creating a "them" in relation to "us," limiting animals to the archetypal and imaginal realms further serves this view of animals as different, and therefore separate and unequal. Psyche's metaphorical language must be valued and honored for full appreciation of our shared soulfulness.

Conclusion

Psychology's project of re-visioning includes a re-imagining of animals that brings nonhuman species into dialogue as partnered equals with humanity. Animals are in our thoughts because of the pictures we paint, the photographs we take, and the dreams we manufacture and remember. "[T]he metaphors drawing animals into the language by which we know ourselves limit the connections to specific, observable characteristics that operate for us in the realm of freedom."[64] As long as animals are used to stand in for human emotions/ ideas/projections, they remain enslaved and kept at a distance. In so doing, we commit a preemptive surgery in our own psyches. There is little hope of healing the human psyche without first healing those whom we have made suffer through domination and exclusion. Although our behavior toward animals may seem to suggests otherwise and that "we may [seem to] be only an inessential part of their habitat, they are an indispensable element of ours."[65]

When "we listen to the dream to see what it is telling us, or look at what it says, we see through it in order to hear its message."[66] Subsequently, if we listen to the animals who appear in our dreams, it is necessary ethically, psychologically, and practically to see through to the lived experience of the real beings that have inspired the image. Changing how we relate to dream animals, namely, by simultaneously acting with comparable respect and care for his/her living counterparts, then we begin to transform our own lives and the culture away from a utilitarian environmental ideology that has dominated modern beliefs about nature.[67] To truly enact one of depth psychology's central tenants then requires a wider lens for "seeing-through our hearing and listen-into our seeing,"[68] one that extends to profound cultural transformation.

Regarding the animal as more than something that stands in for something else is a move toward a subjective relationship with them and is work that needs doing as "a necessary part of our reconceptualization of ourselves as humans."[69] We understand animals as beings like us with histories filled with both joy, suffering, grief, love, and meaning.

I love, respect, and admire the aesthetic, behavioral, affective, and cognitive natures of animals, but above all am convinced of their imaginal nature, evidenced by their playfulness, curiosity, and contemplation. While it is obvious that animals held captive in zoos, in laboratories, at factory farms, or at humane societies, literally cry and reach out to passing humans, those in the wild also speak. Young South African bull elephants, for example, traumatized by witnessing the murders of their parents and family members by poachers, respond in ways that speak volumes about the effects of violence on animal psyches.[70] Another example of the profound impact of disruption of maternal attachment resulting in psychobiological trauma is well documented among chimpanzees.[71] Post-traumatic stress disorders are also evident among dogs, horses, and other species who have been torn from birth families, confined in cages and pens, or forced to behave in ways that are not natural to them.

Hence, we must heed Hillman's methodological caution not to betray the animals, "You can't interpret them; you can't symbolize them; you can't do something that is only human about them. Their presence is felt."[72] The point is to move beyond "the narrow world of human projection"[73] and embrace a kinship that "extends to others, who appear to me as other bodies, to animals whom I understand as variants of my embodiment."[74] As in dream world encounters, it is important to allow the animal to be the animal, to speak for itself, which opens the pathway for dialogue with and access to an affirmation of the universal web.

In this essay I have advocated for an animal imaginal soul lens through which to view simultaneous trauma experienced both by humans and animals in situations of human expansion. This is an urgent call to mind the animal psyche and a needed healing of our ecopsyche and its material manifestation. The environmental crisis, the thousands upon thousands of animals whose minds and lives are stretched to near extinction as a result of the rapacious human psyche, require our attention. The polar ice caps melting, islands shrinking, the weather changing: as organisms who share the planet, we all feel the anguish. However, for nonhuman animals, the experience is even more immediate and felt—starvation, habitat encroachment, hunted, killed, and orphaned—and the causes are not of their doing, but ours.

Psychology is central to conservation, the "human care for nature."[75] This means active engagement and listening in to animals who are in need of our help, particularly those who have experienced forms of trauma and loss such as elephants (wild and zoo'd),[76] dolphins (captive and hunted),[77] wolves and other predators (reintroduced and rejected),[90] chimpanzees (experimented on and isolated),[78] and countless others. Let us re-vision a world where these souls no longer have to fear and fend off the human psyche, a world of healing and reconciliation.

NOTES

1. The term "animal" is used in this essay to refer to other-than-human beings that include birds, mammals, and reptiles. Further "we" refers to modern human cultures.

2. John Berger, "Why Look at Animals?" in *About Looking* (New York: Vintage, 1991), p. 3.

3. Veronica Goodchild, *Eros and Chaos* (Lake Worth, FL: Nicolas-Hays, Inc., 2001), p. xxiv.

DEBRA MERSKIN

4. James Hillman and Margot McLean, *Dream Animals* (New York: Chronicle Books, 1997), p. 2.

5. Hillman and McLean, p. 5.

6. James Hillman, *Re-Visioning Psychology* (New York: Harper Perennial, 1975).

7. Barbara Hannah, *The Cat, Dog, and Horse Lectures, and the Beyond* (Brooklyn, NY: Chiron, 1954/1992).

8. Hillman, *Re-Visioning*, p. xvii.

9. Knute Berger, "Serial Killer Whale?" *Crosscut,* February 24, 2010, http://crosscut.com/blog/crosscut/19353/, accessed February 25, 2010.

10. Hillman, *Re-Visioning*, p. 1.

11. James Hillman, *A Blue Fire* (New York: Routledge, 1990), p. 46.

12. Rene Descartes, "Metaphysics and the Question of Animal Intelligence in the Thought of Descartes," trans. J. Cottingham, R. Stoothoff, & D. Murdoch, *Philosophical Writings of Descartes, Vol. II* (Cambridge: Cambridge University Press, 1984), p. 1.

13. Hillman, *Re-Visioning*, p. 129.

14. "Animal," n. a. *The Oxford English Dictionary* 2nd ed. 1989, OED Online. Oxford University Press, http://dictionary.oed.com.libproxy.uoregon.edu/cgi/entry/50008682?single=1&query_type=word&queryword=animal&first=1&max_to_show=10, accessed January 20, 2010.

15. Hillman, *Re-Visioning*, p. 3.

16. *Ibid.*, p. 13.

17. *Ibid.*, p. 32.

18. *Ibid.*, p. 10.

19. *Ibid.*, p. 32.

20. *Ibid.*, p. 111.

21. *Ibid.*, p. 55.

22. *Ibid.*, p. 99.

23. Robert A. Palmatier, *Speaking of Animals: A Dictionary of Animal Metaphors* (Westport, CT: Greenwood Press, 1995), p. 418, p. 419.

24. *Ibid.*, p. 100.

25. Evelyn Dahl Reed, *Coyote Tales from the Indian Pueblos* (Santa Fe, NM: Sunstone Press, 1988), p. 6.

26. "Project Coyote: Protecting America's Song Dog," *Earth Island Journal* (Autumn, 2009), http://www.earthisland.org/journal/

index.php/eij/article/project_coyote/ (accessed February 25, 2010).

27. *Ibid.*

28. Berger, p. 15.

29. John Roach, "Shrinking sea ice takes deadly toll on Pacific walrus," *San Diego Union-Tribune* (January 10, 2008), http://legacy.signonsandiego.com/uniontrib/20080110/news_1c10walrus.html (accessed February 25, 2010); Preparing for an Uncertain Climate, 22 (United States Office of Technology Assessment: Washington, DC, 1993); William F. Perrin, Bernd Würsig, J.G.M. Thewissen, *Encyclopedia of Marine Animals* (Maryland Heights, MO: Academic Press, 2008).

30. Hillman, *Re-Visioning,* p. 115.

31. *Ibid.*, p. 133.

32. *Ibid.*, p. 144.

33. *Ibid.*, p. 173.

34. *Ibid.*, p. 174.

35. *Ibid.*, p. 189.

36. *Ibid.*, p. 180.

37. Daisie Radner, "Heterophenomenology: Learning about the Birds and the Bees," *Journal of Philosophy* 91(8) (1994): 402.

38. Noel Cobb, *Archetypal Imagination: Glimpses of the Gods in Life and Art* (Herndon, VA: Steiner Books, 1992), p. 237.

39. Stephen Aizenstat, "Nature Dreaming: Depth Psychology and Ecology" (2003), p. 1, http://www.dreamtending.com/articles.html (accessed June 15, 2009).

40. Sally Carless, "Dream Voices: Listening to the Whisperings of the Dream World," http://www.dreamvoices.com/, accessed February 18, 2010.

41. G.A. Bradshaw and Mary Watkins, "Trans-Species Psychology: Theory and Praxis," *Spring*, 75 (Part 1): 71.

42. Radner, "Herophenomenology," p. 403.

43. *Ibid.*, p. 71.

44. Aizenstat, "Nature Dreaming."

45. Cobb, *Archetypal Imagination*, p. 239.

46. Stephen Aizenstat, "Tending the dream is tending the world" (2003), p. 2, http://www.dreamtending.com/articles.html, accessed June 15, 2009.

47. Aizenstat, "Nature Dreaming," p. 4.

48. Lionel Corbett, *The Religious Function of the Psyche* (New York: Routledge, 2001), p. 98.

49. C.G. Jung, "On the Nature of the Psyche," *Collected Works* 8, trans. R.F.C. Hull (Princeton, NJ: Princeton University Press, 1947/1983), § 402.

50. Corbett, *Religious Function*, p. 100.

51. Berger, "Serial Killer Whale?", p. 4.

52. Heraclitus, in *The Art and Thought of Heraclitus*, trans. Charles H. Kahn (New York: Cambridge University Press, 1981), p. 33.

53. Helene S. Lorenz & Mary Watkins, "Depth Psychology and Colonialism: Individuation, Seeing Through, and Liberation" (paper presented at The International Symposium of Archetypal Psychology, Santa Barbara, CA, 2000).

54. Andy Fisher, *Radical Ecopsychology: Psychology in the Service of Life* (Albany: SUNY, 2006), p. 8.

55. Cary Wolfe, "Fathers, Lovers, and Friend Killers: Rearticulating Gender and Race Via Species in Hemingway," *Boundary* 2, 29(1) (2002): 226.

56. "Pythagoras," in Norman Myers, *Gaia: An Atlas of Planet Management* (New York: Anchor, 1993), p. 158.

57. Marcus Bullock, "Watching Eyes, Seeing Dreams, Knowing Lives," in *Representing Animals*, ed. Nigel Rothfels (Bloomington, IN: Indiana University Press, 2002), p. 101.

58. *Ibid.*, p. 102.

59. *Ibid.*, p. 105.

60. Hillman, *Re-Visioning*.

61. *Ibid.*, p. 1.

62. *Ibid.*, p. 2.

63. *Ibid.*, p. 31.

64. Bullock, "Watching Eye," p. 111.

65. *Ibid.*, p. 106.

66. Hillman, *Re-Visioning*, p. 171.

67. Julia Corbett, *Communicating Nature: How We Create and Understand Environmental Messages* (Washington, DC: Island Press, 2006).

68. *Ibid.*, p. 171.

69. *Ibid.*, p. 5.

70. G.A. Bradshaw, *Elephants on the Edge: What Animals Teach Us*

About Humanity (New Haven, CT: Yale University Press, 2009).

71. Jane Goodall, *The Chimpanzees of the Gombe: Patterns of Behavior* (Cambridge, MA: Harvard University Press, 1986).

72. James Hillman, "Animal Presence: Interview by Jonathan White," in *Talking on the Water: Conversations about Nature and Creativity* (San Francisco: Sierra Club, 1994), p. 123.

73. Andy Fisher, "To Praise Again: Phenomenology and the Project of Ecopsychology," *Spring* 76: 159.

74. Maurice Merleau-Ponty, "Husserl at the Limits of Phenomenology," trans. J. O'Neill, in *Themes From the Lectures at the College de France, 1952-1960* (Evanston, IL: Northwestern University Press, 1970), p. 122.

75. Susan Clayton and Gene Meyers, *Conservation Psychology: Understanding and Promoting Human Care for Nature* (West Sussex, UK: Wiley-Blackwell, 2009), p. 5.

76. Bradshaw, *Elephants on the Edge.*

77. Jessica Pierce and Marc Bekoff, *Wild Justice: The Moral Lives of Animals* (Chicago: University of Chicago Press, 2009).

78. Sue Savage-Rumbaugh, *Kanzi: The Ape at the Brink of the Human Mind* (New York: Wiley, 1996).

THE EVOLUTION OF ETHOLOGY: AN INTERVIEW WITH MARC BEKOFF

G. A. BRADSHAW

Marc Bekoff is Professor Emeritus of Ecology and Evolutionary Biology at the University of Colorado, Boulder, where he taught animal behavior for 32 years. He pioneered the study of animal emotions and cognitive ethology and is an internationally renowned author of numerous books, including *The Emotional Lives of Animals*, *Wild Justice: The Moral Lives of Animals* (with Jessica Pierce) and *The Animal Manifesto: Six Reasons for Expanding Our Compassion Footprint*. Together with Jane Goodall, Marc co-founded Ethologists for the Ethical Treatment of Animals. G.A. Bradshaw interviewed Marc for *Spring* to reflect on how ideas about animals—their minds and our own—have evolved over the past three decades.

Spring: Given your experience studying animal minds and behavior, do you think that the field of ethology has changed much over the past three decades?

G. A. Bradshaw, Ph.D., Ph.D., is Executive Director of The Kerulos Center (www.kerulos.org) and founder of the field of trans-species psychology. She holds doctorate degrees in ecology and psychology and is the author of *Elephants on the Edge: What Animals Teach Us About Humanity* (Yale Univ. Press, 2009), an in-depth psychological portrait of elephants in captivity and in the wild. Her research focuses on the traumatic effects of human violence on elephants, grizzly bears, chimpanzees, and parrots and on wildlife cultural recovery.

Marc Bekoff: Yes and no. No, it has not changed because millions of animals are still suffering at the hands of researchers. A lot of animal behavior research is still conducted in old-school traditional ways (animals are numbered, not named, animals are referred to as "the subjects", and papers are written in the third- rather than the first-person perspective—the researcher did this or that rather than I or we did this or that) and biomedical research uses animals as throwaway experimental tools. But the answer is also "yes" because there have been a lot of changes in how scientists view animals compared to the past.

Most ethological research used to focus on what humans wanted to know about animals. We studied animals for our own purposes and not with much thought about what animals needed. Until Donald Griffin, myself, and some others started the field of cognitive ethology, no one in science really thought of animals as having very active minds. Animals were typically treated and used as objects just we might use a piece of laboratory equipment. Animals were taken from the wild, housed in small cages and experimented on, and then often just killed after the study was over. As a result, behavioral research has caused animals a lot of suffering and death. I was involved in some myself, and to this day feel very remorseful for my part. But I saw the light and changed my ways.

Overall, there seems to be a huge shift in attitudes towards animals, but it's slow-going. Today, most everyone agrees that animals have feelings and minds. When I started out as a student, this was considered a crazy idea. Now more and more researchers are aware of the ethical implications of using animals and make efforts to use humane methods so that animals don't suffer as much. But we can do much better because "good welfare" is *not* "good enough". For example, some major universities in India and Russia have stopped performing animal dissection—and there are changes in technology, like the design of radio-collars that are used to track wildlife movements. In some cases, radio collars were so heavy that they caused injuries to animals and also affected their behavior. Also, people now realize that putting an animal in a cage is not natural and that the experiment results are therefore not scientifically valid. Confinement and manipulations cause stress, stress changes behavior and physiology, and these changes can compromise the reliability of the data collected. Another big difference is that now the study of animal emotions is taken seriously.

Spring: Animal emotions—you are one of the main people responsible for making how animals feel a scientifically legitimate research topic. As a result, psychology and ethology are converging into one field.

Marc: Yes, the fact that animals are now understood to have emotions is truly an amazing breakthrough. It reflects a huge change in science. When I first started out, I was the only practicing scientist in this field who really pushed the idea that animals had deep and rich emotional lives and a point of view—they didn't like to be treated like objects and endure unnecessary pain and suffering. Now, you see books and studies in all sorts of places and in many academic disciplines—mainstream journals publish essays on topics such as joy and laughter in rats and empathy in mice. People talk openly and naturally about animals having a sense of humor, feeling grief and joy. It's funny because Charles Darwin wrote about animal emotions years ago, and it has taken that long for science as a whole to accept this idea. Social change is slow to come, but it is coming.

Spring: Has your teaching changed?

Marc: Again, yes and no. My basic lectures have not changed over time. I still talk about how ethological observations and descriptions are critical to any study about animals. I bring in the work of Konrad Lorenz and Niko Tinbergen and talk about how to frame research studies from the perspective of Darwin's theory of evolutionary continuity. And my teaching has always included discussions about the importance of ethics. I was lucky because I was taught about this early on when I was a student, so my courses and lectures always include discussion of *who* we are talking about not *what*. I really stress how important it is to see animals as individuals, not just as members of a species or as property, but as unique sentient beings with feelings and emotions. I encourage students to maintain the highest moral standards in what they do.

But there is one thing that has changed over the past ten years or so. I use more stories about animals with great data to illustrate an idea. I don't want to be a member of the "p<0.05" crowd where we supplant what we know intuitively with numbers. The reality is that people don't really learn through numbers—they learn through stories in combination with solid data. But stories count, and as I like to say, the plural of anecdote is data. For example, whenever I lecture, people want to hear details about how a coyote lives, how a dog plays and how he feels. They want to know the *real* animals, not just what science tells them. People relate to stories because that is how they understand their own lives. It's what Jessica Pierce calls narrative ethology.

Spring: So what you are saying is that people want to be close to other animals and do feel close, but at the same time, they think and do things that keep them apart. Why is that?

Marc: We all have old brains—humans and animals share the same brain structures and neurochemicals, but we live in new sociocultural and technological milieus. You have to remember that our ancestors lived side by side with other animals, and the feeling of closeness with other species is ancient and natural, although our ancestors did kill them for food and other items. It's our old brains that constantly pull us back to nature. We crave contact with animals. But culture doesn't always agree with genetics. Look how most of us live our lives—in front of computers, sitting in houses, surrounded by artificial things. I have friends who tell me "Wow, the day went so fast that I didn't get a chance to take a run or go outside." Our modern society is so packed with human things and demands that it overwhelms us and takes us away from what we would do naturally. We don't take siestas and don't just hang out. We don't take down time, alone time, to look at a tree or marvel at the flight of a bird or an insect. We are busy all the time doing a zillion things and become frustrated and out of touch with natural rhythms and ourselves. So while we want to be close to animals and nature, we just don't make the time. Culture clashes with nature.

Spring: How then do we create a way of living that honors other animals and brings us back to what you call the ancient and more natural ways?

Marc: There are a lot of small simple things to do that can make a big change. The first is to acknowledge that humans are animals and that we should feel lucky to be part of the animal kingdom—treat the expression "behaving like an animal" as a compliment, not something negative. I believe we are born to be good and that includes animals.

"Nature red in tooth and claw" does not hold nor does our assumption that competition is the rule in the wild. In fact, what social ethology studies show is how cooperation, not competition, is the rule rather than the exception. Of course animals compete with one another but not the way we envision it: the importance of competition, without factoring in the significant roles of cooperation, compassion, and empathy, has been overblown.

It's also important to admit that humans cause a lot of unnecessary pain, suffering, and death. We need to strive to become more compassionate to create a larger "compassion footprint" in our interactions with animals and Earth. This includes being more compassionate with ourselves and other people. It's easy to feel overwhelmed with all the bad news and then take it out on others. So we need to treat other humans in a better and more caring way and try not to be so critical of others even if they are doing things in ways we don't like.

To feel empowered and to recognize that each individual can make changes happen—that we all can make positive differences when we make more humane and ethical choices, is equally critical. For example, what you buy and use is a positive vote for change. We need to realize that preventing a cow or pig from suffering is worth a lot more than wearing a new pair of leather shoes or buying a new purse. So at least don't eat factory farmed meat or wear and use leather or fur. Be mindful that what makes the animal feel good makes us feel good too. Animals are asking us to treat them better or leave them alone, and we need to listen to them and look in their eyes, if we dare do so.

And get involved—volunteer at an animal rescue shelter, humane society, or sanctuary, for example. Bring animals into your life. We each have a lot of love to give and so do other animals. Doing those kinds of things makes a huge difference in all our lives—nonhuman and human.

Generally, people need to step back and really smell the roses. When I start to feel really stressed, I usually stop, shift gears, and do something else because I don't want my brain and body to get into that space. I protect myself this way. What each one of us must do is learn our own set point individually and not think we are "wasting time" if we sit by a stream or watch the stars or just sit and do nothing. Going to nature is good for us, of this there can be no doubt.

Spring: You talked about how science has changed over the past three decades, but have you changed?

Marc: Yes. I have shifted philosophically, and it is because of the teachers I have had. Not only wonderful people like Jane Goodall and Donald Griffin, but the animals. Jasper is a moon bear. I aspire to practice what he teaches. Here's why. For fifteen years Jasper was kept in the most inhumane conditions one could imagine. His home was a tiny, filthy "crush cage" on a bear farm in China in which he couldn't move.[1] Imagine being pinned in a phone booth for even fifteen minutes. As if this wasn't enough, Jasper also had a catheter inserted into his gall bladder so that his bile could be collected to treat various ailments in the spurious name of traditional Chinese medicine.[2] How Jasper recovered at the Moon Bear Rescue Centre outside Chengdu, China[3] is beyond belief. Despite all the pain and indignity he endured Jasper is a genuinely compassionate being and peacemaker. He's truly the spokes-bear for forgiveness, peace, and hope. I've met Jasper and looked into his omniscient eyes that say, "All's well, the past is past, let go and move on". Thank you, Jasper, for sharing your journey and your dreams. I bet it's Jasper's optimistic spirit and trust that's allowed him to thrive. His spiritual path is as an inspirational lesson for how we can all be healthy, alive, and connected.

I am much more positive now than I used to be, but I've always been an optimist. I work a lot with kids and their positive energy and focus on what is working, not on what is *not* working, really keeps me going. Over the last fifteen years I feel I have become more patient and have tried harder to understand other people's views. I have stopped expecting that everyone will think the same way I do and agree with me. I'm not trying to change the world overnight because true change can take time. I preach to the unconverted and try to institute change by putting out information in a positive way. I don't try anymore to convince someone that dogs have feelings if people are really resistant to this reality. If they believe it or not, that is fine with me because there are always people who are open to meaningful discussions from which change can emerge. It is up to them to do something to make the world a better place for animals, including other humans. My job is to provide the information and knowledge and let them decide. I really like the saying, "If you take the leap, the net will appear." Put out information and people will absorb it.

Spring: You are involved in prison education programs.

Marc: Yes, and I have learned a lot from this experience, too. For one, it is astounding how, across the board, these men trust and love animals and feel safe with animals. They seek out time and solace with animals and talk about how much they miss the connection with their cat or dog. Also I have learned that you receive what you give. The guys and I spend a lot of time listening to each other. They all have a story. You only have to listen. The time together has made me more empathic and made me appreciative of them as individual beings and my wanting to know what they are feeling. Hearing their stories and how so many love animals has made me reach out to help give them a voice that has been silenced.

Spring: What role do you think psychology and psychologists can play?

Marc: I'm now really active in relatively new and exciting interdisciplinary fields called *conservation psychology* and *conservation social work*. Basically, it's pretty straightforward. Conservation, psychology, and social work are brought together so that we can understand how people form the attitudes they hold and how they can be changed in positive ways. If minds and hearts change, then we can more effectively solve the problems we've caused.

We biologists need psychologists, sociologists, and social workers to partake in this revolution. We need to invite all of them into the discussions and exchange ideas. We can do the best if we share what we know. Studies of animal cognition try to understand how information is processed and used in the myriad social and other situations in which animals find themselves. In a sense, studies of animal cognition can help us understand how attitudes are formed and used. Psychologists can do the same thing with people. Conservation psychology brings to the table ideas about how humans process information about, for example, losses of biodiversity and an understanding of how people perceive these losses and what they mean to them. We can then take these insights and translate them into specific ways to foster positive change in the behavior of individuals. A lot of the work also goes on in communities, and this is where social workers

Fig. 1: Jasper, a Moon bear (*Ursus thibetanus*). Moon bears have been hunted almost to extinction for their body parts which are used in Oriental medicine.
Photo courtesy of AnimalsAsia.

Fig. 2: Marc feeding Jasper.

Photo courtesy of Jill Robinson

and the field of conservation social work can help us along. Teach the children well, for they are the ambassadors for a more harmonious, peaceful, compassionate, and gentle world.

All in all, I remain an optimist and a dreamer that we can make positive differences in the lives of animals, including humans, and in the future of our one and only planet because concentrating on the negative drains time and energy from what needs to be done to make the world a better place for all. I welcome everyone to join me on this journey because everyone counts and everyone can make a difference. The time is now. Negativity is out.

We can and must keep our hopes and dreams alive.

NOTES

1. http://www.newscientist.com/article/mg20227061.400-bear-tapping-a-bile-business.html.

2. For details about bear farming and bear rescue, see http://www.animalsasia.org/index.php?module=2&lg=en.

3. http://www.animalsasia.org/.

Ecopsychology and the Sacred: The Psychological Basis of the Environmental Crisis

David Tacey

I have been calling ecopsychology 'new,' but in fact its sources are old enough to be called aboriginal. —Theodore Roszak[1]

The Shift from Ego- to Eco-centric

There are subtle bonds that connect humans with nature and place. These bonds are hard to describe but this does not mean they should be ignored. In a sense these bonds create the vital link between humanity and the natural environment, and when they are severed, for instance, by excessive rationality or a collapse of awe or reverence toward nature, we are left outside the field of nature and in an alienated state. These subtle bonds are world-creating and world-

David Tacey, Ph.D., is Associate Professor at La Trobe University, Melbourne, Australia, where he teaches literature and depth psychology. He is the author of nine books and over a hundred articles on Jungian psychology, literary and cultural studies, and ecopsychology. His recent books include *Edge of the Sacred: Jung, Psyche, Earth* (Einsiedeln, Switzerland: Daimon Verlag, 2009) and *How to Read Jung* (New York: W. W. Norton, 2007).

destroying; they constitute for us a symbolic world in which we can live in nature as participants in creation. We (by "we" I refer here to modern Western, colonial peoples and cultures) live in a time where these threads are wearing thin and this is cause for alarm, and reason enough to study them. They need support and strengthening, and ecopsychology is one way in which we can achieve this goal.

The subtle threads that bind us to nature have always interested me, and not only recently, as we struggle to find ways to connect with nature in the shadow of the ecological crisis. Ever since I was a child, growing up in central Australia alongside Aboriginal culture, I have been mesmerized by the spiritual bonds that connect indigenous people to place. When I discovered these connections that seemed akin to those of indigenous peoples, I moved to a new place in my relationship with nature. There is no longer a need to be told by outside authorities, or by internal authority for that matter, to *care more* about the environment. Authoritative voices are no longer necessary because there is no longer a drive to mistreat the world or behave thoughtlessly toward it. As a civilization, we need to move beyond the egotism that separates us from the world and cuts us off from the living web of relationships.

To move from *ego-centric* to *eco-centric* is the journey we have to undertake, and as we make this journey we are forced to leave behind the mind that requires a parental authority to teach it how to behave. When we change from ego- to eco-centric, we are connected to the environment and want nothing more than to care for it. What we require is nothing less than a new state of consciousness, one that collapses the old distinction between self and world, which has become for us a hardened dualism preventing the self from participating fully in the world.

Much of the official talk recently about the environment operates mainly at the level of our moral conscience rather than of our consciousness. Everywhere today we find appeals to our conscience and superego, based on fear and scare tactics. Voices of governments and non-government organizations enjoin us to *care more* about nature, but the greatest resource for change is not our *guilty conscience* but *our potential for recovery of a shared unitary consciousness*. This alone, in my view, holds the key to the ecological revolution that is needed. It is true that guilt about our environmental damage must be acknowledged and it can spur us to reparation to some extent. Guilt can be useful if it is shifted toward a cultural grief that brings environmental action. But guilt can also paralyze us and make us unable to do anything.

TOWARD A NEW CONCEPT OF IDENTITY

Environmentalists have made full use of guilt in the past, and rightly so, but in my view punishing people is not enough. To use corporate language, we need less of the stick and more of the carrot. What is the carrot apart from the invitation to a new state of mind, to a new kind of romanticism? People need an alternative vision as to how to live in a different way. We need to reveal that life can be broadened and deepened by opening ourselves to a new concept of identity, one that includes the so-called "external" world as part of our experience of our own subjectivity. In nature, we realize our essential kinship with the whole of creation and our custodianship of the more-than-human world, as Abram calls it.[2] We need to speak up and act on behalf of this other world that is also ourselves. Only by moving beyond the guilty conscience can we move toward an exploration of consciousness, and reach a new awareness that gives us a fuller life. People have to be shown that there is "more" to life than they are living. Ecopsychology can do this, and it can help the environmental movement move beyond its preoccupation with guilt and punishment.

I have written two books on this topic. One is called *ReEnchantment*[3] and the other *Edge of the Sacred*.[4] In writing these books I have thought a lot about the subtle connections between ourselves and the world, and I have reached into my childhood memory and experience to try to articulate as an adult what I could only marvel and wonder at as a child. But strangely enough, I still feel as if I have said nothing about this, as if a vast, new, undiscovered continent of thought lies ahead of us, awaiting our discovery. The whole question of our subtle connection with nature is possibly the most under-researched topic in the field of environmental studies. It requires an intuitive awareness to understand it, and that is possibly why it is under-researched. But I am convinced it is our chief resource in helping us battle our way through the crisis that has arisen from our belief that we are separate from nature.

Our models for unitive consciousness often come from the indigenous people from all parts of the world.[5] In Australia, politicians and media commentators pay lip-service to the "special relationship" to the land that is integral to Aboriginal culture, but frequently fail to take the real message home: unless non-indigenous people have experienced a profound psychic connection to landscape they—we— will not learn to respect the bond between land and indigenous inhabitants. Political goodwill alone will do little to bridge the gap between cultures and our estrangement from self and land. Until we develop a revised sense of identity, which includes the natural world in a broadened definition of self, our best intentions are in vain.

Our love seems to move only toward that with which it can identify, as if caught within a narcissistic frame. Our love finds it hard to move beyond self and its territories or extensions. Our affective bonds unite us with family, home, and personal connections, in small circles of intimacy. There needs to be a shift in the *locus* of our identity, so that what we care about or love, and what we regard as belonging to us, is broadened to accommodate a greater span of reality. We need to broaden our range of intimacy so that it includes the other-than-human and the more-than-human. Put cynically, if humans care only about themselves, then the notion of "self" has to be broadened in the direction of the world to include other selves. The ecological task is not only to repair our damage in the world, but to repair the splits on the inside, to work toward inclusive rather than exclusive concepts of identity. This is why there can be no authentic ecological revolution without an eco-psychology and change on the inside.

LOSS OF SOUL AND REANIMATING THE WORLD

I don't think the change in consciousness must necessarily be *religious*. It is hard to see modern Western people, who are on the whole very secular, becoming religious under any circumstance, or if they are tend to embrace a religion grounded in domination over nature and the indigenous. Subsequently, the revolution may need to be romantic rather than religious. We may need to fall in love with the world, to overcome the myth that says humans are separate from the physical world. In so doing, we may be able to move a long way toward healing the planet and ourselves. The myth of alienation is linked with the myth of individualism—a pernicious myth that keeps us separated from the world and each other. These myths have achieved the status of realities in our time, and they have to be challenged if modern cultures are to recover their mythic bonds with nature. We need a new set of myths, and new understandings of human nature and identity.

The myth of dualism may have suited us once, when we were trying to overcome what we perceived to be the constraints of nature and move toward industrialization and technology. The development of science seemed to require us to adopt a position that was over and above the rest of nature, removed from it and viewing it as an object of study. Now, however, this process needs reversal to return to the primal perception of things where nature is not a dead object, but a living subject. We have to get back to that, somehow. Thomas Berry wrote in his influential work, *The Dream of Nature*, that it is necessary to experience the world "not as a collection of objects, but as a communion of subjects."[6] This is how healing can occur, healing of the planet and of the splits in our human nature.

In Australia, Aboriginal people have used powerful myths of ancestor spirits to facilitate the animation of the world, to turn the world from a collection of objects into a communion of subjects. Rocks, trees, mountain ranges, gullies and gorges are not just geological objects in space, but are physical traces of the movements of ancestral beings in the time of the Dreaming. According to the stories of the elders, nature is experienced as an extended family network, as a field of transpersonal relations that defines the life of the individual and tells him or her who he or she really is.[7] The efficacy of this mythological system can hardly be underestimated seeing that it has nurtured and kept alive a tradition of human cultures that, as Prime Minister Kevin Rudd reminds in his official Apology to Indigenous Peoples, are "the oldest continuing cultures in human history."[8] In other words, the mythic bonds to nature are not to be dismissed by the modern mind, as convention has had it, as archaic remnants of a useless or unscientific way of viewing the world, but are to be respected as important psychological bonds with real survival value.

The *survival value* of mythic bonds has to be emphasized, whereas the scientific view of the world, which encourages the despiritualization of nature, has a questionable record when it comes to survival and environmental resilience. Two hundred years of the scientific world-view has caused unbelievable damage to the earth, let alone the soul, whereas Aboriginal people lived here in Australia for millennia in a state of mutual co-existence with the land. Not that they did not change the land, they did. They cleared the land and changed its face, they used fire-stick farming methods, and archaeological evidence suggests they contributed to the extinction of the original mega-fauna.[9] But they did not cause damage as has been done to the land in the last 200 years of our technological approaches. Indeed it is the landscapes created by their vision and culture to which conservation seeks to restore present-day ecosystems. The problem with our approach is that colonialism, by definition, sought to control the land and not live with it. This is part of the heroic myth, to control and overpower the "other," but eventually the other gives up the ghost and breaks down under the strain. Our consciousness has sought the way of *opus contra naturam*, a work against nature, whereas what is required in Australia is an *opus cum natura*, a work with nature.

Science, so far, has worked to break down the subtle bonds that have kept Australian civilization intact for millennia. In a short time, it has undone the work of spiritual culture that had taken ages to set in place. And what happens to the land eventually happens to the people. Today many Aboriginal people have lost their subtle mythic bonds to the world and to each other through the corrosion of colonization. The devastating effects of their estrangement from spirituality and Dreaming is reflected in the distress of Aboriginal communities in rural, outback, or urban places. White visitors of good will are often appalled at the conditions and at the outbreak of child sexual abuse, incest, alcoholism, glue sniffing, mental illness, and depravity. People often say, "why can't the government do something about this?" "Why can't we throw more money at indigenous cultures, build houses, schools, bridges, and so on?" But this is to miss the point. For a start, these cultures have not needed houses, schools, and bridges for tens of millennia. But the real issue is not about material deprivation but a worse and more fatal condition, which Jung calls "loss of soul." It is perhaps the fact that much of Western culture has lost its own soul that makes many whites incapable of grasping the depths of Aboriginal suffering.

When a people is cut off from what nourishes its soul, the result is always devastation and ruin. In the Judeo-Christian Bible, we read in Proverbs: "Where there is no vision the people perish."[10] We are seeing the indigenous world perish today, as a result of historical violence that has severed connections to nature and society. But let's not be too complacent about this: those of us who derive from the colonizing cultures are next. It is only that indigenous cultures register this loss of soul more quickly, dramatically, and tragically. Practices of the soul are replaced with gadgetry and technology, so that we forget about such vague and subtle things as soul or spirit. But a God-shaped emptiness assails us from within, and is taking its toll in the epidemic of depression, loss of meaning, loss of energy. Indigenous people are, as it were, the canaries in the coalmine; they tell us that the air we are breathing today is toxic and cannot support life.

Something has to be done about reanimating the modern human soul and the soul of the world, but what is it? It is unlikely that contemporary men and women can return to a myth of ancestor spirits such as we find in the Aboriginal Dreaming, but we do need some kind of myth to animate the world and bind us to place. The myth of Gaia might be one such myth, which could be powerful in bringing about the desired change.[11] Mythic visions of connectedness are opening up in science itself, especially in theoretical physics[12] and biology.[13] But I do not believe that appropriating Aboriginal or any other indigenous myths of place is the way forward, as I will explain. But we have to stop thinking of nature as an object, as a resource for mining or farming interests, as real estate for development. Although this view might seem useful for the ego, in that it justifies its expansion, it proves disastrous because it upsets not only the ecological balance, but our physical and mental balance too, insofar as we are part of the same web of life.

The so-called environmental crisis is actually misnamed, in my view. It is not a crisis that begins with the environment, but one that begins with human consciousness. As Einstein famously said, we cannot solve a crisis with the same mental frame that created it in the first place. That is why I distrust a purely rational or scientific approach to the environmental crisis, because these approaches preserve the dualism that created the crisis in the beginning. We need to turn to philosophy, religion, and spirituality, if we are to move to a new place in our relations with the environment. A true ecological revolution requires wisdom, not merely technology. Where can we go to find that wisdom?

Ecopsychology as a Complex Field

Today there are numerous sources for wisdom. We can find it within the context of Western culture in eco-philosophy, social ecology, eco-feminism, deep ecology, Romantic theory, and Jungian ecopsychology. Ecopsychology is, in my view, one of the most important disciplines of our time. It has emerged from the works of Jung and Hillman and has followed their passion for discovering psyche in the world, and not merely inside the human mind. To this day, the core work in this discipline remains *Ecopsychology: Restoring the Earth, Healing the Mind*, edited by Theodore Roszak, Mary Gomes, and Allen Kanner, with forewords by James Hillman and Lester Brown. Hillman's foreword is called "A Psyche the Size of the Earth," and he draws together and extends Jung's ideas about the *anima mundi* or soul of the world.[14]

Roszak's book deserves to be widely read, and he creatively weaves together the little-known Jungian and Neoplatonic notion of *anima mundi* with James Lovelock's world-famous Gaia hypothesis. These theories of world animation have a great deal in common, and much to offer each other, it would seem. The essays in Roszak's book bring together the insights of several disciplines: ecology, depth psychology, psychoanalysis, theology, philosophy, sociology, and the natural sciences. It is significant that ecopsychology cannot be pursued through the lens of a single discipline, but requires a cluster of disciplines to argue its case and construct its field. This is in keeping with the idea of ecology itself, which is inclusive, holistic, and pluralist, always arguing for biodiversity and complexity. Ecology cannot be broken down into compartments, because it urges us to look at the whole of life and explore it in its totality. Hence many views are needed and ecopsychologists must have studied in more than one field to understand the complexity of life as a whole.

However ecopsychology is more likely to emerge from religious studies or theology than it is from scientific psychology, because it assumes a spiritual or soulful view of the world. This is evident as we peruse several texts in this field, including works by Bishop,[15] Roszak,[16] Spretnak,[17] Sardello,[18] and Snyder,[19] all of which share a spiritual point of view. The most recent book in the field is *Nature and the Human Soul* by Bill Plotkin, and he concedes that most psychologists would dismiss ecopsychology out of hand, since the idea of soul has been viewed as marginal or eccentric to science, or, as he wryly puts it, "soul has been demoted to a new age spiritual fantasy."[20] How true this is. In university discourse, soul is put on a par with dryads, fairies, and elves as quaint relics of the past. If students want to study soul in the Psychology Departments of modern universities, they are immediately derided and stereotyped as advocates of the New Age. Plotkin not only draws on Jung and Hillman, acknowledged masters in the study of soul, but he makes extensive use of literary resources such as those of poets David Whyte, David Wagoner, Rainer Maria Rilke, Mary Oliver, and others. He also makes use of Thomas Berry, Brian Swimme, David Abram, and others who are working in the fields of ecotheology, ecocriticism, and deep ecology. In other words, ecopsychology looks outside "psychology" proper to make its connections and to define its field.

THE INDIGENOUS PERSON WITHIN

The basic premise of ecopsychology is that we have a deep-seated layer of our psyche in which we remain "at one" with the world. This layer has been covered over by civilization, education, and modernity, but it is rescuable from the dark dungeons of the past, or from what Jung would call the deeper reaches of the unconscious. If we can take risks with our consciousness, we might be able to dive deep into the psyche and bring up these lost, forgotten, or overlaid layers of mind. Jung refers to this forgotten vestige as the "two-million-year-old man that is in all of us."[21] He personifies it as an archetypal figure and urges the modern man or woman to get in touch with this figure in the psyche, and to draw from it the wisdom that has been lost in the modern period. "It is only possible to live the fullest life when we are in harmony with these symbols; wisdom is a return to them."[22]

But in case we go into rapturous fantasies about this wonderful untapped inner resource, we need to bear in mind that Jung views our psychic proximity to this archaic figure as a danger as well as an opportunity. Jung believed that it can invade us with negative and violent consequences, throwing us and society into instinctual states or archaic longings that can disintegrate the mind and overturn social order. He makes connections, for instance, between the eruption of the archaic figure of Wotan, ancient god of the forest, with the outbreak of National Socialism in Germany.[23] He says we can be "assaulted" by archaic figures, which can impair our functioning and erode our civilization. Jung gives a personal example of this in his autobiography, in his encounter with an archaic inner figure while traveling in Islamic North Africa.[24]

But Jung quotes Hölderlin in this context, arguing that "Where there is danger, there grows also what saves."[25] It is worthwhile to "wrestle" or "have it out with" the archaic figure of the psyche, for if we manage to resist its disintegrative impact and do not succumb to it, we can move to a new place in which the world becomes reanimated with soul. Jung clearly believes there is no other way to reanimate the world. We cannot do it from willpower or conscious intention, much less from the resources of reason. We must call on the archaic figures of the deep, who bring up enchantment and magic in their wake.

Writing after Jung, the contemporary black African writer Malidoma Some has taken up Jung's ideas and advanced the notion of an indigenous "archetype" in the psyche:

> There is an indigenous person within each of us. The indigenous archetype within the modern soul is in serious need of acknowledgment. A different set of priorities dwells there, a set of priorities long forgotten in Western society.[26]

This is the kind of theorizing that causes scientists to groan and wail, since there is no evidence whatsoever for these assertions. Intellectuals fear that such ideas are racially constricting and prescriptive, and set down in stone the typical responses of a so-called "indigenous archetype." However, Jung and Some are aware that there is no predetermined shape to the activation of this archetypal figure. It can express itself differently in various individuals, and there is no simple "stereotyping" of an archaic vestige in the psyche. As with a lot of Jung's ideas, one either accepts this idea in good spirit, or one rejects it as unscientific.

However, if we take our dreams seriously, we might find "evidence" in the activity of our dreams. The archaic part of us that craves a deep connection with nature, animals, and instinct, and which is becoming sickly under the influence of civilization, might represent itself in our dreams as an indigenous person. In my experience, Westerners often dream of an indigenous figure who calls to them for help, assistance, attention, and love. I have had several such dreams myself, and as far as I am concerned, it is advisable to treat this figure as if it were real. I once dreamed that in an abandoned underground car park, beneath a shopping center, an Aboriginal family came up to me from the shadows of the site and urged me to treat them with respect. "Please take us into your life," they pleaded, "please do not forget us." They were neglected figures of my soul, but also transpersonal figures of the soul of my country, which has been neglected by the social order.

SOUL OF THE WORLD AS THERAPY FOR THE WEST

Jung's concept of wholeness was never meant to be confined to the personal or human sphere. Jungians sometimes interpret wholeness as a personal state or goal, but this was never the full extent of Jung's vision. In terms of his concept of the *unus mundus* (one world), wholeness is to be seen as a potential condition of the universe as a totality, or the universe as cosmos. Too much Jungian concern, or activity operating under Jung's name, gets rid of the cosmic dimension of his work in favor of an entirely clinical dimension. Perhaps this is understandable for the clinical applications of Jung's thought, but we must bear in mind that it is an artificial limitation that is imposed on Jung's work for the sake of a clinical style. Jung's concepts spill out beyond the clinic, into a broader concern for world, nature, and the ecology or interrelatedness of all things.

In a sense, we might say Jung's world is concerned with the "ecology of the soul," but his sense of soul is larger than the individual and larger even than the human. Jung's notion of soul, insofar as it encompasses the idea of *anima mundi*, is a soul as big as the universe. The modern belief that the soul is inside us, which is a useful fiction to support the modern ideology of individualism, is not supported by Jung's work. For Jung, as for the alchemists and medieval scholars of old, we human beings are inside the soul. It does not work the other way around, for soul is infinitely larger than the human dimension. What we like to call "our soul" or "my soul" is simply our individual entry into a realm of soul which is greater than we could ever encompass.

Jung was steeped in Neoplatonic philosophy and although some claim that he had an irredeemably clinical notion of the soul, the fact is that he brought the idea of the *anima mundi* to modern attention and explored it in depth in his alchemical writings.[27] Hillman sometimes lumps Freud and Jung together, claiming that both of them confined the soul to human subjectivity and "localized it in individual persons."[28] But I read Hillman's argument not so much as an attack on Jung, whom he respects, as on the Jungian movement that arose out of his work. It is true that the Jungian movement has appeared to engage in a subjective confinement of the soul, at the expense of its objective dimension. But Jung was anything but a subjectivist when it comes to soul. Jung quotes the famous saying of the medieval alchemists: "The greater part of the soul is outside the body," and in his essay on Chinese alchemy, he wrote:

> The psyche is a world in which the ego is contained. Perhaps there are fishes who believe that they contain the sea. It is our responsibility to do away with this pervasive illusion.[29]

From Jung's perspective, it is an illusion to think of the psyche as inside us; rather, we are inside the psyche. The notion that soul is found inside the body is a sign of ignorance. We have Hillman to thank for bringing this lost dimension of soul into recent focus,[30] but Jung is bigger than the Jungian movement that lost sight of this aspect of his work. I can only speculate that this aspect was judged to be too spiritual for psychologists, or not clinically useful.

It is true that Jung's theory of projection gave the impression that psyche originates within the person, but in his late thought, Jung could see that the theory of projection did not explain the existence of psyche in the world, prior to projection.[31] Jung felt that the psyche encompasses the cosmos, and only part of it is confined within the human frame. Psyche provides the foundation for our ability to know the world not only externally in terms of its appearance, but internally in terms of its meaning and purpose. The mature person feels him- or herself to be spiritually connected to the world, and Jung often advocated increased contact with nature to his mentally sick clients. Jung wrote:

> The psyche is not a hormone but a world of almost cosmic proportions... Only the individual consciousness that has lost its connection with the psychic totality remains caught in the illusion that the soul is a small circumscribed area, a fit subject

for 'scientific' theorizing. The loss of this great relationship is the prime evil of neurosis.[32]

When we lose our connection with the largeness of soul and the totality of its nature, we become separated from the foundations of our lives and succumb all the more readily to neurosis. To imagine the soul as vast, wide, and all-encompassing is what keeps the psyche healthy, according to Jung. As an observer of the modern condition, he had written:

> Through scientific understanding our world has become dehumanized. Man feels himself isolated in the cosmos. He is no longer involved in nature and has lost his emotional participation in natural events, which hitherto had a symbolic meaning for him. Thunder is no longer the voice of a god, nor is lightning his avenging missile. No river contains a spirit, no tree means a man's life, no snake is the embodiment of wisdom, and no mountain still harbors a great demon. Neither do things speak to him nor can he speak to things, like stones, springs, plants and animals. He no longer has a bush-soul identifying him with a wild animal. His immediate communication with nature is gone forever, and the emotional energy it generated has sunk into the unconscious.[33]

Although Jung sounds pessimistic here, arguing that the link with the cosmos has "gone forever," his insistence is mainly rhetorical. His main argument is that what we have lost, we have to find again. Even in this statement he concedes that the psychic connection to the cosmos has "sunk into the unconscious." That is why in dreams, he believes, we can still experience the ancient mystical at-one-ment with nature that is lost to our rational or waking mind:

> The symbol-producing function of our dreams is an attempt to bring our original mind back to consciousness, where it has never been before, and where it has never undergone critical self-reflection. We *have been* that mind, but we have never *known* it. We got rid of it before understanding it.[34]

This is important. We got rid of the unitary mind before we understood it. During the rise of science and rationality, it seemed an impediment to our progress, and we threw it away. Now, in our time, the environmental crisis has made us see that the unitary state has survival value, and is not merely a relic of an ancient way of life that modernity has superseded. We have realized, almost too late, the survival value of a spirituality of place, a spirituality of the natural world. In terms that sound remarkably like Jung's, but I am sure are entirely her own, Annie Dillard has explored this problem in her writing. In *Teaching a Stone to Talk*, Dillard wrote:

> It is difficult to undo our own damage, and to recall to our presence that which we have asked to leave. It is hard to desecrate a sacred grove and change your mind.... We doused the burning bush and cannot rekindle it; we are lighting matches in vain under every green tree. Did the wind once cry, and the hills shout forth praise? Now speech has perished from among the lifeless things of earth, and living things say very little to very few.[35]

We seek to "undo our damage," she says, yet we are not sure how to go about it. Working at the purely external or economic level on climate change and environmental matters is not enough. It certainly helps to attend to things from the outside, but since the real problem has to do with our psychological attitude and the absence of sacred feeling, I doubt the capacity of secular governments and well-meaning agencies to resolve the "environmental crisis." In his influential book, *The Dream of the Earth*, eco-theologian Thomas Berry wrote:

> We must go far beyond contemporary culture [to find a solution]. None of our existing cultures can deal with this situation out of its own resources. We must invent, or reinvent, a sustainable human culture by a descent into our pre-rational, our instinctive resources. Our cultural resources have lost their integrity. They cannot be trusted. What is needed is not transcendence by 'inscendence', not the brain but the gene.[36]

To put this in another way, one cannot resolve the ecological crisis using the rational approach that created it. If we work within the old dualism of human subjects and external objects, the crisis is perpetuated. Something further is needed, as James Hillman has argued, and that something is a recovery of the idea of the sacredness of the earth and the exterior or "outside" nature of the soul, which Neoplatonism calls *anima mundi*. Hillman has written eloquently on this, and he wrote with the full knowledge that the recovery of soul in the world was the missing element in the environmental movement.

Hillman, Jung, Berry, and Lovelock all argue in their different ways that we need to recover our "pre-rational, instinctive resources," to bring about the much-needed revolution in our attitude to nature. We need to feel the soul outside us again, to lure us out of our precious interiority, and to allow us to experience the interiority of the so-called outer world. This brings us back to what I called at the start the primal perception of things.

A Personal Encounter with An Indigenous Culture

I had the privilege of growing up in Alice Springs, central Australia, and to live at close range with the kind of consciousness that refused to see any separation between human soul and soul of the world. My family moved to Alice for health reasons. Asthma afflicted family members, and some of us were unable to breath the humid, moist air of coastal Australia. So we went inland and got cured of asthma. But some of us got cured of Western dualism as well, which was a kind of unexpected and dramatic side effect of moving to a place where there were as many indigenous people as European-based people.

The spirit of the land and the spirit of Aboriginal people worked on my life to release me from the dualistic condition. This was quite subtle at first, and I had not even realized that I was partly "going native" or "going black," terms that were often used in a derogatory sense. Mostly "going native" referred to drunks in the park or derelicts who could not hold down a job. Rarely was it seen in the positive sense of seeing the world as native people see it. But the landscape worked on me, drawing me out of the hard-boiled rational ego into a mystical participation with land, earth, and sky. The Aboriginal people of the town were the first to notice this change in my nature. Some claimed I had an "Aboriginal soul" and others said that I had begun to "think like a blackfella."

To think like a blackfella meant to think in vast terms, across aeons of time and space. It meant being able to experience the land as alive, as a living subject. It was to experience the soul as vast and wide, and not to see the soul merely as a pea-sized organ in the brain, as Descartes had argued. Rather than the soul being inside us, the indigenous view was that we were inside the soul, and as we walk through the world we walk through the soul of the world. I slipped into this mysticism rather easily. It appealed to me to think of the world as ensouled, and I had not yet been sullied by a university education or a Cartesian philosophy that would argue otherwise.

Perhaps this resonance came from my Celtic background, because not too long ago, my Celtic ancestors seemed to experience a similar rapport with the environment to that experienced by Aboriginal people. Perhaps they too felt the invisible forces, recognized the spirits of the land, and adjusted their lives accordingly. They too walked not only through the world, but through the soul of the world. I am never sure why or when we Europeans lost this cosmic vision, because without it we inhabit a spiritual wasteland and feel ourselves to be empty and lost. It is to be believed that we all had this spiritual sense once, and I was determined to recover it for my own life. I did not want to live in the sterile reality that saw nature as dead and inanimate.

But I did not, and could not, take on the Aboriginal cosmology as my own. I was always interested in learning about the Dreamings of Aboriginal people, but I recognized that I could not take them into myself. This would be to steal intellectual property that did not belong to me. It would be theft of an unforgivable sort, the theft of the spirit. After my culture had stolen Aboriginal land, and later, their children, and after Europeans dislocated their culture and religion, I had no desire to add insult to injury by asking for their Dreaming as well. I think it is important to understand this point in our time, where many of us are hungrily eyeing off the cosmological wisdom systems of indigenous people. This happens in the United States, where modern Americans, eager to recover the primal connection with the world, idealize the spirituality of the Indian peoples, without connecting this with the fact that the Americans appropriated the North American continent from the Indians. It seems perverse for the "conquerors" or "victors" to now turn to same indigenous peoples for an injection of eco-spirituality, after all the abuses and misdeeds of the past that continue through the present. In society today, various groups seek out indigenous spiritual wealth, while those who are "politically correct" say we cannot go there at all, that the area is taboo and to be avoided. I think both positions are missing the point. The New Age movement responds rightly to the modern hunger, but often goes on a consumerist shopping spree and does not think much enough about deeper processes and implications. Those who are politically correct suppress the hunger for cosmological vision focusing largely on the obstacles to renewed engagement with indigenous cultures. However, the way ahead is to accept the hunger for shared vision, but not to satiate it by extending colonial appetites and devouring indigenous cultures.

LOOKING AFTER THE ANIMAL PSYCHE

I conclude this essay by reflecting on the role of animals in Aboriginal cosmology. The importance of the animal psyche in the Aboriginal worldview cannot be understood without further exploring the concept of the Dreaming. "Dreaming" is an English translation of some key Aboriginal terms, notably *alcheringa* of the Arrernte people and *tjukurrpa* of the Warlpiri, both of the central deserts. The Dreaming is like a mythic carpet that underlies all reality, natural and human. From a Jungian perspective, it is close to what Jungians call psychic reality. The Australian psychoanalyst Craig San Roque interprets it this way:

> The essence of Tjukurrpa is a multidimensional pattern of connectedness … somehow very like the neurological system externalised and set into the geography of the country. It is a poetic calculus … organised to produce and sustain life, animal beings, food, knowledge, relationship … It is psychological.[37]

It is indeed a psychological concept, although it is usually interpreted as a religious one. Jungian psychology can understand how something can be psychological and religious at the same time, and it is surprising that there has not been more Jungian interest in the Dreaming, especially since Jungian practice is based on a similar concept of psychic reality. Perhaps Aboriginal religions are hard for Westerners to comprehend, with the emphasis on ancestor spirits and reincarnation. Jung himself was interested in Aboriginal religions, even if he had only a rudimentary and second-hand familiarity with the field.[38]

However, if we think about Aboriginal "ancestors" as similar in some ways to "archetypes," we can perhaps sense at least an approximation of Aboriginal cultural reality. For instance, the ancestors were felt to come from below the earth, which is an indication of their chthonic nature as forces of the unconscious. Hume writes: "The Ancestors rose up from beneath the earth and sank back down after their travels, but their influence is still felt, and their past actions are still vital in the present."[39] If we replace the word "ancestors" with "archetypes" this could serve as a definition of archetypal forces. Where the ancestors come from nobody knows. Jung says the same about archetypes—he often says they are just there, and we have no way of telling how they came into being. According to Ted Strehlow, a precise definition of *alcheringa* is "eternal, uncreated, sprung out of itself," and he also translates it as "originating from eternity."[40] In a 1891 grammar of the Arrernte language, Kempe defined the same term as "old, very old, something that has no origin, mysterious, something that has always been so, also, always."[41] This again is reminiscent of Jung's archetypes.

But when we are told that the ancestors speak to humans in dreams, do not obey the laws of time, space, or any other category, and appear in symbolic form in rituals and the arts, there appears to be an even greater resemblance to the Jungian archetype. The parallels seem so strong to anthropologist Stanner that he reflected that the Dreaming could just as easily be called "the unconscious."[42] But in the literature on ancestral spirits, their animal or theriomorphic nature is stressed. In *Ancestral Power*, Lynne Hume writes:

> As the Ancestors journeyed across the land they could change their outward appearance at will, sometimes into animals or birds, reptiles or sea creatures, hence they are the prototypes of existing species. As they paused at certain locations and left traces of the essence of themselves, they endowed the country with immanent significance.[43]

The animals of today trace their roots back to the ancestors and that is why they are sacred. In some Aboriginal cultures, the animals *are* the ancestors, and hence so many Aboriginal ceremonies, dances, and rites of passage focus on the lives and movements of animals. In the dances and ceremonies I am familiar with, the typical animals are the emu and the kangaroo, and it is with some irony that the modern nation state of Australia has adopted these animals as its emblems, presumably with little understanding of the sacred background of this symbolism.

Aboriginals believe that the central point of existence is to get in touch with the Dreaming and become part of its reality. This is achieved through the process of initiation. In initiation, the individual's identification with the ego is severed, often in alarmingly violent ways. However, as with Jungian psychology, it is felt that identification with the ego can only lead to personal harm, anxiety, and ecological disturbances. Aboriginal cultures determine that this false identification has to be terminated swiftly and effectively. The initiation ends the ego-centric life and brings about an eco-centric understanding of identity and reality. It is the more-than-human world that paradoxically allows the human being to become fully human. The normal self or ego keeps us in an alienated condition, and so the Aboriginal initiations have to turn against this condition to bring about the larger life. In Jungian terms, these initiations mark a transformation from ego to Self, that is, a fundamental shift in personal identity from the human sphere to the cosmic totality. This is achieved through the use of an animal totem or symbol. The old existence is ended and a new person emerges who is no longer confined to time and space but enters into the expansiveness of the Dreaming.

In accord with the sensitivities of Aboriginal protocol, as a male commentator I am only allowed to speak about "men's business." At around the age of 13 or 14 years, boys are separated from their families and taken to the initiation fields. Here they are subjected to the famous deprivations and trials, such as hunger, sleeplessness, scarifications across the back and chest, the loss of an eye tooth, and circumcision or subincision of the penis. The boys are often placed in a shallow grave and pronounced dead to their former selves. As Erich Neumann correctly reports, the tribal elder holds out a *churinga* or sacred stone to the youth, and says "Here is your body, here is your second self."[44] The implication is that the boy is to *live from* this second self, and not from the ego.

The second self is symbolized by a tribal totem, usually an animal which is sacred to the tribe. In the tribes of my area, the totemic animals were the Red Kangaroo, Honey Ant, and White Caterpillar. The second self is not human or personal, and its theriomorphic symbolism indicates that it is part of the primordial pattern of creation. Animals are not less than human, as they are for most Western people, but more than human. Their sacredness derives from their proximity to the Dreaming, the ability to express and incarnate an ancestral spirit. Therefore the relation to animals is profoundly religious, spiritual, and moral. As Jungians might say, animals express and embody the symbolic function of the psyche and this assures their sacred stature. But the "psyche" of which I speak is not the human psyche but the world psyche, or *anima mundi*. Even in Western culture, the animal is our deepest and most immediate connection to the chthonic world of ancestor spirits.

It is because of this moral sensitivity and sacredness that the hunting of animals for food is such a complex and ritualized activity. Before the hunt, the elders have to give clearance to the hunter, and this is achieved by appeasing the spirit of the animal before he/she is killed. If there has been no sacred ritual, there can be no hunt, because to kill an animal without the due appeasements and liturgies is regarded as sacrilegious. Without these rituals, the hunt is merely a violation of natural law, since in a profane hunt the animal is treated as an object and not as a living subject. Moreover, to kill an animal without due preparations is to damage the ancestral spirit which the animal incarnates. The animals play a double role as food source and incarnation of spirits, and hence the spiritual preparations are vital before a feast can begin. Mindfulness of the sacredness of the animal is as important as the carnal desire to consume the animal for food.

Finally, it is contact with totemic animals that gives Aboriginal people the courage to be fully human. This is explored in the classic anthropological study of Aboriginal culture, *Dingo Makes us Human* by Deborah Bird Rose.[45] At the top end of the Northern Territory, the dingo is the totemic animal that ensures humane existence by pointing to the nonegoic reality. "We cannot be human without learning the lessons from the animals," I was once told as a boy in central Australia. The lesson to be learned is that human existence does not serve merely human ends. There is a broader field of relations that the individual and society has to acknowledge, and this is why Rose defined the Dreaming as a "reflexive moral relationship of care."[46] The concern for animals is simultaneously moral and spiritual, since animals point not only to cosmic origins but to the notion of right conduct in the here and now. The Dreaming is a system of interconnectedness that binds all reality together in such a way that no one part stands out as separate from the whole. As Lynne Hume writes: "The land and the Dreaming are one and are linked by a spiritual kinship: animals, birds, country, human beings and Ancestors are inextricably linked for all time."[47] When Aboriginal elders enjoin us today to "look after the animals," the complexity of their instruction, and its rich field of archetypal associations, is rarely understood by white society.

NOTES

1. Theodore Roszak, Mary E. Gomes, and Allen K. Kanner (eds.) *Ecopsychology: Restoring the Earth, Healing the Mind* (San Francisco: Sierra Club Books, 1995), p. 5.

2. David Abram, *The Spell of the Sensuous: Perception and Language in a More-Than-Human World* (New York: Vintage Books, 1996).

3. David Tacey, *ReEnchantment: The New Australian Spirituality* (Sydney: Harper Collins, 2000).

4. David Tacey, *Edge of the Sacred: Jung, Psyche, Earth* (Einsiedeln, Switzerland: Daimon Verlag, 2009).

5. David Suzuki and Peter Knudtson, *Wisdom of the Elders: Honoring Sacred Native Visions of Nature* (New York: Bantam, 1992).

6. Thomas Berry, *The Dream of the Earth* (San Francisco: Sierra Club Books, 1988), p. 2.

7. Vicki Grieves, *Aboriginal Spirituality: Aboriginal Philosophy: The Basis of Aboriginal Social and Emotional Wellbeing.* Discussion Paper No. 9. (Darwin: Cooperative Research Centre for Aboriginal Health, 2009). This work by an Aboriginal writer can be downloaded for free at: http://www.crcah.org.au/publications/downloads/DP9-Aboriginal-Spirituality.pdf.

8. Kevin Rudd, Prime Minister of Australia, "Apology to Australia's Indigenous Peoples," 2008, http://www.aph.gov.au/house/Rudd_Speech.pdf.

9. Tim Flannery, *The Future Eaters: An Ecological History of the Australasian Lands and People* (Sydney: Reed Books, 1994).

10. Proverbs, in *The Jerusalem Bible* (New York: Doubleday and Company, 1966), 29:18.

11. James Lovelock, *Gaia: A New Look at Life on Earth* (New York: Oxford University Press, 1979).

12. David Bohm, *Wholeness and the Implicate Order* (London: Routledge & Kegan Paul, 1980).

13. Rupert Sheldrake, *The Rebirth of Nature: The Greening of Science and God* (New York: Bantam, 1991).

14. Roszak, *et. al.*, *Ecopsychology*.

15. Peter Bishop, *The Greening of Psychology* (Dallas: Spring Publications, 1990).

16. Roszak, *et. al.*, *Ecopsychology*.

17. Charlene Spretnak, *States of Grace: The Recovery of Meaning in the Postmodern Age* (San Francisco: HarperSanFrancisco, 1991).

18. Robert Sardello, *Facing the World with Soul* (Hudson, New York: Lindisfarne, 1992).

19. Gary Snyder, *The Practice of the Wild* (San Francisco: North Point Press, 1990).

20. Bill Plotkin, *Nature and the Human Soul: A Road Map to Discovering Our Place in the World* (New York: New World Library, 2008), p. 6.

21. C.G. Jung, "The Two-Million-Year-Old Man" (1936), in William McGuire and R.F.C. Hull (eds.), *C. G. Jung Speaking* (London: Picador, 1980), p. 100.

22. C.G. Jung, "The Stages of Life" (1930/1931), in the *Collected Works of C.G. Jung*, eds. Herbert Read, Michael Fordham, Gerhard Adler and William McGuire, trans. R.F.C. Hull (London: Routledge & Kegan Paul; Princeton: Princeton University Press, 1953-1979), vol. 8, § 794 (all future references to Jung's *Collected Works*, abbreviated to CW, will be with chapter titles followed by the original publication dates, volume and paragraph numbers).

23. C.G. Jung, "Wotan" (1936), CW 10.

24. C.G. Jung, *Memories, Dreams, Reflections* (1963), ed. Aniela Jaffé (London: Fontana, 1995), pp. 266-275.

25. Hölderlin, in Jung, *Memories*, p. 274.

26. Malidoma Some, *Ritual: Power, Healing, and Community* (Portland: Swan Raven, 1993), p. 34.

27. C.G. Jung, "The Visions of Zosimos" (1938/1954), CW 13.

28. James Hillman, *Archetypal Psychology: A Brief Account* (Dallas: Spring Publications, 1983), p. 145.

29. C.G. Jung, "Commentary on 'The Secret of the Golden Flower'" (1929), CW 13, § 75.

30. James Hillman, "*Anima Mundi*: The Return of the Soul to the World", in *Spring 1982* (Dallas), pp. 71-93; also in James Hillman, *The Thought of the Heart and the Soul of the World* (Dallas: Spring Publications, 1992); and James Hillman and Michael Ventura, *We've*

Had a Hundred Years of Psychotherapy and the World's Getting Worse (San Francisco: HarperCollins, 1992).

31. David Tacey, *Edge of the Sacred*, p. 27.

32. C.G. Jung, "The State of Psychotherapy Today" (1934), CW 10, § 367.

33. C.G. Jung, "Symbols and the Interpretation of Dreams" (1961), CW 18, § 585.

34. *Ibid.*, CW 18, § 591.

35. Annie Dillard, *Teaching a Stone to Talk* (London: Picador, 1984), p. 70.

36. Thomas Berry, *The Dream of the Earth*, pp. 207-208.

37. Craig San Roque, "Coming to Terms with the Country: Some Incidents on First Meeting Aboriginal Locations and Aboriginal Thoughts," in M. T. Savio Hooke & S. Akhtar, (eds.) *The Geography of Meanings, Psychoanalytical Perspectives on Place, Space, Land and Dislocation* (London: The International Psychoanalytical Association, 2007), p. 121.

38. C.G. Jung, "Mind and Earth," (1927/1931), CW 10.

39. Lynne Hume, *Ancestral Power: The Dreaming, Consciousness, and Aboriginal Australians* (Melbourne: Melbourne University Press, 2002), p. 26.

40. T.G.H. Strehlow, *Songs of Central Australia* (Sydney: Angus & Robertson, 1971), p. 614.

41. Kempe, in Strehlow, *ibid.*, p. 596.

42. W.E.H. Stanner, "Some Aspects of Aboriginal Religion" (1976), in Max Charlesworth (ed.), *Religious Business* (Cambridge: Cambridge University Press, 1998), p. 7.

43. Hume, *Ancestral Power*, p. 25.

44. Erich Neumann, *The Origins and History of Consciousness* (1949) (Princeton: Princeton University Press, 1973), p. 289.

45. Deborah Bird Rose, *Dingo Makes us Human* (Cambridge: Cambridge University Press, 1992).

46. Deborah Bird Rose, "Consciousness and Responsibility in an Australian Aboriginal Religion", in W.H. Edwards (ed.), *Traditional Aboriginal Society: A Reader* (Melbourne: Macmillan, 1987), p. 260.

47. Hume, *Ancestral Power*, p. 29.

FILM REVIEW

The Cove. Screenplay by Mark Monroe. Richard O'Barry, Simon Hutchins, Mandy-Rae Cruickshank, Kirk Krack, David Rastovich. Directed by Louie Psihoyos.

REVIEWED BY VICTORIA C. DRAKE

The Rocks Have Eyes
A Film Review of *The Cove* (2009)

Those images that yet
Fresh images beget,
That dolphin-torn, that gong-tormented sea.

William Butler Yeats, "Byzantium"

If images speak a thousand words, then *The Cove* (Winner, 2010 Academy Award, Best Documentary Feature Film) could fill volumes. It is a tense, claustrophobic night off the coast of Japan. An

Victoria C. Drake is currently working on her Ph.D. in Depth Psychology at Pacifica Graduate Institute. After attending Harvard University (B.A. 1983), she followed her passion to become a life-long international wildlife conservationist and environmental community justice advocate. Victoria lives in Chicago with her husband, James Evan-Cook (from Kent, UK); their three daughters, Angelica, Isabella, and Lily; and assorted animal companions.

inconspicuous phalanx is cautiously climbing up steep rocks in the dark, clinging to the unstable terrain, diving in dangerous waters, blindly setting up illegal film and sound recorders, evading discovery. The perilous reality of this moment is palpable. The immediacy of blurry, night vision cameras casts the otherworldly figures in an eerie, greenish, hazy glow, like aliens. It feels as if we are there, at one with them, also scrambling against time; that we, too, are taking a certain risk, even as voyeurs in the dark. We, too, might get caught in the act of launching a long overdue "coup de dolphin": surreptitiously filming the yearly secret capture and massive killing of dolphins in a hidden Japanese cove.

From the earliest days of Greek lore, dolphins have been interchangeable as messengers of the gods. Their appealing curiosity and sociable intelligence have always attracted the human imagination. Dolphins are closely associated with Poseidon's daughters, the Nereids, and with Aphrodite, Galatea, and Apollo. Poseidon is credited with creating the constellation, Delphinus, in gratitude for a dolphin who found and brought back to him his beloved nymph Amphitrite, who became his bride. (Both "Delphinus" and "dolphin" come from the Greek *delphis*, meaning *womb*). The Greeks probably came to call this constellation Delphinus (meaning "Lord of the Dolphins") from India where it was first identified with the dolphin. Early Christians viewed Delphinus as the Cross of Jesus. A dolphin also rescued the Dionysiac poet, Arion, from drowning, as well as countless lesser-known mortals. The sun god, Phoebus Apollo, masqueraded as a dolphin when he founded his oracle at Delphi on the slopes of Mount Parnassus with a temple to Poseidon and a statue of Arion riding a dolphin. The dolphin that rescued Telemachus, Odysseus' son, later emboldened his family's heraldic shield.

As noted by Bearzi and Stanford, "Intelligence, consciousness and compassion were among the words used by the ancient Greeks to describe their *companions of the sea*."[1] Plutarch regarded dolphins as the only creatures that seem to seek friendly contact for purely altruistic reasons. Greek myths abound with dolphin mythologems and mythemes. Perhaps, the most depth psychologically relevant story involves Dionysus, who was traveling between the islands of Ikaria and Naxos disguised as a commoner. When a band of rogue Etruscan pirate sailors tried to kidnap Dionysus to ransom for the slave trade, Dionysus turned the oars of the boat into snakes and filled it with vines, leopards, lions, and the jarring sound of flutes/pan pipes, so that the sailors leapt overboard in fear. Poseidon promptly turned them into a pod of dolphins, forever destined to assist those in need. Thus, for the Greeks, dolphin-cide was a heinous crime, since dolphins were former humans retaining human-like qualities. Dolphins may assist humans in distress, since they are wired to bring things up to the surface. They are the only wild species known to intentionally rescue people. Byzantine sailors, Arab sailors, Chinese and European explorers all report dolphins rescuing sailors or ships in trouble. The presence of dolphins heralds safe passage and calm seas. As with the albatross, it was an unpardonable offense to harm a dolphin. Additionally, in Hindu mythology, the Ganges River dolphin is associated with Ganga, the goddess deity of the Ganges River. The Boto dolphins in the Amazon River are believed to be shape shifters or *encantados*, capable of bearing children with women.

Against this entangled backdrop of fact and legend emerges *The Cove* (2009), a riveting documentary about dolphins, not in their mythological and historical role as rescuer of humans in distress, but as unwitting sacrifice to human greed. Enter Louie Psihoyos, Ric O'Barry, and Jim Clark: three colleagues who share the same visionary dream of ending the cryptic slaughter of bottlenose dolphins and other cetaceans. Every year for decades (no one knows exactly when this nefarious ritual began) from September-March, a covert group of Japanese fisherman has been illicitly herding whole schools of wild dolphins, which are small whales, into a hidden, protected cove in a National Park off the coast of Taiji, Wakayama, Japan. This is "ground zero" for dolphin capture and slaughter in the world. The enduring economic incentive is to select the most marketable facsimiles of "Flipper," which are then sold to oceanariums all over the world for as much as $150,000. The rest of the targeted dolphins are systematically and brutally harpooned, butchered for their meat. Most of the Japanese population has no awareness of this practice, nor do they realize that the dolphin meat they ingest, often falsely marketed as more desirable whale meat, is heavily laden with dangerously toxic levels of mercury. That is, until now.

Psihoyos, a charismatic, accomplished photographer for *The*

National Geographic Society, had been diving and documenting the persistent decline of coral reefs for the past thirty years. In 2007, when he learned of this systematic, secret dolphin genocide (23,000 dolphins slaughtered per year), he swiftly recruited a passionate posse to do something he had never done before: give voice to the dolphins' haunting death screams in chilling technicolor. Psihoyos enlisted his diving partner and internet entrepreneur, Jim Clark, to fund the project. Eventually, he met Ric O'Barry, who has devoted the past thirty-five years of his life to freeing captive or enslaved dolphins all over the world. O'Barry is driven by an abiding, gnawing guilt that his lucrative ten-year involvement in popularizing the "Flipper" TV series enabled dolphin shows to become monstrous revenue business machines. He now places himself on the front lines of dolphin activism, risking life and limb, allowing himself to be pilloried and targeted in his crusade to redress the irreparable debt he believes that he owes to countless dolphins, past and present. O'Barry's remorse is a cautionary tale of common environmental blinkeredness turned on its side, belly up. His epiphanic grief at witnessing one of the "Flipper" dolphins "commit suicide" has paradoxically become his defining wound and gift, not only for all remaining dolphins, but also for the world at large.

To realize his core intention, Psihoyos enlisted an adroit, guerilla dream team of divers, staging coordinators, and Hollywood-trained camera crew, affectionately dubbed "Ocean's 11." Their plan of action was nothing short of a James Bond film: they had to infiltrate the heavily secluded cove under cover of darkness, attach strategically disguised cameras and sound recorders in the sheltering rocks and underwater crannies, and later return to retrieve the cameras, risking discovery, certain arrest, and torture. The entire drama unfolds with the taut rhythm of a spy caper, except this is the real deal. Our brave eco-heroes emerge to tell the tale intact, but not unscathed. This film elicits affect like no other of its kind. Witnessing the dolphins' plaintive sonar cries of panic, seeing them heroically try to escape certain doom in the blood-red cove waters, the collective trauma of what has happened and is happening there is visceral. To remain passive towards the helpless dolphins' predicament is to be as culpable as the violating fishermen. By watching this film, we are all implicated in this still as-of-yet unfolding event. Clandestine dolphin slaughter poses an ethical dilemma for our collective 21st century psyche at large. *The Cove* is a clarion call to "lift up" the very species that has mysteriously come to our aid for so long.

A formidable barrier to the conservation of dolphins is the projections that are made onto them in current literature and film, especially science fiction. While dolphins have demonstrated superior intelligence, this faculty is often reduced to a simplistic, unthreatening curiosity. For example, dolphins are typically depicted as friendly, curious aliens as in *The Hitchhikers Guide to the Galaxy* (1978), where they vainly try to warn humans of Earth's impending doom before jumping ship. In the second book of P. Watts' "Rifters" trilogy, *Maelstrom* (2001), enhanced bottlenose dolphins act as underwater hunters for a private military. A similar role for dolphins is represented in W. Gibson's short story *Johnny Mnemonic* (1981), in which cyborg dolphins are used during wartime by the military to find submarines and after the war by a group of revolutionaries to decode encrypted information. In *Startide Rising* (1983), D. Brin introduces a Terran spaceship named "Streaker," manned by 150 "uplifted" (advanced) dolphins, whose intelligence matches that of humans. In the science fiction comic *The Ballad of Halo Jones* (1984), dolphins are a peaceful, respected species, which excels at piloting spacecraft. Dolphins also appear frequently in non-science fiction literature. *Into the Deep* (1995) by K. Grimwood depicts a marine biologist struggling to crack the code of dolphin intelligence, including entire chapters written from the viewpoint of his dolphin characters. In his paradigm, humans and dolphins are capable of communicating via telepathy. Finally, "Flipper" was the fictitious dolphin persona that captivated our modern psyche, for better or worse. Akin to Lassie, Flipper obediently rescues accident-prone children.

Recently, there have been several documentary films bearing comparable aquatic environmental themes of urgency, such as *Darwin's Nightmare* (2004), *The 11th Hour* (2007), *Flow* (2008), and *Up the Yangtze* (2008). Yet *The Cove* aspires to be more than the sum of its parts, extending far beyond the confines of a Japanese enclave. The subtle beauty and brilliance of this film is that it is not just about dolphins or metaphorical *daimones*, though they are certainly the driving force, inspiration, and focus. It is not just about the West versus

Japan, us versus them, pitting one against the other by using captivating film image as psychological mediation to repudiate spurious "cultural" practices. Like Paul Watson of Animal Planet channel's *The Whale Warrior: Pirate for the Sea*, Psihoyos seeks to educate, empower, and inspire a global audience, especially the Japanese. Initially, Psihoyos tried to make his film legally, above board, with all the proper permits and cooperation, to no avail. It is notable that there is no Japanese member of his team and no championing Japanese ally. So, like most environmental advocacy in Japan, he went "underground" to expose a topic that evolved from a site-specific project about the shadow activities in an obscure little cove to one that stumbled upon a sleeper environmental catastrophe of untold magnitude: that of Japan's ubiquitous mercury poisoning. The film's labyrinthine net expands even wider to include the overwhelming issue of the global deep sea fishing crisis. In forty years, there will be no fish left in the oceans at the current rates of extraction, yet seventy percent of Japan depends on the sea for subsistence. Japan's empty defense that dolphins are eating all the fish obscures the real culprit with a human face and a bottomless appetite. If Japan fails to curtail dolphin slaughter, as well as develop other viable, sustainable food resources, they may soon be charting desperate straits themselves.

Historically, humans have killed animals for food, clothing, ritual, symbolic sacrifice, survival, and sport. *Killing Animals*[2] analyzes the interdisciplinary complexities of killing other species as the ultimate expression of human power and universal dominance over an *Other*. Psychological slaughter (like soul loss) on a cultural and individual level also exacts a collective, energetic toll. This externalizing, objectifying source of personal power keeps accelerating, especially with respect to dolphins. "Diviner than a dolphin is nothing yet created, for indeed they lived aforetime men and lived in cities along with mortals, but they exchanged the land for the sea..." , once wrote the Greek poet, Oppian.[3] *The Cove* highlights the repetitive cycle of two species locked in an oppressive, downward spiral from which neither can thrive until we stop unnecessarily using dolphins for food, therapy, and entertainment. Dr. L. Marino unilaterally asserts that all dolphin/ cetacean captivity is exploitative, dissociative, and cruel.[4] The latest incident (February 24, 2010) at Sea World involving the untimely, brutal death of an experienced orca trainer is a glaring red flag to investigate the psychological well-being of keeping intelligent cetaceans in confinement. There is no scientific evidence that swimming with dolphins is therapeutic, nor is there any ethical training, oversight, or certification for such a practice.[5] With insatiable greed-driven, technologically advantaged humans at the helm, dolphins are suffering an unqualified cost. Activist or inactivist, friend or foe, this is a cautionary episode in the complex matrix of man's ambivalent relationship with nature. Say not the dolphins die in vain.

> We should learn to consider the world as our home.
> When we realize that we are one, the world will be our home.
> We have to feel responsibility for every part of the world.
> This is the only way to ease the suffering that we encounter
> these days.
>
> Thich Nhat Hanh

NOTES

1. M. Bearzi and Craig B. Stanford, *Beautiful Minds: The Parallel Lives of Great Apes and Dolphins* (Cambridge, MA: Harvard University Press, 2008), p. 18.

2. Animal Studies Group, *Killing Animals* (Champaign, IL: University of Illinois Press, 2006).

3. Oppian, *Halieutica* 12 (Oxford, UK: Diaper and Jones, 1722). First English translation.

4. Dr. Lori Marino, private phone conversation, February 23, 2010.

5. K. Ellison, "Dolphin therapy is booming despite concerns about efficacy and animal treatment," *The Washington Post*, Feb. 23, 2010, http://www.washingtonpost.com/wpdyn/content/article/2010/02/22/AR2010022203637.html.

THE LONG VERSION OF THE WORLD'S SHORTEST OSCAR ACCEPTANCE
SPEECH
by Louie Psihoyos, director of *The Cove*

- We made this film to give the oceans a voice.
- We told the story of *The Cove* because we witnessed a crime; not just a crime against nature, but a crime against humanity.
- We made this movie because through plundering, pollution and acidification from burning fossil fuels, ALL ocean life is in peril, from the great whales to plankton, which incidentally, is responsible for half the oxygen in this theater.
- Thank you…and thank you to the Academy for shining the brightest lights in the world on *THE COVE*
- Japan, please see this movie! *Domo Aragato!*

For more information on cetacean rights, see:
http://cetaceanconservation.com.au/cetaceanrights/signatories.php

LIBER NOVUS, THAT IS, THE NEW BIBLE
A FIRST ANALYSIS OF C. G. JUNG'S
RED BOOK

WOLFGANG GIEGERICH

A fter first finishing Jung's Red Book, an enthusiast might exclaim, to apply the words of Heinrich Heine (1830) from another context: "What a book! As great and wide as the world, extending its roots into the unplumbed depths of creation and towering up into the blue mysteries of the sky.... Sunrise and sunset, promise and fulfillment, birth and death, the whole drama of mankind, all is contained in this book...." But for those who read it with the mind of an analytical psychologist the exclamation point at the end of the initial phrase, "What a book!" will soon change into a question mark: What

Wolfgang Giegerich studied at the University of Würzburg and the University of Göttingen, and obtained his Ph.D. from the University of California at Berkeley. He received a diploma from the C.G. Jung Institute–Stuttgart. After many years in private practice in Stuttgart and later in Wörthsee, near Munich, he now lives in Berlin. He has lectured and taught in many countries (Germany, Switzerland, Austria, England, Italy, the USA, Russia, Japan, and Brazil) and before many professional societies. His more than one hundred and seventy publications in the field of psychology, in several languages, include fourteen books, among them *The Soul's Logical Life: Towards a Rigorous Notion of Psychology* (Peter Lang, 1998; 4th ed. 2007), and the three volumes of his Collected English Papers: *The Neurosis of Psychology*, *Technology and the Soul*, and *Soul-Violence* (all published by Spring Journal Books).

kind of a book is the Red Book? In his Introduction, the editor clearly states: "It is nothing less than the central book in his [Jung's] oeuvre," "the single most important documentary source" (p. 221b). The validity of the second description can readily be granted. But is the Red Book really a *book*, and part of Jung's oeuvre? It is a most curious and puzzling phenomenon.

THE BOOK WHICH IS NOT A BOOK

What makes a book a book is not that it is so many pages bound in one volume, which is only the meaning of "book" as a physical object. It is inherent in the notion of a book that it is aimed at an audience, a public. Jung never published his Red Book, and not only for external reasons, such as that it was not completely finished or that he feared hostile reactions. On the other hand, he time and again did toy with the idea of its publication. And the text of the book itself clearly operates with the idea of a public and frequently explicitly addresses an imaginary ye: "what I must proclaim to you" (229b),[1] "You coming men!" (230r), "Believe me:... I give you news ..." (231a f.), "My friends, ..." (232b), which corresponds to the fact that for long stretches the diction is preachy. About the *Sermones ad mortuos* Jung said to Aniela Jaffé, that they "formed the prelude to what had been his to communicate to the world" (346n, tr.m.). At one point we hear, "Therefore I say this to you, my friend, so that you can tell your friends, and that the word may spread among the people" (254n, tr.m.), a clear indication that *within* the fantasy expressed in the book there is a rather strong wish for promulgation and having an effect, which also comes out in the statement, "What is agonizing, however, is the thought that this must occur solely for me and that perhaps no one will be able to gain light from what I bring up from the depths" (267n, tr.m.).

Jung's lifelong wavering and hesitation, which resulted in the Red Book's remaining secreted away for almost half a century beyond his death, is, I think, a clear sign that he had a distinct (and correct!) feeling for the nature of his *Red Book*, namely that it is an "impossible" book, because of its internal contradiction. In its character it is prophetic preaching and yet at the same time it refuses to be a doctrine for the generality. A recurrent theme is: "I do not want to be a savior, a lawgiver, an educator unto you. After all, you are not little children any more"

(231b, tr.m.), a sentence that itself objectively contains the said contradiction inasmuch as its semantic message ("no teaching") contradicts its syntax (the preaching to a ye), whereas the quote cited above about the agonizing thought that "this must occur solely for me" expresses the same contradiction as a subjective emotion. If one really would not want to be a teacher or educator of others, one would not formally address others. One would leave them alone, solely minding one's own business—perhaps as Blaise Pascal, without breathing a word to anyone, sewed his hand-written record of a powerful visionary experience which he had on 13 November 1654, the *Memorial*, close to his heart into his clothes, where it was found by his servant only after his death.

Jung suggested that his patients prepare their own Red Books. According to Christiana Morgan he told her, "I should advise you to put it [the material of her active imaginations] all down as beautifully as you can—in some beautifully bound book" (216a). And he added: "for you it will be your church—your cathedral," where the "for you" indicates that we have to read "YOUR church—YOUR cathedral," because it would be exclusively hers. The "church" that Jung has in mind and that is embodied in the Red Book is one that by definition has no congregation, but only one single member, the one isolated atomic individual whose personal Red Book it is. It is utterly private, subjective. And this is why it is not a book in the way Augustinus' *Confessions*, Dante's *Divina Commedia*, Nietzsche's *Zarathustra* are books. They, too, may be based on personal experiences, but are unambiguously intended for the generality (even if Nietzsche's book is already a bit on the retreat, explicitly conceiving itself as *A book for all and none*). But Jung's Red Book is exclusively his, neither for all, nor for none. It has no message to be shared, communicated: "It is my mystery, not yours. ... You have your own" (246b, tr.m.). "No one besides you has your God" (329b). Ideally, if there are four billion people in the world, each one should solipsistically have *his or her own* equivalent to Jung's Red Book.

Now that the Red Book has been published after all, it can nevertheless not become public property like other books. And the literal preaching internal to its style is in itself contraceptive, fundamentally self-contained, like a tempest in a teapot. It cannot, indeed ought not, reach the reading public. If we as public were nonetheless to be truly reached and felt that it contained a message for us, we would have misunderstood and *misused* it.

We have to take this insight still further. One main reason why Jung hesitated to publish his Red Book, as we learn from Cary Baynes' notes, is the "difficulty with the form" (212b) that he saw. He could not find "the appropriate form" (213b). "[S]ome of it hurt (his) sense of the fitness of things terribly." He "had shrunk from putting it down as it came to" him (*ibid.*). And decades later he told Aniela Jaffé that he had immediately realized that the material expressed in it would still need to be brought into a suitable form (214a). That Jung was aware of the fact that the problem of the Red Book was one of form confirms the view that he had a fine sense of its true nature. But what is this problem of form? It can become clear through a confrontation of Jung's book with art.

Reflecting about the nature of what he was doing, Jung was certain that it was not science. But then a tempting voice tried to convince him: "That is art," to which he replied emphatically, "No it is not" (199b). The Red Book is not science, not art, but also not *Dichtung* (a poetic work) (213a), nor of course philosophy. This view of Jung's that it is not art and not poetic literature is not so much an observation or assessment as a programmatic statement: his *refusal* to let it be or become art. We have to ask: what is at stake with Jung's adamant warding off of the possibility that his Red Book might have, or might take on, art character? What was to be prevented at all cost? Asked the other way around: what would its turning into art do to the Red Book? What is it that the artist, by which I do not mean here a human being, but rather the art-producing "soul" in a human being, achieves?

If we take a portrait as an example, what turns it into a true work of art is that within itself it successfully manages to perform a radical reversal. Whereas empirically the starting point of a portrait is the real model out there, the work of art deprives this model of being its origin and source and internalizes the source of authority and conviction wholly into the work itself. The portrait as a work of art has its truth not in any likeness with the "original," it is not a copy of the original (as in Plato's idea of art), but it is its own original, containing its truth within itself, and this is why it glows from within. It is, as Hegel saw it, the self-manifestation of the absolute in sensuous form. The mystique of Leonardo's *Mona Lisa* is not derived from the real person depicted;

its truth does not depend on any (in this case presumably existing) likeness with her. Rather, the art work has its ground solely in itself and thus has made itself independent, cut itself loose, from its "referent" so that it turned into a *self* that stands on its own and speaks for itself. The art-making process is the "soul's" or "mind's" performance of this "alienation": the dispossessing of the external real of its authority and the making over of this authority to, and sinking it unconditionally into, the art work. (This sinking "origin" and "authority" into the art work itself is an example of an "absolute-negative interiorization": the creation of an interiority that is not a positivity, does not exist as a positive fact. And this is why art is one instance of soul-making.) The actually portrayed person, rather than merely being literally portrayed, is, together with any likeness that the depiction may have, truly reborn, originally recreated within the painting and by virtue of it, from within its own intrinsic origin, so that any still existing likeness has been reduced to a sublated, secondary moment in the painting's self-display.

If we think of a literary work like Dante's *Divina Commedia*, it is conceivable that its starting point was inner experiences. But this is precisely not what gives Dante's work its greatness. On the contrary, its character as a cultural property of mankind results from the fact that the substance of those experiences was relentlessly released *from* the solipsistic privacy of his personal inner experiences and their factual-event character and released *into* its form *as* fantasy, *as* poetic imagination. The fantasy content was relentlessly let go of and in this way allowed to find its own center of gravity and source of authority solely within *itself as* imaginal or fantastic. At the same time it was freed from its empirical rootedness in the author's subjectivity so that it could truly come into its own, which is tantamount to saying that it was allowed to create itself anew solely from out of its fantasy-internal truth and necessity. This is a truth that it only *obtains* through the art-*making* process which, as we have seen, consists in its being dispossessed of its alleged origin or groundedness in empirical experience and unconditionally interiorized into its fantasy character itself. The psychological difference does not reserve itself. Any great artist lets his experience as well as his subjectivity (the fact that it is he who had this experience) completely go under into the very *form* of fantasy, putting all his eggs in this one basket. Art-making requires taking a plunge. The fantasy (the idea, the image) is precisely allowed to be "nothing but" fantasy. Only this unconditional releasement of the fantasy into itself, into its fantasy character, for what it may be worth, allows it to come home to itself and have its truth exclusively within itself and to be determined solely by its own internal logic. And only through this going under of the artist's subjectivity into the fantasy as self-sufficient and an end in itself does the art-work also obtain true objectivity so that the generality can experience it as its own. Dante's work does primarily not belong to Dante. As a work of art it has truly (not only literally, externally) been *published*, that is to say, its own internal form is such that it is given over to all. This is a manifestation of the psychological difference.

Art comes into being through the relentless interiorization of the positivity of the empirical experience and its "realistic" content into the negativity of the form of mere fantasy. Art-making is the relentless working-off of the *duality* of subject (author) versus object, experience (content) versus representation (form), origin or cause versus result, in favor of the singularity of the work of art that has everything it needs within itself. Dante's work speaks for itself. It comes to us with its own authority. And precisely because it has logically once and for all left behind both its empirical starting point as an experience in a human subject as author and this subject itself. If they, the allegedly "original" experience and the person of the author, nonetheless figure in his work, then only as being freely recreated from within the fantasy according to its own laws. Dante's work is not a report about inner experiences from "the unconscious," not his "individuation process." It is the self-unfolding of a self-sufficient fantasy from out of *its own* internal necessity. (And we could even say that the empirical starting-point, the subjective experience, was only the first and rudimentary immediacy of what only in the finished work of art comes fully to light.) This alone is what gives it both its aesthetic beauty and its power of conviction for thousands of readers, making it truly speak to and deeply move even modern readers, readers who in their own convictions may be fundamentally removed from his early-14th century Christian world-view and cultural and practical life-conditions.

C.G. Jung performs the exactly opposite move to what I described as the art-making process. He preserves the initial duality, dissociating the positive-factual event of a vision here and the general fantasy character of the vision over there. As we hear, he "objected to presenting any of it [the Red Book material] as Dichtung [poetic fiction] when it was *all* Wahrheit [truth]" (212b f.). In other words, he tears fantasy (the form of fantasy) and truth apart as two separate, opposite realities, which comes out all the more clearly because of his allusion to the title of Goethe's work which shows both to be precisely an intricate, inseparable unity: *Dichtung und Wahrheit.* In Jung's Black Book 7 we find the statement, "You concern yourself with the form? Has the form ever been important, when it is a matter of revelation?" (211b, tr.m.). What he experienced is seen as revelation, that is, as a priori *coming* (or *intruding*) *as* truth. It is something that therefore does not need to *achieve* the status of truth by being transposed into the form of art (or any other "symbolic form" in Cassirer's sense), indeed it should not receive such a transformation. About Blake's productions Jung remarked critically, "they are an artistic production rather than an authentic representation [i.e., a mere documentation or "report *about* ..."] of unconscious processes" (*Letters 2*, pp. 513-4). This tells us that for Jung the art-making process distorts that true authenticity which for him resides only in the immediacy of the original experience itself (*Urerfahrung, Urerlebnis*; "the most immediate experience" [*CW* 11 § 396]). The ground of the truth and authenticity of a vision is kept external to its representation, such as in the Red Book, by being declared to have been an experience as factual event. "There was nothing of conscious structure in these fantasies, they were just events that happened" (*Analytical Psychology* 97). Happenings! The positivity of "events and experiences" (*MDR* 182)! The *facticity* of their occurrence!

But all art *is* of "conscious structure" through and through, otherwise dogs would be able to appreciate a statue or painting as art rather than as a mere thing. Fantasies, if they are consciously released into their fantasy character and not deliberately construed as reports about factual events, are in themselves thoroughly illumined, *as* art works events of consciousness.

As we already heard, Jung insisted, concerning his fantasy material: "No, it is not art! On the contrary, it is nature" (*MDR* 186). This is, by the way, diametrically opposed to the thinking of the alchemists, for whom *quod natura relinquit imperfectum ars perficit*. According to this view, truth can only come about through the human processing of what is naturally given as mere raw material, as factual prima materia. Truth is the end-product of a long opus *contra naturam*. What is naturally given is ipso facto precisely not (yet) true. Art *creates* its own origin as and within the work of art. But Jung wants to identify truth with factual existence, as if it were a piece of nature: "An elephant is true because it exists" (*CW* 11 § 5). Ultimately Jung's concept of psychic truth boils down to sheer overwhelmingness, brutal power: "the overpowering force of the original experiences" (360), "quite simply experiences" (365), "The unshakeableness of the experience" (338b). Jung is here a positivist and, in a sense, existentialist. His word truth has nothing to do any more with truth in its authentic sense.

Jung is here committed to a logic of externality and otherness. For him, the Red Book as an object has its truth, origin, and reality not in itself, but fundamentally outside of itself, in the literal experiences that gave rise to it. Because the event of the overwhelming experience is what really counts, he could not radically release the fantasy substance itself of his experience into its own, into logically being fantasy, having the form of fantasy, being art (or, another possibility, being philosophy or *Dichtung*). He needed to emphatically reject the notion of art for his Red Book because what he wanted to cling to and preserve at all cost was the so-called "original" experience external to and underlying the Red Book: the experience which for him was supposed to be the sole locus of truth and authenticity. Unthinkable that he could have released the substance of his experiences from the facticity of the experiences as well as from himself as the subject who had such experience into the negativity of the form of fantasy. Rather than *à corps perdu* plunging into the fantasy world *as* fantasy world and thus as a mental, conscious reality, as speculation, that is, rather than relentlessly releasing his experience, and himself going under, into "the soul," his whole project was precisely to extract from the fantasy the positivity of a literal external cause of it—ultimately "the primal world of the unconscious" (*MDR* 200) and posit it as its a priori. "The unconscious" is the objectified, literalized, externalized—and thus killed—soul: "the soul" by definition deprived of its "being of conscious structure" or its being thought.

The clinging to the factual event of one's experience over against the fantasy character of what has been experienced is at the same time the self-preservation (or initial self-institution) of the ego (the structure or definition of the subject as "the ego" in the sense of personalistic psychology). The I is not willing to let go of itself and go under into its fantasies, so that they might be released into their inherent truth. This is why Jung described this period of his life as (*his*) "Confrontation with the Unconscious," focusing, rather than on the *work* to be *produced*, on the crisis he had to go through and on his tormenting doubts as to his own sanity. And it is why he tried to substitute for the suggestion that what he was doing was art the following theory about the telos of the process: "Perhaps my unconscious is forming a personality that is not I" (199b). This is already *in nuce* the dogma of Jung's psychologistic "personality cult," as one might term it. He circled around *himself* (which might, e.g., be contrasted with mental-illness-plagued van Gogh's dedication to his painting). The creative impulse, which without doubt was at work in Jung, was diverted from its own direction towards the production of truth (in *works* of art, literature, philosophy, music), i.e., towards soul-making, and abused for egoic purposes (self-development). The truth is not allowed to come home to *itself*, but is forced down into the human being as (a new) literal personality.

Cause and telos are in Jung's scheme dissociated and set up as literal and external (past event or future entity, respectively). Art, poetry, philosophical thought (in other words, soul), by contrast, would be what is in between those two: *presence*, because owing to the absolute-negative interiorization of the experienced fantasy into itself, into its truth, into its own internal ground and *archê*, it contains both its cause and its telos only within its absolute negativity.

Because the Red Book has the mystery and truth that it is about fundamentally outside itself in Jung's factual "original" experience, on the one hand, and in the "new personality" to be formed in the positively existing civil man Jung, on the other hand, it is really an *unwritten* book. In Plato scholarship one distinguishes between Plato's exoteric written dialogues made available to the general public and his "unwritten doctrine" (*agrapha dogmata*) made known only orally to the esoteric inner circle of his disciples. Jung's book is esoteric in a much more radical, namely absolute, sense. Plato logically fully *released* his unwritten doctrine out into the open, and thus logically "published" it, even if only orally to select disciples; he could do so because he obviously had relentlessly abandoned himself to the inner truth of his thought experience. Potentially he could therefore also have written down his *agrapha dogmata*. But Jung's Red Book is the paradox of his "*written* unwritten (and on principle unwriteable) truth": literally, factually written, but logically unwritten. It merely *points to* the mystery that is *per definitionem* solely his mystery and not ours. "The myth commences, the one that can only be lived, not sung, the one that sings itself" (328b, tr.m.), we read at one point in the Red Book. The authentic locus of his truth is now the positivity of *Existenz*, real life: "first and exclusively and solely in one's own person" (*CW* 7, p. 5, tr.m.), in man whose nature is now no longer comprehended as his *theoretical* I (classical metaphysics) or his *poietic* soul (Nietzsche), but as what Heidegger would later term his mere *Dasein*.

Just as the authentic locus of the Christian truth is not the church as cathedral, but the human heart, so the authentic place of Jung's truth is not the Red Book, which, as we know, he considered his church, his cathedral. His truth has its authenticity only in the factual events of his "immediate experiences" themselves.

Jung's paintings and calligraphy are only secondary illustrations for the external purpose of satisfying his wish to show his *subjective* esteem. If they were art, they would shine from within themselves. The historistic imitation of a medieval illuminated book is the telltale sign that what the Red Book contains has its worth not in itself, but only in the feeling of the man C.G. Jung. "I always knew that these experiences contained something precious, and therefore I knew of nothing better than to write them down in a 'precious,' that is to say, costly book and to paint the images that emerged through reliving it all..." (360). Decoration. Ego work. It had to be ego work because the fantasy had not been released into its truth, into the *form* of truth. Which is why its truth could not shine forth from it of its own accord. And the fact that the calligraphy and the paintings imitate medieval forms of expression clearly reveals that the visual aspect of the Red Book is not the self-expression, i.e., not the intrinsic form, of the material presented *itself*. Superimposed. An accessory. Inauthentic. Thus Jung's cited critique of Blake ("an artistic production rather than an authentic representation of unconscious processes") reflects upon his own production, if we understand it in a different sense from his. (This is quite apart from the fact that the idea of an *authentic* representation of unconscious processes is in itself fallacious. Authenticity is never the gift of the unconscious processes themselves, of raw natural events, which inevitably come in the state of *imperfection* and *inauthenticity*.

If at all, authenticity can only be the *produced result* of the artist's or adept's *ars*).

The Red Book has meanwhile been published. But published only the way art works can nowadays be *technically reproduced*. We can never get behind the reproduction to the "original"—because Jung's own volume is in itself not, and was not supposed to be, the original. Dante's *Divina Commedia*, by contrast, does not need a costly leather binding. Even if it comes to us in a wretched, cheaply printed paperback copy we have nevertheless the original: because as art and philosophical thought it has its illumining and heart-warming truth absolute-negatively within itself, a truth that freely communicates itself to anybody capable and willing to abandon himself to it. It is everybody's mystery, not only Dante's.

Pitfalls for the Superficial Observer

Madness. In his *Nachwort* (1959) Jung wrote about the Red Book, "To the superficial observer, it will appear like madness" (360). But he remains a superficial observer himself to the extent that he ascribes the not-madness only to the fact that he was secondarily, after the fact, able to capture and contain the overwhelming power of the original experiences. What we have to realize is that the material is not psychotic from the outset. Clinical categories and a psychiatric, diagnostic approach are misplaced. We need a psychological, "final-constructive" approach and to comprehend the whole process as part of a systematic soul opus. About a certain traumatic experience of a hysterical patient Jung wrote: "The fright and the apparently traumatic effect of the childhood experience are merely staged, but staged in the peculiar way characteristic of hysteria, so that the *mise en scène* appears almost exactly like a reality" (*CW* 4 § 364). By the same token, the *apparently* psychotic character of some of Jung's material must be seen through as an *arrangement* (in Adler's sense), as staged, but staged (a) *as* not staged and (b) of course not staged by the experiencing ego personality, but by "the soul"—just as that patient's fright was of course not staged by her ego-personality, but by her neurotic "soul" for *its* neurotic purposes. What in Jung's case "the soul" needed to stage for the benefit of the experiencing Jung through the seemingly psychotic character of the images was the appearance of the *absolutely overwhelming* power of the experiences. It was needed to produce the sense of the absolute immediacy of authentic psychic experience. But with this notion we have already entered the sphere of the second pitfall.

Immediate experience, volcanic eruption, being unintentional. To the superficial observer it might appear as if the fantasy material came to Jung as immediate experience (which was of course also Jung's own view). That he saw it this way shows that he did not look at what happened from the standpoint of soul, but from that of only one half of the whole: the experiencing ego personality. He identified with the latter and therefore took the overwhelmingness that the experiences had for the I at face value, the same way his hysterical patient had taken her fear at face value. In the case of this patient Jung had been able to see the whole picture, but not in his own case.

Psychologically it is a grave mistake to privilege one element of a dream, fantasy, or psychic experience, for example the I, taking it literally by setting it up as a given existing outside the fantasy, in "reality," and thus as already known from "reality," and taking all other elements only as products of fantasy or reactions to the "given reality." The I is just as internal to the fantasy as they are; it is an imaginal, "fantastic" I and needs to be seen through. A dream or fantasy within itself *invents*, just as everything else in it, so also the experiencing I in the particular form that is necessary for *this* fantasy. As psychologists we always have to take responsibility for the whole psychic phenomenon.

However, that Jung here took the I simply for granted "without questions asked" is not so much to be viewed as a failure of his, but rather as a necessary ingredient of what the soul wanted to create with the whole process Jung underwent. Conversely, his *extrajection* of the experiencing I from out of the fantasy character of the experience—his identifying it *tel quel* with himself as the real person that he was—shows that his understanding of it was not a psychological one, but one that paradoxically stayed *fantasy-internal*, enveloped in the external impressions that the fantasy wanted to produce. We could also say that his interpretations of his experiences do the fantasy experiences' bidding and are thus a continuation of them, although in the medium of conscious reflection.[2] They are additional *psychic* phenomena in the same vein, rather than *psychological* interpretations.

The unmediatedness thesis is contradicted by a number of features.

As Shamdasani pointed out in his Introduction and as any reader will see right away, much of the content of the Red Book is directly derived from Jung's reading (200b). It is the work of a scholar and in fact largely took place in his library (203a). The Nietzsche imitation in style, and partly in intent, is striking. The Red Book at one point says, "the soul is everywhere that scholarly knowledge is not" (233b), a radical disjunction! If that were true, then the Red Book would not be an expression of soul since it is steeped in learnedness.

Another point is that the process recorded in the Red Book was started as an experiment, as Jung himself said repeatedly. Experiments are performed by the scientific mind. There was certainly spontaneity within this experiment and for the experiencing subject. But the experiment itself as a whole was a deliberate technical undertaking. Jung uses phrases like: "when I switched off consciousness" (cf. 200b), "I used the same technique of the descent" (*Analytical Psychology* 63), an "insane asylum of my own *making*" (*ibid.* 24, my ital.), "But if we *turn* the God *into* fantasy" (283a, my ital.), which betray an element of purposeful design and artifice.

The experiences were also by no means unintentional. It is the "superficial observer" and fantasy-syntonic I in the Red Book that says, "It has happened thus to me. And it happened in a way that I neither expected nor wished for" (338b, tr.m.). In truth, however, there is from the outset a powerful will or craving underlying it all, which shows itself time and again in the Red Book. "I wanted my God for better or worse [i.e., at all cost]" (289a, tr.m.). "And what wouldn't you give for a single look into the infinite things that are to come? Would they not even be worth a sin for you?" (246a, tr.m.) "And I felt it again to be absolutely certain that my life would have broken in half if I failed to heal my God" (281b, tr.m.). "... an unspeakable greed seizes you..." (270a). There are, more theoretically, apodictic-dogmatic presuppositions like "We need the life of eternity" (253b) or "We lack nothing more than divine force" (281b, tr.m.), which are hardly reconcilable with the truly empirical stance of an unprejudiced experimenter. In general the text is soaked in the rhetoric of wanting, longing, expectation. We hear from one figure of "the excess of my desire" (342a, tr.m.), another felt seduced "desirously stretching my hand after the divine mysteries" (275b). The attitude demanded in the Red Book concerning one particular psychic phenomenon ("joy"), but applying to psychic experience at large, namely that it "should neither be made nor sought; it should come, when it must come. ... (i)t comes and exists of its own accord, and is not sought here and there" (341b, tr.m.) is not corroborated by the Red Book experience as a whole. It is not so innocent. There was from the beginning an unspoken and apparently subjectively unconscious "quod esset demonstrandum," in other words, a hidden agenda, a strategic goal—obvious today but unconscious to Jung, an agenda whose *spelled out execution* occurred in Jung's years-long fantasy process.

Shamdasani rightly characterizes the Red Book material as "dramatized thinking in pictorial form" (200b). The material is in itself highly reflected. *Malgré* Jung's self-stylization, it is a work of speculative thought, thought, however, not presented in the form of thought, but sunk into the form of, and disguised as, spontaneous immediate experiences (and their interpretation). Jung lets his own thought play itself out in dialogue form, as an interplay between different figures, one of which is the I. No doubt, subjectively it probably was overwhelming and in part surprising *for* the fantasizing Jung. But part of the whole project was precisely to create the appearance of a "natural event," spontaneous occurrence, true revelation and to impress the I accordingly in order to take it in. But *we* as psychologists must not be deceived by this superficial impression staged for a particular purpose.

Taking together the strong will as driving force behind the Red Book and its character as dramatized thinking, we could call the process that unfolds in it *wishful thinking* (in the strict, literal sense of this phrase).

Going *in medias res*. The superficial observer, if he is a Jungian enthusiast, might thirdly want to delve directly into the symbolism of the images presented in the Red Book and of the narrative of the successive events, in order to mine them for meaning or wisdom, using the whole process as an authentic model of the individuation process. But the psychological task is to see through. Not to indulge. We are analysts. Not consumers of mysterious images and ideologies.

Gnosticism. In view of names like Abraxas, Phanes, Pleroma and numerous corresponding ideas known from the Gnostics in late antiquity, the superficial observer might jump to the conclusion that these figures or phenomena, just like that, represent the ancient Gnostic ones of the same name. But we must not naively take them at face value.

In modern authors we must not identify sight unseen the ancient names they use with the same-named ancient mythological phenomena. Richard Wagner's Valkyries are not a revival of ancient Teutonic Valkyries. Nietzsche's Zarathustra is not identical with the ancient Iranian sage. And Nietzsche's Dionysos must not be confused with the ancient Greek god by the same name.[3] Psychoanalysis developed the notion of "screen memories." While our case is not one of screen *memories*, the familiar names are nevertheless similarly masks (though not disguises!) representing something unfamiliar, an idea, phenomenon, or reality that in each case needs to be inferred and reconstructed exclusively from the modern text and its modern context. It is fundamentally new wine that ferments in those old bottles. The figures just mentioned are natives of the 19th century. It is a hermeneutic principle that we must not presume any elements in a work (or, for that matter, in a dream) to be already known from outside the work or dream and mechanically insert into it this "known" ready-made meaning. Everything must be understood in terms of its own time. We need to see that the issues debated and at stake in creative works (and thus also in the symbols and figures that appear in them) belong to the particular historical locus that gave rise to those works.

The same applies to Jung's Red Book. It is a child of its own time and on a deep level it is exclusively concerned with the burning deep intellectual issues of his age. It is not a historical study or a book about ancient mythology and the religious speculation of the Gnostics, nor their resumption or revival. In order to find out what the mythological or Gnostic names known from ancient times in fact represent in the Red Book, we must therefore not consult books on ancient mythology and religion, which, although they may give us certain superficial hints, on the main lead astray. We have to look at their actual phenomenology as well as at the function they have within the Red Book.

An example in point is the motif of the dead who come to Jerusalem in the *Septem Sermones* context. This sounds highly "mythological," and Gnostic. We are tempted to think of the dead in terms of the underworld and the ancestor cult of ancient cultures, of Biblical times, of long-bygone ages and a mysterious exotic world. But when we hear that the dead are those who "repudiated Christian belief and hence turned into those that Christian belief likewise rejected" (348b) and that they themselves insist: "We are not miserable, we are intelligent, our thinking and feeling is as pure as clear water. We praise our reason. We mock superstition" (353a), we realize that they are by no means, the way they are represented in the Red Book's mythologizing style, the dead of former ages, but in truth very much alive. They represent the *Inbild* (envisioned quintessence) of conventional modern man at large as a product of the Enlightenment, Jung's contemporaries (including his own father), who are merely interpreted by the Red Book as fundamentally dead souls who waver between their anti-religious convictions and their deep unsatiable craving for religious meaning and inspiration. The dead are the image for *contemporary collective consciousness*, the embodied "spirit of this time."

Jung's Red Book is a work of thought. It is the soul's (or the historical locus's) attempt to provide an answer to the "spirit of this time." In particular it is "Jung's" wrestling with the spiritual situation of contemporary Christianity and at the same time, as it were, *his* "Answer to 'Nietzsche.'" About the anchorites one of the texts states: "they were those who drew the most inexorable conclusion and consequence from the psychological necessity of their time" (267n, tr.m.). This is precisely what the Red Book wants (tries) to do, too.

I said it is a work of thought, indeed, speculative thought. It is not primarily a work of spontaneous inner experience. What it is ultimately and really about is "the last and simplest things" (229b), "the last mysteries of becoming and passing away" (230a), "the infinite things of what is to come" (246a, tr.m.), "the divine mysteries" (275b). Religion and metaphysics (in the colloquial sense of the word).

"It all began then; the later details are only supplements and clarifications of the material that burst forth from the unconscious." To the superficial observer it might seem that Jung's *Collected Works* are, as it were, the outgrowth of the experiences recorded in the Red Book. This is Jung's own thesis ("The first imaginings and dreams were like fiery, molten basalt, from which the stone crystallized, upon which I could work" [219b], from *Erinnerungen* p. 203). And when Shamdasani, as we heard, said that the Red Book is "the central book in his [Jung's] oeuvre," he seems to support the idea of the seamless continuity between, and unity of, this book and Jung's oeuvre.

Now it is obvious that many of the ideas and positions known from Jung's published work in fact already occur in the Red Book, e.g., the idea of psychic objectivity; of the singular importance of the individual;

Jung's special concept of the self; and even his major "theological" (better: theosophical) conceptions published in *Aion* and *Answer to Job*. On a surface level, semantically, there can be no doubt that the Red Book material represents the nucleus of the psychology laid down in Jung's published oeuvre.

So while historically speaking the Red Book is the source of Jung's "written psychology," logically this "written psychology" is, however, ashamed of its factual origin in the experiences underlying the Red Book. This comes out most blatantly in the fact that when Jung used Red Book material (dreams, visions, or mandala paintings) in his published works, he time and again felt the need to do so anonymously, camouflaging his own products as those of other people, of his patients. Incredible for a psychologist who prided himself on his empiricism, and doubly incredibly considering the repeated motif in the Red Book of being forced to speak (229b): "But you should speak. Why have you received the revelation. You should not hide it" (211b), "it also gave me the courage to say all of that which I have written in the earlier part of this book" (336b). [Even if my experience of God were a deception] "I would nevertheless have to *confess* to this experience and recognize the God in it. ... And even if the God had revealed himself in a meaningless abomination, I couldn't help but *avow* that I have experienced God in it" (338b, tr.m., my italics). But the point is that Jung did not have the courage to avow: to make the Red Book available. He did not speak. He hid behind the front of alleged patients. At best he dropped, late in life, some cryptic hints to his personal experiences such as "I do not believe, I know." And when diagnosed by Martin Buber as a Gnostic on account of his *Septem Sermones*, Jung, rather than owning up to this production of his (so precious to him), dissociated himself from his text, brushing it off as "a sin of my youth ..., which consists in my once having perpetrated a poem" (*CW* 18 § 1501). Jung blamed Buber (and other critics) of simply being ignorant of "clinical experience," when in reality the basis of his views was not clinical experience at all, but his own subjective fantasy experiences, his speculations.

As a responsible scientist Jung would have had to present those mandalas etc., as material stemming from his own subjective experience. More than that, precisely if he felt that his scientific work was basically the elaboration of his early personal experiences, he would have had to present all of the Red Book material. An empiricist has to put his cards, all his cards, on the table. Scientifically, self-experiments do not have much value as evidence. They are, as it were, "uroboric," simply displaying the experimenter's subjective presuppositions, predilections and ideological needs. In his "spontaneous" experiences Jung is merely "incestuously" dealing with his own *projections* (not "*revelations*"[4] from "the unconscious"). Even the experiences in the consulting room are not really conclusive in an evidential sense because, as, e.g., Jung himself rightly wrote to James Kirsch on 29 Sept. 1934: "With regard to your patient, it is quite correct that her dreams are occasioned by *you*. ... As soon as certain patients come to me for treatment, the type of dream changes. In the deepest sense we all dream not *out of ourselves* but out of what lies *between us and the other*" (*Letters 1*, p. 172). Science needs blind or even double-blind experiments, not ones in which test subject and experimenter are the same.

Why did Jung feel the need in his oeuvre to deny (not the content of those dreams, painted pictures, and convictions, but) the fact of their having their real origin in his own subjective fantasies (fantasies which, after all, were so precious to him that he needed to put them down in an expensive leather-bound volume and spent years on their calligraphic presentation)? Why did he behave much like Peter, who also denied what he loved dearly, the Lord? The answer is that something in Jung must have been keenly aware of the fundamental discrepancy, indeed incompatibility, between his fantasy experiences and his "scientific" work as a psychologist. This is why he had to supply a false origin to his own material when using it in his works, similarly to how sometimes important witnesses against Mafia bosses are provided with a new identity by the police, namely an origin in his professional work as an analyst who merely objectively reported what he encountered in his consulting room during many years of clinical experience. The inclusion in his work of his private images and ideas involves a real uprooting of those images and ideas from their own ground and their transplantation into a very different ground or discourse, we could say, from the sphere of Jung's "personality no. 2" and its *speculative thought* to that of "personality no. 1." Jung rode two different horses. There is a logical discontinuity between his experiences and his oeuvre.

"I am much amused that you think I have 'become professorial.' Evidently I have successfully deceived [!] even your eagle eye. One must have a good exterior [*eine gute Exoterik*] 'dans ce meilleur des mondes possibles,'" Jung wrote to Hermann Hesse on 18 Sep 1934 (*Letters 1*, p. 171). Like Plato's esoteric "unwritten teaching" versus his exoteric written dialogues (but in very different ways and for different reasons, see above), Jung's Red Book world and the world of his published oeuvre are heterogeneous: his Red Book is *absolutely* esoteric because it is not even addressed to an inner circle of disciples, but only to himself. It is not psychology, not a contribution to psychology as a theory, but only psychic raw material. As such it can of course become an object of psychological examination, but only with a view to learning what was going on in, and what it meant for, the one individual C.G. Jung—and, of course, in the case of a great man like Jung, above all for the historical locus that expressed itself through him.

Psychology, by contrast, in its logical form inevitably belongs to the generality. In it, universal reason is addressed. The psychologist enters the field not as the private individual that he also is, but as a member of the scientific community and thus as his (personal) attempt to be in the logical status of consciousness-as-such. This is why we have the notion of the "psychological *equation*." The logical form of a psychology and a psychologist's style of speaking have to be such that they within themselves accept the task of justifying themselves precisely before the "spirit of this time," whereas the Red Book says: "No one and nothing can justify what I must proclaim to you. Justification is superfluous to me, since I have no choice, but I must" (229b). Compulsion. No *logon didonai*. Of course not, because it is (allegedly) merely a natural event. Explicitly conceived as a revelation coming with brutal force, it is of merely solipsistic significance. A revelation can be neither questioned nor criticized, no more than an oak tree or a thunderstorm. It is the way it is, and as such it leaves no room for the psychological equation's equal sign, which makes only sense if there is a duality of a human person and the theoretical claims it makes.

In his oeuvre, however, Jung objectively spoke in the logical form of psychology. As psychologist he felt responsible for the groundedness and general comprehensibility of his statements (which is also why he disguised his personal material as material coming from patients). As psychologist he spoke from the standpoint of consciousness-as-such, as a member of the scientific community. Whether he was successful or not in doing this, whether his grounds stand up to criticism or not, is another question, of no concern in the present context. What counts in our context is the logical form of the discourse of his oeuvre.

As important as the Red Book is *for historical* "Jung studies," *as psychologists* we are well advised to dissociate ourselves from the Red Book and instead base our work on Jung's published psychology, and *critically* so at that. We have not become psychologists in order to listen to revelations and to adopt a pseudo-religious ideology of "the self" (or each develop our own one). Psychology is not about the self in the first place. It is the study of "the soul," the discipline of absolute-negative interiority. (I gave an example of absolute-negative interiorization above in what I said about art. The Jungian self presupposes a "positivistic" interiorization into the human being, which ends up with "*the* self" as Other, as an It. Soul-making is the interiorization of whatever phenomenon into *itself*, its own logically negative [mercurial] depth.) The fact that Jung himself abruptly discontinued this project altogether and, further, that when decades later adding an "Epilogue" he stopped in the middle of a sentence, can serve us as a supporting symbol of the necessity of such a dissociation from the Red Book. In *MDR* Jung even explicitly dissociated himself from the Red Book in favor of his scientific work: "Therefore I gave up this estheticizing tendency in good time, in favor of a rigorous process of *understanding*. I saw that so much fantasy needed firm ground underfoot, and that I must first return wholly to human reality. This reality consisted for me in scientific comprehension" (p. 188, tr. m.).

THE PROJECT

Utopia. Now we are ready to look at what the Red Book is actually about and wants to achieve. I already called it Jung's "Answer to Nietzsche." The 19th century as the first phase of *modern* thinking had been the century of the great utopias. After Feuerbach's dream of primordial "conversation" in the sense of "man's community with man," Kierkegaard's dream of the solitary individual's "leap into faith," Marx's dream of a "communist society," the last in the row was Nietzsche's hope for a fundamentally new possibility of creativity, true *poiêsis* (in contrast to simulated creativity, the merely reified and *represented* productive potential of man). Nietzsche *imaged* the event of this new creation of creativeness as Dionysus's coming to Ariadne, to the potentially creative, but to begin with deserted, soul. However, Dionysus's Parousia did not, could not happen.

With the fundamental collapse of Nietzsche's hope the potential of utopian thought—as true *thought*—was exhausted, the utopian dream in thought was over; great philosophical thought was once and for all cured of it.[5] This fundamental disappointment gave room to a radically sobered stance. The early 20th century thus saw the triumphant progress of mathematical logic and Wittgenstein's critique of language, on the one hand, and of Husserl's phenomenology as strict science, on the other hand. Husserl's thinking was the philosophical ancestor of the thought of Heidegger, Sartre, Lacan, Lévinas, and Derrida, to mention only a few. The *utopian* impulse could now survive only where it withdrew into the lowlands of thoughtless and literalistic political ideology and practice (communism, fascism), where "ideology" means historically decidedly obsolete thought that is nevertheless held on to dogmatically as a doctrine and subjective belief system to be literally put into practice by *empirical man*.

In this post-Nietzschean situation Jung started his own work. As we see, he could neither take the self-negation of Nietzsche's vision for an answer, nor could he, like Rudolf Steiner, Alfred Schuler, Ludwig Klages, etc., develop a nostalgic *Weltanschauung*, nor become a political activist. He remained a *thinker* and yet insisted on taking over the heritage of Nietzsche's utopian vision and carrying it further, even if in radically altered form. After the collapse of Nietzsche's vision he could rescue the utopian impulse into the new century only because he believed to be able to "correct" and surpass the Nietzschean position and at the same time to transport *essential thought as such*, or the locus of truth, away from its home ground to a fundamentally *new arena*.

But before we can get to this theme of how the utopian project could be continued *as* "thought" even at a time when it had become historically obsolete, let us look at how the utopian character shows in the Red Book.

The new. What is to come. The dominant orientation of the Red Book is toward the future. Already the title Jung gave it, *Liber novus*, emphasizes its utopian character, and the title of its "Liber Primus" makes it explicit once more: "The Way of What is to Come." Unlike

Thomas Morus' *De nova insula U-topia* (1516) or Bacon's *Nova Atlantis* (1626), the predicate "novus" in Jung's book title does not refer to an island or other geographical place. It qualifies "book." Now it is so that every book that is written comes as a new book. *Novus* cannot mean this triviality. The attribute new must be used in an eminent sense. It must indicate that this book is in competition with *the* previous book and enters the scene with the claim of surpassing it and taking its place. *Liber* is the Latin translation of Greek *biblion*, from whose plural *biblia*, the book of books, we have our word "Bible." When Jung told Christiana Morgan that if she made her own Red Book, "for you it will be your church—your cathedral," he could just as well have said, "your Bible." It is fitting that a book which teaches that rather than "Christians" we all ought to ourselves be "Christs" and which claims to bring to completion the mystery of the Christ (left incomplete by Christ himself) calls itself *Liber novus*.

Throughout the text of the Red Book the commitment to the future is determining: "I read the gospels and seek their meaning which is yet to come, ... their hidden meaning which points to the future" (272a f.), one character, Ammonius, says; "You engender and give birth to what is yet to come" (234b); "My friends, if you knew what depths of the future you carry inside you! Those who descend into their own depths behold what is to come" (241n, tr.m.). "[T]hen your God rises from the radiant cradle, to the immeasurable height of the future, to the maturity and fullness of the coming time" (234a). Time and again we hear of the "new God," or of the "newly appearing God" (301n).

Relentless dismissal of the present. In order for the utopia to have a chance, the prevailing reality has to be logically cleared away. Already Jung's earliest visions are visions of the destruction of old Europe. In the name of "the spirit of the depths" the Red Book states, "for the spirit of this time had nothing to give me any more" (252n, tr.m.). The I of the Red Book has broken with the present, opted out of its own time. To be sure, there is also this isolated statement: "Do not ask after the morrow, the present [*das Heute*] shall be sufficient unto you" (238b, tr.m.). But this is precisely what is not practiced in the Red Book. Its true spirit is expressed in that other statement: "We love only what is coming, not what is" (357b).

Part of the rejection of the present is the vehement anti-Enlightenment impulse. "[T]he enlightened live there. ... They're actually dangerous since they cook the strongest poisons from which even I must protect myself" (282b). "[W]hat you call poison is science" (278b) "'Have you no Gods anymore?' I: 'No, words are all we have'" (279a). "This is also the fate of the Logos: in the end it poisons us all" (280b). "Judgment must fall from you.... Utterly poor, miserable, humble, ignorant, go on through the gate" (246b, tr.m.).

The dismissal of the present also includes the diagnosis of the death of God and its inexorable acceptance. "The dear old God has died, and it is good that way" (333b). "The one God is dead—yes, truly, he died" (357b). "He probably does not know—we have no more prayers. How should he know about our nakedness and poverty?" (271a). I already quoted: "'Have you no Gods anymore?' I: 'No, words are all we have'" (279a). "Science has taken from us the capacity of belief" (278a).

By the same token, Christianity is rejected, with a strong affect. Christ is once derogatorily described as "the pale God of Asians [der bleiche Asiatengott] who was nailed to the wood like a chicken marten" (242b, tr.m.). Numerous biblical adages are parodied or reversed, just one example: "for thine is our power and glory" (345b, tr.m.). Christianity is viewed as deceptive, as making us blind. "Do not let the teachings of Christianity deceive you!" (234n). "Your Christian shrouds have fallen, the veils that blinded your eyes" (341b); "then you will be free and beyond Christianity" (235b). "We want to continue living with a new God, a hero beyond Christ" (242n).

Right at the beginning we hear that "God is an image, and those who worship him must worship him in the image of the overmeaning" (229b, tr.m.), which is a slap in the face of Christianity: the reversal of John 4:24 ("God is Spirit: and they that worship him must worship him in spirit and in truth").

> Here I have to insert a comment on this translation. Jung wrote *Übersinn* where the English translation says "supreme meaning." *Übersinn* is a neologism of Jung's and is clearly modeled after Nietzsche's *Übermensch* (overman). It implies a meaning that is "over," "beyond," "in excess of" meaning. If, for this crucial, recurring Red Book term, "supreme meaning" is used as the translation for *Übersinn*, the shock of "overmeaning" is eliminated, the concept is rendered harmless, even wonderful. But what the Red Book has in mind is outrageous, which also comes out in the genesis of "*Übersinn*": it is said (*ibid.*) to come

about through the "melting together of sense [*Sinn*] and nonsense [*Widersinn*]" (lit. "counter-meaning," i.e., the diametrical opposite or violation of meaning, absurdity). The use of "supreme meaning" renders the sentence following the one just quoted unintelligible: "The supreme meaning is not a meaning and not an absurdity [*Widersinn*, counter-meaning]..." (230a). This is wrong on both counts: a supreme meaning is of course still a meaning (the highest one, at that), and it is of course *not* an absurdity, since if it were it would not be supreme meaning. But the "overmeaning" is, as the Red Book rightly says, indeed *not* a meaning; because it exists as the "melting of together" of meaning and its very opposite so that its meaning character is destroyed. For the same reason, but in opposite direction, it is also not an absurdity (*Widersinn*). The overmeaning is—at least allegedly—catapulted beyond the whole level of the opposites of meaning and absurdity.[6]—It is probably not possible to imitate in English Jung's play with the words *Sinn, Übersinn, Widersinn, Unsinn*. But since these words are of terminological significance, it is problematic that the English translation does not consistently use the same English word for one and the same Red Book term. It translates *Sinn* one time as *sense*, at other times as *meaning*, and *Widersinn* likewise sometimes as *nonsense* and at another time as *absurdity*, and also obliterates the difference between *Widersinn* and *Unsinn*.—Another problem with the English translation of this passage is the plural of "in the *images* of the supreme meaning" for Jung's singular "im Bilde des Übersinnes," which is reminiscent of Gen. 1:27 (God created man ... "in the image of ...").

This substitution of image for spirit and truth is of course a most momentous move. It amounts to a programmatic attack on the negativity of logos. It on principle opens the way for the positivity of the image, that is, for Jung's naturalistic stance, for the mere factual event of the emergence of an image *as the successor to truth*. Later we read: "It is not to be thought; it is to be viewed. It is a painting" (357b). The thinker Jung *thinks* the departure from the inwardness of thought proper and replaces it with the factual experience of images as pictures vis-à-vis the viewing subject, thereby regressively returning to an objectifying thinking (and the subject-object split).

In the Red Book the radical cutting off of the present is integrated in a larger conception of a succession of historical stages of consciousness, where the caesura between them is marked by the death of the gods of the old stage. "But this is the bitterest for moral men: our Gods want to be overcome.... When the God grows old, he becomes a shadow, nonsense.... The greatest truth becomes the greatest lie..." (242a, tr.m.). "Everything that becomes too old turns into an evil, this is therefore also true of your highest. Learn this from the suffering of the crucified God that one can also betray and crucify a God, namely the God of the old year. When a God ceases being the way of life, he must fall secretly. The God becomes sick..." (241b). This is the notion of the death of symbols, known from Jung's published work: "then the symbol is ripe to be destroyed, for it no longer covers the seed, which, you see, is about to grow beyond the shell," Jung wrote to Hans Schmid (6 Nov 1915, quoted in the German version p. 335n, my transl.). Christianity's "teachings are good for the most mature minds of bygone time" (234n). "We have outgrown that childhood where mere belief was the most suitable means to bring men to what is good and reasonable.... ... we need knowledge more than belief" (335b). "Mankind has grown older and a new month has begun" (356b). "[T]he world has acquired a new face. A new cover was thrown over it" (357b).

Hyperbole in goal and style. Since, on the one hand, "the spirit of this time had nothing to give me any more" (253n, tr.m.) and, on the other hand, the entire orientation goes towards the future, the question arises: what is hoped for from the future? What is the real concern around which the Red Book circles, the goal for which it strives? The goal is surprisingly not to find or recover the soul, not to explore its depths. It is nothing psychological, not soul-making, psychologizing. The real purpose is to overcome the nihilism and godlessness of the present. In other words, the goal is Meaning and God, where God means what grants Meaning, and Meaning is the fulfillment experienced through *having* a God to be worshiped. But the Red Book does not content itself with meaning plain and simple. No, right from the outset it reaches out for the overmeaning (229b, tr.m.). "That [the overmeaning] is the God yet to come" (*ibid.*). Just as meaning has to appear in its excessive form of overmeaning, so at the end of the Red Book the idea of God appears as Overgod ("a God above [*über*] God" [349a]). Nietzsche had said: "Dead are all the gods, now we want the overman to live." The Red Book says, as it were, "the spirit of this time has nothing to give me any more, now we want the overmeaning and the Overgod to live." Jung follows Nietzsche and departs from him at the same time by not seeing salvation in the overman but in a new religiousness.

Why overmeaning? Why is meaning not enough? Because meaning, even if it were a different one from the one known heretofore, is discredited as part of "this time." It might be a new alternative all right, but it would nevertheless still belong to the *same old status* of consciousness, the level of the opposites. What in the Red Book is striven for, however, has to be really, *absolutely*, new, an unheard-of, fundamentally new level of consciousness: "... if you also live what you have never yet lived" (233b): never yet! "If I have ascended to the highest and most difficult on the one hand, and want to win through to a redemption at an even higher level..." (293b, tr.m.). "... only my other leads me beyond myself" (*ibid*.). Even the superlative, the highest and most difficult, is not sufficient. It, too, has to be superseded, outstripped. Still higher: the absolute extreme. It has to be mind-blowing and world-shattering. The Red Book will not make do with less. It reaches out (not for "the absolute" in the sense of classical metaphysics, but) for absolute extremes. Hubris, inflated claims: the belief to be in contact with the "spirit of the depths" and to have been "forced down to the last and simplest things" (229b), "reaching deep down, down to the kernel of the world" (276b). A Titanic vision: "I hate this pitifulness of the God. ... You force the gates of Hell.... You storm Heaven..." (285b). The Red Book even claims to be able to go back before Adam and Eve and the Fall: "you free yourself from the old curse of the knowledge of good and evil" (301a).

After having been confronted with such a volley of ideas, one is flabbergasted to also find the isolated statement in the Red Book: "I shun far-flying ideas" (249a, tr.m.).

The style of the Red Book is also hyperbolic. Its diction, modeled after Nietzsche (the "Zarathustra form," so Jung according to Baynes [212b]), is stilted, pretentious, unctuous. We experience here how far we are psychologically removed from the early 20th century, when such a style was obviously still felt to be a possible literary form, whereas for us today it is hard to bear. Of course, we also heard that the style of the Red Book already "hurt (Jung's own) sense of the fitness of things terribly" (*ibid*.). But at least the later parts of the Red Book become less bombastic, less inflated (in style!, not in content), and more didactic, theoretical.

Because the Red Book moves into the future and at the same time tries to go way back before Christianity ("thereby you take a step back before Christianity and a step beyond it" [296b, tr.m.] and even back before the Fall), we see that its thinking is around an empty center, a lacuna. What has validity and (alleged) reality for it is two absences, pre-Christian truth, on the one side, and what is to come, on the other. "I lock the past with one key, with the other I open the future" (250a). The present in between has been cast to the wolves. In this regard there is a structural similarity between Jung's stance and that of Schelling who also had to pay the same price of an emptied-out present for entertaining the idea of an infinitely fulfilled past and an infinitely fulfilled future, even though on the very different basis of the premodern logic of classical metaphysics.

One could view the longing for an overmeaning as a compensatory reaction to the experience of the emptied-out present. But it is also possible to see it the other way around. Diagnosing an emptied-out present not as innocent cognition, but as the strategic act of denying that it has any meaning, of depriving it of any meaning. The thus extracted meaning is both retrojected into a lost past and projected into and heaped upon the future where it reappears as a surplus, excess, as overmeaning. The fact that the whole process described in the Red Book gives the impression of being will-driven seems to favor the second view.

The newness of the new. The talk of an overmeaning would itself be an empty claim, a mere word, if what makes it "over-" could not be spelled out. But the Red Book does not let us down. It tells us that overmeaning [*Übersinn*] is the "melting together of sense [*Sinn*] and nonsense [*Widersinn*]" (229b). This is truly mind-blowing. We have long been familiar with the idea of the union of opposites, and indeed, what the Red Book has in mind is just that. But it is easy to think of this union as if the opposites to be united were merely two conflicting, but nevertheless equally legitimate tendencies or values or two opposite natural forces, two enemies, two mythic figures or metaphysical principles at war with each other, such as Shiva and Vishnu. This would be a semantic or ontological opposition. But the Red Book leaves this harmless idea behind. What it has in mind is the union of a concept

and the negation or denial of this *very same* concept: it is the union of
logical opposites, namely contraries. One and the same term is at one
and the same time affirmed and denied[7]: *Sinn* and *Widersinn*! Reason
and unreason (314a), differentiation and nondifferentiation (347a),
"the fullness and the emptiness" (347b), "truth and lying" (350a).
"The highest truth is one and the same with the absurd [*dem
Widersinnigen*]" (242a). "To the extent that the Christianity of this
time lacks madness, it lacks divine life" (238a). As such, this idea of
the union of opposites is nothing less than a fundamental attack on
the law of non-contradiction and thus on logic itself. We always have
to understand the Red Book ideas of the overmeaning and overgod as
well as of the union of opposites in this absolute sense, in terms of logical
contraries.

What the Red Book is therefore indeed capable of is demonstrating
the concrete content of the notion of overmeaning. What it is, however,
not capable of showing is why a reader should find this overmeaning
meaningful, rather than simply nonsense and hypertrophy. Be that as
it may, we see again that the Red Book, far from being a "Modest
Proposal," hyperbolically reaches out for absolute excess. It *has to* do
that in order to let "what is to come" be an absolute break with the
present and to let the Red Book be truly *Liber novus*, the New Bible.

The familiar Jungian idea of the union in God of good and evil, of
Christ and Satan, that is also discussed in the Red Book must also be
understood in this radical sense. But the moment good and evil are
personified and mythologized as Christ and Satan, we are back in the
innocent imaginal or ontological thinking of the opposites construed
as entities or principles. Then this idea of a union might be shocking
for our customary moral convictions, but not mind-blowing. With this
conception we never arrive at the intended radical idea of overmeaning
and overgod. The Red Book attempts to seize the ultimate.

The new arena. The utopian style of thinking had become
historically obsolete after Nietzsche. In order to nonetheless come up
with a new utopia on the level and in the sphere of thought (rather
than as sociopolitical ideology and party politics), the only possible
way was to provide a radically new arena not merely for this particular
new utopia but, much more radically, for *essential thought as such*,
for the locus of truth. So far throughout history, the "arena" or "stage"
of thought and truth had always been a fundamentally public one,

out in the open so to speak, and fundamentally communal. On the stage of mythological consciousness the arena had been the common visible natural world, the cosmos, the *truth* of which was *thought* in the guise of polytheistic mythic gods and *daimones*, where "thought" had not yet come home to itself (to the *form* of thought), but still occurred in the form of visionary seeing and phainomenal image. Since the emergence of philosophy, that is, of thought's having taken on the form of thought, its arena was the mind, reason, *nous*, *intellectus*, *Vernunft*, the *theoretical* I, whose ultimate truth was transcendent (the divine intellect). In this arena, utopian schemes had no chance any more.

But no place existed other than the two mentioned ones that Jung could have availed himself of as a new arena. The *place* for a new arena, if it was to be, therefore had to be newly invented and produced. The only way to create this place for the arena was to revolutionize the very *notion* of "place" and "arena" by forcing the entire substance of the previous arena through the eye of a needle and making it reappear on the other side. This eye of a needle was the atomic, lonely individual, the empirical I. And the new arena thereby established or rather fabricated was each person's *inner world*. Here we get the explanation for why Jung had to reject the idea that what he was doing was art and why instead of releasing his ideas into fantasy and truth he had to aim at the human personality.

The new locus of truth that was needed could not simply be discovered and made use of by Jung, the way America was discovered and then settled by millions of Europeans. He had to fabricate it, and fabricate it as he was making use of it. The Red Book says correctly: "There are no paved ways.... We build the roads by our walking" (299a, tr.m.). Those roads are not already existing entities, indeed they are nothing ontological at all. They are logical roads. By the same token we would have to say: "there is no existing inner, not an existing 'the unconscious.'" There was not an unconscious for Jung into which he ventured forth (or could have ventured forth). Only our "superficial observer" could believe that the Red Book records Jung's "Confrontation with the Unconscious," or his descent into "the unconscious" understood as the modern equivalent to the mythological "underworld," for the purpose of his self-exploration (as, however, Jung himself represented it). The inner had to be fabricated by and in the extended process of moving "into it." Jung's "moving into it" is, however, in reality a process of piece-by-piece interiorizing into himself the spiritual world that has come down to us as our cultural heritage and that was previously out in the open, fundamentally communal. And, mind you, into himself not as the theoretical I of old, as mind or existing thought (which *as* "his" individual *thought* would nevertheless still be part of the public, cultural discourse), but into himself as *positive-factually existing* isolated individual, as *Dasein*, as Heidegger would later call it. And in the Red Book we have the record of this extended fabrication and interiorization process.

The construction of the inner is therefore at the same time also the record of the establishment of literal, empirical, civil man (what we call "the ego") *as* the new stage for truth, since the inner is *empirical man's* inner as the new hiding-place of truth, its last retreat.

For the interiorization to really produce this inner "space" as the new arena of truth, it had to produce it as the one and only arena, the true one, truer than the former arenas, the mind and the mythic cosmos. It had to be their successor and replace them. And it could only become *the* arena *for the new essential thought as such* if one succeeded in making the interiorization nearly total (complete) and correspondingly reinvented even the old forms of mythic and religious-metaphysical thinking as deficient ("still unconsciously-projected") forms of the newly established unconscious. The task was the logical translation, translocation of the locus of truth into the inner, the unconscious.

In other words, what was needed was a kind of *Umstülpung* (usually meaning a "turning inside out," but here: "turning outside in") of the whole traditional intellectual world. What had always been either the natural or the mental cosmos all around us had to be reflected into the human individual (in its positivity) to be "reborn," "reproduced," *simulated* there as an inner world in the individual's so-called (and only thereby created) "unconscious." In addition to this turning outside in, it necessarily also had to be fundamentally radicalized in the direction of overmeaning as the union of meaning and absurdity and of the overgod as the union of good and evil (because, to avoid appearing as rehash it had to offer something semantically absolutely unheard-of). Except for this fact it was a kind of internalized mirror-image of what human culture in its so-far known history had produced before as general ("collective") cultural ideas.

What the Red Book is about and what it achieved has its place in the history of thought. It is a grave mistake to see it primarily as Jung's personal self-exploration, i.e., as belonging to his private biography only. No, it was an achievement for the generality. But of course, because its purpose was to interiorize the arena of essential thought or the locus of truth into the subjectivity of the positive-factual individual, it necessarily had to *present* itself as Jung's personal process.[8] What this process may show about Jung's psychic makeup is, however, no more than a by-product. The Red Book circles around big questions of general importance, about the arena of truth, about Meaning and God, good and evil, the ultimate mysteries, etc., and, above all, it establishes empirical-factual man in his literalness as the locus of truth, truth now comprehended as *Urerfahrung* (original experience).

The Red Book has the emphasis on the future, on engendering and giving birth, in common with Nietzsche's *Zarathustra*. But the two books or worlds are set completely apart. What Nietzsche was struggling with was what would be the conditions for the possibility of a new true creativeness as such and of a new tragic age (in other words, truly philosophical problems in the sphere of absolute negativity and generality that involve the very *definition* of man and the world). The Red Book, by contrast, starts out from empirical man as a fixed given, a positivity, you and me. When it talks of engendering and giving birth, etc., it means experiential processes in an always already presupposed positively existing man, the concrete individual as *Dasein*, literal man.

The interiorization process is psychologistic and not psychological because it amounts to a reflection into the positivity of the human being as civil man and particular atomic individual. A psychological interiorization, by contrast, would be a reflection of each psychic phenomenon into *itself*, its release into its truth, and not a reflection into the empirical person. The turning outside in that the Red Book performs involves (a) a shift from the universal (general) to the particular, (b) a shift from the negativity of "spirit and truth" to positivity and literalism (the literal individual, on the one hand, and the factual event of the experience of images, on the other), and (c) a prolonged, step-by-step process of sinking the *form* of thought into the *form* of the individual's *Leiben und Leben*, its existential experience "in the flesh." This is a process which to a large extent has the nature of painful suffering and torment (up to the point of near-madness) and is accordingly experienced as "cruel," a very frequent word in the Red Book. The torment was absolutely necessary to really, and absolutely convincingly, install the new arena in factual, bodily felt existence, in man as mere *Dasein*.

Just as Jung's "roads" which we only build by walking them are logical roads, so "the unconscious" is not a literal region or layer in the psyche of people, but a logical arena which comes about through the logical translation of cultural truths from the public, universal realm of consciousness into the factualness of literal events, namely existential experiences of images as facts occurring in empirical man. This sinking essential thought both "into the flesh" of the atomic individual and into the *form* of factual events is, as positivization and imprisonment, (d) *logically* making essential thought itself unconscious. Following the Red Book's dictum about the paved ways, we have to say: there is not an unconscious. We construct it by expelling thought from the realm of consciousness and make it (re-)appear as images, i.e., as objects or 'psychic facts,' that is, by sinking it from the theoretical I of classical metaphysics into the literal, civil man of modernity. But of course, although it seems paradoxical, since this transformation is a positivization, "the unconscious," which is actually a logical status in which thought or truth and particular contents may exist, must become ontologized and thus give itself out as if it were indeed a part of the personality.

We already heard examples of the individual as the exclusive eye of a needle (e.g., "It is my mystery, not yours. ... You have your own" [246b, tr.m.]. "No one besides you has your God" [329b]. "... first and exclusively and solely in one's own person" [*CW* 7, p. 5, tr.m.]). Now I want to give a few statements from the Red Book that show the idea of interiorization or swallowing. "Within us is the way, the truth, and the life" (231b, note the twisting of John 14:16!). "But you find manifold meaning only in yourself" (273b). "The God develops through the union of the principles in me" (254b, "in me"!).

The *totalitarianism* of this interiorization (its in principle all-inclusiveness) comes out, e.g., in the following quotations. "I am my own priest and congregation, judge and judged, God and human sacrifice" (327a). "You are an image of the infinite world, all the last mysteries of becoming and passing away live in you" (230a, tr.m.). "All [!] the darkness of all [!] former worlds crowds together in you"

(308a). "You are the will of the whole [*der Gesamtheit*]" (337a). "…
that the spirit of the depths in me was at the same time the ruler of
the depths of world affairs" (230b f.).

Apart from these more global and programmatic statements, the
whole process with the sequence of experiences described in the Red
Book is about the step-by-step integration of all sorts of aspects of being,
all regions of the world, all elements and facets of human existence into
the thus created inner. Over long stretches the book appears to be much
like a subjective recapitulation of what one might find in textbooks of
religious and mythological phenomenology (rituals and ideas), with
the only difference that rather than in dry theoretical form this
phenomenology comes in animated personalized story form and is
serialized. Night after night Jung produced a new episode devoted to
a particular religious, mythic, or moral topic on the stage of *the* inner
represented by his inner. Just as *within the show* the I is its "own priest
and congregation, judge and judged, God and human sacrifice" or, with
reference to Luke 2, "the mother" [who conceived the God] *and* "the
careful father" *and* "the shepherd" (284a), *in reality* Jung is, *malgré
lui*, simultaneously producer, stage, all the actors, and the experiencing
(and reflecting) audience of the show.

The inner, which at Jung's historical locus was still entirely
subjective (the human individual was the *medium* [eye of a needle]),
later found its *objectified, technical* realization in television. Television
is also the interiorization of whatever topics are to be found in the
world, but an interiorization no longer into the human subject as
medium, but objectively into mediality as such. Here the inner ("the
unconscious") has finally become absolute, come home to itself. It has
come of age, having completely emancipated itself from a childlike,
youthful dependence on meaning (let alone overmeaning) characteristic
of the first (industrial) phase of modernity, so that for it anything goes
program-wise, as is appropriate for the second ("medial") phase of
modernity. In retrospect we can comprehend Jung's systematically
induced experiences as his private television shows *avant la lettre*, in
which the subjective imagination takes the place of our technical
apparatuses.

The Red Book gives us the rare chance of witnessing "live" the
primary construction of the unconscious in Jung's sense. It might be
tempting to go through the whole book and describe what all is

394   WOLFGANG GIEGERICH

interiorized and how each element contributes to the whole, but as this is not possible here, I will just list a few individual features without much commentary. I must also mention that the *manner* in which the various realities are internalized is very different. One form is a kind of (alleged) seeing-through. Another one is "to kill" the reality to be integrated. Again another is identification. Then there is imaginally living through something, and there is also distancing oneself from it. "I unsuspectingly absorb what I reject" (279b). There is fighting with it, literally taking possession of it, giving birth to it, and planting a seed ....

The socio-political reality of World War 1 is interiorized by being explained as stemming from internal problems: "But people see the outer quarrel alright, but not the one within, even though it alone is the wellspring of the great war" (253n, tr.m.).—"You should carry the monastery in yourself. The desert is within you" (230b).—The Red Book interiorizes the power to murder: the murder of the blond hero (241b ff.). The hero needs to be gotten rid of since he represents the I's ambitious orientation towards goals in the outer world.—"No one knows what happened during the three days Christ was in Hell. I have experienced it" (243b; what an incredible claim!).—The I is identified with Christ and deified after the model of the hellenistic figure of Aion (252a, f.). "In this deification mystery you make yourself into the vessel, and are a vessel of creation in which the opposites reconcile" (252n, quoting *Analytical Psychology*).—"I was smitten by the romantic [i.e., romantic infatuation]. The romantic is a step backward" (263a).—"The knowledge of death came to me that night" (267a).—"I will also not let him go, the Bull God, who once wounded Jacob's hip and whom I have now lamed. I want to make his force my own" (281b).—The capacity of sacrificial murder: "The sacrifice has been accomplished: the divine child, the image of the God's formation, is slain, and I have eaten from the sacrificial flesh" (291a). "But through the sacrificial murder, I redeemed the primordial powers and added them to my soul" (*ibid.*).—"I am just now ... about to reintegrate into my being human all the ancient wisdom that he who thinks in the spirit of this time lacks, in order to make my life whole, rather than entirely casting this ancient knowledge off even more, as the spirit of this time always demands" (253n, tr.m.).—To the soul's question: "Do you want to accept all this [namely: "all the superstitions hatched by dark prehistory," e.g., "dirty pouches filled with teeth, human hair and fingernails, timbers lashed together, black orbs, moldy animal skins"]?" the I responds: "I accept it all, how should I dismiss anything?" (305b, tr.m.).—"I caught the sun ... and carried it in my hand" (287a).—"If I accept the lowest in me, I lower a seed into the ground of Hell. The seed is invisibly small, but the tree of my life grows from it and conjoins the Below with the Above" (300b): here we see the interiorized world tree, the swallowing of cosmogony.—The urge for the totalization of the swallowing also shows *ex negativo* in the statement: "I have overthrown all the Gods, broken the laws, eaten the impure. ... However, I am not ready, since I have still not integrated into myself that one thing which chokes my heart" (285b, tr.m.).

God "was born as a child from my own human soul, which had conceived him with resistance like a virgin" (244b). "I am the mother, the simple handmaiden, who conceived and did not know how. I am the careful father, who protected the handmaiden. I am the shepherd who received the message as he guarded his herd at night on the dark fields" (284a, tr.m.). The experiencing I of the Red Book as the *theotokos*, the origin of the god, who on his part formerly used to be thought of as the origin and principle of the world. But not only the mother of God. The whole manger scene is interiorized.

Especially also Christ is interiorized, in the manner of identification: "You should all become Christs" (234b). "You ... can only overcome the old God through becoming him yourself and experiencing his suffering and dying yourself" (254n). If for Nietzsche man was something that was to be overcome, for Jung it is God who needs to be overcome. We see here the same Nietzschean dynamic applied to a different content. The Red Book blames the Christians for waiting "for redeemers who should take the agony on themselves for you, and totally spare you Golgatha" (254a). "To be Christ oneself is the true following of Christ" (254n). The mystery of Christ was incomplete. It needs to be completed by the individual in his singularity and positivity.

This shows that at the level of Jung's thought we are no longer dealing with the deep image of exemplary man as the "suffering God-man in the shape of a servant" that was so prevalent during the 19th century (examples are to be found in Kierkegaard, Marx, Alexandre Dumas père, Stefan George, Courbet ... ; also Nietzsche's 1889 postcards signed "The Crucified"). The latter was also an identification, but much more psychological (an identification not of literal empirical man with Christ but of the deep image or concept of man that belonged to the generality, which means that empirical man as such in his individuality was not immediately identified, but remained subject to the logic *imitatio*). The Red Book wants a much more concretistic and immediate, an "existentialist" identification: the individuation process. And whereas the 19th century idea did not go beyond man's com-Passion with Christ, the Red Book radically rejects all *imitatio Christi* and sees as the task to be performed through this identification the completion of the mystery allegedly left unfinished by Christ, that is, our surpassing Christ.

Small wonder that all this culminates in the idea of the self (in the special Jungian sense, substantiated as an Other) which is pictorially represented in numerous mandalas. Small wonder—because the whole so-called "experiment," the project of the Red Book experiences, had from the outset been nothing but the *detailed thinking-through of the (dogmatic!) concept of "the self"* (in Jung's sense), a thinking-through, however, not in the form of thought, but in the form of systematically produced imaginal visions and existential fantasy experiences. The self is the Red Book's initial programmatic presupposition (the exclusive focus on the lonely individual) *and* its final goal (the fulfilled self as reflected in mandalas). The self as the concept of successfully *totalized* interiorization into the empirical individual had to be spelled out, to be gone through experientially with all its ramifications and consequences (going through torment, madness, through all sorts of aspects of human nature and all typical places or regions of the world, through hell, deserts, etc.). This is so because the Jungian self is not so much a given entity, not an anthropological constant existing *depuis la fondation du monde*, but the product of its slow and detailed production through the interiorization process, and as such a modern invention and a specialty of Jung's. The self as the image of totality (the swallowed world, or the world of the mind reconstituted as an "inner" one) can come about only as the result of a fabrication process.

And here we see again that the Red Book, as a book devoted to this totalitarian self, is not a book of psychology. The soul is not its real topic or concern, but occurs only as one of the figures or voices in this dramatized thought on its way to fulfilled interiorization. What the Red Book is about is really *a metaphysic of "the self"*—however, a metaphysic of self not for its own sake, but in the service of the ultimate purpose of (after "Nietzsche") rescuing God, rescuing the God concept in and for modernity by giving him a new hiding-place and a radically new definition.

This comes out especially in Jung's Copernican Revolution. From time immemorial man had always expected his *Heil* (heavenly grace, bliss, salvation) from the gods or from God. But the Red Book, in keeping with its interiorization project, reverses this relation. It lets the I ask concerning the gods: "Can I help? Or is it superfluous that a man elevates himself to being a mediator of the Gods? Is it presumption or should a man become a redeemer of the Gods, after men are saved through the divine mediator?" and asserts point-blank, "the Gods need a human mediator and rescuer" (358a). Earlier the Red Book stated: "Thus my God found salvation" (283a). Obviously, in this text "Gods" and "God" are threatened in their very existence. This is a reflection of the post-Nietzschean situation. The experience of the death of God is irrevocable and, as we have seen, had been relentlessly accepted by the Red Book. But on this very basis it starts its rescue and restoration project by means of the production of the self. The atomic individual is not only the one who engenders and gives birth to the new God, but also, radically new, the new Savior, Savior *for* the Gods. An inverted world.

The price for the metaphysic of the self is that it can (a) only come up with an a priori "pocketed" God (as the only way how the [retained, unchallenged] enlightened-nihilistic ego can rescue the religious impulse for itself) and that "the self" is (b) fundamentally dispersed, atomized. Each self is imprisoned within itself, it has its *idios kosmos*. "No one besides you has your God" (329b). There is no possibility of a shared, communal religious truth any more. What now is shared as a public truth is only the nihilistic stance, the modern ego. There is only one single point where, according to this utopia, there might possibly arise a new *communis opinio* concerning the religious impulse, namely solely about this isolatedness itself (the atomized metaphysic of the self): the belief that each individual in his metaphysical loneliness has to develop this metaphysic of the self in himself.

The process recorded in the Red Book, I have to stress again, has not much to do with Jung's personal self-exploration or his "realizing himself." If it is an example of the individuation process in Jung's sense, then individuation means *objectively* the realization, in each individual, of the metaphysic of *the* self, not subjectively each person's *empirical-subjective* self-cognition and self-realization.

THE CONSTRUCTION OF PSYCHIC OBJECTIVITY

Such a radical and totalitarian swallowing by the human individual would inevitably result in an inflation of consciousness up to the point of psychosis—*unless* the human individual would, paradoxically, be capable of reserving itself, distancing itself from its own identification. The subject has to pull itself out and set itself up vis-à-vis all those experiences and external to them. Disownment. But is this not absolutely incompatible with the whole project of a totalized interiorization? How can the essential claim "But if you watch closely, you will see ... that things live your life, and that they live off you. ... Nothing happens in which you are not entangled in a secret manner; for everything has ordered itself around you and plays your innermost" (273a), on the one hand, be reconciled with the move of getting out, on the other hand (irrespective of the fact that "getting out" and distancing oneself may be absolutely vital to avoid going mad)?

But we have to realize that, far from contradicting the radical interiorization movement, this getting out is the indispensable prerequisite for its completion. The "inner" is "inner" only to the extent that it is "in" some Other outside of itself, "inside" a surrounding vessel or empty container. For there to be an inner the I has to pull itself out of itself, out of its own subjectivity, and thereby establish itself as an external I, as "the ego," who is set up as innocent observer, *or* victim, of the experiences. This amounts to a fundamental self-dissociation of the I's subjectivity, its split into two. The interiorization of the cultural world into the inner and the I's getting out of itself are one and the same process.

And this self-dissociation is precisely what on principle happens in the Red Book (which is also why the diagnosis of psychosis with respect to its material is a misconception from the outset). We hear: "Thoughts are natural events" (250b). "~~I would have to consider myself mad;~~ [; It would be more than inconsistent,] if I thought that I had produced the thoughts of the Mysterium" (250n). If "my thoughts" are events of nature, then they have a separate existence totally independent of the experiencing I, which ipso facto is "ego." "[I]t is nearly impossible for the thinker to differentiate himself from his thought and accept that what happens in his thought is also *something outside of himself*" (255n) (my italics).

An earthquake comes absolutely of its own accord. I am precisely not "entangled in it in a secret manner." A tree stands where it stands regardless of whether I see it or not. Sunshine, rain, and storms happen whether I like it or not. By setting up his thoughts as events of nature, the Red Book construes them as objective facts that merely *happen to* the ego as the innocent victim, and by the same token the I *disowns* its own thoughts, giving them the status of Other, of not being his, the way a man might deny being the father of a child. The Red Book thus established a subject-object dichotomy and operates within it and establishes the I as the untouched container of whatever experiences: as ego.

Underlying the dogma that it would be crazy to think that he had created the thoughts is an ontologizing logic, a logic of things, objects. The Red Book reifies the thoughts of the mystery as entities. Its concept of production or making that it applies to thoughts seems to be taken from the model of manufacturing, such as how a cobbler makes shoes. As long as this is one's schema for understanding "thoughts," one is of course right to say that it would be crazy to claim that one produces them. Goethe said about his poetry, that the poems made him, he did not make them. This view seems at first glance to express the same idea as the Red Book's dogma. But Goethe would not have considered his poems "events of nature." As a matter of course they would have been products of the thinking mind for him. Nor would he have denied that they are *his* productions, and that he was their author. He even explicitly considered all his poetry as "fragments of a great confession," in other words, as fundamentally subjective: his self-expression. With his statement about the poems that made him, Goethe points much rather to the inner dialectic of intellectual, poetic, artistic productivity, namely that it is at once subjective and objective, production and product, active and passive. But this dialectic or contradictory logic is reductively dissolved in the Red Book in favor of an unambiguous placing its two moments over against each other (which is of course necessary for establishing the theory of "the unconscious").

In order to get an understanding of this dialectic let us begin with the more accessible example of life. I do not create my life, and yet it is truly my life, my activity of living, my being and staying alive: my breathing, eating, digesting, protecting myself, etc. My life is not an Other that happens to me or is done to me; life is performative: my performing it. It is fundamentally and exclusively mine and absolutely syntonic with me. Its dialectic consists in the fact that only to the extent that my life lives me do I live my life, and vice versa. The moment it is no longer mine, then my life is gone, i.e., I am dead. Life does not have a separate existence outside living organisms and independent of their actively living. It exists *only* if and as long as it is individually *theirs*. Even my death does not come to me as if it were an Other, like the medieval idea of the Grim Reaper. It is my active performance of my very own finishing my life, my breathing my last.

By the same token, although I certainly do not "manufacture" my dreams the way a shoemaker makes shoes, they are nevertheless my dream thoughts, produced by me, only by me. They are thoughts and not events of nature. They are my thinking, i.e., (1) mine and (2) mental productions, inventions, interpretations, results of the living thinking by me as subject, not the appearance of natural events or existing facts. But here again it is also true that to the same extent that I have and think my dream thoughts they have or think me. "Show me your dreams and I tell you who you are" (Freiherr von Knigge, modified), i.e., I can show you what you are thinking deep down, or better: *as what* thinking, what thoughts, you exist. *You!* There is nobody else.

The anger that may "come over me" is nevertheless my being angry. If I kill someone in my rage, it is my raging, my doing, and thus also my responsibility—nobody else's (which of course is contrary to a widespread present-day judicial tendency to consider people not responsible for what they do).

So one has to flatly contradict the Red Book and say that if "the thoughts of the Mysterium" came to me, then I produced those thoughts; it was I who thought or fantasized them. They are not naturally existing things that I merely stumbled across or that mysteriously happened to pop into my mind from who knows where, the way a loose roofing tile may happen to fall on my head as I am walking by. No, those thoughts exist only on account of my *thinking* them (or having thought them), on my responsibility. Conversely, this does precisely not preclude that they are also "objective" rather than ego-concoctions, just as Goethe's poems were, *as* subjective confessions, nevertheless something that "made" him.

To the extent that man is more than animal organism, that is, that he is mind or soul, he IS speculative thinking, the *unity* of himself as actively thinking and of his thoughts (or poems, or fantasies, dreams) that think themselves and as such come to him. This is what thinking is. The Red Book's fatal fault is that it tears this unity (the unity of the soul's logical life) apart and distributes its two moments, subjectivity and objectivity, to two *toto coelo* separate ontologized realities, the I and nature, the I and "the unconscious"—and even against the spirit of language to the I and the self (as a real Other).

In very ancient times poetry was experienced as the singing of the Muse and prophecy as the coming of God's word to or upon the (often resisting) prophet. But psychologically this has to be understood like Goethe's dictum. When we read: "Then came the word of the Lord to Isaiah," then we have to take this whole sentence as a unity, one single soul truth, not as the coming together of two, the word of the Lord here and Isaiah there. Isaiah is Isaiah only as the one to whom the word came, and the word came only to Isaiah. "Isaiah" and "the word of the Lord" are the unfolding of one Biblical reality, one soul reality, one fantasy. The same applies to the Muse and Homer, as well as to the Red Book's I and its "thoughts of the Mysterium." Each is the reflection of the other. They "invent" each other, because they are both figures in the same fantasy. It even applies to Goethe and his poems and to me and my dreams. *Poiêsis*: the Red Book's "myth that sings itself," our "thoughts that think themselves" in *our* thinking them, life's living itself in *our* living it.

We can see the mechanism by means of which the Red Book performs the dissociation of this dialectical unity and reifies the thoughts of the Mysterium as events of nature "outside of the thinker." Repeatedly the experiencing I meets the figures appearing to it with a denial of their reality. It says, for example, "Surely, you are the symbols of the most extreme opposites" (246b, tr.m.), "You are symbols ..." (249b), "I am basically convinced that Izdubar is not at all real in the ordinary sense, but is a fantasy" (282a, tr.m.). But the answer he gets is: "We are real and not symbols" (246b). "But we are just as real as your fellow men. ... you have to accept us" (249b). "You wretch, how can you doubt that I am real?" (262a). According to Jung himself, through these statements he was taught "psychic objectivity, the 'reality of the soul'" (*MDR* p. 183, tr.m.).

We ask: how does this psychic objectivity come about? Or rather, how is it constructed (for it is artfully constructed)? In a most curious way! Jung enters his fantasies with the categories of external reflection, namely with the distinction between fantasy and reality. *Inside* his fantasies he views them from outside and doubts the reality of their figures. It is as if a novel within itself tried to pull the rug out from under its characters as only imagined, or as if we, while dreaming, turned around to the wild animal or to the murderous criminal chasing us and said to them, "you are only symbols of my shadow." Or as if within a dream we doubted that we really were desperately erring through the labyrinthine halls of a building. This does not make sense. Within the Red Book, within a novel, within our dreams everything occurring in them is real. It is only outside the fantasy, when we have finished the novel, have awakened from our dream, and then look at them as psychic material or texts from outside that we rightly say that they are fantasy in contradistinction to reality and a symbol for this or that. But the condition of the possibility of taking figures as symbols when it is a question of *interpreting* fantasy material is that *within* the fantasies, on the immediate, experiential or text level, they are unquestionably real for us. Jung's trick of confounding the level of experience or text and the level of interpretation, the trick of introducing into the fantasies themselves the standpoint of external reflection, means first of all that the subject does not fully enter its own fantasies, namely as I, but only as "the ego." The I that truly enters the fantasy goes under into fantasy and is as such imaginal I, itself an internal part of the fantasy and not "real" in the sense of external reality.

The figures' answer, "We are not symbols, we are completely real" tears, secondly, the very fabric of fantasy asunder. Defining the intrinsic reality of the fantasy figures in contradistinction to their being symbols gives them a positivistic, literal reality that is incompatible with the original imaginal reality that fantasies, visions, dreams naturally come with. It is what construes them as natural objects. Years later Jung said, "we cannot go back to the symbolism that is gone. No sooner do you know that this thing is symbolic than you say, 'oh, well, it presumably means something else.' Doubt has killed it, has devoured it" (*CW* 18 § 632). But here this very doubt is surprisingly the starting-point within this fantasy. The killing of the innocent truth and conviction of the fantasy has already occurred. The spiteful assertion, "we are completely real" thus comes as a secondary reaction to this doubt and cannot really undo it. All it can do is establish a dogma *against* the already attained better judgment, against the higher standpoint of reflection.

The I's doubt is an absolutely essential ingredient of the establishment of the inner as the new arena of truth. The fictions must not be innocently released into their fictional or fantasy character. Their immediate sense of realness must be dissolved. The I is not allowed to simply swing itself onto Pegasus in order to let itself be carried wherever Pegasus wants, in the same way as the Red Book is not freely released into fantasy, as I showed above. This possibility has to be once and for all prevented in the Red Book by the intrusion into the fantasy itself of the critical reflection that the fictional figures are merely "symbols of" (this or that). The purpose of this operation, however, is by no means the undoing of the fantasy world. On the contrary, it has to supply a springboard for an all the more radical fictionalization: critical reflection is needed to prevent this fictionalizing from wasting itself on nothing but fictional *contents* (figures and happenings)—this would be one's riding on Pegasus—and to force it instead to reach out even for *the very form (logical status) of fiction or image as such*, so as to now set it up as absolutely real in a naturalistic or positivistic (already reflected) sense. Fantasy has to *simulate* the character of hard-core reality for its fictions ("But we are just as real as your fellow men" [249b]), much like the new 20th century *technical* medium of movies simulates reality so convincingly as to fool everyone.

The inner has only truly become the new arena of essential thought and truth if in its logical form it succeeds in *simulating* nature, reality, positivity, and is no longer innocently *fantasy*. Only now can we fully appreciate what the Red Book's turn against "spirit and truth" in favor of image aims for ("God is an image, and those who worship him must worship him in the image of the overmeaning"). For some it may seem paradoxical, but the *attack* on the reductive "*nothing but* fantasy" idea IS the fight *against* fantasy proper, against mythic or poetic imagination, and *for* the inner or *the* unconscious as a "second" (reflection-produced) *positive-factual reality* that is supposed to have the same, or rather a higher, dignity than the "first" reality.[9]

This "psychic objectivity," *this* "reality of the soul" is reactionary: set up in contradiction to its own underlying denial. It is not our precious psychological concept of psychic objectivity, but a psychologistic and ideological one. In other words, here we are again at a point where we have to make a clear cut between the Red Book and Jungian psychology. Although the psychological concept of the reality of the soul has, in Jung, its biographical origin in the Red Book experiences, its logical origin for us has to be fundamentally different. Psychic objectivity as a concept of true psychology means that precisely and only as symbols, as dream or fantasy figures, as *not* "just as real as your fellow men," i.e., as logically negative, are they real. And not completely (i.e., positivistically) but psychologically real. But they are symbols and fantasy only if they are *imaginatio vera*: if they are the self-display of the inner logic of actually lived life rather than *active imaginations*, deliberate fantasy concoctions.

The Red Book's notion of psychic objectivity is all the more discredited in one very telling, but bizarre episode. "[O]n the border between morning and evening" (280a) the I in search of the East meets its own opposite, a God coming from the East, Izdubar. The latter is lamed through the encounter with the scientific, enlightened awareness of the I coming from the West. The I wants to help its God, which can happen only in that world that the I comes from, but to expose him to that world would be deadly for Izdubar. So the I comes up with the following solution: it first reduces him to a fantasy that he can carry on his back, and later it shrinks him to the size of an egg that he puts into his pocket. "Thus I enter the hospitable house where Izdubar is supposed to find healing. / Thus my God found salvation. The salvation occurred through his being subjected to the very thing that one would have to consider absolutely fatal, namely that one declares him a figment of the imagination. How often has it been assumed that the Gods have been brought to their end in this way. This was obviously a great illusion: since this is precisely how the God is saved. He did not pass away, but became a living fantasy... But I loved my God, and took him to the house of men, since I was convinced that even as a fantasy he really lived..." (283a, tr.m.).

Here we see the other side of the same coin. The simulation of positive realness has become so certain of itself that it now can be playfully ironized. Before, the predicate "symbol" or "fantasy" had had the function of derealizing a fantasy experience (although only for the higher purpose of thereby precisely establishing "psychic objectivity" in its positivistic sense). Now, the derealization through the reduction of the God to the status of mere fantasy has the opposite function of precisely rescuing the reality of something that is already known to be historically obsolete, and of smuggling it, in this immunized (encapsulated) form, into the world of modern consciousness. Both moves are manipulative, tricks (the Red Book: "Out of love I devised the trick" 286a), and show the presence of (fantasy-external) ego reflection within the fantasy itself. The second one, with its image of pocketing the God reduced to the size of an egg, thanks to its crude literalism also (involuntarily) caricatures the entire Red Book procedure of interiorization or swallowing. The pocketed and only *as* pocketed rescued God has been reduced to a commodity, a Marxian fetish. Again we see that this type of "psychic objectivity" is unsuitable for a true psychology. The rescue of this God is phony because it is only secured at the price of keeping it concealed from the very consciousness into which it is transported (the world of Enlightenment), in other words, by a *sacrificium intellectus*.

The positivistic objectifying is carried to its extreme when it is directed at the I itself, so that the I appears as an Other, a thou or it. "The taming begins with you, my I, nowhere else. Not that you, stupid [in the sense of dull, dumb] brother I, had been particularly wild..." (334b). "I felt my I squirm in pain" (336b). It is inherent in the concept of I that it can never be a "you" and a "brother." Both "brothers" are one and the same. The I is in itself self-relation, self-reflection and not the relation of two separate entities or beings. The phrase "my I" is a meaningless combination of words because it pretends that the one I owns the other I as its property. But by means of it, the uroboric unity of the I, its by going away from itself precisely returning to itself, is split into two. The objectified "you, stupid brother I" amounts to a fundamental disownment, the I's deliberate self-alienation and self-cloning. Both this stupid brother and the I who has such a stupid brother (as an Other) should rightly be called "the ego." The ego is the I's self-dissociation, the split of the uroboric, dialectical unity of subjectivity or thinking into two, who are not really "brothers" because their relation is hierarchical. The one looks condescendingly and contemptuously down upon the other.

Only by the I's having pocketed *itself* and converted the very notion of I into a thou or it, an object, has the opus of swallowing been truly completed: become absolute. And now it again comes out for us that the interiorization is not merely a shoving of things in from outside, but also the reverse (namely externalizing) movement of the I's getting out of its being living thought, subjectivity, the soul's life and its expanding itself to such an extent that it can become the positive-factual container for the whole world (including the I itself) as its object or content, indeed, for the whole world as likewise totally cut off from living thought: as "images" of "the *unconscious*." "Unconscious" means: everything in "the unconscious" is, in its *logical form*, just as "dumb," just as mindless as the ego's "stupid brother": nothing but images to be observed and, on top of it, fundamentally private, by definition incommunicable (even if they are factually communicated, as in the now "published" Red Book). It means basically what we heard from Jung earlier: "There is nothing of conscious structure in these fantasies, they are just events that happen."

We have to see this objectification (disidentification) very critically, because it means the eviction of subjectivity or the soul from itself as living speculative thought and the reifying of what it is concerned with. The epitome of this eviction is the concept of a substantiated self as an Other. But at the same time, we must guard against throwing out the baby with the bathwater. The capability to see oneself objectively, to distinguish oneself from oneself (without reifying!), and to appreciate psychic material in its (true) psychic objectivity is indispensable for true psychology.

* * *

After this analysis of the character of the Red Book itself I want to add a few words about the published versions. Production-wise, both the German and the English editions are superb volumes. Sonu Shamdasani's introduction and annotations deserve high praise. They give valuable, very helpful background information, especially because they also use much unpublished material not accessible to the general public. At times Shamdasani also adds his own critical judgment to his introduction, such as when he rightly notes: "However, from an evidential standpoint, given the breadth of his learning, Jung's own material would not have been a particularly convincing example of his thesis that images from the collective unconscious spontaneously emerged without prior acquaintance" (220a f.). But at other times he simply adopts at face value Jung's self-interpretation, where a critical comment might have been in place. One example: after relating 12-years-old Jung's thought of the destruction of the beautiful Basel cathedral through an almighty turd falling from God's throne on its roof, he continues, "He felt alone before God, and that his real responsibility commenced then. He realized that it was precisely such a direct, immediate experience of the living God, who stands outside Church and Bible, that his father lacked" (194a). This sounds as if there had in fact been "a direct, immediate experience of the living God." Here one would have expected a word of contradiction, especially since this problematic interpretation sets the course for all of Jung's later thinking about "God" and "immediate experience," also for that occurring in the Red Book.

In addition to noting the changes between Jung's "Black Books," the Drafts of the Red Book, and the Red Book itself, to explanatory comments on certain names, symbols, psychological ideas occurring in the Red Book, to parallels between Red Book ideas and passages in Jung's other works, the notes also identify Jung's numerous unreferenced quotations or allusions. Considering the huge number of allusions it is small wonder that a number of them escaped the editor's attention (just two examples, in addition to the above-mentioned "God is an image, and those who worship him must worship him in the image of overmeaning" [229b]: "We asked earth. We asked Heaven etc." [285a]: Augustinus, *Confessions* 10,6; "Bear ye each your own burden" 324a, tr.m.: Gal. 6:2). A few seem not really to the point or even a bit misleading (also just two examples: "the spirit of this time," a phrase expressing Jung's cultural criticism, has nothing to do with the "spirit of the times" quote from Goethe's *Faust* [229n], which is concerned with the totally different topic of historical hermeneutics; "the ram that should bear our sin" [241b, tr.m.]: the more appropriate reference would be John 1:29, because with the Leviticus passage Jung's anti-Christian sting is missed). "*Ecclesia catholica et protestantes et seclusi*

in secreto" (320n) means "the Catholic Church, the Protestants, and
those who are secluded in loneliness [or secrecy]" rather than "A church
both Catholic and Protestant shrouded in secrecy." But these are small
flaws in an otherwise highly scholarly and helpful apparatus of notes.

In the German version, the translation of the English Introduction
and notes is accurate and reads quite well (minor errors
notwithstanding: e.g., omission of "at Herisau" in the sentence "In
November, while on military service ...," [210b German ed., 209a Engl.
ed.]; "The Comparative Study of the Individuation Process" [219a]
does not mean here "Die vergleichende Studie zum..." [220a], but
"Vergleichende Erforschung des...").

It is, however, a pity that, concerning the English edition, in such
a handsome, costly volume the English translation of Jung's text leaves
much to be desired. The translation is unreliable. It does not
consistently convey the sense and feel of the Red Book text. Of course,
not all mistakes are of equal importance, some may be oversights, as
can easily happen, but they all contribute to a loss of precision over
against the original. Often they even distort the meaning and seem to
reflect an insufficient understanding of the particular German
sentences. Just a few examples, mostly from passages quoted above:
"*demütig, unwissend*" is not "unknowingly humiliated" (246b), but
"humble, ignorant." "Höre auf" means "Stop," not "Listen" (342a).
"*Ich will ... sein*" means "I want to (be)" instead of "I will (be)" (231b
and elsewhere). There is a difference between "I would prefer not to
tell you" (275b) and "*Ich liebe es nicht, mit dir zu sprechen*" ("I do
not like to speak with you"), as also between "May each go his own
way" (231b), a hope or wish, and "*Ein jeder gehe seinen Weg*" ("Each
shall [or should] go his own way," an imperative). "*Ich wollte meinen
Gott auf Gnade und Ungnade*" means "I wanted my God at all cost/
unconditionally/for better or worse," but not "for the sake of grace and
disgrace" (289a). In the phrase "*Das Gesetzgeben, das
Bessernwollen...*" the second noun should not be rendered as "wanting
improvements" (231b). "*Bessern*" in this context means to reform
(people!), to improve them (above all morally), and we can be sure that
somewhere in the back of Jung's mind there was the memory of the
relevant passage from *Faust*, "I do not entertain the illusion that I would
be able to teach something to improve and convert people (*die
Menschen zu bessern und zu bekehren*)." In the sentence (and

paragraph) beginning "But if you watch closely, you will see ..." (273a) it should read "that things live *your* life," not "*their* life." It is not completely wrong to translate "*aus dem, was ich emporschaffe*" with "from my work" (267n). But what an abstraction, what a flattening! What the German suggests (a bringing up from the depths through his efforts) is lost. Above I already pointed to the same flattening that occurred with the translation of *Übersinn* as "supreme meaning," but in that case it is also a fatal mistake.

* * *

I began with the Heine quotation: "What a book!" I hope that it has become a bit clearer *what* kind of a book the Red Book is. It is a new publication, but it should not be *Liber novus* for us. Its value is twofold: it provides us with a rich source for gaining insight into the formation of and deeper motivation behind Jung's thought and, beyond Jung, into one episode of intellectual history, and it is a mine of interesting symbolism and theosophic speculation.

C.G. Jung, *Das Rote Buch. Liber novus*, herausgegeben und eingeleitet von Sonu Shamdasani, Düsseldorf (Patmos) 2009, 372 pages.
C.G. Jung, *The Red Book. Liber Novus*, edited and introduction by Sonu Shamdasani, New York and London (Norton) 2009, 371 pages.

NOTES

1. I quote indiscriminately from all versions of the material given in the main text as well as in the footnotes (Black Books, Drafts, etc.), since I consider all of it as being part of the same matrix. Numbers in parentheses refer to pages, the letters "a" and "b" indicate left and right columns, respectively, of the English Red Book; "n" stands for footnote, "tr.m." for "translation modified."
2. Following a suggestion by Greg Mogenson (personal communication), this, Jung's sense of fantasy, could be referred to, in keeping with his idea of "overmeaning" (see below), as: overfantasy.
3. Jung felt that Nietzsche, a classical philologist, misnamed

Dionysus. He suggested that the god in fact experienced and meant by Nietzsche was much rather the Germanic Wotan. Thus on the one hand, Jung is aware of the fact that the name must not be taken at face value. On the other hand, by simply foisting *another archaic* God on him he changes the particular object of reference, but retains the same logic of "external referent" that also prevails in the other case of seeing in the 19th century figure a veritable archaic reality.

4. Whereas "projection" only formally (neutrally) denotes that something (e.g., an unconscious presupposition or prejudice) has been "thrown" out so that it now appears to consciousness "out there" in objectified form, "revelation" is primarily a religious term implying (ultimately divine) authority, truth, and higher meaning.

5. On this whole theme of 19th century utopian thinking and on Nietzsche in particular see especially Claus-Artur Scheier, *Nietzsches Labyrinth. Das ursprüngliche Denken und die Seele*, Freiburg/München (Alber) 1985 and *idem*, "Einleitung," in: Friedrich Nietzsche, *Ecce auctor. Die Vorreden von 1886*, Hamburg (Felix Meiner) 1990, pp. vii–cxxiii.

6. This conception would actually require to have been worked out in terms of a dialectical logic, the logic of sublation. But as a prophetic and religious thinker, Jung is content to dogmatically assert the overmeaning just like that as a fact without bothering to *think* it and this means to get really into it by reconstructing its logical genesis. The way it comes in the Red Book it is an unthought claim.

7. Here we see again how indispensable a dialectical approach would be to give validity to these ideas.

8. My assessment that the Red Book must not be seen primarily "as Jung's personal self-exploration" seems to contradict my earlier statement that "it is utterly private, subjective." The point here is, however, that inasmuch as Jung's task is to *think* the idea of absolutely personal experience, his Red Book takes place on the level of the generality; but since *what* he has to think is the idea of *absolutely personal experience*, the Red Book has to be utterly private.—But the private self aimed at is itself only the *general abstract form* of self: the Red Book more or less completely omits details from Jung's personal childhood and his private life, his relations to his parents, wife, children, his love-life, his personal complexes and subjective emotions, etc., that would be such an essential part of any ordinary analysis.—

This is also a point where I can at least briefly mention that the same dialectic prevails with respect to the question of whether the Red Book is art or not. I showed above why it is not. But now we have to realize that inasmuch as Jung *relentlessly abandons himself* to the thought or fantasy of the utterly private inner in himself (and precisely also to the fantasy that "It is not art!" but the creation of another literal personality in him) and releases this fantasy *of* the *not*-fantastic but *positively real* I into itself, the Red Book is, after all, "art" (of sorts; or literature/philosophy): "art," of course, only on the level of what Mogenson termed "overfantasy." Or, as already hinted at above, it is, *malgré* Jung, indeed "an artistic production rather than an authentic representation of unconscious processes," namely, the artistic production precisely *of* the fantasy of "an authentic representation of unconscious processes." Though this be madness, yet there is method in it. What in Jung was indeed an *artistic production* of this "authentic representation of the unconscious process" is, after Jung, in all the many Jungian analyses focusing on the individuation process no more than a literalizing re-production or better *simulation* of an "authentic representation of an unconscious process."

9. Cf. "It is *psychic reality* which has at least the same dignity as physical reality" (*CW* 15 § 148, tr.m.).

BOOK REVIEWS

Elena Liotta. *On Soul and Earth: The Psychic Value of Place*. London: Routledge, 2009.

REVIEWED BY ANNE NOONAN

This collection explores the intermingling themes of place and migration, and the relationship of psyche and environment. The main body of the work is by Elena Liotta, a Jungian analyst in Italy. The themes she proposes, which include origins, space, place, journey, exile, and loss of identity, are met, echoed, considered, and amplified by nine other contributors. Most allude to Jung or the post-Jungians tacitly or overtly as points of reference. All emphasize the relationship of mind and body—the latter intended in the widest possible sense, from physical soma to cosmos, and including the man-made

Anne Noonan is a psychiatrist and a Jungian analyst. She is a founding member and training analyst of the Australia and New Zealand Society of Jungian Analysts (ANZSJA). Her Jungian training was undertaken under Paolo Aite and Robert Grinnell in Rome where she also trained in group work with Claudio Neri at the University of Rome, La Sapienza. She has written on the interdependence of psyche and environment, including a paper on the effects on Indigenous Australians of British nuclear testing in Australia, which was presented at the "Moruroa e tatou" conference in Tahiti in 2006. A recent essay "Stardust" is published in *Depth Psychology, Disorder, and Climate Change* (Jung Downunder Books, 2009). A former president of the Jung Society of Sydney and lecturer at the University of Western Sydney in Analytical Psychology, she currently works in private practice in Sydney and in remote Indigenous communities in Central Australia.

environment. The mind is intended to be seen through the lens of soul as understood through the complex meaning of the German word "seele" = mind/soul and as homage to Jung's essay "Mind and Earth."

Liotta opens her work by talking of her own personal experience of moving from her birth place and the advantages and disadvantages of such moves, which involve change and loss of culture, language, systems, and custom with consequent attack/rearrangement of past identity.

Her basic premise is that we are extensions of our environment, and Jung's essay "Mind and Earth," a seminal inspiration for the collection, is the backbone of this argument. She cites his aporic advice that every man should have his own piece of land and his personal observations following his visit to America that land/living place quickly induces morphic and behavioral change or, seen less literally, that as humans we have the capacity to interiorize our community and ecosystems.

She discusses the importance of the transitional object and its extension into memory, culture, and language whilst eschewing the conventional psychoanalytic dyad of the mother-child as the sole reenactment of therapeutic temenos. She stresses the importance of the move from "there and then" to the "here and now" as determining factors in psychic development, particularly when there are dramatic environmental changes.

She warns against the seduction of symbol and interpretation as set formulae of psychic engagement and stresses the need for change in points of view on the "journey." She gives a concise short piece on *genius loci* and sacrality of place.

Her understanding and experience of the suffering and disorientation of the migrant, particularly when finding himself as the unwanted guest, scapegoated victim, is evocative. She manages to convey this dangerous world well, and in it I recognized my own work with Indigenous, remote-area Australian Aboriginals. This is a world where a misunderstanding of language or custom may be taken as madness or criminal behavior, where there is a constant need for watchfulness to mitigate against exclusion and shame, where the habitual and reliable no longer exists, where there is possibility of adaptation but with a consequent loss of the ancient and obligations of loyalty to those who have fallen.

Throughout the work Liotta manages to synthesize a number of approaches traditionally considered outside the realms of therapy. She is also opening onto one of the most pressing problems of our times—the plight of the refugee as a casualty of the twin-headed monsters of war and climate change. She implicitly proposes the problem of the individual analyst in dealing with such enormous collective problems.

Liotta is extremely well informed culturally, politically, and psychologically. She takes us on a number of journeys where we explore real and fantasy places and spaces with her. There are some light side trips—including a delightful vignette of a child, Ariosto, and trips to the moon.

Whilst reading her I sometimes had feelings of being in a maze, a labyrinth of unknown and lost things. On pondering this experience I believe my response reflected a kind of parallel process of the subject matter, the journey to the unknown with attempts to find one's bearings, the impotence of the analyst in certain grave situations with a consequent tendency to fall into excessive didactism. For me the thread of Ariadne, and understanding and clues to my reactions, came with the chapter on the foreign patient (I myself was analyzed in Rome) where Liotta helps us recognize the foreign, alienated parts in all of us.

Indeed as Liotta says in a premise to this chapter "in the end it all came down to an unexpected return"—an enantiodromia occurs when she is working with the foreign patient. Here she is on home ground—transference with words and images of desire and memory arrive, familiarity and engagement are reclaimed.

I found the other nine contributors stimulating—to coin an Italianism, "each one more beautiful than the other." Their task is, by and large, easier than the first part of the book. Metaphors and containers are offered with fairly clear ideas on remedies for contemporary displacement—of course how to bring them into practice is another question!

Whilst the majority of contributors describe particulars of place and space, the journey is implicit in each as images of containing bodies are offered. Afflictions of alienation are observed: the mechanization of the body and the loss of its ancient role of symbolic actor and physical representative of the creation story (still seen in some traditional cultures), the analysis of contemporary cities producing fragmentation, isolation, and individualism.

We are offered particular ways of considering these contexts, the natural world as *succus vitae* of our existence with its supportive background of many species, the vegetative and mineral world—those elements and creatures who encourage and sustain us imaginatively and physically.

We look at the garden as a safe place where human needs and emotions can be tolerated and worked with as well as the need for recognition of dark places and the use of inherited, ancient knowledges to mitigate and work with them. The inspirational motto for a community in the Italian village of Pari is Carlo Levi's observation "the future has an ancient heart."

Of particular use for therapists were the discussions on:

"Places of Healing": the importance of the setting and the comfort and well being of the operator/ therapist, particularly if working in repressive conditions, and the need to remain faithful to the space as a place of healing.

"Exile an impossible return?": Therapists are being increasingly called to work with refugees, be they political, affective, environmental /climate, or economic. The recogniton of the manifold reasons and outcomes for the flight and the response of the flyer/fleer are essential.

Last, but not least, I would like to comment on the chapter "The earth, the song, the symbol" on the importance, *inter alia*, of one's own song, the healing song, the reflection and day dreaming of one's experience as it occurs "that incessantly creates and recreates the earth." The background song as an example of the fusion of movement and place, action, and repose is indeed a most therapeutic insight. Bruce Chatwin's book *Songlines* is cited. Again to be taken as metaphor or to know one is again in the realm of aporia. If taken literally, *Songlines* is an overidealization of the lives of Australian Indigenous people who have suffered and continue to suffer enormously from internal displacement, loss of land, language, and custom. Nevertheless, I have observed that Indigenous people are at least aware of their losses and will prefer to seek help where possible from their traditional healers, the songmen and women who still know the stories that heal them through their creative singing of the land.

This is a generous book which at times risks excessive density and "overfill." It is at its best when it allows space for imaginative engagement with the reader. It is at all times informative, generally thought-provoking, and multi-layered, emerging as a response to the pressing contemporary issues of a global world.

REFERENCES

Bion, W.R. "Bion's Brazilian Lectures." Sao Paolo. 1973.

Derrida, J. "Deconstruction Engaged." *The Sydney Seminars*. 1999.

Noonan, A. "Psyche and Environment." *Landmarks*. Published ANZSJA, 2000.

Noonan, A. "The Effects of Colonisation." Lecture. IAAP Conference. Cambridge. 2001.

Noonan, A. "British Nuclear Tests in Australia and their effects on Indigenous people." Lecture. COSCEN, Moruroa e Tatou, colloque de Papeete, Tahiti. 2006.

Noonan, A. "Stardust." *Depth Psychology, Disorder and Climate Change*. Jung Downunder Books, 2009.

BOOK REVIEWS

Virginia Apperson and John Beebe. *The Presence of the Feminine in Film*. Newcastle: Cambridge Scholars Publishing, 2008.

REVIEWED BY ELENORA BABEJOVA

Virginia Apperson and John Beebe describe their collection of essays on the feminine in film as a "montage" that takes a "patchwork" approach to show different faces of the feminine. For Apperson, the aim of these reviews is to show how the feminine has been rejected and might be reinstated. Movies are an excellent medium to reflect on the feminine, mirroring conscious and unconscious aspects of their time and culture. Film is a field for the different types of the feminine, including those denied by the patriarchal culture, to find their expression; a place where they can morph, shift, and contort.

This approach invites questions about what the archetypal feminine means in the contemporary world and whether it has been entirely emptied of meaning by feminist deconstruction in recent decades. Where does cultural and social conditioning end and archetypal qualities begin? The Western world has split apart the feminine and the masculine as irreconcilable opposites; yet anybody

Eleonóra Babejová, Ph.D., is training as a Jungian analyst at ISAPZURICH. She explores imaginal spaces through writing, movement, and ritual. She is a poet, dancer, and teacher who has worked with adults and teenagers with learning disabilities.

who knows the Chinese symbol of Tao knows that it is impossible to separate yin and yang. Can one even talk about the feminine without relating it to the masculine, and vice versa?

Although the authors clarify that the feminine belongs to both women and men, in most of the twenty-four reviews in this book the feminine is embodied in female characters, mirroring how characteristics attributed by our culture to the feminine have been mainly carried by women. As Apperson points out, patriarchal assumptions about the feminine become internalized "to form unconscious working models." Patriarchy is understood as "an unconscious cultural complex that insists on asserting power" at the cost of anything else. The patriarchal worldview wrenches apart opposites and neatly organizes the "masculine" and "feminine" into a binary model of positives and negatives. Reading through these reviews is a good opportunity to contemplate how much each of us carries such assumptions in our deep psyche, in spite of ideological commitment to equality. The reviews highlight some of the recurrent motifs defining how the feminine has been seen in western civilization: vulnerability, body, relating and feeling/emotion.[1]

Vulnerability in the feminine is the ability to risk spontaneous emotional life and remain true to one's feeling values without unnecessary defenses (which are part of patriarchal masculinity). However, this vulnerability can be either weakness or strength, depending on whether it is supported by other feminine and masculine aspects in the psyche. In *Wide Sargasso Sea*, for example, the vulnerability of the young feminine becomes her downfall. The heroine of this moving film lacks a strong ground, the connection to gut instinct that would give her the basic confidence in valuing herself just the way she is. Lacking supportive mothering (the divine mother-daughter bond represented by Demeter-Persephone), when rejected by the patriarchal masculine, she tragically lapses into madness. Furthermore, as Apperson stresses, apart from good mothering, the young feminine needs "paternal and fraternal safeguards," in other words, the support of the masculine. With no such support available, her vulnerability becomes the place of disintegration.

Beebe refers to Gareth Hill's distinction between the dynamic and static masculine and feminine, a four-fold model that captures the dynamic interaction between the feminine and the masculine and the movement of one into another. Hill's conceptualization makes it easier to take a step back and start thinking outside the stereotypical gendered opposition, found even in Jung, between the feminine (women, Eros, feeling, anima) and the masculine (men, Logos, thinking, animus).[2]

Yet even the neat symmetry of Hill's model derives from a binary model. Most people today toss coins six times (heads or tails) to divine a hexagram from the I Ching. However, the ancient yarrow stick method yields entirely different mathematical probabilities, capturing more exactly the qualitative difference between the archetypal masculine and feminine (the old yang and old yin in I-Ching, corresponding to Hill's static masculine and feminine). The old yang line transforms into its opposite three times more often than an old yin line.[3] In other words, the old yin is far more resistant to change than the old yang. For me, this implies we cannot construct symmetric models of masculine and feminine. Perhaps Jung's sense of a basic difference between anima and animus came from an intuition of this essential asymmetry even though the concept of animus was born from his own need for symmetry.

Similarly, Toni Wolff's four structural forms of the feminine psyche come into mind. They work as pairs of opposites (mother-hetaira, medial woman-amazon), setting up a four-fold model that functions similar to Jungian typology. "Mother" and "medial woman" correspond to Hill's static feminine, and "hetaira" and "amazon" fit with the dynamic feminine. Yet the reality of the feminine is hard to capture in any model. Perhaps a refusal to be categorized is its most pronounced quality. Perhaps it is this elusive quality that is so unnerving.

The feminine needs to retain its feisty quality in order to hold its ground with the masculine. As the review of *Wide Sargasso Sea* points out, the feminine has the potential to be "impetuous and effervescent, eager to love and to be loved, wildly expressive and profoundly sensitive." This quote captures accurately what Hill calls the "dynamic feminine," which is most at risk in the patriarchal culture. There are other kinds of feminine (inertia-laden, preferring life to recreate itself in the same cycle) that have supported the long rule of patriarchy, as Marion Woodman also points out.[4] The dynamic feminine has been denied in patriarchal culture by both men and women. It is projected onto others as feebleness, weakness, emotionality, and madness. During the patriarchal era it was mainly projected onto women and others who did not fit a preferred model of heroic strength that never displays weakness or emotion.

Jane Alexander Stewart's guest review of *Silence of the Lambs* shows how vulnerability can also be a different kind of strength that comes from one's ability to remain open and related to the other, no matter how dark the other is. Clarice Starling exemplifies a new female heroine who stays true to her feminine values in a role where the heroic masculine approach is preferred and even seen as the only possible way to success. She is not an action/adventure character. She considers feelings an asset, easily handles emotions, dares to reveal herself, is receptive and responsive. She goes deep within herself and retreats to feeling images as a source of strength. Yet she is also conscious of the boundary between revealing herself and allowing emotional exploitation. She uses her "feminine orientation as inner authority" and manages to descend to the truly Stygian underworld to meet evil—a realm that the patriarchal authority chooses to keep hidden, locked away and dealt with only across many safeguards which don't allow any true communication. The level of sheer terror experienced when watching this movie indicates how different this kind of strength is and how difficult it is for us to conceive of it as strength rather than foolish risk-taking.

It is this "feminine" vulnerability that is the most denied, diminished, and unintegrated part of the feminine in our culture. As Apperson points out, the patriarchal masculine is intolerant of difficult feelings and painful experiences and wants to keep in control so that they don't surface. Feeling is either ridiculed or pathologized while a heroic ideal of strength is idealized. We still find it hard to imagine that being receptive and yielding does not mean being weak, and so we fail to see the yin is just as valuable and strong as the yang. Yet in the Taoist world view, the yielding quality of the yin does not mean disability, weakness or servility as we tend to see it in the western world, but purely an attitude that "allows one to prevail against odds with minimum wear and tear."[5] The idea of dynamic equilibrium and right timing is central, so yielding in the right moment is a stronger action than fighting and pushing.

Beebe's review of *Crouching Tiger, Hidden Dragon* offers an interesting example of vulnerable "yang–femininity" in the young heroine Jen. She manages to move against the patriarchal rules of her culture and manifests the initiative and autonomy of the "dynamic feminine." Beebe uses the interesting term "female puer" to denote Jen's ability, as a martial artist, to move into a realm that her culture defines as male.

The body as an aspect of the feminine has also been suppressed by the patriarchal worldview. The body and its pleasures are strongly present in the *Wide Sargasso Sea* through its lush Caribbean paradise-like environment, the heroine's sensuality, and the gutsy wisdom of the indigenous women, who stand in contrast to the patriarchal and rigid world of the English. It is also present in *Chocolat* in the seductive and healing power of chocolate that changes the Christian patriarchal milieu of the village ruled by the domineering patriarch. It is there in the unruly and spontaneous behavior of Jane Austen's girls in *Pride and Prejudice*. *Monsoon Wedding* presents us with a sensual environment and with a "splendidly corporeal" feminine, in Apperson's words. In all of these movies we see women heroines grounded in their bodily selves and female ways of knowing.

As Apperson says, the female body has been objectified, corseted, and anesthetized in western (and other) cultures. But I would argue that the body has been anesthetized for both men and women, although in different ways. The body has been seen as another unruly and chaotic Other that needs disciplining, whether in a "feminine" corset, an overdeveloped Terminator-like musculature, or the rigidity that follows from the inhibition of spontaneous expression and breath. Both men and women need to rediscover the vitality locked in their bodies.

Pleasure cannot ever be fitted into the corset of political correctness.[6] Only in North America can chocolate be described as "a tad sinful" (as in the review of *Chocolat*). There is a strong anti-pleasure tendency in North American culture that betrays an underlying Puritan cultural complex.[7] Pleasure is simply not something that is appreciated or valued, although it might grudgingly be allowed when it does not interfere with efficiency. Perhaps the fear is that one might drown in the dark sea of chocolate/pleasure as in the Sargasso Sea. The idea that what gives us pleasure must be sinful is another consequence of the denial of the body and its need for loving care (rather than corseting discipline).

Conversely, the fascination with the "extraverted sensation panorama of contemporary India" seen in *Monsoon Wedding* derives from a western fascination with its opposite, a kind of unruly, emotional, bright-colored feminine. Locked in the often sterile uniformity of urban environments, we seek a sensuous capacity for pleasure in idealized exotic settings. If we took this manifestation of the feminine out of its culture and transplanted it into a western context, I suspect that it might not fit our tastes. As Beebe observes in his review of *Vertigo*, as the audience we have to recognize that, at least in this film, we prefer the patriarchal elegant anima style of the heroine to her more colorful and "florid" personification that looks like a "vulgar theater mask."

Similarly, while the heroine of *Dangerous Beauty*, a highly paid courtesan, is portrayed as bright, delightful, and authentic, it seems to me that she is idealized by Apperson in the same way as she is envied by the "good women of Venice," as the independent "bad" woman who can have forbidden delights that "good wives" may not—freedom from their husbands' domination, pleasures of body and mind, excitement and adoration of powerful men. The fact that she serves men for her livelihood and her pleasure is subservient to theirs makes it hard to conceive of the heroine as a "self-realized woman," even if we watch the movie as just a cultural fairy tale.

The patriarchal worldview affects men as well. Many of the male characters in these films lack the capacity for feeling without lapsing into familiar defenses that are mostly based on a hierarchy of patriarchal values. For instance, Beebe's review of *Brokeback Mountain* makes me wonder where is the potential for men to relate and feel their own vulnerability. Beebe talks about "the inexplicable unadaptedness of men in relationships." The failure of male characters to connect with their anima figures "symbolic of a deeper aspect of [their] suffering" is also captured in his essay on "The anima in film" which offers different aspects of this archetypal mediatrix of the masculine psyche. In Beebe's review of *Letter to an Unknown Woman*, the heroine fully devotes herself to "mirror the masculine" up to the point of self-destruction, for a man who is unable to relate to her or the anima that she represents.

Perhaps the key lies in the archetypal Great Mother and her "orgiastic emotionality". The male character in *Wide Sargasso Sea* is terrified of being drowned in the overwhelming sensuality and emotionality of the Great Mother whether symbolized by the Sargasso Sea itself or the uninhibited and, to his eyes, uncontained and embarrassingly uncivilized island ways of his young wife. In *Marnie,* the main character reveals the background of the "demonized mother", the "resistant unconscious" that can be held in "active imaginal dialogue." Conversely, in *The Queen,* the "Queen" (in her capacity as the "mother of the nation") is challenged to find the right feeling attitude in the critical moment of Princess Diana's death. The unmothered mother is unable to provide the necessary grounding for her daughter in *Wide Sargasso Sea.* Does the return of the shadow feminine mean simply lifting inhibition from powerful emotions? How does one deal with the fear (carried by both women and men) of annihilation by these wild waves of feeling?

What we are talking about above is the free flow of feelings. Beebe notes a shift in men's consciousness with movies like *Kramer vs. Kramer,* "the first men's weepie," where this flow is allowed. He sees this new category of male heroes as a response to the appearance of tough female heroines. Apperson expresses the hope that as more men learn to "cultivate their emotive skills", "emotional privilege will be shared by both genders in and outside the cinema." I think we also need to cultivate the capacity to be with whatever emotion (image, idea) arises, without evaluation. It is a simple "being with" similar to the way of a mother with her infant and comes closest to what Erich Neumann termed "matriarchal morality," an unconditional affirmation of the wholeness of being which exists prior to the patriarchal moral codes.[8] If mother complex can inhibit spontaneous expression of feeling and mark the way we use our feeling function in our life,[9] application of masculine differentiation too soon squashes new birth before it can reveal its potential. Once we are able to suffer the heat of emotions and digest them, we can cultivate a more differentiated feeling function which weighs and sorts and goes far beyond merely permitting feelings to flow. Allowing "orgiastic emotionality" may be less threatening when there is a mode of being modeled for us that can also work with the released emotions rather than simply becoming their victim.

To suffer and endure has been seen as the path of the archetypal feminine. In patriarchal culture women carry men's unconscious feminine side and thus their feeling function. Yet this does not mean that feeling belongs exclusively to women. Apperson notes the feminine on the face of the male character in *The Lives of Others.* To me his appeal comes from staying in his human integrity and allowing his vulnerability to co-exist with his masculinity. He also possesses a strong Eros which is not the prerogative of any particular gender. Here again thinking within the categories of the feminine/masculine duality does not seem to clarify for me but confine. Can one say that integrity or being human are feminine or masculine qualities? And perhaps it is not a mere question of reclaiming feeling but of opening to Eros, the primordial force that pulls us into engagement. It requires that we reclaim our imagination and longing and enter a space where there are no ready answers. This is where Gogol ends up in *The Namesake*.

The challenge of staying deeply human, engaging with feeling in everyday relationships, both in its introverted and extraverted aspects, is beautifully shown in Beebe's review of *Rhapsody in August*. He weaves together visual imagery with the feeling landscapes of the characters, showing how the natural and psychic landscapes reflect each other. Beebe's final reviews on the soul of the world demonstrate how anima figures in films (such as Anna in *The Heart of the World*) call attention to the factuality of the world dying because it is losing its heart. As Beebe points out, Anna becomes the *anima mundi*, at present incarnated in cinema itself as she offers liberation from the literal perspectives that our culture has been increasingly locked in.

Both Apperson and Beebe point out the transformative potential of film. They see movies as the most readily available fairy tales of the 21st century. We are affected by their images, stories, and symbols as if experiencing a fairy tale. Beebe describes "auteur films" as a kind of active imagination by directors who use film as a medium for the creation of consciousness (for example, *Schindler's List*.) He emphasizes that mass audiences are in pursuit of transformative films. Yet, paradoxically, if this pursuit becomes yet another form of passive consumption, the transformative power of film will be reduced.

Despite their fascinating range, intellect, and dynamic quality, some of Beebe's reviews can be challenging for a reader who is unfamiliar with film studies terminology. Similarly, he sometimes uses typology as self-explanatory, which may not be obviously the case. However, this is a thought-provoking and worthwhile book. Apperson and Beebe's reviews capture the many faces of the feminine and at the same time create a space to manifest in her own ways. The book shows the richness of the feminine and its interactions with the masculine in many different layers. The book gives us many paths to become thoughtful about what we have seen and offers different ways of looking beyond the images. It is a rich invitation to reflect on what moves us and why. And if we allow the images to move us, we are participating, in Beebe's words, in a "healing rite of vision." That movement connects us not only with our feminine soul but also with the soul of the world.

NOTES

1. I was curious to find that in contemporary feminism which has gone through deconstruction of the patriarchal discourses the realm of the "feminine" (used in parentheses by the authors) is seen as "negotiated through the figure of the mother, the body, the void and the image…" Grieselda Pollock, Victoria Turvey Sauron, *The Sacred and the Feminine, Imagination and Sexual Difference* (New York: I.B. Tauris & Co Ltd., 2007), p. 7.

2. Gareth Hill, *Masculine and Feminine: The Natural Flow of Opposites in the Psyche* (Boston & London: Shambhala, 1992), p. 21-2. Aspects of the static masculine: positive—order, rules, systems of meaning, hierarchies of value, theories of truth, standards, persona; negative—order for its own sake, rigid expectations, dehumanizing righteousness, complacency. Aspects of the dynamic feminine: positive —transformation, "altered states," imagination and play; negative— chaos, emptiness, despair, depression, alcohol and drug intoxication, hysteria, identity diffusion. Aspects of the static feminine: positive— organic, undifferentiated wholeness, uterus, the cycles of nature, being and self-acceptance; negative—smothering entanglement, inertia, routine, stuporousness. Aspects of the dynamic masculine: positive— initiative, goal-directedness, grandiosity, linearity, technology; negative —inflation, rape and directed violence, willfulness, life-taking technologies, disregard for nature and ecology.

3. Rudolf Ritsema, Shantena Augusto Sabbadini, *The Original I-Ching Oracle* (London: Watkins, 2007), p. 13.

4. Marion Woodman, Robert Bly, *The Maiden King: The Reunion of Masculine and Feminine* (New York: Holt and Company, 1998), p. 27-8: "The old petrifying mother is like a great lizard lounging in the depths of the unconscious. She wants nothing to change. If the feisty ego attempts to accomplish anything, one flash of her tongue disposes of the childish rebel. Her consort, the rigid authoritarian father, passes the laws that maintain her inertia… The effort of centuries to kill the

dragon has ended in the worship of mother in concrete materialism. The sons and daughters of patriarchy are, in fact, motherbound."

5. Thomas, Cleary, Sarta Aziz, *Twilight Goddess: Spiritual Feminism and Feminine Spirituality* (Boston: Shambhala, 2002), p. 75.

6. Siri Hustvedt wrote a delightful essay about our very human tendency to objectify what we desire and the hopelessness of any projects trying to make our fantasies of others correct, proper, good, or "psychologically healthy." Siri Hustvedt, *A Plea for Eros* (New York: Picador, 2006), pp. 45-60.

7. See Manisha Roy, "Religious archetype and cultural complex," in Thomas Singer, Samuel L. Kimbles (ed.), *The Cultural Complex: Contemporary Jungian Perspectives on Psyche and Society* (Hove and New York: Brunner-Routledge, 2004), pp. 64-77.

8. Erich Neumann, *The Child: Structure and Dynamics of the Nascent Personality* (London: Maresfield Library, 1973), pp. 90-93.

9. Marie-Louise von Franz, James Hillman, *Lectures on Jung's Typology* (Putnam, Connecticut: Spring Publications, 2006), pp. 137-145.

BOOK REVIEWS

Avis Clendenen. *Experiencing Hildegard: Jungian Perspectives*. Chiron
Publications, 2009.

REVIEWED BY URSULA WIRTZ

Avis Clendenen, Ph.D., D. Min., is a pastoral theologian and the
Sister Irene Dugan Scholar in Spirituality and professor of religious
studies at Saint Xavier University in Chicago, where she works at the
interface of psychology and theology. Her book is about a wise old
woman and a wise old man (Hildegard von Bingen and C.G. Jung),
and it is not utterly clear which of the two the author sides more
passionately with.

Avis Clendenen writes with remarkable clarity about "one of the
most prolific female authors of the medieval era" (p. 32). She attempts
a synthesis of the spiritual insights of Hildegard "who could have been
a twentieth-century depth psychologist" and their relation to the
theories of Jung, "[who could have been] a twelfth-century mystic/
scientist/ artist" (p. 39). Hildegard's life and creative work is understood

Ursula Wirtz, Ph.D., is a Jungian training analyst with a diploma from the C.G.
Jung Institute Zurich (1982). She received her doctorate in philosophy from the University
of Munich and a degree in Clinical and Anthropological Psychology from the University
of Zurich. She is currently on the faculty of ISAPZURICH. She has taught at various
European universities and published on trauma, ethics, and the spiritual dimension of
analytical psychology. She is also involved in the training of fledgling Jungian groups in
Eastern Europe and is a member of the ethics committee of the IAAP.

as an embodiment of what Jung meant by individuation. Avis Clendenen's goal is to bring the contributions of Hildegard and Jung into our contemporary life, in order to guide those who are on some spiritual quest in search of the soul. The creative genius of the courageous, intuitive, and visionary medieval nun, who called herself "God's mouthpiece" and "little trumpet" (p. 14), shines through her multidisciplinary work. We learn about her spiritual awakening and her "illuminations", her rich legacy, including a theological trilogy, two scientific works, and the first known morality play of the West, as well as composing seventy-seven liturgical songs, biographical works, poetry, letters, and medical treatises. Her vast knowledge of nature and the curative powers of plants and herbs, and her elaborations on holistic healing made her "the first published female doctor".

Throughout the whole book theological, historical, and psychological scholarship are intertwined. Avis Clendenen uses the theoretical framework of Jungian psychology, for her "a sacred science," (p. 3), as the lens through which she views "the Sybil of the Rhine". The author believes that Hildegard and Jung were guided by a similar *spiritus rector*, that both were deeply concerned with "the inbreaking of the divine" (p. 74), and attempted "to heal a Christianity in crisis" (p. 179). She sees Hildegard and Jung as companions on the via *negativa*, sharing the experience of the dark night of the soul that ultimately brings about spiritual transformation, the awakening of one's consciousness to the infinite and a sense of wholeness. For Jung, Hildegard was "a verdant inner ancestor, scientist, and seer" (p. 165).

Both experienced the pressing need to name and to attend to their inner visions, to remain true to their own myth at any cost. The author believes "that Hildegard could easily have been the poster woman for the invention of modern depth psychology and a good friend of Carl Gustav Jung." (p. 36)

Avis Clendenen's portrait of Hildegard, a "female warrior", and in her own words, "a feather on the breath of God", is artfully blended with contemporary reflections on how we as individuals can make this global world a better and wiser place to live in, more "live-giving and life-saving" (p. 170). This book is not only about Christian theology, mysticism, and female visions; it is also an urgent plea for a global awakening, a coming to consciousness in a time of peril, a call to face our "existential estrangement" (Tillich) from what we are meant to be.

Just as Hildegard related her prophetic insights to contemporary theological and political issues, Avis Clendenen also views the personal and the spiritual as truly political, an utterly feminist stance. Consequently, many of Clendenen's secondary sources and "almost archeological endeavor of Christian feminism" (p. 125) are feminist scholars from different fields. She discusses Hildegard, a "master at gender inversion" (p. 107) in medieval religious culture, and Hildegard's relevance to the contemporary dialogue with reference to gender and religious leadership today. We are introduced to Hildegard's theology of the Feminine and how her visionary works established a foundation for creative thinkers in our century, "developing an eco-spirituality based on the interdependence of all aspects of the created universe." (p. 147)

On her own account, Avis Clendenen—like Hildegard—makes a strong point of our interconnectedness and the interdependency of humanity and creation, prompting us to reconnect through Hildegard with our own feminine roots and our own creative imagination to lend us wings for the future. Meaningful quotations from Hildegard, Jung, Jacob Böhme, the scriptures, various writers, and some beautiful poetry of Mary Oliver are woven into the text, so that the book is easily readable and also provides a wealth of resources to revisit for further contemplation and reflection.

The seven chapters of the book cover major themes of Hildegard's thinking, writing, and her visionary interior life. Each chapter relates her insights to major tenets of analytical psychology, particularly to the reality of the soul and the life of the unconscious. They illustrate how the wise woman and the wise man ponder the same ideas. The first two chapters place Hildegard's work into historical context and give us a better understanding of the shaping events of her life's journey. They also address the reasons for her reemergence into contemporary consciousness.

In Chapter three, "Confrontation with the Unconscious," the author explores Hildegard's and Jung's experience of "The numinous in the guise of pathology" (p. 73), an encounter which did not lead to splitting, fragmenting, or becoming psychotic but was perilous and painful. They shared the belief that" suffering is an endemic part of the human, spiritual experience." (p. 74) Hildegard often reported the suffering associated with her visionary experiences, but her "debilitating symptoms evaporated each time she released what was inside her" (p. 72). Just as Jung thought of the approach to the numinous as the real therapy, Hildegard shows that "*even the very disease can take on a numinous character.*" (p. 73)

Some colorful plates from Scivias, an illuminated manuscript of twenty-six visions, are included in the book. They reveal the depth of Hildegard's cosmological visions of man at the center of the universe. In the approach to the numinous as a liberation from the curse of pathology and in the shared conviction of the reality of evil, discussed in the fourth chapter of "The Interplay of Light and Shadow" Jung and Hildegard meet. Her acute sense of the dark side of life and human's destructiveness foreshadows Jung's notion of the personal and collective shadow.

In search of further meeting points, Avis Clendenen examines in depth the seven references to Hildegard's work found in seven volumes of Jung's *Collected Works* and situates them in the context of his thinking.

In chapter five Avis Clendenen explores Hildegard's pro-female orientation to Christian theology and claims that "the feminine divine" in her visions "foreshadowed the important role that the feminine plays in Jungian depth psychology." (p. 108) Like a trickster Hildegard transcended the limits imposed on her as a female. Clendenen notes with empathy how courageous it was of Hildegard to address publicly a corrupt negligent clergy, and a misogynic tradition of the church, where women were "first in order of sin and second in order of creation." (p. 64)

The author devotes the sixth chapter to a "churchy" (p. 127) discussion of Hildegard, as a religious and ecclesial leader with a very independent mind, who exercised extraordinary influence, following her own myth. Drawing on Hildegard's positive evaluation of the feminine and female nature relative to the Divine, she raises the provocative question of gender and female religious leadership in the life of the church today. (p. 119) Avis Clendenen's effort to raise to consciousness a previously submerged strand of the Christian tradition and to remind us that Hildegard's timeless voice "continues as an urgent cry for a new future whose destiny we hold within us" (p. 152) is acutely felt throughout the book.

Her study culminates in the final chapter with Hildegard's compelling ecological theology and spirituality, the famous concept of *viriditas*, the greening power, a green life force, intimately connected with creativity, love, and fecundity, elaborated in her *Book of Divine Works*. The author claims that Jung's appreciation of *viriditas* (Jung's use of "green" and" greenness" appears twenty times in the index to the *Collected Works*, as Clendenen points out) relates to his understanding of the interpenetration of psyche, nature, and spirit.

In dealing with Hildegard's "green vision of humanity in relation to the cosmos" (p. 146), one can feel the core concern of Avis Clendenen, the plea for personal, societal, and clerical transformation and the search for "twenty-first-century guides among us who can illuminate contemporary ways of being monastic" (p. 170) and help us to move out of our half-consciousness.

She encourages the reader after each chapter to what she refers to as "Application" to engage in guided exercises such as journal writing and meditations that deepen psychospiritual insights and personal transformation. With her emphasis on deepening one's experience of one's own interior life, she is rooted not only in spiritual, catholic contemplative practice but also in analytical psychology, viewing experience as sacred. Her pastoral identity flares fiery, in her probing questions and passionate recommendations of subscribing to "Chittisters's 'Monastic Way', a monthly publication with daily reflections to help you walk through life whole and holy" (p. 172) to online organizations like "Vital signs" or "State of the World" from the Worldwatch Institute, and to use the existing road maps to "find our way back to a Sabbath from all the busyness that fills our days" (p. 171). These are meant to challenge us as individuals, help us to wake up just as Hildegard did with her teachings, to force us to take responsibility for the condition of our inner world and to make choices that contribute to the "transformation of our postmodern, fragmented, unprecedented, turbocharged life." (p. 181)

There is one point I want to take issue with. Clendenen's statement, that "Hildegard is a model of an Animus Woman" (p. 139), may be meant by the author's eye as homage to Jung, an example of renewed appreciation for animus in woman, but in my understanding this sounds like reductionism, similar to a recent biographer's attempt to explain her visions and divine inspirations as caused chiefly by migraine attacks. Putting Hildegard, the prophet of cosmic wisdom, into the Jungian Procrustian bed of animus theory, does not do justice to her, a woman, who transcends dualism, and speaks with a voice that reminds us of the wisdom literature. I do not think, "It is fair to say" that her affiliations with men surrounding her, "mentors, secretaries and superiors... constellated the creative animus in Hildegard." (p. 138) Such derivative understanding does not give justice to the sophianic wisdom this liminal, prophetic woman embodies. As a "Sister of Wisdom", she deserves to be seen in relation to Sophia, the embodiment of wisdom and love. Sophia, Lady Wisdom, appeared also in the last of her illuminations, *"The end of Time"* when she was over 70 years old, but Wisdom had a prominent place in all her works and visions. She praised *Virtus Sapientiae* also in her songs. I was therefore more than surprised that "wisdom" and "Sophia" did not make it into the otherwise very helpful Index of Clendenen's book. As a Jungian, I had also wished for a more searching treatment of the complexity of Hildegard's Mandala symbolism, a deeper consideration of her spiritually rich images of egg, circle, cosmic wheel, and cosmic Tree, together with her highly differentiated symbolism of colors.

Apart from these lacunae, Avis Clendenson's book is an example of "greening", a confessional passionate engagement with what has seized her in the work of Hildegard and Jung. Reading her text, I received the deep impression of an erotic bond between the writer and her subjects, the old wise woman and the old wise man, who model for us the connection to the numinous within. *Experiencing Hildegard from a Jungian Perspective* meant for me revisiting those who were "not the graspers but the grasped" (p. 168), possessing the great treasure of religious experience, "that has given a new splendor to the world and to mankind". (C. G. Jung, *Collected Works* 11, para. 167)

BOOK REVIEWS

Pia Skogemann. *Where the Shadows Lie*: *A Jungian Interpretation of Tolkien's* The Lord of the Rings. Chiron Publications, 2009.

REVIEWED BY RUTH LEDERGERBER

At the outset let it be said that Pia Skogemann not only meets with flying colors the expectations that she evokes with the subtitle, *A Jungian Interpretation of Tolkien's* The Lord Of The Rings, but also the expectations that are attached to the book's title itself, *Where the Shadows Lie*. The author demonstrates how exciting it can be to reflect on the personal and collective shadow. She also reflects in the final chapters on the extent to which Tolkien's book still addresses our contemporary *Zeitgeist* and the shadows of the last two hundred years. Although she stresses that she considers Tolkien to have had no political intentions in mind in his work, she nevertheless attaches at the end of her book an engaged effort to look at shadow sides in a political context completely in the sense of C.G. Jung. Outer events and outer shadows always correspond also to internal affairs, and vice versa. As long as the collective shadow remains unconscious, we all remain a part of the events and are therefore participants in the collective shadow (and the collective guilt). I shall return to this point later.

Ruth Ledergerber is a graduate of the C.G. Jung Institute and has a private practice in Zurich, Switzerland. She is currently a training analyst at ISAPZURICH.

First, a word about the author. Pia Skogemann is Danish, has studied Comparative Religion, and has worked as a psychotherapist and counselor from a Jungian perspective in private practice for more than thirty years. She is a founding member of the C.G. Jung Institute in Copenhagen, and has taken an active role in the *Journal of Jungian Theory and Practice*. She has been publishing her work for 25 years and has written on fairy tales, dreams, individuation, archetypes, and the feminine in twelve books. In itself, these numerous areas of interest indicate an engaged person who is at home in religious, cultural, and spiritual areas, both in the here and now and also in the fantastic, enchanted world of possibilities.

The book discussed here is her first work in English.

At the outset, the author says that *The Lord of the Rings* polarizes and triggers two opposing reactions. The one type of reader struggles mightily and then with a shrug of the shoulders puts the book to the side, while the others are enthralled from the first sentence and remain gripped to the end. Pia Skogemann, who has read this book again and again for thirty years and understands it ever anew, belongs to the latter type. I confess that I belong to the first and was therefore restrainedly curious to see if the author would manage to arouse interest also outside of the fandom. She was successful.

The author interprets Tolkien's masterpiece from two perspectives, among others: The Shire, the place where things happen, represents for her the territory of consciousness as the uppermost level of our soul. Its boundaries are the furthest edges of consciousness. In this beautiful, quiet space live the four hobbits, whom she looks upon as the ego in all its possible aspects and in its various developmental stages.

This is the point of departure for Pia Skogemann's impressive description of the individuation process.

In the first ten chapters she is able, figuratively speaking, to create a *Perpetuum mobile* or to sketch an enchanted house in which friend and foe, little ghosts and powerful forces, live and interact. It is a spacious structure that is, at the outset, occupied by the four Hobbits who initially—still speaking figuratively—are barely familiar with two rooms and have set these up as a cozy and comfortable home. Windows and doors are tightly closed. Then, a first door to an adjoining room is opened by Bombadil, which introduces movement into the tranquil scene. The remaining rooms on same floor are occupied by personal shadow figures.

There is, however, still plenty more space. On other floors live, unbeknownst at the outset, other beings from other lands, even kings and nobles, as well as ordinary folks and all their shadow figures. In the basement and attic, hugely powerful, archetypal forces are waiting for action, and outside the door lies the unexplored landscape. By the end of the book not only are the entire house and its residents turned upside down during a productive developmental process, but also the area around the house transforms itself into a garden, a park, which the Hobbits can shape and fence in. As such, it stands for an individual and collective consciousness process. There remains, however, another infinitely larger unexplored space beyond the Shire that embodies the collective unconscious.

Pia Skogemann manages brilliantly to unlock Tolkien's dense book and to illuminate the images behind the book's images.

As it plays out everywhere, so it also happens in this house: The Hobbits are unwillingly pulled out of their rooms by the pulsating life outside. Barely have they left their fortress than they are both oppressed by their own shadows and overwhelmed by powerful forces. They are forced, as are the many other creatures in the book, into a learning process and suffer the major feelings of abandonment, aloneness, emptiness, helplessness, envy, and desire, and they are oppressed, harassed, and terrorized by dark powers. Yet the good archetypal figures, who support love, togetherness, loyalty, friendship, and tenacity, also stand ready to help them. The author refers readers to, among other things, the embodiment of the world soul and the figure of the old wise one. Together with the great shadow, he is described as Mercurius Duplex and acts as such throughout all of history.

The author illuminates Tolkien's figures. She clarifies what stands in the background, what is alluded to, and when she lifts Tolkien's images up she shows the omnipresent symbolic character: A river-crossing is an irreversible event, entering the gloomy forest leads deeper into the unconscious, facing the present chaos stand the fortresses and landscapes in the form of mandalas that can ever again establish order.

Every movement inside this house and in its surroundings triggers a further movement, and like a magician, Pia Skogemann reveals that

the whole story of *The Lord of the Rings* can be seen as a dynamic process
in which everyone's individuation process affects the whole. Although
this story takes place outside of ordinary space and time, that is, in a
dreamlike world of fantasy, the author extends the boundaries, in an
almost playful fashion, also to our human world and, like the master
Tolkien himself, dissolves the boundaries between inner and outer. In
a most vivid and convincing way, she shows that an individual person's
individuation process has an effect on the collective individuation
process of humanity as a whole and vice versa, and that every
development is also a molting in which the old must be shed in order
to allow for something new. Thus the author shows that all the main
characters of the story go through a process of maturation. The four
Hobbits, for example, return to their rooms changed and only then
are enabled to occupy the whole house, to recognize the potential for
conflict, and to resolve immediate problems. In that they now
continuously integrate their shadows and give form to the archetypal,
they have become able to distinguish between what is to be included
in their existence and where to set boundaries, either porous or closed.
They have gained new friends, lost old ones, and can now use the house
and park for the benefit of the community. They have become whole.

The Lord of the Rings basically reflects the male psyche, the author
claims. Nevertheless, inasmuch as a psyche means both male and female
sides, Pia Skogemann finds the feminine in Tolkien's novel in green
nature, in the holistic way of thinking, in the tender relational ability,
and in the meaning of community. She compares the situation to those
fairy tales that begin with: "Once upon a time there was a king who
had three sons..." As in these tales the youngest son comes home with
a bride and the female can assume a place, so it also happens in Tolkien
that women are found by the protagonists and marriages take place.

   This section seems to me to be the weakest point in the book. The
question occurred to me if Pia Skogemann could not grant that her
revered Tolkien was, in relation to the feminine, completely imprisoned
in the masculine *Zeitgeist* of the early 20th Century, wherein there can
be only a single Jeanne d'Arc because several of them would be
unbearable. However, this writer is not qualified to pursue this point
further because she does not belong to the fan club and has not read
The Lord of the Rings.

Pia Skogemann's book becomes most exciting when in the final chapters she bends her bow with a light touch toward the present. She writes about the collective developmental process and the powerful shadows of the last centuries that still heavily burden our shoulders and await a collective process of recognition.

Although *The Lord of the Rings* is not a political allegory, the author directs readers repeatedly back to themselves and their history with the question of where our collective western Predator is hidden that could make possible the exploitative colonialism, the inhumane capitalism, a Holocaust, and that continues to make possible today a debasing, racist attitude.

What kind of shadow is it that brought whole nations to identify with the Self, to become overwhelmed by the Self and inflated all the way to a narcissistic, grandiose Self?

In *The Lord of the Rings*, it is Mordor who embodies the shadow side of the last two centuries and who accompanies us still today. Neither the common good nor human rights nor the world as a whole are of any concern to him. In narcissistic grandiosity all of our internal feelings of abandonment and emptiness, of anxiety and darkness, can be evaded and lead inexorably to inner and outer destructiveness.

The author pleads for dynamic processes: that, as with the Hobbits it is not possible to maintain the status quo which hinders development, integration and becoming conscious of the fearful darkness is elementary for the individual and collective development toward wholeness. She puts forward the hypothesis that *The Lord of the Ring* fascinates precisely because it addresses the collective unconscious of our time. Since we all belong to our *Zeitgeist* and its shadow, we intuit and sense in this story something that moves us but is not yet conscious. For a long time, the West rested on linear progress and only today realizes how much of life and of what is essential for life was thereby killed off.

She observes an interesting reversal that she has found not only in *The Lord of the Rings* but also in other fantasy novels such as *Momo, The NeverEnding Story,* and *The Golden Ball.* Whereas in the old fairy tales the devil or evil power sought to exchange gold or power for the soul—that is, the material for the spiritual—in today's stories the virtual, the perfect, and the controlling try to devour the individual. This presents itself as chaotic, untamed, and wild. The immaterial threatens matter. As examples the author mentions the invisible grey eminences in this world and the tightly organized Mafioso forces. In contrast, the spiritual shows itself as material, in that today the issue is to preserve the little globe of earth and in the globalized world to set up firm, visible signs of community.

Pia Skogemann reflects on whether children and youth today are any longer being taught about good and evil as before from the Bible, or whether the questions about good and evil are not being much more answered for them in fantasy fiction, whose masterpiece is *The Lord of the Rings*. Since time immemorial, fairy tales have shown that heroes can only successfully achieve their goals if they set out on a quest, confront their fears, integrate their shadows, and unswervingly persevere. The fantasy novels distinguish themselves from the traditional fairy tales insofar as their heroes, while needing to develop an individual approach, also move within a community context, find themselves within a network of friendships, develop a sympathy for the whole, and concern themselves with the welfare of the community. In this fashion, these novels reflect the spirit of our times, its collective development, and its threatening shadows.

To work on "the ring" as Tolkien develops this concept in his book is the task of our time. It is a personal and also a collective process of individuation. Pia Skogemann names this task that of developing the archetype of the Anthropos or Compassion.

BOOK REVIEWS

Naomi Ruth Lowinsky. *The Sister From Below: When the Muse Gets Her Way*. Hanford, California: Fisher King Press, 2009.

REVIEWED BY DAVID H. ROSEN

*T*he Sister From Below: When the Muse Gets Her Way* by Naomi Ruth Lowinsky is an original and very creative form of active imagination. Lowinsky has written a healing memoir as dialogue with her muse (soul and shadow). It's a type of ethno-autobiography and the author adds an aesthetic depth that only a mature Jungian analyst could do, who is also a poet. She explores and transforms inner delusions and demons, which qualifies her for "One Bright Pearl" (I've come to realize that Shin Buddhism is similar to Jung's psychology).[1] Naomi Lowinsky exhibits an openness that is rare among published Jungian authors.

Lowinsky begins her volume with an Introduction *On the Muse* with Robert Graves' view of the muse as "The White Goddess or...

David H. Rosen, M.D., is the McMillan Professor of Analytical Psychology, Professor of Humanities in Medicine, and Professor of Psychiatry and Behavioral Science at Texas A&M University. He is the author of over one hundred articles and eight books, most recently, with Joel Weishaus, *The Healing Spirit of Haiku*. He is currently completing a memoir *Lost in Aotearoa: Finding My Way Home*.

Mother of All Living."[2] She posits that the muse is a soulful "trouble-maker" who is "essential to the creative process" and one's "imagination" and "deeper life."[3] Lowinsky is also a scholar and she discusses the nine muses of the ancient Greeks. She then writes of multiple manifestations in which the muse has visited her: stirred up creative ferment, unearthed her voice as a poet, filled her with "stories of ghosts, mysteries, erotic teachings, [and] the old religion."[4] In addition, the muse appeared as an inner figure, a fleeting memory from early childhood, an ancestor, an image from myth, dream, culture, dead poet or ghost from the personal past. She sums it up, "The muse makes weird things happen, excites your passions, moves your soul, lifts the veil on other realities [and] can send you into agony or ecstasy depending on her mood."[5] She even includes a male muse, which is an example of how Lowinsky stretches your mind. She imagines her book as a mandala; a flower with each petal representing a different experience in her life.

This book contains ten unnumbered chapters. The first, *The Argument*, includes "The Woman You're Not." Lowinsky records "Making a shambles of my life," when she "married too young and for all the wrong reasons."[6] The muse ripped Naomi out of that world through divorce and she was a single mother with young children. She then stopped, listened to the muse, went back to school, and became a psychotherapist as well as a Jungian analyst. The muse appeared as a soulful poet, but the wild and dangerous shadow kept disturbing her psyche and way of life.

The 2nd Chapter, *When the Sister Gets Her Way*, encompasses "A Soul at the White Heat," which is an example of the courageous dialogue that takes place between Naomi and her sister from below. Lowinsky's dialogue with her muse takes us through her childhood in Florence, New York City, and Princeton (where her father worked as a humanist along side of Einstein). Finally, she settled in Berkeley in 1957, when President Eisenhower sent troops to Little Rock to facilitate desegregation, the Russians launched Sputnik, *Howl* was published, and Alan Ginsberg visited the San Francisco Bay area. As a teenager and young woman, Naomi loved poetry and read Walt Whitman and Emily Dickinson.

Through a poem called "Red Fire," published in 2000 in *red clay is talking,* Lowinsky writes about being possessed by ghosts who demanded babies and of her long ago dissolved first marriage and lovely children. In the university she studied English and persuaded her professor to let her translate a German short story by Herman Broch (imprisoned by the Nazis as a political prisoner in 1935) as her Senior Honor's Thesis. In this story she read "Can poetry change the world?" Lowinsky then had the image of the poet as a musical instrument to be played by the muse. Following this came a dream of her dying grandmother Oma, which led to a later poem. Undergoing a deep depression, while ill with high fevers, she became conscious of death. The myth of Inanna (recounted by Sylvia Perera in *Descent to the Goddess*)[7] helped her to "die" and be reborn as her fledgling true self. Studying Jung's psychology and "Longing for Poetry to Arrive,"[8] the return of the feminine helped her to move closer to her real self.

Chapter 3, *Lady of Florence: First Muse*, recalls the seeds of Lowinsky's early childhood in Florence. On revisiting Florence as an adult she knew that she was "home in my heart."[9] She owns the poetic seed in herself, "Everyone is a poet when they are four!"[10] Naomi answers her own question "How does one get to the bottom of oneself?"[11] She returns through poetry to the lost nurse of a childhood in Florence.[12]

In Chapter 4, *How Eurydice Tells It*, Naomi shares that Orpheus was embodied by her father as his myth and she owes her love of Eurydice and Orpheus to him. The Orpheus of her childhood was her father's Renaissance version, that is, Orpheus could charm the wildest animals, the most unruly children and settle them down as well as get them to sleep. Even the terrible King and Queen of the Underworld were charmed by Orpheus' music on the lyre. Eurydice hardly made an appearance in her father's version. She "was pale, disappearing into darkness, a sexless angel."[13] Through active imagination Lowinsky characterized Eurydice as an independent empowered woman who breaks from her father, and her muse helped transform her rage at father and Orpheus. Jung assisted Naomi by honoring that "Emptiness is the great feminine secret."[14] She lauds Hilde Doolittle who was her poetic mid-wife bringing her back to life from the dead.

Chapter 5, *A Grandmother Speaks from the Other Side*, concerns her muse's focus on Clara, her father's mother who died in Westerbork, a concentration camp in Holland. Lowinsky wrote about her family history of the Shoah in her book *The Motherline* (1992). However, it was the tragedy of September 11th that pulled her into darkness and led to contact on the internet from a cousin named Sjoera. This catalyzed a visit to Holland where she saw a list of Dutch Jews who had been killed by the Nazis, which included four Lowinskys. She and Sjoera, sharing the same last name, wept together in Anne Frank's house. Lowinsky then takes us into moving melancholic holocaust poetry by Nelly Sachs, the Nobel Prize winning Poet of 1966, and Paul Celan. She shares Sachs' "Chorus of the Orphans" and Celan's "Black Milk..." Both poets understandably suffered from severe depression following World War II and after Celan committed suicide, Sachs died of cancer on the same day Celan was buried. I have deep respect for Naomi Lowinsky for writing a poem "muse" to bring her grandmother Clara, who died of cancer in Westerbork, out of the darkness of death into the light of rebirth.

Old Mother India, Chapter 6, involves Lowinsky's visit to India as a young mother and her return thirty years later with her daughter Shanti who was adopted at birth in India. Her poem for Shanti "We return to Mother India" is lovely. Naomi's transitory identity as a novelist was no more as the culture of India blew her mind and she entered a trance-like state. It also opened her up to the archetypal realm.[15] She asked and answered her own question: "What to do after that but become a Jungian?"[16] Lowinsky writes of the Hindu "Elephant Blessing" as an example of synchronicity as well as a link to the heart, breast milk, and orgasm. The night after the elephant blessing Naomi and Shanti both dreamt of rainbows.[17] Another moving synchronicity was finding Esther, a woman who had worked in a no longer existing missionary hospital when and where Shanti was born. The uncanny thing was that Esther looked like an Indian woman that Shanti had dreamt of years ago. Naomi ends this chapter with the story of how poetry began in India. The first Indian poet was Valmiki who saw, "A pair of love birds singing in a tree...suddenly the male bird falls, hit by a hunter's arrow. The cry of the female seeing her lover fall, filled Valmiki with the sound and rhythm of lyric poetry."[18]

Sappho at Midlife, Chapter 7, is about the erotic muse. Lowinsky informs us that 2600 years ago, "a young woman's education included the arts of love as well as of poetry, dance, and music."[19] Sappho knew "the archetype of sacred sexuality."[20] Lowinsky was tempted by her muse, "Every woman needs to know the passion for the goddess."[21] Naomi is "fierce" about her work and writes a poem for Sappho titled

"Midsummer passages at 12 and 50."[22] Lowinsky addresses a woman's blood, both the first (menarche) and the last (menopause) in a new way and encourages women to "feel your hot flashes."[23] Her muse claims it's "erotic to make poems."[24]

Chapter 8, *Helena is a Root Vegetable*, concerns visiting Dionysus' homeland of Thrace. Naomi was invited to go to Bulgaria when Dan, her second husband of 20 years, contacted her from "the plain of Thrace."[25] Earlier Lowinsky had been primed to go to Thrace when Tedy Petrova, the Jungian analyst from Bulgaria, informed her that "Thrace was not only the home of Dionysus, but also of Orpheus and Eurydice!"[26] The root of Mandragora is Helena's root, which is eaten in the spring in nature as part of an ancient ritual to cause "a spell for love, for marriage."[27] Naomi recounts an arduous and exciting trip into the Rhodope Mountains to the birthplace of Dionysus from the Great Mother herself, who then couples with her son to give birth to Orpheus.[28] Dionysus and Orpheus are torn to pieces as both are "shamanic figures."[29] Naomi sees a mysterious creature who appears to be a Centaur in the mountains.[30] She imagines that it is "Cheiron [Chiron]...a great teacher of healing and the tutor of Aesclapius."[31] She realizes that Cheiron is her "spiritual ancestor as a Jungian, for Cheiron is the archetype of the wounded healer and sacred to the discipline of analysis."[32] The epiphany of this chapter is Naomi's visit to the cave of Orpheus where he came to get his Eurydice out of the underworld.[33] Though fearful, Naomi goes down into the cave, which is "womb, tomb"[34] and feels "the darkness...the cold of the rock...and then she is "reborn into light...one in the darkness with Orpheus, god of poetry, and one in the darkness with Eurydice."[35] "I have exploded into many joyous pieces like Dionysus, god of green things, growing into sunlight."[36] Lowinsky clearly participated in "an initiation mystery."[37]

In Chapter 9, *The Book of Ruth: Naomi's Version*, Lowinsky examines the mystery of her name. Her Jewish parents called her "Ne ohm." When she was divorced with three children the man who became her second husband called her "Na oh mi" and she responded to the Hebraic pronunciation on a soul level.[38] A dream of standing up to a patriarchal Rabbi allows Lowinsky to give voice to a spiritual Jewish independent woman through Ruth and knowledge of "the loss and redemption of the feminine principle in Judaism."[39] She learned about the "secret forsaken god story" by reading a book by an Israeli Jungian analyst Rachel Hillel.[40] Naomi realized that her name came from the Canaanite people and meant "lovely one" and "delight of the gods."[41] Lowinsky's namesake Naomi and her family left patriarchal Judea and went to Moab, a Canaanite land where the goddess was still worshipped. Based on this story of "ancient Naomi," Lowinsky meditates on *The Book of Ruth* and writes her own version with the assistance of her muse.[42] The ancient Naomi's husband, Elimelech, died and due to harsh conditions and cries from Elimelech to return, the widow Naomi returns to Bethlehem, Judea with Ruth who knows the secrets of the feminine. Boaz was struck by the beauty of Ruth and her erotic ways and they married. He died shortly thereafter, but Ruth gave birth to Obed. This baby boy was fed by the miracle milk of Naomi who became his nurse. Obed was the father of Jesse and Jesse was David's father. So these children all honored the goddess.[43] The spirit of Ruth lives on in the Kabbalah as Shekinah and in Gnosticism as Sophia, and in hermetic alchemy as Soror Mystica.[44]

The book ends with Chapter 10, *Beloved of the Beloved*, which begins with the "male muse" and how the masculine is needed for all creativity. In "A Ghost of My Youth" Naomi rekindles memories of her old friend and lover John Gardner.[45] John was with Naomi after she left a conventional marriage and set out to find her true self. He supported her early development as a poet. She quotes two lovely poems of his which include these lines: "The history of the forest in her eyes/ she falls into me /[and] My spirit drifted into skies of you."[46] Then Lowinsky separates the male muse from John, her brilliant father, and all men. Naomi realizes that the male muse "understood [her] journey to unearth the goddess [and] was the first to support [her] creativity and wildness."[47] Naomi recounts that her second husband Dan is "a male who loves the goddess, knows how to worship her, joins her in all the worlds [and] is in touch with [the] Spirit Ancestor [or the male muse]."[48] Naomi recounts a dream in which "a shaman…came to her and showed [her] older brother stones…then, he had even older sister stones. He showed [her] that when a stick was drizzled in menstrual blood, and used to write with, it would burst into flame."[49] She realized that this was the male muse initiating her into her own writing process from the deep feminine. In a return trip to Bulgaria, Naomi and Dan venture to the Rhodope Mountains in order to visit the temple of

Dionysus at Perperikon in Thrace where there was an oracle in ancient times that rivaled Delphi in Greece.[50] A final act of courage is Naomi's heroic climb up and into "the Womb of the Rock," when Boris the guide says, "You are the first woman to get into this cave."[51] Her male muse allowed her—not Dan—to be in the cave where the sun god marries mother earth.[52]

In closing this book and its review, I am moved to say that this healing memoir is a mandala as the author said at the beginning. Naomi Ruth Lowinsky has written a remarkable autobiography about her individuation process, that is, her journey toward wholeness. I wholeheartedly recommend this original and immensely creative book—it's one of a kind and full of integrative honesty.

NOTES

1. Taitetsu Unno, *River of Fire, River of Water* (New York: Doubleday, 1998), pp. 115-117.

2. Naomi Lowinski, *The Sister From Below: When the Muse Gets Her Way* (Hanford, CA, Fisher King Press, 2009), p. 1.

3. *Ibid.*

4. *Ibid.*, p. 3.

5. *Ibid.*, pp. 2-3.

6. *Ibid.*, p. 5.

7. Sylvia Perera, *Descent to the Goddess* (Toronto: Inner City Books, 1981).

8. *The Sister From Below*, pp. 32-36.

9. *Ibid.*, p. 40.

10. *Ibid.*, p. 38.

11. *Ibid.*, p. 48.

12. *Ibid.*, pp. 45-48.

13. *Ibid.*, p. 59.

14. *Ibid.*, p. 65.

15. *Ibid.*, pp. 97-101.

16. *Ibid.*, p. 101.

17. *Ibid.*, p. 111.

18. *Ibid.*, p. 119.

19. *Ibid.*, pp. 123-124.

20. *Ibid.*, p. 126.

21. *Ibid.*, p.129.
22. *Ibid.*, pp. 133-135.
23. *Ibid.*, p. 136.
24. *Ibid.*, p. 139.
25. *Ibid.*, p. 144.
26. *Ibid.*, pp. 145.
27. *Ibid.*, p. 145.
28. *Ibid.*, p. 149.
29. *Ibid.*, p. 150.
30. *Ibid.*, p. 151.
31. *Ibid.*, pp. 151-152.
32. *Ibid.*
33. *Ibid.*
34. *Ibid.*, p. 157.
35. *Ibid.*
36. *Ibid.*
37. *Ibid.*
38. *Ibid.*, p. 163.
39. *Ibid.*, p. 167.
40. Rachel Hillel, *The Redemption of the Feminine Erotic Soul* (York Beach, Maine: Nicolas-Hays, 1997).
41. *The Sister From Below*, p. 171.
42. *Ibid.*, pp. 170-176.
43. *Ibid.*, p. 179.
44. *Ibid.*, p. 180.
45. *Ibid.*, p. 185.
46. *Ibid.*, p. 186.
47. *Ibid.*, p. 187.
48. *Ibid.*, p. 190.
49. *Ibid.*, p. 192.
50. *Ibid.*, p. 194.
51. *Ibid.*, p. 198.
52. *Ibid.*, p. 199.

TO LEARN ABOUT THE MYSTERY OF THE SOUL
READ JUNG'S RED BOOK

TO ENCOUNTER THE MYSTERY OF *YOUR* SOUL

ARCHETYPAL DREAMWORK

FIND OUT MORE

"**Submit a Dream**" free at our website.

UPCOMING WORKSHOPS

**The International Association
for the Study of Dreams
Annual Conference**
June 27-July 1, 2010

**Kripalu Center
for Yoga & Health**
Weekend Workshop
November 26-28, 2010

WE OFFER

• One-on-One Therapy (available via Phone Sessions)

• Five-Day Dreamwork Retreats in northern Vermont

• Programs and Online Classes at

The Center for Archetypal Dreamwork
Visit our website for our full course schedule

Books about Archetypal Dreamwork

*The Deep Well Tapes * The Secret of the Pomegranate * Hubris of the Heavens*
by Marc Bregman * *Sex, Trauma and Conjunctio*
by Marc Bregman with Christa Lancaster's *Vessel*

The History of Last Night's Dream by Roger Kamenetz
as featured on **Oprah's** Soul Series

North *of* Eden

**To learn more, call Susan Marie Scavo or
Bill St.Cyr ~ 802.229.4785
www.northofeden.com**

Announcing the release of a new film about Jungian analyst, author, and lecturer, Lyn Cowan

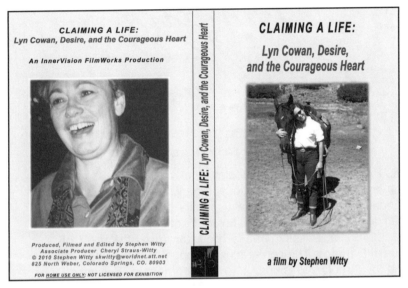

CLAIMING A LIFE:
Lyn Cowan, Desire, and the Courageous Heart

An InnerVision FilmWorks Production

Produced, Filmed and Edited by Stephen Witty
Associate Producer Cheryl Straus-Witty
© 2010 Stephen Witty skwitty@worldnet.att.net
825 North Weber, Colorado Springs, CO. 80903

FOR HOME USE ONLY; NOT LICENSED FOR EXHIBITION

CLAIMING A LIFE: Lyn Cowan, Desire, and the Courageous Heart

CLAIMING A LIFE:

Lyn Cowan, Desire, and the Courageous Heart

a film by Stephen Witty

Claiming a Life: Lyn Cowan, Desire, and the Courageous Heart

a fifty-one minute documentary about Dr. Lyn Cowan and the process of individuation; about allowing Eros, god of desire, to be part of one's life, summoning the courage to follow his lead, and living life with integrity.

The film weaves interviews with *Spring* author Dr. Lyn Cowan (*Masochism*, 1982, *Tracking the White Rabbit*, 2002, *Portrait of the Blue Lady*, 2004), highlights from her recent public lectures on *Eros* and the racehorse *Seabiscuit,* and scenes from the films *American Beauty* and *Seabiscuit.* The filmmaker, Stephen Witty, Ph.D., is a Jungian Analyst in Colorado His previous film, *Where We Are: Jungian Analysts in the 21st Century,* is also available from *Spring Journal and Books*

Claiming a Life:
Lyn Cowan, Desire, and the Courageous Heart,

available from springjournalandbooks.com for
$39.95(USD) plus shipping and handling.

A LITERARY FEAST IN NEW ORLEANS
NOVEMBER 17 - NOVEMBER 21, 2010

The Pirate's Alley Faulkner Society, Inc., a (501) (c) (3) non-profit literary and educational organization, is pleased to announce that it will once again sponsor its annual multi-arts festival, **Words & Music, A Literary Feast in New Orleans.** The 2010 Humanities theme is **The Literature of War & Collateral Damage**. The conference will open on November 17 and run through November 21, with programming designed for multiple audiences: students and scholars, developing writers, established authors, readers, and patrons of the arts.

Tim O'Brien, Winner National Book Award

The five-day festival will include daily **Literature & Lunch** sessions, evening entertainment, film events and live New Orleans music events.

Among important speakers will be National Book Award winner, **Tim O'Brien**, author of the moving account of the soldier's experience in war, **The Things They Carried**, and other books and stories on the Vietnam War.

This year for the first time the Faulkner Society is inviting academics, scholars, psychologists, physicians, music critics, film directors, attorneys, artists, and environmental activists to register and present papers during **Words & Music, 2010** on topics related to the 2010 theme. For suggested theme topics for papers, guidelines, and registration details, see opposite page.

For complete information on **Words & Music, 2010** visit the web site of the Faulkner Society: **www.wordsandmusic.org** or e-mail us: **Faulkhouse@aol.com**

Call For Papers: The Literature of War & Collateral Damage

The Pirate's Alley Faulkner Society cordially invites the submission of papers on **The Literature of War & Collateral Damage** for **Words & Music: A Literary Feast in New Orleans** November 17 -November 21, 2010. **Suggested topics:**

The Psychology of War:

As Old as Humanity: Why is War the Longest Running Show in Literature?
Romance & War: Why Do We Associate War with Romance in our Storytelling?
Patriotism: How Does It Originate? It's Impact on Literature?
War & Peace: Is There a Way To Make Peace the Norm Instead of War?
Why Are So Many of the Great War Books Written Decades, Generations After the Battles are Over?
The Collateral Damage of War to the Psyches of Ordinary Non-combatants
War & Dreams: What do our Dreams of War Mean?
War's Destruction of Social Structures and the Impact on Literature
Women at War: Emotional and Social Consequences as Inspiration for Literature
Do Women Love War as Much as Men?
War and Mass Idolatry: Why an Osama Bin Laden?
Post-traumatic Stress of War As Inspiration for Literature
Psychological Warfare in the 21st Century and its Place in 21st Century Literature

War & The Arts:

War As a Creative Well of Inspiration for the Visual Arts
War and Architecture: Out With the Old, In With the New. Why?
Music to Inspire Warriors
Music as Audio Symbols of Various Wars
Music to Make Us Forget About Wars: On the Front & At Home
War-inspired Music of Lasting Impact
Music for Propaganda in War
Music for War Movies

War And The Environment

War: An Environmental Disaster for All Species
The Environmental Impact of War as Inspiration for Literature
If Man Can't Give Up His Terrible Love of War, Can There Be Such a Phenonemon as The Greening of War?

Guidelines, Publication Details, and Registration

For information about how to register, guidelines for presentation of papers, and information about publication of the proceedings, contact Rosemary James, Faulkner Society Co-Founder, by e-mail: **Faulkhouse@aol.com.** Visit our web site for details about the program, pricing, schedule: **www.wordsandmusic.**

Attend the Premiere Graduate School for Depth Psychology and Jungian Studies

M.A. & PH.D. PROGRAMS IN DEPTH PSYCHOLOGY, THE HUMANITIES, AND MYTHOLOGICAL STUDIES

Pacifica Graduate Institute is an accredited graduate school with two campuses in the coastal California foothills south of Santa Barbara. Both campuses have outstanding educational resources and offer ideal settings for contemplation and study.

For more information:
☒

or ☒   ☒

Pacifica is accredited by the Western Association of Schools and Colleges (WASC).

- Degree programs informed by the work of C.G. Jung and other noted scholars in the tradition of depth psychology

- An interdisciplinary curriculum

- Monthly three-day residential class sessions or a hybrid low-residency/online educational format

- Small, interactive classes that are led by a talented and dedicated faculty

- An academic community that celebrates diversity and fosters a spirit of collaboration and open expression

PACIFICA
GRADUATE INSTITUTE

249 Lambert Rd.
Carpinteria,
California 93013
www.pacifica.edu

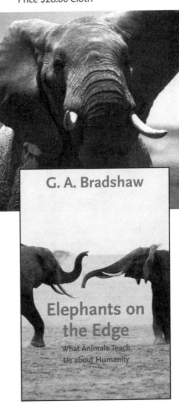

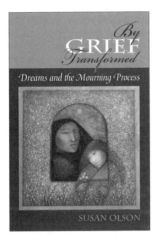

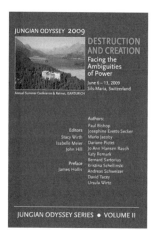

THE PLAYFUL PSYCHE

THE 6TH JUNGIAN ODYSSEY ANNUAL CONFERENCE & RETREAT

"In all chaos there is a cosmos, in all disorder a secret order." *CG Jung*

"It is on the edge between order and chaos that the subtle dance of life takes place." *I Ching*

ISAPZURICH

THE INTERNATIONAL SCHOOL OF ANALYTICAL PSYCHOLOGY ZURICH
AGAP POSTGRADUATE
JUNGIAN TRAINING

Entering Chaos, Coincidence, Creation

Monte Verità
Switzerland
May 28-June 4, 2011

Keynote Address
F. David Peat, PhD

Special Guests
Prof. Reinhard Nesper, Dr.sc.nat.ETH
Beverly Zabriskie, LCSW
Prof. Lisa Sokolov, MA, CMT
Joseph Cambray, PhD
with other guests and faculty of ISAPZURICH

www.jungianodyssey.ch
info@jungianodyssey.ch